Lecture Notes in Business Information Processing

521

Series Editors

LNBIP reports state-of-the-art results in areas related to business information systems and industrial application software development – timely, at a high level, and in both printed and electronic form.

The type of material published includes

- Proceedings (published in time for the respective event)
- Postproceedings (consisting of thoroughly revised and/or extended final papers)
- Other edited monographs (such as, for example, project reports or invited volumes)
- Tutorials (coherently integrated collections of lectures given at advanced courses, seminars, schools, etc.)
- Award-winning or exceptional theses

LNBIP is abstracted/indexed in DBLP, EI and Scopus. LNBIP volumes are also submitted for the inclusion in ISI Proceedings.

João Paulo A. Almeida · Claudio Di Ciccio ·
Christos Kalloniatis
Editors

Advanced Information Systems Engineering Workshops

CAiSE 2024 International Workshops
Limassol, Cyprus, June 3–7, 2024
Proceedings

 Springer

Editors
João Paulo A. Almeida ⓘ
Federal University of Espírito Santo
Vitória, Brazil

Claudio Di Ciccio ⓘ
Utrecht University
Utrecht, The Netherlands

Christos Kalloniatis ⓘ
University of the Aegean
Mytilene, Greece

ISSN 1865-1348   ISSN 1865-1356 (electronic)
Lecture Notes in Business Information Processing
ISBN 978-3-031-61002-8   ISBN 978-3-031-61003-5 (eBook)
https://doi.org/10.1007/978-3-031-61003-5

Preface

Over the last four decades, the Conference on Advanced Information Systems Engineering (CAiSE) has been established as a leading venue for information systems engineering research on innovative topics with rigorous scientific theories. The theme of this year's CAiSE reflected the interdisciplinary and diverse nature of information systems engineering as in the tradition of the conference, focusing on "Information Systems in the Age of Artificial Intelligence". CAiSE 2024 was held in Limassol, Cyprus on 3–7 June 2024.

Every year, CAiSE is accompanied by a significant number of high-quality workshops. Their aim is to address specific emerging challenges in the field, to facilitate interaction between stakeholders and researchers, to discuss innovative ideas, and to present new approaches and tools. Six workshops were held at the conference this year:

– 3rd International Workshop on Agile Methods for Information Systems Engineering (Agil-ISE);
– International Workshop on Blockchain for Information Systems (BC4IS24) and Blockchain for Trusted Data Sharing (B4TDS);
– 2nd International Workshop on Hybrid Artificial Intelligence and Enterprise Modelling for Intelligent Information Systems (HybridAIMS);
– 2nd International Workshop on Knowledge Graphs for Semantics-Driven Systems Engineering (KG4SDSE);
– 16th International Workshop on Enterprise & Organizational Modeling and Simulation (EOMAS);
– International Workshop on Digital Transformation with Business Process Mining (DigPro).

HybridAIMS, KG4SDSE, EOMAS, DigPro, BC4IS24 and B4TDS followed a presentation-oriented track, while Agil-ISE opted to be discussion-oriented and, hence, without the publication of the accepted papers in this volume. The presentation-oriented workshops received a total of 60 submissions, of which 25 were accepted for publication as full papers and 5 as short ones. The selection was based on the scrutiny of three reviewers per paper from the program committee of each workshop following a single-blind scheme. We would like to thank the organizers of the workshops for their excellent job. Also, we express our gratitude to the reviewers for their timely and constructive work, as well as the publicity chairs for their activities that helped to attract submissions. We thank the Proceedings Chair, Sander Leemans, and Springer for the swift communication and support of the proceedings production process. Finally, we warmly thank Pnina Soffer

and Haris Mouratidis—the General Co-chairs of CAiSE 2024—, George A. Papadopou-
los—Local Organizing and Finance Chair—, and Giancarlo Guizzardi and Flavia Maria
Santoro—the PC Co-chairs of CAiSE 2024—for continuously helping us in the process.

June 2024

João Paulo A. Almeida
Claudio Di Ciccio
Christos Kalloniatis

Organization

Workshop Chairs

João Paulo A. Almeida   Federal University of Espírito Santo, Brazil
Claudio di Ciccio   Utrecht University, Netherlands
Christos Kalloniatis   University of the Aegean, Greece

Contents

KG4SDSE

EOMAS

DigPro

BC4IS+B4TDS

International Workshop on Blockchain for Information Systems (BC4IS) and Blockchain for Trusted Data Sharing (B4TDS)

Blockchain technology enables distributed parties to share data and business logic in a trusted way, without requiring trusted third parties. It provides a form of shared database and execution environment with additional trust guarantees compared to more traditional solutions. Among other things, blockchain and smart contracts can improve the management of trusted evidence for the information stored and exchanged. This is a core element in processes involving mutually distrusting participants and is also valuable for auditing, verification, and sharing purposes. The relatively new nature of blockchain technology and its distinctive characteristics such as decentralization and immutability raise new challenges from an information systems perspective. Important challenges revolve around requirements engineering, development, integration, use, governance, and evolution for and of such systems. Specific challenges arise also from the data perspective of blockchain-based information systems. Among other things, there is a need for innovative solutions and research around the storage, organization, retrieval, and sharing of data in a decentralized and trusted way. This would be a step towards strengthening decentralized access to data for businesses, organizations, or participants in worldwide distributed networks.

This year, we joined the "International Workshop on Blockchain for Information Systems (BC4IS)" and "Blockchain for Trusted Data Sharing (B4TDS)". The joined event received seven submissions. Each paper was assigned to three members of the PC and we collected at least two single-blind reviews. Considering the reviews and the maximum acceptance rate of Springer (set around 50%), three papers have been accepted as full papers and one as a short paper. Finally, we had the chance to have a keynote, presented by Claudio Di Ciccio on the topic of "Blockchain for Processes". We thank the program committee members for their high-quality reviews contributing to the quality of the workshop.

June 2024

Victor Amaral de Sousa
Sarah Bouraga
Felix Härer
Alessandro Marcelletti

Organization

BC4IS Workshop Co-chairs

Sarah Bouraga   University of Namur, Belgium
Victor Amaral de Sousa   University of Namur, Belgium

BC4IS Workshop Program Committee

Pierluigi Plebani   Polytechnic University of Milan, Italy
Nicolas Herbaut   Université Paris 1 Panthéon-Sorbonne,
                                       France
Wim Laurier   University of Saint-Louis - Brussels,
                                       Belgium
Jean-Noël Colin   University of Namur, Belgium
Felix Härer   University of Fribourg, Switzerland
Claire Deventer   University of Namur, Belgium
Giovanni Meroni   Technical University of Denmark,
                                       Denmark
Georgios Palaiokrassas   Yale University, USA

B4TDS Workshop Co-chairs

Alessandro Marcelletti   University of Camerino, Italy
Felix Härer   University of Fribourg, Switzerland

B4TDS Workshop Program Committee

Johannes Sedlmeir   University of Luxembourg, Luxembourg
Marco Comuzzi   Ulsan National Institute of Science and
                                       Technology, South Korea
Julius Köpke   University of Klagenfurt, Austria
Francesco Tiezzi   University of Florence, Italy
Andrea Morichetta   University of Camerino, Italy
Yue Liu   Data61, Commonwealth Scientific and
                                       Industrial Research Organisation,
                                       Australia

Blockchain in E-Learning Platform to Enhance Trustworthy and Sharing of Micro-credentials

Alessandro Bigiotti[1](✉)[iD], Maria Paola Francesca Bottoni[2](✉)[iD], and Giacomo Nalli[3](✉)[iD]

[1] Division of Computer Science, University of Camerino,
Via Madonna Delle Carceri, 9, 62032 Camerino, Italy
`alessandro.bigiotti@unicam.it`
[2] Legal and Social Science, International School of Advanced Studies,
University of Camerino, Via Andrea D'Accorso, 16, 62032 Camerino, Italy
`mariapaolafrancesca.bottoni@unicam.it`
[3] Computer Science, School of Science and Technology, Middlesex University
London, The Burroughs, London NW4 4BT, UK
`g.nalli@mdx.ac.uk`

Abstract. Blockchain is a disruptive technology and interest in its adoption is growing across many market sectors in Industry 4.0. However, the blockchain adoption is limited by the difficulty in managing private keys and wallets to interact therein. This paper describes the integration of a consortium blockchain within e-learning platforms. The adoption of blockchain in the e-learning platform maximises the reliability, verifiability and sharing of micro-credentials. The proposed solution aims at eliminating the difficulties of managing keys and wallets. The enhancement in the reliability of micro-credentials is particularly important in learning environments and in companies that want a guarantee of effective training of employees. The present article, in line with the European privacy framework, exploits the potential of blockchain without compromising user data protection.

Keywords: blockchain · smart contract · online learning · micro-credential · industry 4.0

1 Introduction

Industry 4.0 was launched in 2010 by the German government as a strategic initiative aiming to integrate new technologies derived from "Information and Communication Technologies" into the industrial environment [29]. Among the technologies of interest in Industry 4.0 we find artificial intelligence, the Internet of

This research was funded by Ministero dell'Università e della Ricerca (MUR), issue D.M. 351/2022 "Borse di Dottorato" - Dottorato di Ricerca di Interesse Nazionale in "Blockchain & Distributed Ledger Technology", under the National Recovery and Resilience Plan (NRRP).

J. P. A. Almeida et al. (Eds.): CAiSE 2024 Workshops, LNBIP 521, pp. 5–17, 2024.
https://doi.org/10.1007/978-3-031-61003-5_1

Things and certainly the blockchain. In particular, the blockchain is an emerging and potentially disruptive technology due to its transparency, decentralisation, and security properties. The significant features of blockchain technology are the use of cryptographic primitives, to manage authentication and data integrity, and the use of distributed algorithms, to conduct peer-to-peer communications. The adoption of blockchain technology in Industry 4.0 was favoured by the introduction of so-called smart contracts, digital contracts executed within the blockchain [2]. The blockchain began as a public peer-to-peer network, used as a public distributed ledger without restrictions. However, the lack of restrictions is problematic in corporations where privacy requirements and access control mechanisms are needed. To fill this gap, recently advanced frameworks have been implemented to build private blockchains such as Hyperledger Fabric and Hyperledger Besu [8] which are capable of meeting privacy and access control requirements. The adoption of private blockchain allows the application of blockchain in Industry 4.0 and generates several benefits in many sectors.

For instance, the blockchain in the energy market can streamline energy production and consumption, helping to monitor pollution levels while promoting a peer-to-peer energy market [5]. In the manufacturing sector, the blockchain along with the integration of IoT devices, can optimise production processes. In agribusiness, the adoption of blockchain can help to monitor the food supply chain and guarantee access to healthy food, in terms of secure and safety food [17]. Similarly, blockchain adoption could have some beneficial impacts in the educational field and specifically in the e-learning platforms, e.g. Learning Management Systems (LMS) and Course Management Systems (CMS), used for professional training in several different companies that adopted the Industry 4.0 policies. Industry 4.0 requires specialising professionals with specific skills and knowledge of their job sector. Many researchers observe the lack of trained employees with adequate training, including lifelong learning, creates the risk of a transition from technological unemployment to structural unemployment [19]. To train their employees, many institutions and many businesses offer them online training courses and digital technologies designed for distance education, and remote and online learning. However, the use of online training courses can lead to the risk of counterfeiting of the results [26]. Moreover, the methods used for the verification process can be cumbersome and too slow [23]. In this way, the adoption of blockchain technology in the business oriented to the Industry 4.0 policies can produce several benefits, e.g. the increasing the trustworthiness of the certificates issued and to accelerate the verification process, facilitating the sharing of the certificates itself.

This paper aims to explore the potential of integrating blockchain with micro-credentials in online courses delivered through e-learning platforms, to increase the trustworthiness of the certificates in the labour market and the education system. The paper is structured as follows: Sect. 2 describes the main features of micro-credentials and blockchain, followed by some related works. Section 3 deeps the potential of micro-credentials through a case study of an e-learning platform. Section 4 proposes the adoption of blockchain in the e-learning environment as a tool to improve the reliability of certificates, simplify their verification and improve sharing. Section 5 demonstrates that the smart contract-driven approach implemented aims to run the blockchain invisibly to the end user while also protecting user privacy. Finally, Sect. 6 by the European regulatory framework in this field summarises the reasons for the adoption of micro-credential in Industry 4.0 and illustrates the conclusion.

2 Background, Related Work and Contribution

2.1 Micro-credentials

The wide increase of Massive Online Open Courses (MOOC) and the innovation in online learning led to the development of micro-credentials. Micro-credentials represent small-scale learning programmes aimed at acquiring specific knowledge and skills in selected topics that meet the needs of learners to increase their abilities in specific sectors that can involve not only professional development but also personal, social and cultural goals. The need to attract specialists in the new emerging technologies and the rapid potential problems of unemployment make the Micro-credentials particularly suitable for the Industry 4.0. Indeed, the micro-credential provides specific knowledge, skills and competencies that meet labour market needs [20] and offer to both provider learners and provider employers, the assurance that the promised learning outcomes will be achieved. The European Union (EU) adopts the micro-credential approach for lifelong learning and employability to develop quality education and implement a vocational training policy. Additionally, the EU recommends certifying learning objectives, such as short e-training courses, through the adoption of micro-credentials. Micro-credentials can help individuals fill skill gaps necessary for success in a fast-changing environment, without replacing traditional qualifications. Various providers could design and issue these credentials in different learning settings, including e-learning courses. Despite the EU sponsoring the adoption as a tool to acquire new professional knowledge and skills and despite their increasing use [9], in the legal field and IT area, there is no common definition or standard for micro-credentials in Europe. This lack of clarity limits the understanding and uptake of micro-credentials, undermining their potential to facilitate flexible learning and career pathways. The increasing and diverse use of micro-credentials raises a debate on evaluating, certifying, and ensuring micro-credentials. The current debate throughout Europe is centred on the incorporation of micro-credentials into national qualifications systems and frameworks, as well as the establishment of conditions for their recognition. However, in the Member European States, there are notable differences in approaches, with varying national perspectives on the description and assessment of qualifications.

2.2 Blockchain

The blockchain is a disruptive technology that aims at maximising the transparency, traceability and security properties of the actions carried out by the participants of the blockchain itself. The cornerstones of the blockchain lie, firstly in the use of distributed algorithms to manage peer-to-peer communications between network participants, and then in the use of cryptographic primitives that guarantee authentication in the interaction and integrity of the data. Given these characteristics, the blockchain is an ideal technology to overcome the validity criticism of the certificates provided by e-learning platforms [4].

Furthermore, the advent of smart contacts allows to extend the basic functionality of the blockchain, making it possible to define complex logics that go beyond the simple movement of an asset. However, although several types of blockchains exist today and frameworks for building custom blockchains suitable for corporate and private contexts are also emerging, at the same time the adoption of blockchain in numerous contexts faces several barriers. The barriers are technical, due to the lack of experts to support the management of the blockchain, and functional, as users do not have the necessary knowledge to understand the functioning of the blockchain and the management of public and private keys, and wallets needed to interact with the blockchain itself [27].

The public blockchains are distributed databases that seek to achieve decentralisation by replacing a unitary actor with many different users. In this mean, for private blockchains is easier than their public counterparts to comply with some aspects of General Data Protection Regulation (GDPR) [12,13].

2.3   Related Work

The authors in [10] propose a feasible integration of the Ethereum public blockchain with an educational institution in order to register the students' achievements and verify it through a QR code. Similarly, the authors in [15] propose the architecture of a feasible model that aims at integrating the blockchain with an education system. The architecture aims to make the educational process more transparent, traceable and easily verifiable by companies or other interested parties.

The authors in [22] propose a possible integration of the Moodle platform with the public Ethereum blockchain for the validation of the documents produced by the platform itself, storing the hash of the documents produced on the blockchain. In the same way, the authors in [18] propose the integration of the Moodle platform with the Ethereum blockchain to store the metadata associated with the digital certificates produced by the platform, while the authors in [21] provide an integration of the blockchain for the verification of the badge as a certification.

Regarding micro-credentials, the authors in [16] propose EduCTX, a system in which users interact directly with the blockchain and keep their skills as points obtained via ERC20 tokens.

We did not find other works with concrete proposals, but only surveys that partially inspired the present work [1,3].

In the examined approaches, the use of blockchain has been proposed for maintaining the metadata relating to any certificates. In many of the works presented, the integration of a public blockchain was proposed and the issues of costs and privacy were not adequately expressed or were not expressed at all.

2.4   Contribution

Our approach involves implementing a consortium blockchain that enables users to interact with the blockchain without managing private keys and wallets, maintaining user privacy. Moreover, the skills gained by the users are kept in specific smart contracts that aim to be real CVs. The main outcomes of this study can be summarised as follows:

1. Integrate a consortium blockchain in e-learning education systems, specifically applied to Micro-Credentials, to maximise the trustworthiness of the certificates and speed up their verification processes.
2. Present the design of smart contracts to make digital certificate verification faster, transparent and accessible, and enable end users to interact with the blockchain indirectly.
3. Propose a system for recording and sharing training curricula based on the micro-credentials certificates collected by users, safeguarding the privacy of the individuals involved.

3   E-Learning Platform and Micro-credentials

In the field of e-learning platforms related to micro-credentials, a consortium of organisations offers online courses aimed at acquiring specific knowledge and skills required in the labour market, in line with the needs of Industry 4.0. The platforms offering online services, the institutions registered, the courses provided by the institutions and the candidates wishing to improve their knowledge are the main actors currently involved in e-learning platforms based on micro-credentials. Different institutions can co-exist in a single platform. Each institution offers specific short-term training online courses aiming at helping people to develop specific knowledge and skills, allowing users to tailor their learning to the topics they are interested in and to open up the training available from different countries. Several instructional designers during the design of the micro-credentials consult the learners to find out what topics meet their professional learning needs [30] according to the vision of Web 2.0 pedagogy that allows the learners to become more active and co-producers of the teaching material. The design of micro-credentials based on LMS, indeed, is usually characterised by features that encourage the applications of pedagogical strategies such as the peer learning and wiki [24]. These features can include not only traditional text documents but it can also include exercises, quizzes blogs, discussion board [25]. The actors involved in the e-learning consortium are represented by the institutions and the learners, identified as "candidates".

Figure 1 (left side) shows the main actions that an institution can perform within an e-learning platform. Institutions can register their affiliation with the e-learning consortium and then they can create new courses including learning contents, provide a final assessment and set badges criteria. The on-line courses have been designed as self-learning, without the need for instructors to be involved in assessments or issuing certificates.

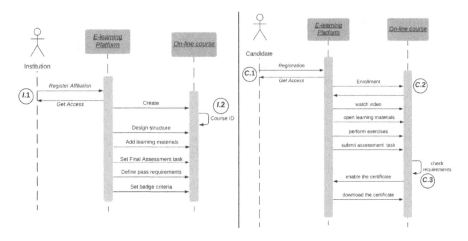

Fig. 1. The sequence diagram shows the interactions and operations that an institution (on the left) and a candidate (on the right) can carry out on e-learning platforms for Micro-Credentials.

Figure 1 (right side) shows the main actions that a candidate can perform within an e-learning platform. The learners, once registered, can improve their knowledge and skills by enrolling in new courses, attending the course in self-learning and completing the required tests to obtain the certificate that represents the acquisition of new skills. The certificate can be downloaded from the platform.

However, LMS platforms are still managed by humans and the risk of counterfeiting certificates remains a concern [14], although the issue of fake diplomas has increased in recent years thanks to advanced graphics editing software. Because of the increasing certification demand and the fake qualifications in the labour market, today it needs major control on the credentials [7]. The verification process could depend on the staff's experience in investigating credentials and a trusted network of professionals who may have knowledge of how to verify the documents. In addition and unfortunately, it is possible that some staff members in different institutions such as administrators, instructors, and office employees may be involved in the production of fake certificates and diplomas [28]. The combination of these factors demonstrate the need to develop tools able to combine credibility and agility in labour market data. Furthermore, the qualifications held by various students generally become fragmented and difficult to share efficiently. The next section explores blockchain integration, aimed to increase the trustworthiness of the certificates issued, speed up the verification processes and simplify the shareability of the qualifications held by students.

4   Consortium Blockchain Within E-Learning Platforms

The integration of a consortium blockchain within e-learning platforms represents a possible solution to overcome the issues described in the previous section. The proposed solution aims at facilitating the management of private keys and wallets for end-users when interacting with the blockchain. This task is delegated to the e-learning platform which is the first manager of the blockchain. Once registered, institutions can request to participate in the management of the blockchain, making it more decentralised. In this way the security of the proposed solution and the credibility of all the actors involved should be increased. Figure 2 shows the structure of the smart contracts implemented to increase the trustworthiness of the certificates issued by the different institutions and to speed up the verification of the qualifications obtained by the different candidates. The relationships between the smart contracts shown in Fig. 2 represent the actions of the institutions ($I.1$, $I.2$) and the actions of the candidates ($C.1$, $C.2$, $C.3$) in the case study illustrated in Fig. 1. The management of smart contracts follows a tree structure. The smart contract placed at the root of the tree is the only access point to the blockchain, and therefore the only access to all other smart contracts. The other smart contracts are dynamically assigned and managed by the *ELearningPlatform.sol* smart contract, allowing the registration of institutions *Institution.sol* and candidates *Candidate.sol*. An institution sends a request to the platform when it wants to make the registration on the platform. Once the platform receives the request, it registers the institution on the *ELearningPlatform.sol* which dynamically allocates a new smart contract. Each institute is placed at the first level of the tree and can create new courses. When an institute adds a new course, it is registered to its *Institution.sol* smart contract, which dynamically allocates a new *Course.sol* smart contract. The smart contracts located at the second level of the tree, identified as leaves of the

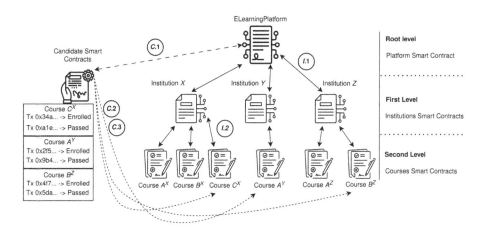

Fig. 2. Smart Contracts architecture.

tree, represent the various courses created. The main actions performed by the *ELearningPlatform.sol* are listed below:

Register an institution (*I.1*): This action allows the registration of a new institution.

Register a course (*I.2*): This action allows an institution to create a new course.

Register a candidate (*C.1*): This action allows the registration of a new candidate.

Course subscription (*C.2*): This action enables the enrolment of a candidate into a course.

Course passed (*C.3*): This action enables a candidate to complete the assessment and obtain a certificate upon passing the exam.

Course verification : This action aims to simplify the verification process. The verification process requires the involvement of both the platform and a third party to verify the certificate obtained by the candidate. The third party checks the candidate's skills through a simple query to the e-learning platform providing the candidate identifier, the institution identifier, and the course identifier.

The interaction between the user and the blockchain must be invisible. In particular, the user continues to interact with the platform as if the blockchain doesn't exist. A Solidity implementation of all smart contracts shown in Fig. 2, along with relevant details, can be inspected thoroughly in a dedicated repository[1].

The proposed approach is designed for a consortium blockchain that might be implemented using Hyperledger Besu [8]. This solution is not feasible for public blockchains due to the size of the byte-code of the *ELearningPlatform.sol*, which requires specific customisation. Furthermore, a public blockchain approach could discourage participants due to privacy issues and high transaction costs.

The *Candidate.sol* smart contract represents a starting point for creating an effective curriculum vitae recorded on the blockchain. This approach increases the credibility and verifiability of Micro-Credentials obtained by candidates. Candidates can easily be shared between different institutions via the *ELearningPlatform.sol*. Two actions are taken to preserve privacy. Firstly, during the registration phase (Fig. 1 - *C*.1), the user's sensitive data is kept off-chain within the e-learning platform. Secondly, only one identifier is stored in the *Candidate.sol* smart contract (Fig. 2 - *C*.1).

4.1 Institutions and Candidates Actions

The main actions performed by an institution consist of the registration into the e-learning platform and the creation of new courses. The initial operation that an institution can take is the registration on a platform (*I*.1). Then, the

---

[1] https://github.com/alessandrobigiotti/micro-credentials-smart-contracts.

e-learning platform needs to associate the institution's access credentials with a pair of keys. The pair of keys allows the identification of the institution within the blockchain. The platform uses the newly created keys to invoke the function `registerInstitution` through the *ELearningPlatform.sol* smart contact. This smart contract dynamically allocates a new *Institution.sol* smart contract, owned by the institution and registered on the platform. After the registration phase, the institutions can create new courses (I.2) available for various candidates. When a new course is created, the platform invokes the `registerCourse` function using the credentials associated with the specific institution. This institution dynamically allocates a new smart contract *Course.sol* associated with the specific institution.

The *Candidate.sol* smart contract aims to be an effective digital curriculum vitae because it collects all the qualifications and skills acquired by each candidate. When a user registers on the platform (C.1), the system invokes the function `registerCandidate` via the *ELearningPlatform.sol* smart contract, which dynamically allocates a *Candidate.sol* smart contract. The user registration phase is a sensitive process as it involves sharing personal information such as name, surname, address, and tax code, or other data depending on the platform's requirements. In this study, all sensitive data is kept off-chain within the platform. A unique code that identifies the student is kept within the blockchain and no sensitive data is shared. The *Candidate.sol* smart contract tracks the activities carried out by the candidate during its interactions with the platform. After the candidate registration, the main actions needed to be maintained on the blockchain are the enrolment in a course (C.2) and the final test to issue the certificate (C.3). When a candidate enrols in a course, the platform sends a transaction. This transaction updates the status of the smart contract *Candidate.sol*, and indicates the enrolment in a new course through the `courseSubscription` function. Similarly, the platform updates the status of the same smart contract by recording a transaction indicating the successful completion of the selected course through the `passCourse` function.

5   Discussion

The use of blockchain technology in the education sector raises several challenges. According to the authors in [11], a big challenge is the functional adoption of the blockchain technology. The involvement of trainees, educators, instructors and managers in the use of blockchain is not currently easy and sustainable. Therefore, this study aims to enable users to interact with the blockchain indirectly with a silent integration of this technology into e-learning platforms. However, in the future each user will need to manage their own keys, as if they are the access credentials to the e-learning platform.

Other challenges to consider are the verification of the authenticity of a certificate and the need to use third parties solutions [31]. In this work, the blockchain acts as a validator for the certificates held by candidates, without the need to implement third parties. The e-learning platform must guarantee the reading access to the blockchain, linking sensitive data with the related smart contracts, allowing third parties to carry out checks on the status of the certificates held by the various candidates. This feature makes the verification process fast and efficient. Moreover, the *Candidate.sol* smart contract acts as a collector of all the certificates received by the candidate. It also eliminates the fragmentation of the different certificates and facilitates their sharing with any interested third party. Furthermore, based on recent research involving interoperability protocols between blockchains [6], this smart contract implementation can allow the sharing of students between different platforms. It can also improve the sharing of candidate training data and overcome the fragmentation criticism potentially associated with micro-credentials.

This case study presents a crucial aspect in terms of user privacy, paying attention to the privacy of the final users [11, 31]. In fact, sensitive candidate data is not stored within the blockchain, but is saved off-chain and managed directly by the platform. Candidates have a unique identifier that will be stored within the blockchain, creating a link to the user's sensitive data. This approach permits to track the certifications held and holdable by candidates without keeping sensitive data on the blockchain. The main advantage of this approach is the real data protection, because those using micro-credentials in the blockchain do not use or share sensitive data, but use an anonymous identifier. The results illustrate the significant impact of blockchain to enhance the reliability of micro-credential in the light of the European regulatory framework. Similar results need synergetic work between lawyers, computer scientists and institutions to create a specific regulatory framework for a disruptive technology, such as blockchain.

6   Conclusion

In this work, a consortium blockchain is integrated with micro-credentials through an e-learning platform to increase the trustworthiness, verifiability and sharing of completion certificates. The proposed solution aims to make the interaction with the blockchain invisible to the users involved, facilitating its adoption. In addition, the solution proposes a new approach that allows the collection of micro-credentials to realise a certified curriculum vitae, validated by the blockchain. The adoption of blockchain technology ensures that the value of micro-credentials is known, understood and recognised both in the labour market and the education system such as stable, reliable material. In this way, the knowledge and skills of learners and the employers' proposals strengthen their validity and increase the user's trust. Currently, the European Commission is developing tools, software and services that will form part of the European Digital Credentials (EDCI) Infrastructure and the experimentation of the blockchain in the micro-credentials field can be a good way to implement the vocational training policy (IGG), combining credibility and agility in labour market.

References

1. Ahsan, K., Akbar, S., Kam, B., Abdulrahman, M.D.A.: Implementation of micro-credentials in higher education: a systematic literature review. Educ. Inf. Technol. **28**(10), 13505–13540 (2023). https://doi.org/10.1007/s10639-023-11739-z
2. Alharby, M., Aldweesh, A., Moorsel, A.V.: Blockchain-based smart contracts: a systematic mapping study of academic research. In: 2018 International Conference on Cloud Computing, Big Data and Blockchain (ICCBB), pp. 1–6 (2018). https://doi.org/10.1109/ICCBB.2018.8756390
3. Alsobhi, H.A., Alakhtar, R.A., Ubaid, A., Hussain, O.K., Hussain, F.K.: Blockchain-based micro-credentialing system in higher education institutions: systematic literature review. Knowl.-Based Syst. **265**, 110238 (2023). https://doi.org/10.1016/j.knosys.2022.110238
4. Ayub Khan, A., Laghari, A.A., et al.: Educational blockchain: a secure degree attestation and verification traceability architecture for higher education commission. Appl. Sci. **11**(22) (2021). https://doi.org/10.3390/app112210917
5. Bigiotti, A., Mostarda, L., Navarra, A.: Blockchain and IoT integration for air pollution control. In: Barolli, L. (ed.) Advances on P2P, Parallel, Grid, Cloud and Internet Computing, 3PGCIC 2023, LNDECT, vol. 189, pp. 27–38. Springer, Cham (2024). https://doi.org/10.1007/978-3-031-46970-1_3
6. Bigiotti, A., Mostarda, L., Navarra, A., Pinna, A., Tonelli, R., Vaccargiu, M.: Interoperability between EVM-based blockchains. In: Barolli, L. (ed.) Advanced Information Networking and Applications, AINA 2024, LNDECT, vol. 200, pp. 98–109. Springer, Cham (2024). https://doi.org/10.1007/978-3-031-57853-3_9
7. Brown, G.M.: Degrees of doubt: legitimate, real and fake qualifications in a global market. J. High. Educ. Policy Manag. **28**(1), 71–79 (2006)
8. Capocasale, V., Gotta, D., Perboli, G.: Comparative analysis of permissioned blockchain frameworks for industrial applications. Blockchain: Res. Appl. **4**(1), 100113 (2023). https://doi.org/10.1016/j.bcra.2022.100113
9. Cedefop: Microcredentials: Striving to combine credibility and agility. Publications Office of the European Union (2024). https://data.europa.eu/doi/10.2801/966682
10. Cheng, J.C., Lee, N.Y., Chi, C., Chen, Y.H.: Blockchain and smart contract for digital certificate. In: 2018 IEEE International Conference on Applied System Invention (ICASI), pp. 1046–1051 (2018). https://doi.org/10.1109/ICASI.2018.8394455
11. El Koshiry, A., Eliwa, E., Abd El-Hafeez, T., Shams, M.Y.: Unlocking the power of blockchain in education: an overview of innovations and outcomes. Blockchain: Res. Appl. **4**(4), 100165 (2023). https://doi.org/10.1016/j.bcra.2023.100165
12. European Parliamentary Research Service: Blockchain and the general data protection regulation: Can distributed ledgers be squared with european data protection law? Technical Report, European Parliment (2019)
13. Filvà, D.A., García-Peñalvo, E.A.: Privacy and identity management in learning analytics processes with blockchain. In: Proceedings of TEEM 2018, pp. 997-1003. Association for Computing Machinery (2018). https://doi.org/10.1145/3284179.3284354
14. Go, A.: Stopping fake certificates and transcripts - is digital and blockchain technology the answer? In: An Anthology of Selected Papers of APQN Annual Academic Conference, pp. 191–201. Asia-Pacific Quality Network (APQN) and Eduvalue Pte Ltd, Singapore (2021)

15. Han, M., Li, Z., He, J.S., Wu, D., Xie, Y., Baba, A.: A novel blockchain-based education records verification solution. In: Proceedings of the 19th Annual SIG Conference on Information Technology Education, SIGITE 2018, pp. 178–183. Association for Computing Machinery (2018). https://doi.org/10.1145/3241815.3241870

16. Hölbl, M., Kamisalić, A., Turkanović, M., Kompara, M., Podgorelec, B., Herićko, M.: Eductx: an ecosystem for managing digital micro-credentials. In: 2018 28th EAEEIE Annual Conference (EAEEIE), pp. 1–9 (2018). https://doi.org/10.1109/EAEEIE.2018.8534284

17. Javaid, M., Haleem, A., Pratap Singh, R., Khan, S., Suman, R.: Blockchain technology applications for industry 4.0: a literature-based review. Blockchain: Res. Appl. **2**(4), 100027 (2021). https://doi.org/10.1016/j.bcra.2021.100027

18. KARATAŞ, E.: Developing Ethereum blockchain-based document verification smart contract for moodle learning management system. Bilişim Teknolojileri Dergisi **11**(4), 399–406 (2018). https://doi.org/10.17671/gazibtd.452686

19. Kuzior, A.: Technological unemployment in the perspective of industry 4.0. Virt. Econ. **5**(1), 7–23 (2022). https://doi.org/10.34021/ve.2022.05.01(1), https://virtual-economics.eu/index.php/VE/article/view/140

20. Kušić, S., Vrcelj, S., Zovko, A.: Micro-credentials - improvement or fragmentation in higher education? Educ. New Dev. 2022 - **2** (2022). https://doi.org/10.36315/2022v2end033

21. Mikroyannidis, A., Domingue, J., Bachler, M., Quick, K.: Smart blockchain badges for data science education. In: 2018 IEEE Frontiers in Education Conference (FIE), pp. 1–5 (2018). https://doi.org/10.1109/FIE.2018.8659012

22. Morais, A.M.D., Correia Neto, J.D.S., Medeiros, R.W.A.D., Nóbrega, O.D.O., Lins, F.A.A.: A solution for integrating virtual learning environments with blockchain. Res. Soc. Dev. **10**(12), e210101220354 (2021).https://doi.org/10.33448/rsd-v10i12.20354

23. Mudiyanselage, A.K., Pan, L.: Security test moodle: a penetration testing case study. Int. J. Comput. Appl. **42**(4), 372–382 (2020)

24. Nalli, G., Amendola, D., Smith, S.: Artificial intelligence to improve learning outcomes through online collaborative activities. In: European Conference on e-Learning, vol. 21, pp. 475–479 (2022)

25. Nalli, G., Culmone, R., Perali, A., Amendola, D.: Online tutoring system for programming courses to improve exam pass rate. J. E-Learn. Knowl. Soc. **19**(1), 27–35 (2023)

26. Perera, P., Sirisuriya, S., Gunathilake, H.: Security vulnerabilities and security elements of frequently used e-learning platforms: a review (2022)

27. Prewett, K.W., Prescott, G.L., Phillips, K.: Blockchain adoption is inevitable-barriers and risks remain. J. Corp. Account. Finan. **31**(2), 21–28 (2020)

28. Sayed, R.H.: Potential of blockchain technology to solve fake diploma problem (2019)

29. Silva, T.B.D., Morais, E.S.D., Almeida, L.F.F.D., Rosa Righi, R.D., Alberti, A.M.: Blockchain and industry 4.0: overview, convergence, and analysis. In: Rosa Righi, R., Alberti, A., Singh, M. (eds.) Blockchain Technology for Industry 4.0. Blockchain Technologies, pp. 27–58. Springer, Singapore (2020). https://doi.org/10.1007/978-981-15-1137-0_2

30. White, S.: Developing credit based micro-credentials for the teaching profession: an Australian descriptive case study. Teach. Teach. **27**(7), 696–711 (2021)
31. Yumna, H., Khan, M.M., Ikram, M., Ilyas, S.: Use of blockchain in education: a systematic literature review. In: Nguyen, N., Gaol, F., Hong, TP., Trawiński, B. (eds.) Intelligent Information and Database Systems, ACIIDS 2019, LNCS, vol. 11432. Springer, Cham (2019). https://doi.org/10.1007/978-3-030-14802-7_17

A Conceptual Model for Blockchain-Based Trust in Digital Ecosystems (Short Paper)

Yuntian Ding[1] , Nicolas Herbaut[2(✉)] , and Daniel Negru[3]

[1] Aquitaine Science Transfert, 33405 Talence, France
yuntian.ding@nseven.xyz
[2] Centre de Recherche en Informatique, Univ. Paris 1 Panthéon-Sorbonne,
Paris, France
nicolas.herbaut@univ-paris1.fr
[3] LaBRI, UMR 5800, Univ. Bordeaux, 33400 Talence, France
dnegru@labri.Fr

Abstract. In inter-organizational business processes, divergent interests among participants often result in trust deficiencies. The question of how to initiate trust remains a largely unresolved theoretical issue. However, the advancement of Blockchain technology has led to an increase in its application for establishing trust among stakeholders in these processes. This paper introduces a conceptual model that leverages an ontology of trust to examine its significance within digital ecosystems and suggests a method to promote the integration of blockchain. We exemplify our approach with a practical industrial case study and outline prospective developments in the field of trust facilitation through blockchain technology.

Keywords: blockchain · trust · ontology · inter-organizational business process · content distribution

1 Introduction

The increasing complexity and interconnectedness of the business environment mean that no single entity controls the entire process, leading to trust issues among partners with potentially conflicting interests. Trust is crucial for encouraging collaboration, as fear of unmet expectations can hinder joint efforts. Identifying and addressing trust issues is therefore essential.

A shift towards flexible, trust-establishing methods can open new market opportunities. Centralized systems, constrained by reliance on a central authority, lack this flexibility. Blockchain technology, offering a decentralized ledger system, is seen as a breakthrough for industries needing decentralized decision-making.

Yet, defining and measuring trust remains challenging, with research on blockchain's effectiveness in addressing trust issues lacking empirical validation. This paper proposes a conceptual trust model based on ontology, exploring blockchain's potential to resolve trust issues within digital ecosystems (DEs).

J. P. A. Almeida et al. (Eds.): CAiSE 2024 Workshops, LNBIP 521, pp. 18–24, 2024.
https://doi.org/10.1007/978-3-031-61003-5_2

The paper is organized as follows: related work on trust and blockchain is reviewed (Sect. 2), followed by the introduction of a blockchain-based trust model (Sect. 3), leading to a discussion on the findings and future research (Sect. 4), and concluding remarks.

2   Related Work

Trust's abstract nature and its variability across disciplines pose challenges in developing a unified definition. Various trust ontologies have emerged to address this, critical for designing systems deemed trustworthy. Research has increasingly focused on blockchain's role in trust management.

McKnight et al. introduced a typology of trust in e-commerce, featuring disposition to trust, institution-based trust, trusting beliefs, and trusting intentions [1]. Amaral et al. expanded on this, proposing a detailed ontology of trust using the ROT model, based on the foundational theory UFO and OntoUML language, to distinguish between social and institution-based trust [2]. They emphasized that trust inherently involves uncertainty and risk, delving into the complexity of trustors' intentions and the evidence needed for trustworthiness [3]. Luhmann discussed how modern society's complexity leads to trust as a crucial outcome for social order, highlighting the role of trust in managing uncertainty [4].

Hawlitschek et al. reviewed the transformative potential of blockchain in decentralizing markets and reshaping trust dynamics [5]. Sayed et al. noted blockchain's ability to eliminate intermediaries, enhancing transparency and trust among stakeholders [6]. Despite these findings, research on how blockchain can specifically enhance system trustworthiness remains limited.

3   Conceptual Model

In this section, we present a framework for understanding trust in business processes within a DE, focusing on the challenges of sharing trust among opportunistic organizations. We distinguish between scenarios where trust is internally generated by stakeholders and externally supplied by a third party. To clarify, we reference the N7 model.

3.1   N7: Running Example

The N7 platform aims to create a DE for distributing multimedia content, involving Content Owners (COs, who produce the content), Content Providers (CPs, who retail the content), and Service Providers (SPs, who ensures technical support and maintain the quality of the viewer's experience). These entities collaborate to deliver content while maintaining its quality and accessibility. Traditional content distribution often relies on complex agreements that depend on a form of trust in the judicial system to enforce contracts (Social Trust [2]), which may not always be effective. Additionally, niche content often struggles with establishing such partnerships due to economic and legal constraints. The existence

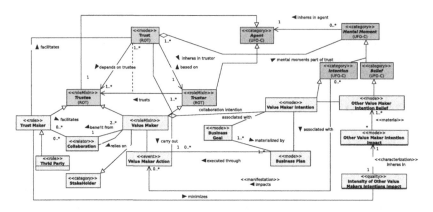

Fig. 1. Ontology of trust in digital ecosystems (Color figure online)

of pirate distribution ecosystems further complicates the landscape, as they illegally stream content, harming content owners financially and exposing users to risks like malware. N7 addresses these challenges by integrating blockchain technology to establish a trust-based system through cryptographic evidence, aiming to secure and enhance cooperation among all parties involved.

3.2   Ontology of Trust in Digital ecosystems

We formalize trust in DEs in the OntoUML shown in Fig. 1, focusing on the particular roles played by process stakeholders and third parties in trust formation. We utilize the ROT [2] as a foundation for our trust mental model (in orange), which in turn employs the UFO foundational ontology proposed by Guizzardi et al. (in blue) [7].

DE consist of at least two `Value Makers` intending to benefit from the outcome of the `Collaboration` in the execution of an Interorganizational Business Process (IBP). They are the IBP `Stakeholders`. For instance, in the Uber Eats DE, the Value Makers are the customers, restaurants, delivery personnel, and the Uber platform itself, as they all benefit from payments or services provided through the "food ordering" IBP. Since every value maker relies on the collaboration of others yet also benefits from this collaboration, they are considered both `Trustor` and `Trustee` from the perspective of the IBP, marking a significant novelty in relation to ROT. The `Trust` in DE characterizes the relationship between `Trustors` and `Trustees`, embodying a complex mental state consisting of a set of `Beliefs` regarding the intentions of other `Value Makers` and the specific `Intentions` of each one. The `Other Value Maker Intention Belief` also considers the impact on our own `Intentions` through their respective `Intensity`. For example, when ordering a product online from a merchant with a contractual return policy, even if we harbor the `belief` that the product may not meet our needs, the `Intensity` of this belief's impact is minimized by our entitlement to a refund. In other words, some intentions are based on the self-interests of a Value

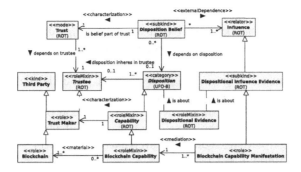

Fig. 2. Ontology of Capabilities Manifestation for Blockchain trust systems

Maker, while other intentions depend on what we believe other Value Makers' intention, and these intentions regarding the other Value Maker can affect ours depending on their importance. The **Intentions** of **Value Makers** consist of a set of **Business Goals**, which represent the desired outcomes of the collaboration. To achieve these goals, Value Makers devise **Business Plans** executed through a series of **Value Maker Actions**. These actions can affect (positively or negatively) the **Intentions** of other **Value Makers**. For example, if an airline overbooks its flights as part of a business plan to optimize profit, we might be negatively affected by being unable to join our family for Christmas (our intention). **Value Makers** are not solely responsible for fostering trust within the framework. Our conceptualization introduces **Trust Makers** as a distinct category of **Trustee** that does not contribute to the value creation of the process. Unlike **Stakeholders**, **Trust Makers** hold no intention within the IBP, serving exclusively to facilitate trust without deriving benefits from the process itself. As an illustration, consider the process of selling a painting through an auction house: the seller may seek an independent appraisal to determine a potential selling price. Here, the independent expert acts as a **Trust Maker**, enhancing trust without participating in the value generation of the auction.

The N7 platform acts as a **Trust Maker** helping CO, CP and SP building up trust to make the collaboration possible. However, deriving trust is particularly difficult and the role of a third party is paramount, but comes with significant drawbacks, as we show in the next section.

3.3 The Problems of Third Parties and How Blockchain Can help

Achieving trust within DEs presents a significant challenge as agreements between companies are fleeting, yet these ecosystems open new avenues for collaboration and value creation across increasingly complex value chains.

In practical terms, establishing trust anew for each transaction within a DE is inefficient. Consequently, these ecosystems often depend on **Third Parties** to act as trust facilitators. However, it is rarely that case that third party is just **Trust Makers**. In most cases, they also act as **Value Makers** by regulating the ecosystem to such an extent that other participants lack the flexibility to tailor the IBP to their needs. A significant concern arises when these trust facilitators, due to the high value of trust as an asset, accumulate it, leading to monopolistic conditions. For instance, the general public is typically reluctant or unable to bypass major platforms like Google for installing applications on Android phones. A notable case involved the application provider Epic Games challenging Apple for the right to sell their games outside of the App Store, culminating in legal action to demonstrate that the platform was in breach of the EU's Digital Markets Act regulations.

Blockchain solutions are increasingly recognized for their potential to address the issues mentioned earlier, through their distinctive capabilities: Blockchain technology facilitates the development of customized IBPs through smart contracts, enhancing the flexibility and versatility of the DE. It allows for the transparency of code execution on blockchains, providing auditable processes. Furthermore, blockchain systems are capable of recording all process execution traces, ensuring data auditability for Value Makers. This capability fosters an indirect form of trust through the control and oversight of transactions and interactions within the ecosystem

Given these features, blockchain can be viewed as a reliable and "intentionless" **Trust Maker** that decentralizes trust requirements by providing tools to run business processes on a decentralized infrastructure. This constitutes our primary contribution as we link existing blockchain capabilities with the role of Trust Maker, explaining how blockchain can substitute for third parties in establishing trust among Value Makers who initially lack mutual trust in digital ecosystems. However, as an emerging technology, established best practices and deployment strategies are still limited. Moreover, the effective utilization of blockchain's capabilities hinges on specific prerequisites, the absence of which could significantly undermine its trust-enhancing proposition. In the next section, we propose a description of how we can think of ensuring those capacities to the stakeholders.

3.4   The Need for Capabilities Manifestation For Blockchain

Amaral et al. expanded the ROT [3] by incorporating the beliefs and intentions of a trustor, as well as evidence indicative of a trustee's trustworthiness. They argued that **Trust** is shaped by the **Trustee's Disposition. Disposition** refers to properties that manifest only in specific situations and may not always be evident, such as a magnet's tendency to attract metal. However, as illustrated in Fig. 2, **Capabilities** generally cannot be directly assessed by the **Trustor**. Instead, it is the **Trustor**'s belief in these dispositions that influences **Trust**. The case of **Blockchain** serving as a **Trust Maker** is unique. As a **Trustee**, blockchain exhibits no **Intention** or business goals, owing to its inherently trustworthy design. This limits the necessity for belief in **Capabilities** to specific **Blockchain Capabilities**, demonstrated through **Blockchain Capability Manifestation**. Consequently, careful and targeted design of capability manifestations through `Dispositional Evidence` is essential to promoting trust in blockchain systems.

In the N7 case, based on our system requirements analysis, privacy, integrity and traceability were identified as required blockchain capacities to enhance the system's trustworthiness. We gathered relevant literature, whitepapers providing theoretical evidences for the blockchain platform used in N7, and results from automated testing serving as dispositional evidence. These reveal how type of blockchain, consensus, network state and smart contracts satisfy requirements, thereby foster trust in the ecosystem.

4   Conclusion and Future Work

In summary, this paper presents a conceptual framework leveraging blockchain technology to address trust issues in DEs, illustrated through the N7 DE for content distribution. Our findings reveal blockchain potential to enhance trust by ensuring data privacy, integrity, and traceability.

Our conceptual framework represents an initial effort to understand the benefits of utilizing blockchain technology to enhance trust in DE. However, there are opportunities for refinement and improvement. Firstly, the relationship between risks and the evidence provided is somewhat broad and needs to be tailored more closely to specific risks in DE, rather than addressing only high-level, general risks. Further research is necessary to identify these specific risks and develop a deeper understanding of the most impactful evidence to present. Additionally, we may have underestimated the significance of code auditability. In practical terms, it might not always be feasible for stakeholders to confirm whether the implemented smart contract accurately reflects the IBP. This is crucial because any flaws in the smart contract could undermine the reliability of its execution records. Establishing a collection of trusted, standard patterns could mitigate this risk [8]. Moreover, the introduction of blockchain-based trust could influence the intentions of "value makers" within the ecosystem. If these actors perceive that they must adhere strictly to predefined rules and cannot leverage their market power to "adjust" business processes for their benefit, they may see reduced gain from participating in the DE. This could potentially deter their involvement. Lastly, it remains to be determined who should deploy and maintain the blockchain solution and how its governance should be organized. Ideally, a consortium of stakeholders would oversee these tasks. However, this approach carries the risk of a dominant group seizing control of the blockchain system and exploiting it for their own interests. Further work in understanding the governance of blockchain for DE is required.

References

1. McKnight, D.H., Chervany, N.L.: What trust means in e-commerce customer relationships: an interdisciplinary conceptual typology. Int. J. Electron. Commer. **6**(2), 35–59 (2001). https://doi.org/10.1080/10864415.2001.11044235

2. Amaral, G., Sales, T.P., Guizzardi, G., Porello, D.: Towards a reference ontology of trust. In: Panetto, H., Debruyne, C., Hepp, M., Lewis, D., Ardagna, C., Meersman, R. (eds.) On the Move to Meaningful Internet Systems: OTM 2019 Conferences, OTM 2019, LNCS, vol. 11877, pp. 3–21. Springer, Cham (2019). https://doi.org/10.1007/978-3-030-33246-4_1

3. Amaral, G.C.M., Sales, T.P., Guizzardi, G., Porello, D: Ontological foundations for trust management: extending the reference ontology of trust. In: Proceedings of 15th International Workshop on Value Modelling and Business Ontologies (VMBO 2021), vol. 2835 (2021)

4. Luhmann, N.: Social Systems. Stanford University Press, Redwood City (1995)

5. Hawlitschek, F., Notheisen, B., Teubner, T.: The limits of trust-free systems: a literature review on blockchain technology and trust in the sharing economy. Electron. Commer. Res. Appl. **29**, 50–63 (2018) https://doi.org/10.1016/j.elerap.2018.03.005

6. Sayed, B., ORAL, H.V.: A review on blockchain operations in construction management. J. Sustain. Constr. Mater. Technol. **8**(2), 146–152 (2023). https://doi.org/10.47481/jscmt.1244244

7. Guizzardi, G.: Ontological foundations for structural conceptual models (2005)

8. Six, N., Herbaut, N., Salinesi, C.: Blockchain software patterns for the design of decentralized applications: a systematic literature review. Blockchain: Res. Appl. **3**(2), 100061 (2022). https://doi.org/10.1016/j.bcra.2022.100061

High-Performance Confidentiality-Preserving Blockchain via GPU-Accelerated Fully Homomorphic Encryption

Rongxin Guan[1], Tianxiang Shen[1], Sen Wang[4], Gong Zhang[4], Heming Cui[1,3], and Ji Qi[2(✉)]

[1] The University of Hong Kong, Hong Kong, China
`rxguan@cs.hku.hk`
[2] Institute of Software, Chinese Academy of Sciences, Beijing, China
`qiji@iscas.ac.cn`
[3] Shanghai AI Laboratory, Shanghai, China
[4] Huawei Technologies, Hong Kong, China

Abstract. Data confidentiality is essential for safety-critical blockchain applications such as digital payment. A promising approach for preserving confidentiality is to encrypt transaction data using homomorphic encryption (HE) and prove the correctness of transaction execution through non-interactive zero-knowledge proofs (NIZKPs). However, prior work on this approach suffers from poor performance caused by the costly HE computation, hindering their adoption for real-world applications. In addition, prior work is restricted by the use of HE schemes that only support either addition or multiplication, making it challenging to implement business logic involving both types of arithmetic operations.

We present GAFE, a high-performance confidentiality-preserving blockchain that carries a GPU-accelerated transaction execution workflow. GAFE encrypts transaction data with FHE, allowing both addition and multiplication on ciphertexts. For high performance, GAFE leverages parallel execution on GPUs to accelerate FHE computations. For result correctness, GAFE generates lightweight NIZKPs that incur low overhead. Evaluations show that GAFE is highly performant, achieving a $3.1\times$ increase in throughput (258 transactions per second) and a 37% reduction in latency (1.61 s), surpassing the baseline without GPU acceleration.(GAFE stands for GPU-Accelerated Fully Homomorphic Encryption Blockchain.)

Keywords: Blockchain · Confidentiality Preserving · GPU Acceleration · Fully Homomorphic Encryption

1 Introduction

Blockchain has been a transformative force for both industry and academia [3] due to its exceptional characteristics, such as immutability [18]. However, notable

J. P. A. Almeida et al. (Eds.): CAiSE 2024 Workshops, LNBIP 521, pp. 25–36, 2024.
https://doi.org/10.1007/978-3-031-61003-5_3

blockchains like Hyperledger Fabric [2] (HLF) face a serious confidentiality issue as they process and store transaction data in plaintext, exposing sensitive information to anyone with access to the blockchain. This confidentiality issue impedes the widespread adoption of blockchain, especially in safety-critical applications such as finance [30], where data confidentiality is crucial.

A promising approach to addressing the confidentiality issue is using homomorphic encryption [1] (HE) and non-interactive zero-knowledge proofs [24] (NIZKPs). HE enables arithmetic computation to be performed directly on ciphertexts. NIZKPs allow a prover to prove that a statement is true without revealing any information beyond the validity of the statement itself. In this approach, clients encrypt transaction input data using an HE scheme, and nodes execute transactions directly on ciphertexts. Then, clients generate NIZKPs to prove the execution correctness, without disclosing the plaintexts of the results.

However, prior work on this approach faces two prominent deficiencies. Firstly, they suffer from low performance due to the intensive computational costs of HE. For instance, the notable confidentiality-preserving blockchain ZeeStar [23] exhibits a long commit latency of tens of seconds. As a result, prior work fails to meet the high-performance requirements of many blockchain applications, such as digital payment [30]. Secondly, prior work has serious limitations in expressing complex business logic due to its reliance on partially homomorphic encryption [1] (PHE). PHE supports either addition or multiplication on ciphertexts, making prior work unsuitable for applications like finance [30] that involve both types of arithmetic operations. Although fully homomorphic encryption (FHE) offers a promising alternative that allows arbitrary computation on ciphertexts, its adoption is impeded by its even higher computation costs.

Our key insight to address the deficiencies is that, *we can efficiently integrate FHE and blockchains by introducing GPU acceleration for transaction execution and FHE computation*. Blockchain transactions that invoke the same smart contract are highly parallelizable, thus enabling parallel computations of FHE across multiple transactions. These parallel computations are well-suited for GPUs, which offer superior parallel processing capabilities and are widely available in modern commodity machines. Hence, employing GPU-accelerated FHE is both beneficial and feasible for blockchains, as it enables high performance, confidentiality preservation, and the implementation of complex business logic.

Nonetheless, the trivial combination of FHE and blockchains leads to the problem of inconsistent ciphertext results. Specifically, when given identical inputs, different nodes may generate inconsistent ciphertexts for the same plaintext result. This inconsistency occurs because FHE schemes intentionally introduce random noise to ciphertexts. This noise serves as a protection against attacks aimed at extracting information from the ciphertext [25].

To solve the problem of inconsistency, our second insight is *to integrate lightweight NIZKPs with the trusted execution mechanism of the execute-order-validate blockchain workflow* [2]. This mechanism first executes a transaction on multiple nodes and considers it correct iff a majority of nodes produce consistent results. Inspired by this mechanism, clients can generate NIZKPs that decrypt all ciphertext results and check the consistency of the majority of plaintexts. The

Table 1. Comparison of GAFE and related confidentiality-preserving blockchains. "❖/◆" represent general-purpose and specific-purpose blockchains, respectively.

System	FHE Support	GPU Acceleration	High Performance
❖ ZeeStar [23]	✗	✗	✗
❖ Ekiden [9]	✗	✗	✓
❖ Hawk [17]	✗	✗	✓
❖ Arbitrum [15]	✗	✗	✓
◆ Zcash [14]	✗	✗	✗
◆ Monero [20]	✗	✗	✗
◆ FabZK [16]	✗	✗	✓
◆ Zether [7]	✗	✗	✗
◆ RFPB [27]	✗	✗	✓
◆ GAFE	✓	✓	✓

generation of NIZKPs is lightweight as it does not perform costly HE arithmetic computations like existing studies [23, 27].

These two insights lead to GAFE, a high-performance confidentiality-preserving blockchain. GAFE carries a *GPU-accelerated transaction execution workflow* in four phases. First, the client encrypts transaction input data using FHE and sends the encrypted transaction to all executor nodes. Second, each executor uses a GPU to execute FHE computation for multiple transactions in parallel, then the client generates NIZKPs to prove the execution correctness. Third, the orderer nodes run a consensus protocol to determine the transaction order within each block. Finally, the executors validate and commit the transactions in the determined order. In short, this workflow achieves high performance while ensuring the provably correct execution of confidentiality-preserving transactions.

We built GAFE on top of HLF [2], a notable execute-order-validate blockchain framework. We compared GAFE with a baseline that performs FHE computation solely on the CPU. The results show that GAFE achieves high performance, with an effective throughput of 258 transactions per second and a commit latency of 1.61 s. Compared to the baseline, GAFE achieved a 3.1× increase in throughput and a 37% reduction in latency.

In summary, we make the following contributions: (1) We propose a GPU-accelerated transaction execution workflow that integrates GPU-accelerated FHE into blockchain and ensures execution correctness through lightweight NIZKPs. (2) We implement GAFE, a high-performance confidentiality-preserving blockchain that incorporates the aforementioned workflow. (3) We conduct evaluations on GAFE, demonstrating its effectiveness and high performance.

2   Related Work

2.1   Confidentiality-Preserving Blockchains

We categorize prior work on confidentiality-preserving blockchains into two groups, as shown in Table 1.

General-purpose Blockchains. ZeeStar [23] uses ElGamal encryption [19], which only supports HE addition. While ZeeStar extends addition to emulate multiplication, this extension is inefficient and not applicable to ciphertexts encrypted by different keys. Ekiden [9], Hawk [17], and Arbitrum [15] present substantial vulnerabilities due to their reliance on trusted managers or hardware. Note that GAFE is a general-purpose blockchain.

Specific-purpose Blockchains. To conceal sensitive digital payment information, Zcash [14] employs NIZKPs, while Monero [20] uses ring signatures and stealth addresses. However, their poor performance has impeded their broader adoption [7,22]. FabZK [16] combines NIZKPs with a specialized tabular data structure to realize confidentiality, but this data structure restricts FabZK to performing only HE addition. Zether [7] and RFPB [27][1] also support only HE addition due to the use of PHE schemes.

2.2 GPU-Accelerated Fully Homomorphic Encryption

Much prior work leverages GPU acceleration for FHE computations to unlock the potential of FHE in real-world applications. HE-Booster [26] accelerates polynomial arithmetic computation by mapping five common phases of typical FHE schemes to the GPU parallel architecture. It also introduces thread-level and data-level parallelism to enable acceleration on single-GPU and multi-GPU setups, respectively. Ozcan et al. [21] presents a library that makes efficient use of the GPU memory hierarchy and minimizes the number of GPU kernel function calls. Yang et al. [28] provides GPU implementations of three notable FHE schemes (BGV [6], BFV [5,12], and CKKS [10]) along with various optimizations, including a hybrid key-switching technique and several kernel fusing strategies. Note that GAFE is orthogonal to the implementation of GPU-accelerated FHE schemes, allowing GAFE to leverage the latest advancements in this field.

3 Overview

3.1 System Model

GAFE comprises three types of participants: *client*, *executor*, and *orderer*. Executors and orderers are referred to as *nodes*. GAFE uses permissioned settings, where all participants are organized into distinct *organizations* and explicitly identified. Each organization runs multiple executors and orderers, as well as possesses a set of clients. We built a prototype system of GAFE on top of HLF. Specifically, each type of participant is described as follows:

Client. Clients encrypt transaction input data, submit the encrypted transactions to the nodes for execution and commitment, and prove the execution correctness. Each client is identified by a unique string *id* and owns a public-private key set for performing FHE computations. In addition, each client is associated with FHE ciphertexts, such as the client's balance *bal*.

---

[1] We refer to the system proposed in [27] as RFPB for convenience.

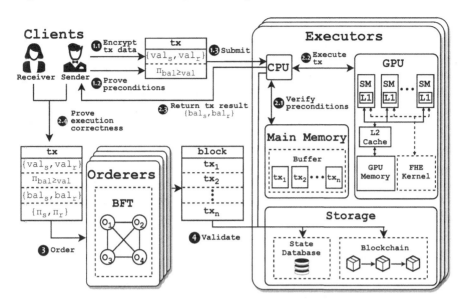

Fig. 1. GAFE's GPU-accelerated transaction execution workflow. Each executor utilizes multiple Streaming Multiprocessors (SM) of a GPU to concurrently execute FHE computations for multiple transactions.

Executor. Each executor is responsible for three main tasks: (1) executing encrypted transactions, (2) validating transaction results, and (3) maintaining the latest local copy of blockchain and state database. Each executor is equipped with a GPU to accelerate FHE computations during transaction execution. We provide a detailed discussion of GAFE's transaction execution workflow in Sect. 4.2.

Orderer. Orderers determine the order of transactions within each block via a Byzantine-Fault-Tolerant consensus protocol (e.g., PBFT [8]).

3.2 Threat Model

GAFE adopts the Byzantine failure model [4,8], which tolerates up to N malicious orderers out of $3N + 1$ orderers. Each client is limited to accessing only the plaintext of its own data and is unable to access the plaintext of other clients' data. Nodes are incapable of revealing the plaintext of any client's data. We make standard assumptions on FHE and NIZKP.

3.3 GAFE's Workflow Overview

GAFE carries a *GPU-accelerated transaction execution workflow* (Sect. 4.2) that consists of four phases, as shown in Fig. 1. We take digital payment as an example to illustrate our workflow.

Phase 1: Construction. The client constructs a transaction tx by encrypting the transaction input data (e.g., payment amount val) and generates an NIZKP $\pi_{bal \geq val}$ to demonstrate that the client's balance bal is greater than or equal to val. Finally, the client submits tx and $\pi_{bal \geq val}$ to all executors for execution.

Phase 2: Execution. The executor verifies $\pi_{bal \geq val}$ and continues execution iff $\pi_{bal \geq val}$ is valid. Next, the executor buffers tx along with other transactions received within a specific time frame. These buffered transactions are moved to a GPU for concurrent FHE computations, and then the execution results are returned to the submitting clients. Upon receiving the results from all executors, the client generates NIZKPs to prove the execution correctness. Finally, the client sends both the execution result and the correctness NIZKPs to the orderers.

Phase 3: Ordering. All orderers run a BFT consensus protocol to determine the order of transactions within each block. Once the order is determined, the orderers disseminate the generated block to all executors for validation.

Phase 4: Validation. On receiving a block from the orderers, the executor sequentially validates each transaction within the block in the determined order. The executor commits a transaction iff the transaction has valid correctness NIZKPs and has no write conflict with previously committed transactions within the same block. Otherwise, the executor aborts the transaction.

4   Workflow Description

4.1   Client Key Generation

Each client must generate a unique public-private key set for conducting FHE operations. This key set consists of (1) an encryption key pk, (2) a decryption key sk, and (3) an evaluation key ek used for on-ciphertext arithmetic computation. While both pk and ek are open to all participants, sk must remain private to the client. Specifically, GAFE runs the key generation algorithm associated with the chosen FHE scheme (e.g., CKKS [10]), which initially generates sk, and then derives pk and ek from sk. In addition, GAFE derives a unique fixed-length string id based on sk to serve as the client's unique identifier.

4.2   GPU-Accelerated Transaction Execution

GAFE's *GPU-accelerated transaction execution* workflow co-designs the execute-order-validate workflow [2] with GPU-accelerated FHE schemes. It consists of four phases, as outlined in Fig. 1 and Algorithm 1.

Phase 1: Construction. For confidentiality preservation, GAFE processes and stores transaction data in the form of ciphertext. Thus, the client is required to construct an encrypted transaction before submitting it for execution.

Phase 1.1: Encrypting Transaction Data. The client encrypts transaction input data using the encryption keys. In digital payment, a transaction involves a sender client c_s and a receiver client c_r. Thus, c_s encrypts the payment amount val into two ciphertexts, val_s and val_r, using c_s's and c_r's encryption keys, respectively. The reason why two different ciphertexts are generated for val is

---

Algorithm 1: Transaction execution workflow of the client.

---

input: Plaintext transaction input data val
// Phase 1: Construction
1 $pk_s \leftarrow$ GetEncryptionKey(id_s); $val_s \leftarrow$ Encrypt(val,pk_s);
2 $pk_r \leftarrow$ GetEncryptionKey(id_r); $val_r \leftarrow$ Encrypt(val,pk_r);
3 $bal_s \leftarrow$ GetBalance(id_s);
4 $\pi_{bal \geq val} \leftarrow$ GenerateNIZKP($bal_s \geq val_s$, sk_s);
5 $tx \leftarrow \{val_s, val_r, \pi_{bal \geq val}\}$;
   // Phase 2: Execution
6 $results \leftarrow \varnothing$;
7 **For every executor e; do in parallel**
8 | $bal'_s, bal'_r \leftarrow$ SendForExecution(e,tx);
9 |_ $results \leftarrow results \cup \{bal'_s, bal'_r\}$;
10 $\pi_s \leftarrow$ GenerateNIZKP(a majority of bal'_s in results are consistent);
11 $\pi_r \leftarrow$ GenerateNIZKP(a majority of bal'_r in results are consistent);
   // Phase 3: Ordering & Phase 4: Validation
12 $tx \leftarrow tx \cup \{bal'_s, bal'_r, \pi_s, \pi_r\}$;
13 SendForOrderingAndValidation(tx);

---

that GAFE employs single-key FHE, which restricts computation to be performed on ciphertexts that are encrypted with the same encryption key. GAFE does not use multi-key FHE, which enables computation on ciphertexts encrypted with different encryption keys. This is because multi-key FHE incurs an extremely high computational overhead [29], impractical for real-world applications.

Phase 1.2: Proving Preconditions. In certain applications, the client generates NIZKPs to prove the satisfaction of preconditions that are compulsory for the correct execution of transactions. For instance, digital payment demands that the sender client c_s's balance bal_s must be not less than val. To prove this precondition, c_s generates an NIZKP $\pi_{bal \geq val}$ that takes c_s's decryption key as private input, decrypts the two ciphertexts bal_s and val_s, and compares the resulting plaintexts. Thanks to the zero-knowledge property of NIZKPs, GAFE preserves the confidentiality for c_s's decryption key and the two resulting plaintexts.

Phase 1.3: Submitting Transactions. Lastly, the client submits the transaction to all executors, including the encrypted input and precondition NIZKPs.

Phase 2: Execution. As shown in Fig. 1, the execution phase comprises four steps. Algorithm 2 outlines Phase 2.1, 2.2, and 2.3 from the executor's viewpoint.

Phase 2.1: Verifying preconditions. Upon receiving a transaction, the executor first verifies the precondition NIZKPs associated with the transaction (e.g., $\pi_{bal \geq val}$). If $\pi_{bal \geq val}$ is invalid, the executor terminates the transaction execution.

Phase 2.2: Executing transactions with GPU-accelerated FHE. Each executor independently executes transactions. Internally, the executor maintains a buffer that stores the transactions received within a predefined time frame (e.g., 500 milliseconds). When a timeout occurs or the number of buffered transactions reaches a specific threshold, the executor (1) moves the encrypted data of all buffered transactions from main memory to GPU memory, (2) launches the corresponding

---

Algorithm 2: Execution phase of the executor.

---

1 buffer ← ∅;
   // Phase 2.1: Verifying preconditions
2 **Upon reception of transaction tx from client; do**
3     $\{val_s, val_r, \pi_{bal \geq val}\}$ ← tx;
4   bal_s ← GetBalance(id_s); ek_s ← GetEvaluationKey(id_s);
5   bal_r ← GetBalance(id_r); ek_r ← GetEvaluationKey(id_r);
6   **if** VerifyNIZKP($\pi_{bal \geq val}$,bal_s,val_s) = *true* **then**
7 | buffer ← buffer ∪ $\{val_s, val_r, bal_s, bal_r, ek_s, ek_r\}$;
8   **else**
9 | Terminate();
10

   // Phase 2.2: Executing transactions with GPU-accelerated FHE
11 **Upon timeout or |buffer| ≥ threshold**
12   MoveFromMainMeoryToGPUMemory(buffer);
13   **For every transaction tx in buffer; do in parallel on GPU**
14 | bal'_s ← FHESub(bal_s,val_s,ek_s); bal'_r ← FHEAdd(bal_r,val_r,ek_r);
15   └ buffer ← buffer ∪ $\{tx, bal'_s, bal'_r\}$;
16   MoveFromGPUMeoryToMainMemory(buffer);
17   └ buffer ← ∅;
   // Phase 2.3: Returning transaction results
18 **For every transaction tx in buffer; do in parallel**
19   └ ReturnResultToClient(tx,id_s)

GPU kernels of FHE computation, and (3) copies back the resulting ciphertexts back to main memory. Taking the example of digital payment, the executor first moves the following data to GPU memory: the ciphertexts of the payment amount $\{val_s, val_r\}$, and the sender's and receiver's balances $\{bal_s, bal_r\}$. Next, the executor launches the GPU kernels for FHE addition and subtraction to compute the updated balances: $bal'_s = bal_s - val_s$ for the sender, and $bal'_r = bal_r + val_r$ for the receiver. Inside each kernel, we concurrently perform polynomial arithmetic computations that are highly parallelizable and pervasive in FHE schemes, such as Number-Theoretic Transform [26]. Note that GAFE is independent of FHE implementation and open to various GPU acceleration techniques [21,26,28]. Once the FHE computation is completed, the executor copies the updated balances $\{bal'_s, bal'_r\}$ back to main memory.

Phase 2.3: Returning transaction results. After execution, the executor returns the results to the client who submits the transaction. In the case of digital payment, the executor returns the updated balances $\{bal'_s, bal'_r\}$ to the sender.

Phase 2.4: Proving execution correctness. Upon receiving the results of a transaction from all executors, the clients of the transaction must prove the execution correctness. To achieve this, the clients must be online and generate NIZKPs to prove the consistency of the majority of the results. In digital payment, the sender c_s generates an NIZKP π_s that takes c_s's decryption key as private input, decrypts c_s's updated balance ciphertexts from all the results, and checks the consistency of the resulting plaintexts. The receiver c_r follows a similar procedure and generates an NIZKP π_r using c_r's decryption key to ensure the consistency of c_r's updated balance. Lastly, c_s sends the following materials to the orderers for ordering: the input data $\{val_s, val_r\}$, the precondition NIZKP $\pi_{bal \geq val}$, the consistent results $\{bal_s, bal_r\}$, and the correctness NIZKPs $\{\pi_s, \pi_r\}$.

Phase 3: Ordering. GAFE orderers run a BFT consensus protocol (e.g., PBFT [8]) to collectively determine the transaction order within each block. Once a consensus is reached among all orderers, they proceed to generate the block and disseminate the block to all executors for validation.

Phase 4: Validation. When receiving a block from the orderers, the executor sequentially validates all transactions according to their order in the block. The executor will only commit transactions that satisfy two conditions. First, the transaction must not have any write conflict with previously committed transactions within the same block. Second, the transaction must be associated with valid correctness NIZKPs (e.g., $\{\pi_s, \pi_r\}$), which serve as proofs of the transaction's execution correctness. If a transaction fails to meet either of these conditions, the executor aborts the transaction and does not commit it to the state database. Once the executor has validated all transactions, the executor permanently appends the block to the local copy of the blockchain.

5 Evaluation

5.1 Settings

Implementation. We built a prototype system of GAFE based on HLF v2.5 [2] and simulated the business logic of digital payment. We implemented the CKKS scheme [10] for GAFE based on the state-of-the-art studies on GPU-accelerated FHE [21,26,28]. GAFE adopted the gnark [11] library's implementation for the Groth16 NIZKP system [13] and employed our Golang implementation of the PBFT [8] consensus protocol. We also developed a baseline system called GAFE (w/o. GPU) that follows a similar transaction execution workflow as GAFE, except that the baseline does not buffer transactions for concurrent execution and performs all FHE computations exclusively on the CPU.

Metrics. We evaluated two metrics: (1) *effective throughput*, which indicates the average number of transactions per second (TPS) committed to the blockchain; and (2) *commit latency*, which measures the time duration from transaction construction to commitment. Additionally, we also reported the cumulative distribution function (CDF) of commit latency for all committed transactions and the latency of each phase in the transaction execution workflow (§4.2).

Testbed. We ran all evaluations on a cluster of 4 machines, each with an Nvidia RTX 3090 GPU, a 3.1GHz AMD EPYC 9754 CPU, and 64GB of main memory.

5.2 End-to-End Performance

We evaluated the end-to-end performance of GAFE and GAFE (w/o. GPU). For each evaluation, we created three executors, four orderers, and one thousand clients. Next, we constructed and submitted 100,000 digital payment transactions. To prevent transaction aborts caused by write conflicts, we explicitly

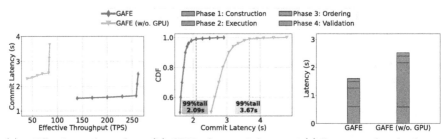

(a) Effective throughput (b) CDF of commit latency. (c) Latency of each phase.
and commit latency.

Fig. 2. End-to-end performance of GAFE and the baseline.

ensured that no two transactions in the same block shared identical clients. We
ran the evaluation ten times and reported the average values of the metrics.

GAFE exhibited exceptional end-to-end performance, as shown in Fig. 2a.
GAFE achieved a high throughput of 258 TPS and a low average latency of
1.61 s. In contrast, GAFE (w/o. GPU) displayed a significantly lower average
throughput of 83 TPS and a notably longer average latency of 2.53 s. These
results highlight the substantial performance advantage of GAFE over GAFE
(w/o. GPU), with a 3.1× increase in effective throughput and a 37% reduction in commit latency. Additionally, Fig. 2b illustrates that GAFE achieved a
shorter 99% tail latency (2.09 s) compared to the baseline (3.67 s). This suggests
that, even in worst-case scenarios, GAFE is capable of completing transaction
execution in significantly less time.

GAFE's high performance is attributed to the concurrent FHE computations
on GPU. Figure 2c compares the latency of each phase between GAFE and the
baseline. Note that GAFE achieved notably lower latency in the execution phase.
The reduced latency is enabled by GPUs' optimized parallel processing capability, facilitating concurrent execution of a significant portion of arithmetic computations in typical FHE schemes. As a result, GAFE avoids performing FHE
computation on the CPU, which has significantly fewer cores and is less efficient
in executing a large number of compute-intensive computations in parallel.

6   Conclusion

We present GAFE, a confidentiality-preserving blockchain that achieves high performance via the novel GPU-accelerated transaction execution workflow. GAFE
protects data confidentiality by encrypting transaction data using FHE, ensures
execution correctness by generating lightweight NIZKPs, and achieves high performance by leveraging GPUs to execute transactions concurrently. We implemented GAFE on the codebase of HLF. Our evaluations demonstrated the superior performance of GAFE compared to the baseline, with a significant 3.1×
increase in effective throughput (258 TPS) and a notable 37% decrease in commit latency (1.61 s).

Acknowledgements. The work is supported in part by National Key R&D Program of China (2022ZD0160200), National Key R&D Program of China (No. 2023YFB4503902), HK RIF (R7030-22), HK ITF (GHP/169/20SZ), the Huawei Flagship Research Grants in 2021 and 2023, and HK RGC GRF (Ref: HKU 17208223), the HKU-SCF FinTech AcademyR&D Funding Schemes in 2021 and 2022, the HKU-CAS Joint Laboratory for Intelligent System Software, and the Shanghai Artificial Intelligence Laboratory.

References

1. Acar, A., Aksu, H., Uluagac, A.S., Conti, M.: A survey on homomorphic encryption schemes: theory and implementation. ACM Comput. Surv. **51**(4), 1–35 (2018)
2. Androulaki, E., et al.: Hyperledger fabric: a distributed operating system for permissioned blockchains. In: Proceedings of the thirteenth EuroSys Conference, pp. 1–15. ACM, New York, NY, USA (2018)
3. Aste, T., Tasca, P., Di Matteo, T.: Blockchain technologies: the foreseeable impact on society and industry. Computer **50**(9), 18–28 (2017)
4. Bessani, A., Sousa, J., Alchieri, E.E.: State machine replication for the masses with BFT-smart. In: 2014 44th Annual IEEE/IFIP International Conference on Dependable Systems and Networks, pp. 355–362. IEEE, IEEE Computer Society, 1730 Massachusetts Ave., NW Washington, DCUnited States (2014)
5. Brakerski, Z.: Fully homomorphic encryption without modulus switching from classical GapSVP. In: Safavi-Naini, R., Canetti, R. (eds.) Advances in Cryptology - CRYPTO 2012. CRYPTO 2012, LNCS, vol. 7417, pp. 868–886. Springer, Berlin (2012). https://doi.org/10.1007/978-3-642-32009-5_50
6. Brakerski, Z., Gentry, C., Vaikuntanathan, V.: (leveled) fully homomorphic encryption without bootstrapping. ACM Trans. Comput. Theor. (TOCT) **6**(3), 1–36 (2014)
7. Bünz, B., Agrawal, S., Zamani, M., Boneh, D.: Zether: towards privacy in a smart contract world. In: Bonneau, J., Heninger, N. (eds) Financial Cryptography and Data Security, FC 2020, LNCS, vol. 12059, pp. 423–443. Springer, Cham (2020). https://doi.org/10.1007/978-3-030-51280-4
8. Castro, M., Liskov, B., et al.: Practical byzantine fault tolerance. In: OSDI, vol. 99, pp. 173–186. ACM, New York, NY, USA (1999)
9. Cheng, R., et al.: Ekiden: a platform for confidentiality-preserving, trustworthy, and performant smart contracts. In: 2019 IEEE European Symposium on Security and Privacy (EuroS&P), pp. 185–200. IEEE (2019)
10. Cheon, J.H., Kim, A., Kim, M., Song, Y.: Homomorphic encryption for arithmetic of approximate numbers. In: Takagi, T., Peyrin, T. (eds.) Advances in Cryptology -ASIACRYPT 2017, ASIACRYPT 2017, LNCS, Part I, vol. 10624, pp. 409–437 Springer, Cham (2017). https://doi.org/10.1007/978-3-319-70694-8_15
11. consensys: Gnark (2023). https://docs.gnark.consensys.net/
12. Fan, J., Vercauteren, F.: Somewhat practical fully homomorphic encryption. Cryptology ePrint Archive, Paper 2012/144 (2012). https://eprint.iacr.org/2012/144, https://eprint.iacr.org/2012/144
13. Groth, J.: On the size of pairing-based non-interactive arguments. In: Fischlin, M., Coron, J.S. (eds.) Advances in Cryptology - EUROCRYPT 2016. EUROCRYPT 2016, LNCS, vol. 9666, pp. 305–326. Springer, Berlin (2016). https://doi.org/10.1007/978-3-662-49896-5_11

14. Hopwood, D., Bowe, S., Hornby, T., Wilcox, N., et al.: Zcash protocol specification. GitHub: San Francisco **4**(220), 32 (2016)
15. Kalodner, H., Goldfeder, S., Chen, X., Weinberg, S.M., Felten, E.W.: Arbitrum: Scalable, private smart contracts. In: 27th USENIX Security Symposium (USENIX Security 18), pp. 1353–1370 (2018)
16. Kang, H., Dai, T., Jean-Louis, N., Tao, S., Gu, X.: Fabzk: supporting privacy-preserving, auditable smart contracts in hyperledger fabric. In: 2019 49th Annual IEEE/IFIP International Conference on Dependable Systems and Networks (DSN), pp. 543–555. IEEE, IEEE, Portland, Oregon, USA (2019)
17. Kosba, A., Miller, A., Shi, E., Wen, Z., Papamanthou, C.: Hawk: the blockchain model of cryptography and privacy-preserving smart contracts. In: 2016 IEEE Symposium on Security and Privacy (SP), pp. 839–858. IEEE (2016)
18. Landerreche, E., Stevens, M.: On immutability of blockchains. In: Proceedings of 1st ERCIM Blockchain Workshop 2018. European Society for Socially Embedded Technologies (EUSSET) (2018)
19. Meier, A.V.: The elgamal cryptosystem. In: Joint Advanced Students Seminar (2005)
20. Monero: the monero project https://www.getmonero.org/
21. Özcan, A.Ş, Ayduman, C., Türkoğlu, E.R., Savaş, E.: Homomorphic encryption on GPU. IEEE Access **11**, 84168–84186 (2023)
22. Raczyński, M.: What is the fastest blockchain and why? analysis of 43 blockchains, January 2021. https://alephzero.org/blog/what-is-the-fastest-blockchain-and-why-analysis-of-43-blockchains/
23. Steffen, S., Bichsel, B., Baumgartner, R., Vechev, M.: Zeestar: private smart contracts by homomorphic encryption and zero-knowledge proofs. In: 2022 IEEE Symposium on Security and Privacy (SP), pp. 179–197. IEEE (2022)
24. Sun, X., Yu, F.R., Zhang, P., Sun, Z., Xie, W., Peng, X.: A survey on zero-knowledge proof in blockchain. IEEE Network **35**(4), 198–205 (2021)
25. Viand, A., Jattke, P., Hithnawi, A.: Sok: fully homomorphic encryption compilers. In: 2021 IEEE Symposium on Security and Privacy (SP), pp. 1092–1108. IEEE, San Francisco, CA, USA (2021). https://doi.org/10.1109/SP40001.2021.00068
26. Wang, Z., et al.: He-booster: an efficient polynomial arithmetic acceleration on GPUs for fully homomorphic encryption. IEEE Trans. Parallel Distrib. Syst. **34**(4), 1067–1081 (2023)
27. Xu, L., Zhang, Y., Zhu, L.: Regulation-friendly privacy-preserving blockchain based on zk-SNARK. In: Ruiz, M., Soffer, P. (eds.) Advanced Information Systems Engineering Workshops. CAiSE 2023. LNBIP, vol. 482, pp. 167–177. Springer, Cham (2023). https://doi.org/10.1007/978-3-031-34985-0_17
28. Yang, H., Shen, S., Dai, W., Zhou, L., Liu, Z., Zhao, Y.: Phantom: a cuda-accelerated word-wise homomorphic encryption library. IEEE Trans. Depend. Secure Comput. 1–12 (2024). https://doi.org/10.1109/TDSC.2024.3363900
29. Yuan, M., Wang, D., Zhang, F., Wang, S., Ji, S., Ren, Y.: An examination of multi-key fully homomorphic encryption and its applications. Mathematics **10**(24), 4678 (2022)
30. Zhang, T., Huang, Z.: Blockchain and central bank digital currency. ICT Express **8**(2), 264–270 (2022)

A Blockchain-Based Approach for Model Card Accountability and Regulatory Compliance

Ankur Lohachab$^{(\boxtimes)}$(iD) and Visara Urovi(iD)

Institute of Data Science, Department of Advanced Computing Sciences, Maastricht University, Maastricht 6229 GT, Limburg, The Netherlands
{ankur.lohachab,v.urovi}@maastrichtuniversity.nl

Abstract. This paper introduces an approach that utilizes smart contracts to facilitate the trustworthy sharing and management of Machine Learning (ML) and Artificial Intelligence (AI) models, as described using model cards. To this end, the proposed approach incorporates Account Abstraction for authentication, enabling role-based access control. This control allows stakeholders to share, track, and validate model cards transparently and securely while tailoring visibility and interaction to preserve privacy in accordance with each role's privileges. The approach further delineates the conceptualization and lifecycle management of model cards, spanning from creation to deprecation, all within a blockchain-based framework. Additionally, the paper discusses the state parameterization of model cards, formalizing the operational dynamics and constraints associated with each phase of their progression. The proof of concept, implemented to evaluate our approach, suggests that it is capable of effectively capturing and maintaining an immutable record of the various states of model cards, thereby providing a robust and verifiable trail. Overall, our approach is designed to ensure the integrity of model cards and establish accountability, thereby strengthening trust among stakeholders, particularly those relying on AI and ML models as described in model cards.

Keywords: Model Card · Decentralized Trust in AI · Account Abstraction · Non-Fungible Tokens (NFTs) · Blockchain Technology · AI and ML Model Provenance · Smart Wallet

1 Introduction

The proliferation and utilization of open-source machine learning (ML) frameworks have streamlined the process for a diverse array of stakeholders, including non-expert analysts [1], to efficiently share, customize, and deploy artificial intelligence (AI) and ML algorithms across domains. This encompasses a broad

---

A. Lohachab and V. Urovi—Contributing authors.

J. P. A. Almeida et al. (Eds.): CAiSE 2024 Workshops, LNBIP 521, pp. 37–48, 2024.
https://doi.org/10.1007/978-3-031-61003-5_4

spectrum of models, from large-scale language models leveraging transformer architectures [2] to convolutional neural networks for image processing [3] and recurrent neural networks for sequential data analysis [4]. Indeed, while these advancements facilitate the integration of AI capabilities into various applications, they also give rise to issues such as errors, bias, and failures [5]. This juxtaposition emphasizes the critical need for mechanisms that ensure transparency and accountability in these models. Addressing this challenge, model cards [6] offer a pragmatic solution by facilitating a standardized documentation format for AI models. This format typically encompasses essential details such as the model's architecture, training data, performance benchmarks, ethical considerations, and potential limitations. Moreover, a significant focus is placed on evaluating the model's human-centric performance across diverse individuals, phenotypic or demographic groups, and conducting intersectional analyses that combine two or more of these groups [6]. Considering this, it can be said that model cards significantly enhance transparency for ML models, benefiting both experts and non-experts alike.

Despite model cards being a significant step toward improving transparency among developers, users, and stakeholders of machine learning models, their effectiveness is contingent upon the creators' integrity. This highlights the risk of potentially misleading model representations, whether unintentional or intentional [6], and underscores the importance of not relying solely on model cards. Furthermore, a similar challenge arises from the lack of a mechanism to maintain the versioning of a model card, potentially leading to reliance on outdated versions. Our literature review identifies a significant gap: there is a notable lack of work on developing trusted, transparent, and secure provenance mechanisms for model cards that ensure accountability and meet regulatory compliance in specific scenarios. One reason for this gap seems to be the relatively recent adoption of model cards, which has brought their limitations, especially in ensuring their integrity, into focus as areas of concern.

Considering this, our work aims to address such underlying concerns, with focus on ensuring the trustworthiness and enabling the provenance of the sharing of model cards. It is important to highlight that, from perspectives of accountability and compliance, our work conceptually builds upon our previously proposed architecture, LUCE [7]. This paper proposes a distributed approach, termed as m-LUCE, that leverages blockchain functionalities to establish a seamless workflow between model card owners/publishers and analysts/users. This facilitates efficient interactions and inherently enhances accountability to mitigate potential risk scenarios, such as backdoor attacks on model cards. More specifically, central to m-LUCE is the tokenization of model cards, utilizing smart contracts in accordance with EIP-1155-a multifaceted standard that provides a robust mechanism for the traceability of model cards. With this, the aim is to inherently support accountability by directly linking actions and changes to the model cards' underlying states within m-LUCE. Furthermore, to facilitate a seamless UI/UX experience for model card owners, analysts, and all involved entities, m-LUCE employs Account Abstraction (AA), providing smart wallet contracts to registered users. For the efficacy of m-LUCE, a proof of concept has been tested using the Thirdweb SDK [8,9], IPFS (InterPlanetary File System), and the Polygon testnet network. In summary, this paper makes the following contributions:

- This paper introduces an approach designed to ensure the trustworthy management of model cards, enabling stakeholders to securely share and transparently track the provenance of underlying AI and ML models, thereby improving integrity and strengthening accountability within the ecosystem.
- This paper employs Non-Fungible Tokens (NFTs) to represent model cards, a key aspect of our approach that ensures their lifecycle is immutably recorded and facilitates detailed tracking and auditing of state changes. Additionally, our approach implements AA to improve the end-user experience and enhances the security and usability of model card management, thereby allowing more refined control over access and permissions.
- This paper delves into the conceptualization and lifecycle management of model cards, from their inception to deprecation, emphasizing governance and state transitions as orchestrated by the ERC-1155 standard, particularly through state parameterization. This exploration aims to elucidate the operational dynamics and constraints embedded within the proposed approach, highlighting the importance of governance and temporal parameters in shaping conditions and limitations on state transitions.

2   Background

2.1   Model Cards

More recently, the imperative for shared understanding and transparency in AI, ML, and associated datasets has garnered significant attention [10]. In response to these imperatives, several solutions have been proposed. For example, Pushkarna et al. [11] introduced a framework termed *Data Cards*. These Data Cards are designed to support transparency reporting by generating documentation that is scalable for production environments and enhances readability. Similarly, other studies, such as [12–15], have focused on establishing standardized methodologies for communicating the characteristics of datasets used in ML research and applications. Nevertheless, despite the diversity in the concepts underlying these approaches, they all share a common goal: to enhance transparency and comprehensibility. It should be noted that although exploring the unique capabilities of each model presents an interesting research direction, such exploration lies beyond the scope of this work, which instead focuses on *Model Cards* [6]. The reasons for zeroing in on model cards are manifold, encompassing not only their intrinsic functionalities—such as facilitating better decision-making and promoting increased collaboration—but also their recognition by several key stakeholders, including Google Cloud and Kaggle, as a foundational step towards transparency in AI. In other words, *Model Cards* serve as concise documents, as exemplified in Table 1, for trained machine learning models; they offer benchmarked evaluations across a range of conditions, including various cultural, demographic, or phenotypic groups (for example, race, sex, and location) as well as intersectional groups (such as combinations of race and sex), which are crucial for the models' intended application domains.

Table 1. Overview of Model Card sections.

a) **Model Details**	d) **Metrics**
- Person or organization developing model	- Model performance measures
- Model date, version, type	- Decision thresholds, Variation approaches
- Information on training algorithms, parameters, fairness constraints	e) **Evaluation Data**
- Paper or other resource for more information	- Datasets, Motivation, Preprocessing
- Citation details, License	f) **Training Data**
- Contact for questions or comments	- Details on the distribution over various factors
b) **Intended Use**	g) **Quantitative Analyses**
- Primary intended uses and users	- Unitary and intersectional results
- Out-of-scope use cases	h) **Ethical Considerations**
c) **Factors**	i) **Caveats and Recommendations**
- Relevant and evaluation factors	

2.2   Tokenization of Model Cards

Despite the aim of Model Cards to offer a comprehensive overview of a model's capabilities and limitations, several concerns persist. One such concern is the challenge of maintaining synchronous updates with their corresponding Model Cards, which could lead to discrepancies between the model's current functionality and the information detailed in the Model Card. Furthermore, ensuring that the information within Model Cards is both accessible and verifiable remains a concern, particularly in scenarios requiring regulatory compliance or third-party audits. In response, m-LUCE employs smart contracts; for instance, to efficiently manage the states of the Model Cards, we propose taking the Model Card as input and storing it as an NFT on the blockchain, specifically using ERC-1155 [16], a multi-token standard. The primary reason for selecting this standard over ERC-721 [17], which necessitates the creation of a separate NFT for each instance, is to enhance scalability. ERC-1155 enables the creation of multiple copies of the same NFT, beneficial in scenarios where multiple copies of a Model Card are required, thus significantly enhancing the scalability of m-LUCE. Beyond the tokenization of Model Cards, m-LUCE's approach to authentication employs AA, specifically adhering to the EIP-4337 standard [18]. This allows for gasless transactions for certain operations, with the consortium serving as the paymaster in m-LUCE. Additionally, it enhances the UI/UX experience through user-friendly login and recovery mechanisms, role-based authentication, and the use of pull transactions in specific scenarios. It is crucial to highlight the importance of establishing key infrastructure components, such as the Bundler, which demands meticulous planning and execution. Consequently, for the implementation of m-LUCE, we have utilized the Thirdweb SDK [9] and adapted the Managed Account Factory contract [8] to meet the specific needs of our proposal.

2.3 Motivating Scenario

Consider a scenario where an entity publishes a model card for an AI system designed to predict patient outcomes from healthcare data. The card details the algorithm's performance across demographic groups, claiming high accuracy and low bias. Later, another entity using this model for clinical decision-making finds performance discrepancies not disclosed in the model card, possibly due to data distribution changes, model updates, or overlooked biases. This underscores the need for dynamic management capable of real-time updates and provenance tracking for model cards, ensuring stakeholders have access to trusted records at all times.

3 Proposed Approach: m-LUCE

3.1 Approach Overview

m-LUCE extends our previous work, LUCE [7], as outlined in Sect. 1, by enhancing it from a compliance and accountability perspective and introducing transparent provenance for model cards. Below, we outline m-LUCE's key steps (illustrated in Fig. 1a):

1. **Smart Wallet Contract Deployment (Managed Smart Wallet - EIP-4337):** m-LUCE begins with the deployment of an adapted managed factory contract, specifically tailored to the EIP-4337 specification (as mentioned in Sect. 2.2). This step underpins the creation of individualized smart wallets, aimed at providing m-LUCE users—Publishers, Analysts, or Admins—with a mechanism for seamless and secure interactions across the blockchain network. Adhering to EIP-4337, m-LUCE enhances user autonomy by abstracting complex blockchain operations and offers features such as transaction batching, sponsored transactions, and improved security measures, essential for a positive user experience in managing model cards. Furthermore, the underlying authentication strategy is straightforward; for example, as highlighted in Fig. 1b, the React component (Listing 1) initiates the connection by requesting user login, which, upon successful authentication, triggers a smart contract function in Solidity (Listing 2) to register or verify the user's identity within m-LUCE. Additionally, m-LUCE enables the upgradeability of smart wallets, managed by designated administrators, exemplified by the *updateImplementation* function in the *ManagedAccountFactory* smart contract, ensuring seamless and secure updates to wallet contracts within the system.

Listing (1) Wallet Connection

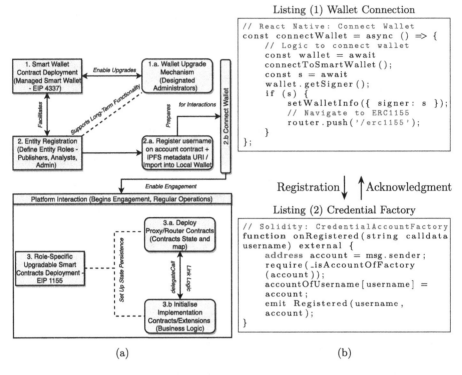

```
// React Native: Connect Wallet
const connectWallet = async () => {
    // Logic to connect wallet
    const wallet = await
    connectToSmartWallet();
    const s = await
    wallet.getSigner();
    if (s) {
        setWalletInfo({ signer: s });
        // Navigate to ERC1155
        router.push('/erc1155');
    }
};
```

Registration ↓   ↑ Acknowledgment

Listing (2) Credential Factory

```
// Solidity: CredentialAccountFactory
function onRegistered(string calldata
username) external {
    address account = msg.sender;
    require(_isAccountOfFactory
    (account));
    accountOfUsername[username] =
    account;
    emit Registered(username,
    account);
}
```

(a)   (b)

Fig. 1. (a) An overview of m-LUCE. (b) A snippet illustrating the authentication mechanism using AA.

2. **Entity Registration:** For entities to participate in m-LUCE, registration is a prerequisite. In this context, the *connectToSmartWallet* function (as mentioned in Listing 1) serves as a pivotal example, illustrating how it securely establishes connections for both new and returning users to m-LUCE. By utilizing the *SmartWallet* and *LocalWallet* classes, this function adeptly manages user authentication and subsequent smart wallet connections, laying the groundwork for secure and efficient entity interactions. Moreover, the *grant-Role* function from the *ManagedAccountFactory* smart contract plays a crucial role; it facilitates the assignment of specific roles to users' m-LUCE accounts.

3. **Role-Specific Upgradable Smart Contracts Deployment - EIP-1155:** At the center of m-LUCE is the utilization of role-specific upgradable smart contracts, conforming to the EIP-1155 standard. This approach facilitates a multitude of functionalities. For instance, through the *mintBatch* function, m-LUCE enables the issuance of multiple instances of a model card with controlled quantities, allowing for the distribution of a model card to multiple analysts simultaneously. Moreover, m-LUCE incorporates extensions from ERC-4907 [19] to enrich the customizable aspects of ERC-1155, notably introducing the capability to rent model cards. For example, through the *setUser*

function from ERC-4907, it automates the accessibility of model cards by allowing data providers to specify the duration for which a model card remains accessible on the platform. This functionality enables setting a specific access timeframe for a particular analyst, with the potential to automatically revoke access once the period expires. Additionally, m-LUCE has conceptualized the deployment of proxy or router contracts for upgradeability (as depicted in Fig. 1a).

3.2 Modeling State Parameterization for Model Cards

This section delves into the conceptualization and lifecycle of model cards within m-LUCE, viewed through state parameterization. The lifecycle spans from creation to deprecation, governed by the ERC-1155 standard, which ensures secure recording of state transitions on m-LUCE. Figure 2 illustrates various states and transitions in a model card's lifecycle, emphasizing operational dynamics and constraints, such as time-bound availability for actions like validation. Having said that, to formally describe the states involved in managing model cards on m-LUCE, we define the underlying system model $\mathcal{M}$ as a tuple $\mathcal{M} = (S, A, T, \Sigma, \prec, \mathcal{F}, \mathcal{C}, \mathcal{D})$, where:

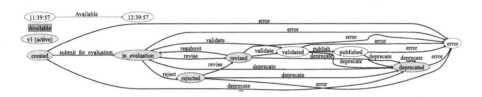

Fig. 2. An illustration of the Model Cards possible states managed using ERC-1155.

- S is a finite set representing the possible states of a model card within the system. This set encapsulates each distinct phase a model card might undergo, from its creation to its potential deprecation, reflecting its lifecycle within the m-LUCE environment. For example, $S = \{\text{created}, \text{submitted\_for\_evaluation}, \text{in\_evaluation}, \text{validated}, \text{rejected}, \ldots\}$ defines the finite set S of distinct states that a model card can occupy throughout its lifecycle.
- A denotes the finite set of actions executable on model cards, directly affecting their state. Actions in A cover all operations enabled by smart contracts that can alter a model card's lifecycle stage, such as creation, evaluation, and validation. Examples of actions include `create`, `submit_for_evaluation`, `validate`, `reject`, `publish`, `revise`, and `deprecate`. Each action triggers specific state transitions as defined by the system's logic and is governed by the ERC-1155 smart contract.

- $T : S \times A \to S$ defines the transition function, mapping a pair consisting of a current state and an action to a subsequent state within the system. This function embodies the core logic dictating how actions, when executed on model cards at particular lifecycle stages, deterministically lead to transitions to new states. For example, if a model card in the `created` state undergoes the `submit_for_evaluation` action, T dictates the resulting state as `in_evaluation` (as detailed in Table 2).
- Σ represents the set of all valid sequences of actions, underpinning the operational semantics to which model cards are subject within the system. Simply put, each element in Σ is a sequence that adheres to the logical and operational rules established by the transition function T and the action set A, ensuring that each sequence is not only possible but also valid within the constraints of the m-LUCE environment.
- $\prec$ is a binary relation over Σ that defines the causal order of actions, ensuring the logical progression of state transitions. For any two elements x, x' in a sequence, $x \prec x'$ indicates that x causally precedes x'. Causal dependencies between elements are divided into two categories: *Message Dependency* $(x \to_M x')$, which occurs if one element x involves sending or inserting a message that x' receives or processes—crucial for actions like submitting a model card for evaluation; and *Local Dependency* $(x \to_L x')$, which occurs when both elements are part of the same smart contract operation sequence, with x occurring before x' in this sequence. This mechanism describes sequential state changes within a single transaction, such as updating a model card's status from `submitted_for_evaluation` to `in_evaluation`.
- $\mathcal{F}$ delineates the fairness constraints integral to the system's operational ethics, ensuring equitable consideration and execution of all actions within a bounded timeframe. We leverage Sequential Consistency, which guarantees that all transactions appear to be executed sequentially in a single global order, even though they might be processed concurrently on m-LUCE. This enforces specific fairness properties: *Freedom from Starvation* ensures every submitted model card (`submit_for_evaluation`) eventually reaches a final state (e.g., `validated` or `rejected`) within a reasonable timeframe. *No Unfair Prioritization* mandates that the order of execution for actions on different model cards respects the causal dependencies defined by $\prec$, preventing any single actor from unfairly monopolizing resources like evaluations.
- $\mathcal{C}$ delineates the set of constraints integral to the operation and governance of the system, ensuring that all interactions with model cards adhere to a predefined framework. These constraints include: *Regulatory Compliance*, ensuring adherence to legal standards; *Business Logic*, defining operational rules for model card management such as eligibility criteria for evaluation; and *Temporal Constraints*, employing Linear Temporal Logic to reason about time-dependent propositions. For instance, *Model Validation Deadline*: G (`submit_for_evaluation` $\to F$ `validated`, T_{max}) specifies that all model cards submitted for evaluation must be validated within a maximum timeframe T_{max}. Additionally, *Expiration Threshold*: G (`created` $\land \neg$ `validated`

$\wedge T_{expire}$ elapsed) $\rightarrow$ deprecated indicates that any model card not validated within T_{expire} after creation will automatically be deprecated.

Table 2. State transitions in Model Card management based on event triggers.

Trigger (Event)	created	in_evaluation	rejected	revised	validated	published	deprecated	error
submit_for_evaluation	in_evaluation	–	in_evaluation	in_evaluation	–	–	–	–
reject	–	rejected	–	–	–	–	–	–
revise	–	revised	revised	–	–	–	–	–
resubmit	–	–	–	in_evaluation (version++)	–	–	–	–
validate	–	validated	–	validated	–	–	–	–
publish	–	–	–	–	published (transfer_ownership)	–	–	–
deprecate	deprecated (applies to all statuses)							–
error	error (applies to all statuses)							

- $\mathcal{D}$ encompasses a set of decision functions, formalized as $\mathcal{D} : S \times A \rightarrow \{true, false\}$, which systematically assess the permissibility and advisability of executing given actions in particular states. Each decision function within $\mathcal{D}$ integrates comprehensive logic derived from the system's operational constraints, regulatory guidelines, and the intrinsic business rules governing model card transactions.

To sum up, the state transition matrix presented in Table 2 illustrates the lifecycle of model cards managed under the ERC-1155 smart contract within m-LUCE. It highlights the various states a model card can assume and the corresponding triggers. For instance, the *submit for evaluation* trigger exemplifies the fairness property of freedom from starvation, as outlined in $\mathcal{F}$. Similarly, *resubmit* reinforces fairness principles, while *validate* and *publish* actions are in line with m-LUCE's operational ethics and fairness constraints. Moreover, *deprecate* and *error* states exemplify the implementation of temporal constraints and error handling mechanisms, respectively.

4   Evaluation and Discussion

To evaluate m-LUCE's effectiveness and efficiency, we focus on its core functionalities: provenance and lifecycle management of model cards. Evaluation criteria include the system's handling of state transitions, permissions enforcement, and maintaining a transparent, auditable trail of actions on model cards.

Fig. 3. A snippet of the proof-of-concept implementation.

4.1 Functional Testing

We conducted functional tests to assess m-LUCE's management of the model card lifecycle, from creation to potential deprecation. To this, a key test involved submitting a model card for evaluation, demonstrating the system's processing of submissions. As shown in Fig. 3, upon submission, all registered entities, including the publisher, can view the model card's status. An admin or authorized entity then must decide (accept or reject) within a predefined timeframe, showcasing the system's governance. For example, in our scenario, illustrated in Fig. 2, the admin has a 1-hour decision window. Figure 3 shows a model card rejected based on evaluation criteria. Besides, Listing 3 details functions `submitForEvaluation` and `rejectModelCard`, underpinning these processes.

The `submitForEvaluation` function allows the owner (typically the model card provider) to transition a model card's state from `Created` to `InEvaluation`, provided the model card is currently in the `Created` state. Similarly, the `rejectModelCard` function enables the transition of a model card's state from `InEvaluation` to `Rejected`, adhering to the system's governance that a model card can be moved to `Rejected` only if it is currently under evaluation. Put simply, functional testing of m-LUCE underscores its capability to seamlessly manage the lifecycle of model cards within a blockchain environment. Moreover, the testing highlights the system's adherence to fairness constraints and decision-making processes within a bounded timeframe, ensuring that no action is unduly delayed or ignored.

Listing 3. A snippet of ERC-1155 for managing Model Card lifecycle.

```
// Function to submit a model card for evaluation
function submitForEvaluation(uint256 modelCardId) public onlyOwner {
    require(modelCardStates[modelCardId] == ModelCardState.Created,
    "Model card must be in Created state.");
    modelCardStates[modelCardId] = ModelCardState.SubmittedForEvaluation;
}

// Function to reject a model card
function rejectModelCard(uint256 modelCardId) public onlyOwner {
    require(modelCardStates[modelCardId] == ModelCardState.InEvaluation,
    "Model card must be in evaluation.");
    modelCardStates[modelCardId] = ModelCardState.Rejected;
}
```

4.2   Discussion

m-LUCE introduces an approach to managing the lifecycle of ML and AI model cards on the blockchain, enhancing features such as tamper evidence, incremental updates, and snapshots for state versioning and provenance tracking with minimal structural overhead. Below are some key benefits that m-LUCE provides:

1. **Enhanced Provenance and State Management:** m-LUCE implements a state management system for detailed tracking and tamper-evident recording throughout the model card lifecycle—from creation, through validation or rejection. This feature is crucial for reliability and accountability in sensitive applications such as healthcare, offering an immutable audit trail.
2. **Lineage Creation and Traceability:** By facilitating the reconstruction of a model card's history, m-LUCE enhances the integrity and credibility of the ML and AI models it documents. This level of lineage creation and traceability is essential in fields like medical research and clinical applications, where the link between accountability and outcomes—such as patient safety and treatment efficacy—is critical.

5   Conclusions and Future Work

This paper has highlighted the benefits of model cards for enhancing transparency and efficacy in ML models while aiming to address their integrity and accountability concerns. To this end, we introduced m-LUCE, an approach for ensuring trusted provenance and secure sharing of model cards, developed through a proof of concept that utilizes EIP-1155 for managing model cards as NFTs and EIP-4337 for enabling Account Abstraction in authentication. Furthermore, we also explored the operational dynamics and constraints of model cards, emphasizing their lifecycle management from inception to deprecation via state parameterization. Nonetheless, the proof of concept opens several avenues for further inquiry, especially concerning the system's efficiency and a deeper understanding of its functionality. It is important to note that while the approach is designed to be generic, its current implementation and testing have focused on a subset of potential functionalities. Additionally, future efforts will aim to broaden the tokenization scope and improve the approach's applicability. Recognizing model cards as merely one method to enhance transparency, future investigations will explore how blockchain technology can amplify the utility and impact of other transparency-enhancing AI and ML methodologies.

Acknowledgements. This work was supported by the REALM project (Grant No. 101095435).

References

1. Yang, Q., Suh, J., Chen, N.-C., Ramos, G.: Grounding interactive machine learning tool design in how non-experts actually build models. In: Proceedings of the 2018 Designing Interactive Systems Conference, pp. 573–584 (2018)

2. Zhao, H., Chen, H., Yang, F., Liu, N., Deng, H., Cai, H., Wang, S., Yin, D., Du, M.: Explainability for large language models: a survey. ACM Trans. Intell. Syst. Technol. **15**(2), 1–38 (2024)
3. Browne, M., Ghidary, S.S., Mayer, N.M.: Convolutional neural networks for image processing with applications in mobile robotics, pp. 327–349 (2008)
4. Lipton, Z.C., Berkowitz, J., Elkan, C.: A critical review of recurrent neural networks for sequence learning. arXiv preprint arXiv:1506.00019 (2015)
5. Osoba, O.A., Welser IV, W., Welser, W.: An Intelligence in our Image: the Risks of Bias and Errors in Artificial Intelligence. Rand Corporation, Santa Monica (2017)
6. Mitchell, M., et al.: Model cards for model reporting. In: Proceedings of the Conference on Fairness, Accountability, and Transparency, pp. 220–229 (2019)
7. Urovi, V., Jaiman, V., Angerer, A., Dumontier, M.: Luce: a blockchain-based data sharing platform for monitoring data license accountability and compliance. Blockchain: Res. Appl. **3**(4), 100102 (2022)
8. Thirdweb: managed account factory. https://portal.thirdweb.com/contracts/build/base-contracts/erc-4337/managed-account-factory. Accessed 19 Feb 2024
9. Thirdweb: account abstraction. https://portal.thirdweb.com/connect/account-abstraction Accessed 18 Feb 2024
10. Nicenboim, I., Giaccardi, E., Redström, J.: From explanations to shared understandings of AI (2022)
11. Pushkarna, M., Zaldivar, A.: Data cards: purposeful and transparent documentation for responsible AI. In: 35th Conference on Neural Information Processing Systems, pp. 1776–1826 (2021)
12. Bender, E.M., Friedman, B.: Data statements for natural language processing: toward mitigating system bias and enabling better science. Trans. Assoc. Comput. Linguist. **6**, 587–604 (2018)
13. Gebru, T., et al.: Datasheets for datasets. Commun. ACM **64**(12), 86–92 (2021)
14. Holland, S., Hosny, A., Newman, S., Joseph, J., Chmielinski, K.: The dataset nutrition label. Data Protect. Priv. **12**(12), 1 (2020)
15. Stevens, L.M., Mortazavi, B.J., Deo, R.C., Curtis, L., Kao, D.P.: Recommendations for reporting machine learning analyses in clinical research. Circ. Cardiovasc. Q. Outcomes **13**(10), 006556 (2020)
16. Radomski, W., Cooke, A., Castonguay, P., Therien, J., Binet, E., Sandford, R.: ERC-1155: multi token standard. Online serial (2018). https://eips.ethereum.org/EIPS/eip-1155
17. Entriken, W., Shirley, D., Evans, J., Sachs, N.: ERC-721: non-fungible token standard. Online serial (2018). https://eips.ethereum.org/EIPS/eip-721
18. Buterin, V., et al.: ERC-4337: account abstraction using alt Mempool [DRAFT] (2021). https://eips.ethereum.org/EIPS/eip-4337. Accessed 13 Mar 2024
19. Anders, Lance, Shrug: ERC-4907: Rental NFT, an Extension of EIP-721. Online serial (2022). https://eips.ethereum.org/EIPS/eip-4907

HybridAIMS

2nd International Workshop on Hybrid Artificial Intelligence and Enterprise Modelling for Intelligent Information Systems (HybridAIMS 2024)

Hybrid Artificial Intelligence is the research direction that focuses on the combination of two prominent fields: sub-symbolic AI (e.g., statistical learning methods, such as Bayesian learning, deep learning such as large language models based on transformer networks) and symbolic AI (e.g., knowledge-based systems such as knowledge graphs, rule-based reasoning, automated planning). Approaches from both fields have complementary strengths and, especially when suitably integrated, can enable the creation of Intelligent Information Systems (IIS). For example, whilst neural networks can recognize patterns in large amounts of data, knowledge-based systems contain domain knowledge and enable logical reasoning, enforcement of constraints, and explainability of conclusions. AI approaches are typically integrated with application systems, which provide data for the AI approaches and use the results of these approaches for further processing. Thus, the creation of IIS requires high expertise in both AI approaches, and familiarity with the application domain and IT requirements. An early inclusion of domain experts in the engineering process is beneficial as it promotes high quality. Such an early inclusion is, however, challenging because stakeholders from business and IT have complementary skills and speak different languages: one more technical and one more business-oriented. Enterprise Modelling (EM) can tackle this challenge as it supports business and IT alignment. It is an established approach for the conceptual representation, design, implementation, and analysis of information systems. This is of relevance for AI approaches. Graphical notation of enterprise models fosters human interpretability, hence supporting communication and decision-making involving stakeholders from the application domain, IT, and AI. The convergence of Hybrid Artificial Intelligence and Enterprise Modelling promises to deliver high value in the creation of Intelligent Information Systems.

This International Workshop on Hybrid Artificial Intelligence and Enterprise Modelling for Intelligent Information Systems (HybridAIMS) brought together researchers and practitioners from machine learning, knowledge representation and reasoning (incl. semantic technologies), and enterprise modelling to reflect on how combining the three fields can contribute to engineering intelligent information systems across various application domains.

HybridAIMS 2024 received ten high-quality international submissions. Each paper was single-blindly reviewed by two to four members of the Program Committee. Of all the submitted manuscripts, the top seven were accepted to be presented on 3 June 2024. In the proceedings, five of those are published as full research papers and two as short papers.

Steven Alter gave the invited talk to open the workshop with a presentation entitled "How six levels of enterprise modelling could help in visualizing applications and limitations of symbolic and sub-symbolic AI". Steven, in his talk, addressed the challenge of combining enterprise modelling with symbolic AI and sub-symbolic AI in the development or operation of information systems by introducing the Work system-centric enterprise modelling (WSCEM). This includes a new RAVC framework (Resources, Activities, and Value for Customers) that can be applied in different ways across six levels, from enterprise capabilities to roles and responsibilities of digital agents within specific activities. According to Steven, RAVC ideas imply a series of flexible analytical "lenses" that focus on a specific level but can be adapted for understanding work system and IS operation at other levels. Those lenses help in visualizing applications of both symbolic and sub-symbolic AI independently or in combination. Recognizing possible degrees of "smartness" at the various levels helps in describing the contribution of Artificial Intelligence along multiple dimensions related to information processing, action in the world, internal regulation, and knowledge acquisition.

Anne Füßl *et al.* presented an explanation user interface for a knowledge graph-based XAI approach to process analysis.

Václav Pechtor explored the convergence of Neuro-Symbolic AI and Enterprise Modelling applied to the public sector.

Jack Daniel Rittelmeyer and Kurt Sandkuhl presented a survey study to evaluate the completeness and correctness of a morphological box for AI solutions.

Joachim Ehrenthal *et al.* proposed an approach that integrates generative Artificial Intelligence into Supply Chain Management using the SCOR Model.

David Mäder *et al.* presented a student performance prediction model based on course description and student similarity.

James Allan *et al.* envisioned a hierarchical knowledge framework for Digital Twins of buildings and their energy systems.

Knut Hinkelmann *et al.* proposed an ontology-based modeling approach of argumentation in the Research Problem Modelling Language (RPML) to enhance research clarity.

We thank the authors for their noteworthy contributions and the members of the Program Committee for their invaluable help in the reviewing and discussion phases. We hope that the reader will benefit from reading these papers to learn more about the latest advances in research about the convergence of hybrid artificial intelligence and enterprise modelling.

June 2024

Emanuele Laurenzi
Hans Friedrich Witschel
Alessandro Oltramari
Paulo Shakarian
Peter Haase

Organization

Workshop Chairs

Emanuele Laurenzi   FHNW, Switzerland
Hans Friedrich Witschel   FHNW, Switzerland
Alessandro Oltramari   Carnegie Bosch Institute, USA
Paulo Shakarian   Arizona State University, USA
Peter Haase   Metaphacts, Germany

Program Committee

Karsten Böhm   FH Kufstein Tirol, Austria
Robert Andrei Buchmann   Babeș-Bolyai University of Cluj Napoca, Romania
Yoojung Choi   University of California, USA
Sergio de Cesare   University of Westminster, UK
Arianna Fedeli   University of Camerino, Italy
Fabrizio Fornari   University of Camerino, Italy
Giancarlo Guizzardi   University of Twente, Netherlands
Knut Hinkelmann   FHNW, Switzerland
Stephan Jüngling   FHNW, Switzerland
Andreas Martin   FHNW, Switzerland
Heiko Maus   Research Center for AI (DFKI), Germany
Uwe Riss   University of Hertfordshire, UK
Ben Roelens   Ghent University, Belgium
Kurt Sandkuhl   University of Rostock, Germany
Gerardo Simari   Universidad Nacional del Sur and CONICET, Argentina
Pnina Soffer   University of Haifa, Israel
Hua Wei   Arizona State University, USA

A Hierarchical Knowledge Framework for Digital Twins of Buildings and Their Energy Systems (Position Paper)

James Allan[(✉)], Edrisi Munoz, Sergio Acero González, Hassan Bazazzadeh, Federica Bellizio, Hanmin Cai, Reto Fricker, Philipp Heer, Mina Montazeri, Sascha Stoller, and Georgios Mavromatidis

Urban Energy Systems Laboratory, Empa, Überlandstrasse 129, 8600 Dübendorf, Switzerland
james.allan@empa.ch

Abstract. This position paper explores applying the Data, Information, Knowledge, Wisdom (DIKW) framework to Digital Twins of buildings and their energy systems. The DIKW framework provides a basis for applying hybrid artificial intelligence (AI) by illustrating where symbolic elements, such as knowledge graphs and sub-symbolic, ML-based approaches, are combined to represent the behavior of complex systems to support decision-making. Several established processes and technologies (BIM, BMS, EMS) are also used in the built environment that often operate in isolation and would benefit from modularization and interconnectivity. Adherence to the DIKW could provide a basis for evaluating interoperability by identifying the data requirements and outputs of each process and technology that work with the data.

Keywords: Digital Twins · Energy · Knowledge Management · Buildings

1 Introduction

Significant advancements in digitalization have been made in the built sector; however, a lack of semantic interoperability hinders the development of scalable energy applications in buildings [1]. Semantic interoperability is a critical consideration of Digital Twins (DTs), where a real-time data connection is established between a physical entity, e.g. a building, and its digital replica, e.g. a simulation model. DTs aid operational and strategic decision-making by learning from the past and predicting the future. DT There are several established practices and technologies widely used in the built environment: Building Information Modelling (BIM) for information management, Building Management Systems (BMS) for automation and control, and Energy Management Systems (EMS) for analytics and forecasting. Many data requirements and functionalities of these services are either shared or complementary to that of a DT; therefore, a conceptual framework helps identify common data requirements to support the interoperability of technologies and services. To achieve this, we have organized commonly used data and services by mapping them onto the DIKW knowledge hierarchy to compare their

© The Author(s), under exclusive license to Springer Nature Switzerland AG 2024
J. P. A. Almeida et al. (Eds.): CAiSE 2024 Workshops, LNBIP 521, pp. 53–58, 2024.
https://doi.org/10.1007/978-3-031-61003-5_5

functionality regarding their data needs and relationships. This approach recognizes that DTs do not exist in isolation but can exchange data with existing services in the built environment to augment their functionality.

2   BIM, BMS and EMS and Digital Twins

Building Information Modelling (BIM) is a process used in the Architecture, Engineering & Construction (AEC) sector to manage a digital representation of an asset throughout its lifecycle, from planning and design to construction and operation. BIM aims to facilitate communication and information exchange across the diverse stakeholders involved throughout a building's lifecycle. Building Management Systems (BMS) are a technology used to control building systems, and Energy Management Systems (EMS) are used to monitor, analyze, and provide insight into improving performance. A BMS is often directly connected to the raw data and signals of the sensors and actuators, whereas an EMS works on knowledge about building and system performance. Despite having different objectives, it is common for an EMS to cooperate with the BMS. The Digital Twin is a newer concept, and as a result, DTs have suffered ambiguity. Various interpretations and applications of the term exist across academia and industry. Most agree that DTs are a digital replica of a physical entity; however, inconsistencies about the importance of a real-time data connection in the twinning process tend to occur. DTs are particularly mature in the manufacturing sector; a highly cited article by Aheleroff et al. describes a DT Reference Architecture Model for Industry 4.0 [2]. The reference architecture defines levels of integration based on their real-time connection: Model (no real-time), Shadow (one way), Twin (bi-directional) and Predictive (bi-directional powered by distributed computing technologies). In terms of the relationship to the existing services, a DT goes beyond the functionality of EMS by incorporating adaptive models that emulate the behavior of the physical system while remaining connected to real-time data to update itself during its lifecycle [3].

3   Physics-Based Simulation and Artificial Intelligence

Artificial intelligence (AI) and physics-based simulation models forecast the energy demands of buildings and energy systems. Physics-based simulations are also known as white-box models. They model the energy balance of a building by considering internal gains and losses, and the thermodynamic properties of components such as walls, windows, and roofs. They require information to parameterize the model, which often carries uncertainty. Data-driven, AI-based approaches are increasingly applied in energy system research to forecast future conditions, modeling the dynamics of the underlying physical systems to facilitate decision-making and strategic planning [4]. However, AI that uses pure black-box models and other approaches beyond the state of the industry (e.g. optimization-based strategies/controllers) present significant challenges. More specifically, they obscure the decision-making process and hinder the ability of stakeholders to interpret and trust the outcomes [5, 6], raising concerns, particularly in applications where transparency and understanding the rationale behind decisions are crucial for social acceptance. In addition, pure black-box models have been shown to have low sample efficiency, requiring extensive amounts of data to train the model [7, 8]. Integrating knowledge graphs and the infusion of expert knowledge or physical information into AI models is a promising approach to address these challenges. With their graph-based structure, knowledge graphs can facilitate advanced data analysis and insight generation, potentially enhancing the explainability of AI models. Moreover, the AI community applying solutions in the energy system sector is increasingly leveraging expert knowledge and physical insights to improve AI models' sample efficiency and accuracy [9].

4   From Data to Wisdom, a Paradigm for Digital Twins

DTs aim to generate higher value insights than the data and information they are based on; and the Data, Information, Knowledge, Wisdom (DIKW) framework conceptualizes the flow from data into wisdom [10]. Therefore, applying the DIKW framework to DTs seems logical if we assume the knowledge and wisdom segments represent insight. The DIKW framework has been considered for DTs by Aheleroff et al., who criticized the linear progression of data into wisdom, whereas in reality, data can flow between any of the segments [2]. Another author, Grieves, criticized the DIKW as fatally flawed for DTs due to ambiguity, inconsistency and simplicity [11]. Nevertheless, Grieves does not abandon the framework due to humanity's reliance on data, knowledge and wisdom. Instead, they propose a new DIKW framework that incorporates a system-oriented approach, defining and highlighting the relationship between the different layers of the pyramid.

4.1   The NEST Demonstrator

The NEST is a modular research and innovation building showcasing innovative building materials, constructions, and energy technologies and systems [12]. It is a living demonstrator containing residential and office spaces. A network of decentralized energy technologies supplies the energy needs as part of an energy hub. Interconnected sensors and actuators enable researchers and operators to isolate, automate and control individual technologies and components in the network. The NESTCloud is an Azure-based cloud architecture providing real-time and historical data access through an API[1]. The digital infrastructure and applications developed for NEST are supported by the Digital Hub initiative[2], which is focused on accelerating digital technologies in the building, energy and mobility sectors. A knowledge graph is hosted on the cloud architecture to enable dynamic and flexible data representation so that additional information, such as geometrical adjacencies, zoning, HVAC loops, system configurations and demand flexibilities, can be added to the graph and queried. BIM models and schematics are available for all units in the NEST; however, the current BIM models only contain geometrical entities. Researchers at NEST are working on a combination of physics-based and ML-based approaches to modelling and operational control of the building and its systems.

---

[1] Https://visualizer.nestcloud.ch.

[2] https://www.empa.ch/web/digital-hub.

4.2   An Implementation of the DIKW for Buildings and Energy Systems

An implementation of the DIKW framework for buildings and energy systems is shown in Fig. 1. Each segment is associated with processes and systems (listed on the left) and specific questions related to the operation of buildings and energy systems (listed on the right). This follows the systems-based vision of Grieves in applying the DIKW for DTs [11]. In addition, AI approaches (symbolic vs non-symbolic) and performance forecasting techniques (data-driven, physics-based and rule-based) are positioned on the outer slopes of the pyramid, aligned against the segments that typically contain inputs to each methodology. The contents of the pyramid contain several pieces of information: Sources are shown in grey boxes (sensors, signals and actuators); data formats and schemas are shown in white boxes (csv, IFC, OWL etc.); and the established processes and technologies (BMS, BIM, EMS, DTs) are placed above the segment deemed most fitting. In the Data layer, raw data is represented at the bottom of the pyramid as unprocessed signals and text-based data formats. Data positioned higher in the pyramid is increasingly structured as csv, json and xml data formats. The data layer is considered to be most closely linked to the operation of the BMS.

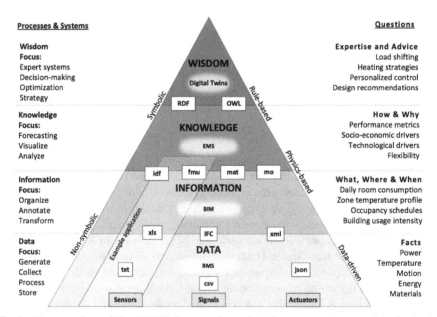

Fig. 1. The mapping of the DIKW framework to data formats, systems, and technologies commonly used in buildings and the built environment.

BIM is the most closely related to the Information segment, where conformance to data models and schemas is typical. IFC is a commonly used reference schema used in BIM. In the Knowledge segment, data can be represented using linked data, using technologies such as RDF, which enables linking entities and concepts, and OWL, which allows the definition of ontologies to describe a specific domain. Adherence to semantic technologies enables enhanced analytics and reasoning of the stored knowledge. The Wisdom segment is most closely associated with the functionality of DTs, which aid decision-making applications by learning from the past and predicting the future. DTs also appear at the top of the pyramid as they can incorporate and augment the functionality of the existing established technologies.

4.3 Analysis of a Specific Application

As a demonstration, we use the framework to classify the approach published in [13], where a digital replica was created as an EnergyPlus simulation model (.idf) and calibrated using data recorded by sensors installed in the physical NEST counterpart. The calibrated high-fidelity model was serialized as an FMU, a format for co-simulation of physics-based models and then used to benchmark controllers. When applying the Reference Architecture [2], this would be considered a model rather than a twin due to the absence of a real-time connection. An outline of the example application is shown on the DIKW framework in Fig. 1. And shows the approach intersecting with the Data, Information and Knowledge segments. This indicates the interoperability of the example application. The proposed framework also indicates which AI or performance forecasting approaches are available to establish bridges and interconnections across the segments. While it is possible to be classified as a DT based on the requirements of the DT reference architecture or from a systems perspective, the proposed DIKW framework could reveal synergies with technologies that could bring benefits in impact, scalability and efficiency of application.

5   Conclusion and Outlook

In this work, we proposed a framework for DTs of buildings and their energy systems based on the DIKW knowledge hierarchy. DTs are considered at the top of the hierarchy as existing technologies such as BMS, BIM, and EMS can support the functionality of the DT. The proposed framework is designed to augment rather than replace existing frameworks and architectures, focusing on evaluating interoperability and identifying connections and approaches that support impact, scalability and efficiency. This approach could help determine whether DTs use the best available data and technology to support its functionality. Further research will analyze a variety of different use cases to build robustness and applicability. Possible areas for improvement include the quantification of interoperability and the representation of data flows. Nevertheless, digitalization brings many challenges in interoperability, and the proposed approach provides a framework to evaluate and improve the interoperability of systems used to implement DTs of buildings and their energy systems.

Acknowledgements. A special thanks to Dr Emanuele Laurenzi and Wolfram Willuhn for their productive collaboration in building the knowledge graph and developing applications.

References

1. Pritoni, M., et al.: Metadata schemas and ontologies for building energy applications: a critical review and use case analysis. Energies **14**, 2024 (2021). https://doi.org/10.3390/en14072024
2. Aheleroff, S., Xu, X., Zhong, R.Y., Lu, Y.: Digital twin as a service (DTaaS) in industry 4.0: an architecture reference Model. Adv. Eng. Inform. **47**, 101225 (2021). https://doi.org/10.1016/j.aei.2020.101225
3. Semeraro, C., Lezoche, M., Panetto, H., Dassisti, M.: Digital twin paradigm: a systematic literature review. Comput. Ind. **130**, 103469 (2021). https://doi.org/10.1016/j.compind.2021.103469
4. Antonopoulos, I., et al.: Artificial intelligence and machine learning approaches to energy demand-side response: a systematic review. Renew. Sustain. Energy Rev. **130**, 109899 (2020)
5. Xu, C., Liao, Z., Li, C., Zhou, X., Xie, R.: Review on interpretable machine learning in smart grid. Energies **15**, 4427 (2022)
6. Chen, Z., Xiao, F., Guo, F., Yan, J.: Interpretable machine learning for building energy management: a state-of-the-art review. Adv. Appl. Energy. **9**, 100123 (2023)
7. Morel, G.: Neuro-symbolic AI for the smart city. J. Phys. Conf. Ser. **2042**, 012018 (2021)
8. Bünning, F., et al.: Physics-informed linear regression is competitive with two machine Learning methods in residential building MPC. Appl. Energy **310**, 118491 (2022)
9. Stiasny, J., Chatzivasileiadis, S.: Physics-informed neural networks for time-domain simulations: accuracy, computational cost, and flexibility. Electr. Power Syst. Res. **224**, 109748 (2023)
10. Ackoff, R.L.: From data to wisdom. J. Appl. Syst. Anal. **16**, 3–9 (1989)
11. Grieves, M.: DIKW as a general and digital twin action framework: data, information, knowledge, and wisdom. Knowledge. **4**, 120–140 (2024). https://doi.org/10.3390/knowledge4020007
12. Richner, P., Heer, P., Largo, R., Marchesi, E., Zimmermann, M.: NEST-A platform for the acceleration of innovation in buildings. Inf. Constr. **69**, e222 (2017)
13. Khayatian, F., Cai, H., Bojarski, A., Heer, P., Bollinger, A.: Benchmarking HVAC controller performance with a digital twin. In: Presented at the Applied energy symposium (2022)

Integrating Generative Artificial Intelligence into Supply Chain Management Education Using the SCOR Model

Joachim C. F. Ehrenthal[1]([✉]) [ID], Phillip Gachnang[1] [ID], Louisa Loran[2],
Hellmer Rahms[2], and Fabian Schenker[2]

[1] University of Applied Sciences and Arts Northwester Switzerland FHNW, 5210 Windisch,
Switzerland
`joachim.ehrenthal@fhnw.ch`
[2] Google Cloud Platform, Mountain View, CA 94043, USA

Abstract. Bridging rule-based Supply Chain Management (SCM) systems with
Generative Artificial Intelligence (GenAI) presents a novel approach towards overcoming persistent SCM challenges. This study introduces a novel approach that
integrates GenAI with the Supply Chain Operations Reference (SCOR) Model,
a widely accepted quasi-ontology in SCM, through Retrieval-Augmented Generation (RAG). Utilizing Google's Vertex AI Search as an implementation case
in an educational context, we demonstrate the practical application of resulting
generative SCM (GenSCM), which seeks to combine the advantages of both symbolic and sub-symbolic AI. Our study contributes to the literature by outlining an
approachable pathway for integrating GenAI in SCM, and it provides insights on
a domain-specific integration of symbolic and sub-symbolic AI. While the findings illustrate the potential of GenSCM in education, future research is needed
on superior SCM problem-solving and operational execution in real-life SCM
settings.

Keywords: Generative Artificial Intelligence · Supply Chain Management ·
Retrieval-Augmented Generation · Ontology · Supply Chain Operations
Reference (SCOR) Model · Google Cloud Platform

1 Introduction

This study pioneers an approach to integrate Generative Artificial Intelligence (GenAI),
AI that creates new content by learning patterns from data, into Supply Chain Management (SCM), the business function in charge of networked value co-creation overseeing
procurement, production and distribution, focusing on the synergy between GenAI's
sub-symbolic capabilities and the structured, domain-specific, symbolic Supply Chain

© The Author(s), under exclusive license to Springer Nature Switzerland AG 2024
J. P. A. Almeida et al. (Eds.): CAiSE 2024 Workshops, LNBIP 521, pp. 59–71, 2024.
https://doi.org/10.1007/978-3-031-61003-5_6

Operations Reference (SCOR) Model[1], the dominant reference framework of SCM, via Retrieval-Augmented Generation (RAG) in an educational setting as a case study.

Over the last decades, the Achilles' heel of SCM has been data complexity and overload [2] combined with a shortage of skilled talent [3]. While supply chains generate vast amounts of data [4], companies struggle to extract meaningful insights out of mostly siloed data and to keep pace with market dynamics [5, 6], leading to limitations in adopting traditional methods of AI with their pre-defined logic, rules, and highly structured approaches [7], giving rise to the need for new tooling to analyze messy, large, real-world SCM problems [8]. Recent research suggests that GenAI may offer new solutions for these issues [9, 10]. However, the usefulness of GenAI in addressing the of day-to-day challenges of SCM—such as increasing complexity [11], pressure to accelerate operations [12], handling supply disruptions [13, 14], and navigating geopolitical tensions [15] while mitigating effects of climate change [16]—depends on its ability to process the complexities of SCM, and to guide execution.

Therefore, our research objective is to form Generative SCM (GenSCM) by integrating symbolic AI's domain-specific knowledge and structured data processing to complement sub-symbolic GenAI's pattern recognition and generative capabilities, leading to improved and contextually aware solutions to SCM problems. Specifically, we propose to connect the capabilities of sub-symbolic GenAI with the well-defined, rule-based interactions of SCM using the SCOR Model. While not a fully formalized ontology, SCOR exhibits quasi-ontological characteristics due to its methodical organization and representation of SCM knowledge, as well as its adoption as the global standard, and is thus a prime candidate for our approach.

The remainder of the paper is organized as follows: In Sect. 2, we provide a background on GenAI and its use in SCM. In Sect. 3, we detail our case study, a university

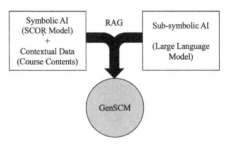

Fig. 1. Higher-level representation of integrating GenAI and SCM via RAG towards GenSCM in an educational setting (hence course contents as contextual data).

---

[1] Please see [1]. SCOR, in the current 'Digital Standard' version, is a comprehensive and relational, organising SCM processes (orchestrate, plan, order, source, transform, fulfill, return) and mapping them onto a hierarchical taxonomy (strategic to operational), including performance metrics (resilience, economic, sustainability) and human resources (skills, experiences, training), making it a foundation for strategic and operational excellence in SCM.

course focused on SCM, for which we developed and implemented a GenSCM application.[2] We evaluate our approach with exam-inspired questions, which is good practice for evaluating GenAI when initially applied to specific domains. In Sect. 4, we outline implications and directions for future research. Figure 1 illustrates our overall approach.

2 Background

GenAI is a type of AI designed to create multi-modal content and is based on advances in the Transformer Model [18]. It creates content by interpreting and generating tokens based on learned representations such as sequences of characters and text, and thus differs from non-generative AI methods which rely on predefined solution paths and require specific data inputs. GenAI consists of three main components: foundational models, large-scale machine learning models like neural networks trained on extensive data sets capable of adapting to various tasks; a supporting infrastructure that provides the necessary storage and computing power; and practical applications that use GenAI's capabilities to solve business problems. Recent advances have made GenAI capable of parsing, natural language processing, and text generation [19–21], enabling "conversational AI," i.e. *interactive and adaptive communication between users and GenAI* using a natural language paradigm.

GenAI represents a shift from the conventional optimization, AI, and Machine Learning (ML) methods on which SCM practice and research rely today. Instead of focusing on specific SCM tasks such as supplier selection, forecasting, scheduling, predictive maintenance, routing, or automation, GenAI offers a broader range of capabilities, including conversational search, document synthesis, enhancing, and personalizing product or content discovery, simplifying knowledge management, process automation in customer service, compliance checks, generating product and process documentation, and aiding content creation for presentations [22]. Moreover, by automating analysis and facilitating communication, GenAI models can help supply chain managers make faster, more informed decisions and communicate action items more effectively. However, GenAI must be properly set up, integrated, and used to be efficient and not lead to unwanted effects, most notably a potential lack of currentness (when constant model retraining is unfeasible), and hallucination, where GenAI may provide seemingly plausible information and guidance out of scope with instructions and the underlying trained data [23], as well as bad business decisions based on bad GenAI suggestions and resources wasted while interacting with a GenAI where well-trained humans would have obtained better results faster [24].

3 Case Study: A SCM University Course

This Section presents our case study, where we explore the practical application of GenSCM within an educational setting. The case study approach enables the secure examination of how integrating sub-symbolic GenAI capabilities with the symbolic SCOR

---

[2] While this does not involve real-time supply chain data analysis and execution, it serves as a suitable environment to test the integration of GenAI with the SCOR model and to explore its capability in understanding the interconnected elements of SCM as empirical evidence of on GenAI in SCM is limited [17].

Model can enhance SCM education, before further exploring it in business settings. While not focused on near-time or real-time SCM data, our application establishes a foundation for assessing GenSCM's potential to integrate the SCOR Model. Inspired by how Google's MedPaLM, a medical Large Language Model (LLM), underwent testing through a series of medical question-answering evaluations, our approach tests Gen-SCM against a set of exam-inspired questions, and thus follows an established means of assessment to ensure its relevance and applicability.

3.1 Generative AI Course Companion Requirements and Goals

To demonstrate integrating GenAI and SCM to form GenSCM, we created a GenAI application (app) as a companion for an SCM course. Student users enter questions ('prompts') on anything about in the SCM course and receive results as summary, with source documents, and the opportunity to ask follow-up questions. Table 1 provides an overview of the use case and problems to be solved, and the relation to SCM practice.

Table 1. *GenSCM demonstrator use case details and persistent SCM issues addressed.*

Theme	Details	*SCM issue*
Setting/Context	University of Applied Sciences Northwestern Switzerland FHNW School of Business course "SCM & Sustainability"	***Talent shortage***
Actors	Students of business and business information systems in Bachelor's programs, mostly part-time, and their educators, a team of PhDs with backgrounds in life sciences SCM, industrial manufacturing, and global logistics	
Challenges/Problems	Guided by a sophisticated learning management system, optimized using learning analytics, students struggle with the breadth and depth required to master SCM, as is common in SCM courses [25]. Also, student usage of consumer GenAI has led to frustration due to lacking reliability	***Data complexity and overload***
Solution/Action	Deploy GenAI using the materials provided via e-learning and used in class as data sources,[a] grounded in the SCOR Model	

(continued)

Table 1. (*continued*)

Theme	Details	*SCM issue*
Expected Outcome	Enhanced student learning success with a 24/7 study companion, leading to better access to course knowledge	***Increasing effectiveness***
Validation	Validate results with a combination of concepts, methods, and instruments prompts related to procurement, production, distribution, and sustainability, and common terminology	***Sustainable development***

[a] Please note that full educational usage rights exist, and that data is free from harmful and discriminatory content as per university rules.

3.2 Introduction to Vertex AI Search

For our case study, we selected Vertex AI Search [26], an enterprise-grade component of Google Cloud to bridge the gap between the capabilities of GenAI and the practical needs of SCM via the SCOR Model. It uses Google's foundational language models, search capabilities, conversational AI technologies, and provides enterprise-grade security. This approach overcomes the data privacy, security, and control issues associated with the use of widely accessible consumer GenAI platforms. Furthermore, a Vertex AI Search makes use of RAG [27] to ground answers in the data provided as the search source, offering more granular control by grounding the model with the data provided, and ensuring the data is current as per our needs. We deliberately used the Vertex AI Search out-of-the-box, without any coding or alteration, using publicly available capabilities as of October 2023 (running on PaLM 2 for Text, specifically text-bison, cf. [28]) to make this demonstration universally accessible to non-technical practitioners, researchers, and educators in SCM alike. Moreover, our approach transcends traditional data management and knowledge retrieval in SCM, which is characterized by fragmented information across disparate

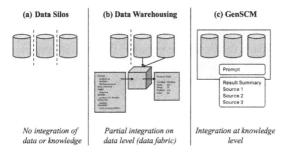

Fig. 2. Differences in Data and Knowledge Management: From Data Silos to Integration at the Knowledge Level.

systems, resulting in various well-known inefficiencies.[3] Figure 2 illustrates how our approach (c) departs from the traditional means (a, b) of organizing data and extracting knowledge in SCM.

3.3   Setting up the Vertex AI Search

After setting up a Google Cloud account, we navigate to the Google Cloud Console and add a new project with a unique project name (depending on organizational security settings, Google Cloud locations may have to be selected). To invite collaborators, we search the navigation bar for "IAM & Admin" and select "Grant Access," adding our team with appropriate permissions.

Before we build the GenAI app, we upload the data we want the GenAI to use to a Google Cloud Storage bucket, by searching the navigation bar for "Cloud Storage." Within Cloud Storage, we created a New Bucket and followed a predefined workflow: We select a name for the Bucket, select "eu" as multi-region location type (which is best-fit for our location Switzerland), select the default standard storage class for our data, use the default access setup (enforcing public access prevention), and select default data protection (as we have no special requirements for object versioning or retention). After the setup is completed, we are taken to the newly created Storage Bucket, and select "Upload Files" to upload our course content as source data for the GenAI. We upload our course data, all as Portable Document Format (PDF), with a total size of around 4GB of non-storage optimized teaching materials in both German and English, and the SCOR Model. Note that these data are in our environment, to which no one except us has access.

Now that the data are in Cloud Storage, we can build a GenAI app. To do so, we search for "Gen App Builder" in the navigation bar, and once we're inside the Vertex AI Dashboard, create a "New App." This takes us through the workflow setup is as follows:

For our Search app, we select "Search" as the app type. In the configuration step, we left all default features turned on. Then, we give our app a name, and again select "eu" as the location for the app. Then, we define the data to be used. We do so by creating a new "Data Store." We select "Cloud Storage" and browse to the location of the data Storage Bucket we had just created for the project. We select it and then specify the kind of data. In our case, we use unstructured documents. We could also use structured JavaScript Object Notation (JSON) data and unstructured JSON with metadata, but we do not have such data for our course.[4]

To finalize the configuration, we give the GenAI's "Data Store" a name, and select that "Data Store" to create the GenAI Search app. That's it. Depending on the size of the data, we only need to wait for the data to be indexed and processed in the background. Once this is done, we can move on to the Preview Widget, which we can configure to

---

[3] The most well-known information management related issue in SCM is the bullwhip effect, in which small variations in demand amplify through the supply chain, leading to substantial overstock and/or shortages due to a lack of information-sharing and synchronized decisions.

[4] To unify data without tooling such as Vertex AI, a common approach is using vector databases, which convert data into vectors for efficient analysis of complex datasets across different data types.

provide results as a search with a list of results, as a generative summary above the search results, or as a conversational search with generative summaries and support for follow-up questions. The latter is the default value that we select. For us, the entire process, including data upload, required a few minutes.

3.4 Evaluation

To evaluate the GenSCM app, we built a test set of prompts and evaluated it against the expected results not known to GenSCM using grading keys, which is line with standard academic assessments and thus ensures a familiar evaluation mechanism to the evaluating researchers. Our test set encompassed the four central SCM domains: procurement, production, distribution, and sustainability. We assessed GenSCM in line with the course goals, specifically:

- Concepts: Comprehension of core principles.
- Methods: The ability to explain practices.
- Instruments: Proficiency in using analytical tools.

For instance, in evaluating concepts, we prompted GenSCM to explain 'dual sourcing' and its pros and cons, anticipating a balanced discussion on supplier diversification (Prompt: "Explain dual sourcing. What are advantages and disadvantages?" Expected answer: "Dual sourcing involves procuring an item from two distinct suppliers. This strategy balances the pros and cons of having fewer (innovation capacity, integration, and trust, yet: dependency and missed opportunities elsewhere) or multiple suppliers (risk reduction, better prices, yet: higher administrative cost, and less focused relations."). Under methods, for instance, we asked about 'Total Quality Management (TQM)' and its distinction from traditional quality frameworks (Prompt: "What is TQM? How is TQM different from traditional quality management?"), expecting a comprehensive delineation of TQM's holistic approach. Instrument testing involved applying, for instance, the 'Economic Order Quantity (EOQ) model', where an accurate calculation would demonstrate proficiency in analytical tools (Prompt: "Apply the EOQ model: A company needed 10,000 units of item A last year. For ordering and transporting the item, the company incurs costs of CHF 1,000 per order. The storage cost rate is 10% per board. The value of a single unit of item A is CHF 50." Expected answer: "2,000.").

An additional set of prompts assessed the ability of GenSCM to explain SCM terminology. To this end, we use abbreviations, from broad terms like 'SCM' to more specialized abbreviations like 'JIT/JIS' and 'CPFR' (Prompt "What is <abbreviation>?", in the case of JIT/JIS expecting the expanded for Just-in-Time/Just-in-Sequence and a short explainer like "Synchronized production and delivery of items in the time/sequence needed for production", and in the case of CPFR expecting "Collaborative Planning, Forecasting and Replenishment" as expanded form and "Joint business planning and execution approach for collaborative supply chain management." as explainer). All concepts, methods, instruments, and terms occur in the data provided to GenSCM, and are tailored to fit the course participants, as does our prompting. Thus, we can assess GenSCM's focus on our datasets as opposed to its foundational model. GenSCM's responses were graded on the four categories of correctness, completeness, clarity, and conciseness in three-tier rubrics of exceeding expectations, meeting expectations, and not meeting expectations (leading scores of 3, 2, and 1 respectively), with expectations formulated ex ante, as is good practice in examinations. Overall, the evaluation was designed to assess the out-of-the-box usability of GenSCM on our data, integrating the SCOR Model and course contents.

3.5 Results

The results of the GenSCM evaluation are as follows: The average scores for all categories exceeded 85%, indicating that the responses were acceptable and well above average long-term student performance in similar exam questions. However, there is room for improvement. Overall, the highest scores were obtained for clarity and accuracy. The average score for terminology was higher than that for procurement, production, distribution, and sustainability questions relating to concepts, methods, and instruments. This is in line with expectations as terminology questions do not require nuanced answers to complex interconnected issues if the terminology is properly picked up on. Table 2 details the scoring of our validation experiment regarding concepts, methods, and instruments. These results are consistent and balanced. Three deviations from this observation exist: (a) a procurement instrument question expecting a numerical answer (which is not what the foundational model selected is trained to do); (b) a conceptually difficult distribution question on economies of scale, scope, and density unknown to the SCOR Model; and (c) a specifically granular method-related question regarding sustainability metrics that do not exist in the SCOR Model.

Table 2. Scoring results as per Concepts, Methods, and Instruments prompts (3 is highest).

		Correctness	Completeness	Clarity	Conciseness	Avg.
Procurement	Concept	3	3	3	2	**2.75**
	Method	3	3	3	2	**2.75**
	Instrument	1	1	2	3	**1.75**
Production	Concept	3	2	3	2	**2.5**
	Method	2	2	3	3	**2.5**
	Instrument	3	3	3	3	**3**
Distribution	Concept	2	1	2	1	**1.5**
	Method	2	2	3	2	**2.25**
	Instrument	3	2	2	2	**2.25**
Sustainability	Concept	3	2	2	2	**2.25**
	Method	1	2	3	3	**2.25**
	Instrument	3	2	3	3	**2.75**
	Average	**2.42**	**2.08**	**2.67**	**2.33**	**2.38**

Table 3 shows the scoring of terminology-related questions, which in approximately 25% of all cases deviated slightly as either lacking some details (completeness) or being slightly verbose (conciseness), which can be explained by not specifying the output length, and not interfering with standard agent instructions and behavior. Accurate terminology processing, particularly the use of abbreviations, is essential for GenSCM, as such shorthand is prevalent and vital for precision and efficiency in SCM where interacting across business units, company boundaries, borders, and continents is the norm.

Table 3. Scoring results as per Terminology prompts (3 is highest).

Terms	Correctness	Completeness	Clarity	Conciseness	Avg.
BOM, CFPR, ERP, MRP, RFQ, SCM, VMI, WMS	3	3	3	3	**3**
DMAIC, JIT/JIS, MES, PPI, RFID	3	2	3	3	**2.75**
ECR, EOQ	3	3	2	2	**2.5**
Average	**3**	**2.67**	**2.87**	**2.87**	**2.85**

3.6 Enhancement Strategies

Our analysis indicates that our GenSCM app answers domain-specific questions accurately and effectively. With GenAI evolving rapidly, especially in areas such as extended conversation memorization, the results are likely to improve. However, also for applications beyond our educational case, there are several avenues for refinement and enhancement of the out-of-the-box solution. Table 4 organizes these by suggesting improvements to the underlying model, prompting, and data, as well as different approaches to integrating symbolic AI.

Moreover, implementing mechanisms to incorporate user feedback and monitor performance linked to the use of insights generated by GenAI may further improve its performance (including ML), such as incorporating standard supply chain metrics as outcome measurements. Also, we know from entry assessments that students are largely unfamiliar with SCM, and hence matching student skills with GenSCM capabilities is not an issue – whereas in business practice novices and experts may respond to and differently use the same GenSCM, requiring more consideration in matching user and app capabilities, and unlike specialized SCM software, GenAI's everyday use creates diverse user knowledge and attitudes, presenting novel and unique challenges in GenSCM integration and new opportunities to improve SCM.

Table 4. Enhancement strategies to improve on the out-of-the-box solution.

Category	Strategy	Description
Model	Improving prompt understanding	Enhance prompt comprehension by fine-tuned embeddings, i.e. vectors that capture semantic meaning
	Improving answering style	Enhancing response style to align with desired outcomes through fine-tuning for answering
	Hallucination reduction	Despite not identified as a problem in our data, using methods like Chain-of-Verification [29]
	Tailored SCM Model	Developing specialized models for SCM, its sub-disciplines, and industry-specific verticals to provide more nuanced responses for supply chain professionals in various functions and industries
Prompting, Agent, and Data	Improving prompting	Automatically enhancing user prompts for improved results and generating 'Chains of Thought' to break down complex tasks for enhanced outcomes [30]
	Adjusting agent behavior	Instructing the GenAI agent's behavior, like defining a response persona, common goals, or to include visualizations and examples
	Shifting to chat-like format	Better capture specific user intents, and to extract or request data necessary in follow-up questions to the user
	Ontology-based grounding	Using frameworks to improve responses like the SCOR Model, complemented by methods for structured knowledge organization and extraction [31]
	Integrations	Adding more/real-time data sources and function calling (e.g. for executing forecasts on large data)

4   Implications and Further Research

This study has pioneered integrating GenAI into SCM, using RAG and the SCOR Model to form GenSCM. It shows the capability of GenAI to accurately interpret and use domain-specific knowledge representations, such as SCOR, illustrating the benefits of combining sub-symbolic and symbolic AI. For supply chain managers, this means prioritizing data organization to enable the implementation of GenSCM, and to expand employee skills to use the new generative capabilities, since without the ability to execute upon it, the potential of GenSCM will remain untapped.

While our study may serve as an accessible design template, it is limited in scope and context, and thus paves the way for further research. First, research could investigate whether specialized models offer advantages to using, including more elaborate and larger scale experiments, as well as examining advanced prompting and tuning techniques to enhance the interpretative capabilities and performance of GenSCM. Second, the role of ontologies warrants further examination, both for guiding GenAI as well as integrating and retrieving and using real-time SCM data and enabling system-to-system interactions in GenSCM. Third, research could work towards enhancing GenSCM by bridging the gap between the reliability and factual consistency of traditional AI/ML systems and GenAI through function calling, for which combinations of symbolic and sub-symbolic AI also hold promise.

Lastly, looking at current advancements in GenAI, the emergence of multimodal models and their ability to process information across diverse data types and thereby learn, may extend the reach of GenSCM to self-enhancing supply chain solutions that span from digital planning to physical execution [32].

To operationalize the proposed future research, we suggest considering knowledge graph representations for data, and of ontologies, as shown in [33], and to embrace multimodal capabilities for building more advanced GenSCM applications, and to test their performance and reliability in supply chain strategy and operations.

References

1. SCOR Digital Standard. https://scor.ascm.org. Accessed 05 Sept 2023
2. Jackson, T.W., Farzaneh, P.: Theory-based model of factors affecting information overload. Int. J. Inf. Manag. **32**(6), 523–532 (2012). https://doi.org/10.1016/j.ijinfomgt.2012.04.006
3. Birou, L., Hoek, R.V.: Supply chain management talent: the role of executives in engagement, recruitment, development and retention. Supply Chain Manag.: Int. J. **27**(6), 712–727 (2022). https://doi.org/10.1108/SCM-08-2020-0418
4. Baah, C., et al.: Effect of information sharing in supply chains: understanding the roles of supply chain visibility, agility, collaboration on supply chain performance. Benchmarking: Int. J. **29**(2), 434–455 (2022). https://doi.org/10.1108/BIJ-08-2020-0453
5. Sodhi, M.S., Tang, C.S.: Supply chain management for extreme conditions: research opportunities. J. Supply Chain Manag. **57**(1), 7–16 (2021). https://doi.org/10.1111/jscm.12255
6. Sharma, M., Alkatheeri, H., Jabeen, F., Sehrawat, R.: Impact of COVID-19 pandemic on perishable food supply chain management: a contingent resource-based view (RBV) perspective. Int. J. Logist. Manag. **33**(3), 796–817 (2022). https://doi.org/10.1108/IJLM-02-2021-0131
7. Cannas, V.G., Ciano, M.P., Saltalamacchia, M., Secchi, R.: Artificial intelligence in supply chain and operations management: a multiple case study research. Int. J. Prod. Res. (2023). https://doi.org/10.1080/00207543.2023.2232050
8. Stank, T., Esper, T., Goldsby, T.J., Zinn, W., Autry, C.: Toward a digitally dominant paradigm for twenty-first century supply chain scholarship. Int. J. Phys. Distrib. Logist. Manag. **49**(10), 956–971 (2019). https://doi.org/10.1108/IJPDLM-03-2019-0076

9. Richey, R.G., Jr., Chowdhury, S., Davis-Sramek, B., Giannakis, M., Dwivedi, Y.K.: Artificial intelligence in logistics and supply chain management: a primer and roadmap for research. J. Bus. Logist. **44**, 532–549 (2023). https://doi.org/10.1111/jbl.12364

10. Hendriksen, C.: Artificial intelligence for supply chain management: disruptive innovation or innovative disruption? J. Supply Chain Manag. **59**(3), 65–76 (2023). https://doi.org/10.1111/jscm.12304

11. Hearnshaw, E.J.S., Wilson, M.M.J.: A complex network approach to supply chain network theory. Int. J. Oper. Prod. Manag. **33**(4), 442–469 (2013). https://doi.org/10.1108/01443571311307343

12. Camargo, L.R., Pereira, S.C.F., Scarpin, M.R.S.: Fast and ultra-fast fashion supply chain management: an exploratory research. Int. J. Retail. Distrib. Manag. **48**(6), 537–553 (2020). https://doi.org/10.1108/IJRDM-04-2019-0133

13. Pournader, M., Kach, A., Talluri, S.: A review of the existing and emerging topics in the supply chain risk management literature. Decis. Sci. **51**, 867–919 (2020). https://doi.org/10.1111/deci.12470

14. Spieske, A., Gebhardt, M., Kopyto, M., Birkel, H.: Improving resilience of the healthcare supply chain in a pandemic: evidence from Europe during the COVID-19 crisis. J. Purch. Supply Manag. **28**(5), 100748 (2022). https://doi.org/10.1016/j.pursup.2022.100748

15. Bednarski, L., Roscoe, S., Blome, C., Schleper, M.C.: Geopolitical disruptions in global supply chains: a state-of-the-art literature review. Prod. Plan. Control (2023). https://doi.org/10.1080/09537287.2023.2286283

16. Dai, T., Tang, C.: Frontiers in service science: integrating ESG measures and supply chain management: research opportunities in the postpandemic era. Serv. Sci. **14**(1), 1–12 (2022). https://doi.org/10.1287/serv.2021.0295

17. Fosso Wamba, S., Guthrie, C., Queiroz, M.M., Minner, S.: ChatGPT and generative artificial intelligence: an exploratory study of key benefits and challenges in operations and supply chain management. Int. J. Prod. Res. (2023). https://doi.org/10.1080/00207543.2023.2294116

18. Vaswani, A., et al.: Attention is all you need (2017). https://doi.org/10.48550/arXiv.1706.03762

19. Cheng, H.T., Thoppilan, R.: LaMDA: towards safe, grounded, and high-quality dialog models for everything. https://ai.googleblog.com/2022/01/lamda-towards-safe-grounded-and-high.html. Accessed 05 Sept 2023

20. Kadavath, S., et al.: Language models (mostly) know what they know (2022). https://doi.org/10.48550/arXiv.2207.05221

21. Ouyang, L., et al.: Training language models to follow instructions with human feedback (2022). https://doi.org/10.48550/arXiv.2203.02155

22. GCP: Hey Google, what's up with generative AI? https://cloudonair.withgoogle.com/events/gen-ai-for-startups. Accessed 05 Sept 2023

23. Ortega, P.A., et al.: Shaking the foundations: delusions in sequence models for interaction and control (2021). https://doi.org/10.48550/arXiv.2110.10819

24. Krinkin, K., Shichkina, Y.: Cognitive architecture for co-evolutionary hybrid intelligence. In: Goertzel, B., Iklé, M., Potapov, A., Ponomaryov, D. (eds.) AGI 2022. LNCS, vol. 13539, pp. 293–303. Springer, Cham (2023). https://doi.org/10.1007/978-3-031-19907-3_28

25. Birou, L., Lutz, H., Walden, J.L.: Undergraduate supply chain management courses: Content, coverage, assessment and gaps. Supply Chain Manag.: Int. J. **27**(1), 1–11 (2022). DOI: https://doi.org/10.1108/SCM-07-2020-0309

26. GCP: Vertex AI. https://cloud.google.com/vertex-ai. Accessed 05 Sept 2023

27. Lewis, P., et al.: Retrieval-augmented generation for knowledge-intensive NLP tasks. In: Advances in Neural Information Processing Systems (NeurIPS 2020), vol. 33, 9459–9474 (2020). https://doi.org/10.5555/3495724.3496517

28. GCP: Model Information. https://cloud.google.com/vertex-ai/docs/generative-ai/learn/models. Accessed 05 Sept 2023
29. Dhuliawala, S., et al.: Chain-of-verification reduces hallucination in large language models (2023). https://doi.org/10.48550/arXiv.2309.11495
30. Wei, J., et al.: Chain-of-thought prompting elicits reasoning in large language models (2022). https://doi.org/10.48550/arXiv.2201.11903
31. Caufield, J.H., et al.: Structured prompt interrogation and recursive extraction of semantics (SPIRES): a method for populating knowledge bases using zero-shot learning. Bioinformatics **40**(3), btae104 (2023). https://doi.org/10.1093/bioinformatics/btae104
32. Ahn, M., et al.: AutoRT: embodied foundation models for large scale orchestration of robotic agents (2024). https://doi.org/10.48550/arXiv.2401.12963
33. Pan, S., Luo, L., Wang, Y., Chen, C., Wang, J., Wu, X.: Unifying large language models and knowledge graphs: a roadmap. IEEE Trans. Knowl. Data Eng. (TKDE) (2024). https://doi.org/10.1109/TKDE.2024.3352100

An Explanation User Interface for a Knowledge Graph-Based XAI Approach to Process Analysis

Anne Füßl[(✉)], Volker Nissen, and Stefan Horst Heringklee

Technische Universität Ilmenau, Institute for Business and Information Systems
Engineering, Helmholtzplatz 3, 98693 Ilmenau, Germany
anne.fuessl@tu-ilmenau.de
https://www.tu-ilmenau.de/wid

Abstract. In consulting practice, effective use of AI technologies pre-
supposes consultant's and client's ability to understand generated results.
Our knowledge graph-based approach to explainable process analyses
represents a hybrid AI approach that integrates symbolic approaches of
structured knowledge and interactive machine learning methods for making algorithmic procedures traceable and representing analysis results in
a human-readable form. In order to display identified weaknesses and
suitable improvement measures of analyzed business processes in a user-
understandable way and to enable human-in-the-loop interactions, an
explainable, user-friendly interface is required. While much attention is
paid to the computational aspects of generating explanations, there is a
need for further research into the design of explanation user interfaces.
A systematic literature review was conducted to derive a design catalog,
which was demonstrated and evaluated by developing a suitable XUI for
our knowledge graph-based explainable process analysis.

Keywords: Explanation user interface · Hybrid XAI · Knowledge
graph · Process analysis · Consulting self-service

1 Research Background and Objective

Explainable Artificial Intelligence (XAI) aims to develop explanation models for
generating results and decisions that can be interpreted by human users through
a form of explanation. Thereby, an explanation model exposes the algorithmic
decision paths in an XAI system [2]. In order to present results from explanation models in a readable, comprehensible and understandable way for users,
XAI approaches also require an eXplanation User Interface (XUI) [11]. XUIs
provide the user with the sum of all outputs in the form of explanations, enable
a simplified description of generated results that can be interpreted by humans
and allow interactions between the system and the user [3].

The majority of XAI research is concerned with the computational aspects of
generating explanatory models, while there is still little research on the human-
centered design of XUI [3,17]. However, users need to understand how results are

J. P. A. Almeida et al. (Eds.): CAiSE 2024 Workshops, LNBIP 521, pp. 72–84, 2024.
https://doi.org/10.1007/978-3-031-61003-5_7

produced in order to use and adapt them optimally. XUIs make it easier to receive high-quality human feedback and enable it to be used for learning algorithms [10]. The design of XUIs is therefore a suitable way to provide explainable and usable AI [20] and contribute to cognitive support in human-AI interaction.

Consulting services belong to the area of personal services and are characterized by intensive consultant-client interactions. The use of AI technologies in the consulting industry has steadily increased in recent years, driven in part by the Corona pandemic [15]. Complex consulting technologies, such as process mining for analyzing business processes based on event log data, or analytical self-service tools, require technical and analytical expertise to interpret the results in a customer-oriented manner. XUIs can help to present AI results in an understandable way to both consultancies and their clients, and to improve interactive learning models through result verification based on user feedback.

Our hybrid Knowledge graph-Based eXplainable AI approach to Process Analysis (KBXAI-PA) enables comprehensible results on deficiencies and suitable improvement measures depending on deduction algorithms and traversed result paths [7,8]. In previous design cycles, an explanation component was created in order to provide traceability of process analysis results [7] and an interactive machine learning model was integrated to consider user feedback [9]. For a comprehensible result presentation, which makes it easy to understand why which weaknesses have been identified and why which improvement measures appear suitable, even for those unfamiliar with process analysis, a human-understandable XUI with user interaction is now required.

The aim of the present paper is to develop a generic design framework for XUI, which is demonstrated and evaluated using KBXAI-PA as an example. The research method follows the Design Science Research (DSR) process according to Peffers et al. [16]. First of all, we introduce the basics of XAI interactions and user interfaces in the context of interactive learning methods. Section 3 presents a systematic literature review according to Webster and Watson [19] for the identification of existing XUIs, their analysis and the derivation of suitable design components in a design catalog. In Sect. 4, we first describe the current state of development of our KBXAI-PA approach followed by a demonstration of selected design components through the development of an XUI for KBXAI-PA and finally evaluate it through several expert interviews. Section 5 summarizes key findings, provides a critical appraisal and highlights future research efforts.

2 Basics of Human Interactions for XAI

The term XAI describes explainable Machine Learning (ML) approaches that provide interpretable explanations for the behavior and predictions of ML models [11]. XUIs are used to make explanations of an XAI system interpretable to the user and to enable them to develop better mental models [5]. The utility of XUIs depends on their design, what should be explained (content of an explanation) and in which form (presentation form of an explanation) [12]. Originally, XUIs were used for decision support in expert systems, in recommender systems as well as in Interactive Machine Learning (IML) [5].

IML forms an intersection between the design of an XUI and an XAI system [10]. The user is involved in the training process by using human input in the selection, creation and labeling of instances [4]. IML was introduced to the Human Computer Interaction (HCI) community in 2003 by Fails and Olsen [6]. Compared to classic ML, IML is characterized by faster (model adaptation at the time of user feedback), more targeted (adaptation of specific aspects of the model) and incremental (small adaptations without major model changes) model adaptations [1]. This allows users to interactively examine the effects of their actions and adjust subsequent inputs to achieve a desired behavior.

Chromik and Butz [3] supplement the description of an explanation support according to Moore and Paris [14] with interaction strategies and design suggestions for interactive XUI and consolidated them into four design principles. Design principle 1, *complementary naturalness*, aims to complement visual explanations (which exactly illustrate the internal mechanisms of an AI) with natural language explanations. The combination of visual cues and textual explanations can promote user understanding, user interaction and the adaptation of learning models. *Responsiveness through progressive disclosure* is design principle 2 and involves an iterative approach, based on previous explanations, in a user-specific manner. Studies have shown that there is a fine line between "no explanation" and "too much explanation" depending on user's individual need [13]. Design principle 3 describes *flexibility through multiple ways to explain* by combining several forms of explanations (e.g., local, global, or counterfactual explanations, charts, textual and colored highlights) in order to allow the recipient of the explanation to verify findings [3]. The last design principle 4, *sensitivity to the mind and context*, aims to provide functions to personalize and adapt XUI explanations to the user's mental model and the context of the explanation recipients. Users react differently to various forms of explanation, depending on prior bias and existing prejudices.

However, the design principles only provide an abstract overview rather than suggesting concrete design requirements for an XUI. The following section examines existing XUIs with the aim of determining suitable design components for an XUI by considering the design principles of Chromik and Butz [3].

3   Design Catalog for Explanation User Interfaces

XUIs comprise various design components for result presentation and interaction, which must be selected, described and implemented during development. For specifying design requirements and developing XUIs, a generic design catalog with components was developed following a systematic literature review [19], see Table 1. We used the following search query to identify existing design components in the literature: "design" AND "explanation interface" AND "interactive" OR "interactive machine learning" AND "user interface" AND "explainable". Starting in 2003, when Fails and Oslen [6] first mentioned the linking of IML methods in the context of HCI, through early 2023, we initially examined the following databases in terms of title and abstract and afterwards in terms of recognizable design components (the first number in brackets indicates the number

Table 1. Design catalog with components and their frequencies.

Category	Design component	DP	Frequency (n=28)	KBXAI-PA
form of explanation	visual	#1	89.3%	x
	textual	#1	75.0%	x
	multiple views	#2	60.7%	x
	numerical	#1	46.4%	
	table	#2	39.3%	
	dependency diagram	#2	32.1%	
	chat-based	#1	14.3%	
	why-explanation	#2	14.3%	
content of explanation	global	#3	89.3%	x
	local	#3	85.7%	x
	counterfactual	#3	50.0%	
	example-based	#3	21.4%	
interaction	feature relevance	#3	60.7%	x
	search function	#2	28.6%	x
	accuracy indicator	#3	28.6%	x
	feature distribution	#3	28.6%	
	visualization of changes in feature values	#3	28.6%	
	quick-info	#3	28.6%	x
	filters	#2	25.0%	x
	sorting	#2	25.0%	x
	comparison of multiple instances	#3	25.0%	
	slider	#4	25.0%	
	feature selection	#2	21.4%	
	control elements	#4	21.4%	
	prioritizing	#4	7.1%	
adaption	instance correction	#4	67.9%	x
	feature correction	#4	53.6%	x
others	font design	#4	14.3%	
	video	#3	3.6%	

of overall search results, the second reflects the identified papers): ACM Digital Library (68|4), IEEE Xplore (49|3), Science Direct (70|5), Springer Link (139|2), and Google Scholar (95|7). A further seven articles were identified through forward and backward searches. Finally, the literature review resulted in 28 interactive XUIs, which are based on different XAI methods such as decision trees, neural networks, graphs, support vector machines, random forest, and different methods for black- and white-box models.

The analysis of the existing XUIs resulted in a design catalog with 29 design components that are assigned to the respective objective of the design principles (DP) according to Chromik and Butz [3], see Table 1, column three. Thus, DP 1 includes the combination of visual and textual forms of explanation, DP 2 aims at an user-oriented, interactive explanation process, DP 3 combines different explanation contents and DP 4 covers individual adaptations. By analyzing the design components, four categories for structuring purposes were derived and are indicated in the first column: form of explanation, content of explanation, interaction and adaptation. Two components were not assigned to any category and are listed under others. The categories represent essential parts of XUIs, from which design components for the development of XUIs are to be selected.

The frequency of occurrence of the identified components in the literature can be used for assessing their relevance and is structured as follows: Components with a frequency of over 75% are assigned a value of 1: ●, while components between 50 and 75% are weighted with a value of 3/4: ◕. Elements with a frequency of less than 50% and more than 25% are assigned a value of 1/2: ◑ and components with a frequency of less than 25% are rated 1/4: ◔. Table 1 lists the design components for each category in descending order to their frequencies. It should be noted that the design catalog is not intended to be exhaustive.

From the literature analysis it becomes clear that visual and textual forms of explanation are most frequently used in multiple views for global and local explanations in combination. Whereas tables of explanation were only used eleven times, primarily with numerical values. At least over 60% of the identified papers use multiple views of explanation forms in combination. Counterfactual explanations, in which what-if scenarios are used as explanations, are used in half of the papers analyzed. Adaptations to the feature (53,6%) or an analyzed instance (67,9%) are also part of an XUI in the majority of the papers. Instance adaptations refer to a concrete result or decision, whereas feature adaptations refer to an underlying machine learning model. That shows that the user-centered modification of the learning model is an essential aspect in the development of an XUI. A look at the interactions shows that various functions were identified with medium frequency. For the majority of XUIs (60,7%), the relevant features/indicators that led to a result and on which an explanation is based can be retrieved by user interaction. All other functions are used to varying degrees in 20% to 30% of the papers, which may be due to the respective area of application. Interactions for search functions, filters, sorting and feature selection were counted six to eight times for each, although these should be main functionalities. Chat-based and why-explanations that provide information about the consequences of a recommended result have been used less frequently according to the results of the literature review. Individual font design to emphasize special attributes in explanations or explanation videos are also rarely used.

The design catalog provides an overview of XUI components used so far and their frequencies. XUI designers are able to select XUI components with regard to the design principles for XUI [3] and to specify requirements. In the following, an XUI for our KBXAI-PA is developed and evaluated using the design catalog.

4   Demonstration and Evaluation of an XUI

4.1   Current State of KBXAI-PA

In consulting projects, process analyses aim to achieve a consistent understanding of actual processes to identify weaknesses and recommend suitable improvement measures. One form of automated process analysis is process mining, which analyzes existing data in IT systems and uncovers hidden process information using digital traces [18]. Neither manual process steps nor implicit knowledge of process participants are automatically taken into account. In addition, the interpretation of the analysis results frequently requires expert knowledge.

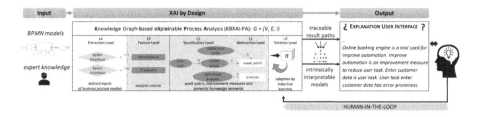

Fig. 1. Concept of KBXAI-PA according to [9] with an example result output.

The KBXAI-PA approach supports the automated identification of process deficiencies and suitable improvement measures based on expert knowledge in a knowledge graph. KBXAI-PA combines symbolic approaches of formal knowledge through an ontology-like knowledge graph architecture and IML methods by integrating implicit knowledge into machine learning methods [9]. In this way, user feedback can contribute to the improvement of results in subsequent analyses and lead to the enrichment of the knowledge graph.

The architecture consists of a directed, edge-labeled knowledge graph in five layers (see Fig. 1) with deduction algorithms that perform the analysis procedure and inductive learning mechanisms to continuously expand the knowledge base through new knowledge elements and inheritance of attributes (abstract elements inherit attributes of concrete elements) [8]. L4 represents the data input layer to integrate expert knowledge and start a process analysis with a business process model of the standard notation BPMN. L3 as data transfer layer contains analysis criteria to use analysis relevant information of a process model. Layers L2 and L1 form the information processing and knowledge representation of weak points, associated improvement measures and semantic correlations. The solution layer L0 contains all nodes activated by a process analysis in the form of result paths π. In conclusion, the knowledge graph comprises factual knowledge about analysis criteria, process deficiencies, and their improvement measures, which provides global explanations, as well as domain knowledge of an analyzed process that can be used for local explanations, see Fig. 1.

The analysis procedure is based on the use of deduction algorithms that run through linked nodes in the graph depending on association classes and calculation formulas, and check which weaknesses and which improvement measures can be identified [8]. The analysis criteria for identifying weak points include, for example, the number of existing manual tasks or message flows, or the occurrence of specific task activities such as print, sign, scan of upstream or downstream tasks. The analysis of suitable improvement measure relies on rule-based calculation formulas. If, for instance, a manual task for entering customer data from a CRM system into a booking form is identified, the abstract improvement measure "automate data transfer" should be inferred. The calculation formula between the nodes "enterCustomerData" and "automateDataTransfer" is as follows: $r(v_{automateDataTransfer}) = true \leftarrow r(v_{enterCustomerData}) == true$. A result path π in which a user task was identified as a media break and the improvement measure of automating data transfer using an online booking engine as improvement tool was derived is as follows:

$$\pi = v_{mediaBreak} \rightarrow v_{existingUserTask} \rightarrow v_{enterCustomerData} \rightarrow v_{bookingRequest}$$
$$\rightarrow v_{handleMediaBreak} \rightarrow v_{automateDataTransfer} \rightarrow v_{onlineBookingEngine}.$$

By reconstructing the result paths run through, intrinsically interpretable models in the form of stochastic decision trees are derived with the help of Bayes' theory [7]. In this way, path probabilities are calculated depending on the traversed result paths in the knowledge graph. The association classes between activated nodes of a result path enable result outputs in the form of natural language structured statements, see Fig. 1 on the right. By taking user feedback into account via an interactive learning loop of the process analysis, human users can verify process analyses results, check their relevance and improve them [9]. The weighting w of a result node of an improvement measure, such as *online booking engine,* learned through interaction is calculated using the mean value of all assessments A of these depending on the respective weak point specification. However, a correct assessment of analysis results also requires a full understanding of the process analysis and how results were generated.

4.2   Designing and Demonstrating of an XUI for KBXAI-PA

The aim of designing an XUI for KBXAI-PA is to present the analysis process and its results in a readable, comprehensible and understandable manner, as proposed in the XAI goals by Gunning and Aha [11]. The explanation should be understandable to the extent that the user see indicators (e.g. concrete user tasks) that justify the identification of a weakness (e.g. media break) by considering the path of result generation. Improvement measures (e.g. improve automation) should be argued in detail in view of identified weaknesses. The user should be able to interact with the system in order to query detailed descriptions and carry out verifications and corrections to a process analysis, which are considered in subsequent analyses. For a first design of an XUI for KBXAI-PA, selected design components with a frequency of 1/2 to 1 were considered regarding the analysis procedure, so that every design principle is represented by at least one component, see Table 1, marked in last column. Nevertheless, all other components should also be investigated in future research.

The design of the interactive XUI includes a backend with an administration view for analysis and system experts and a frontend with the process analysis view for domain experts and end users. The administration view is used to set up analysis procedures including applicable deduction algorithms and the creation of knowledge graphs. The process analysis view contains an overview of generated analysis results and functions for executing new process analyses. Starting a new process analysis requires uploading a process to be analyzed in BPMN format. For this, we use a sample order-to-cash process model with several user tasks, repeatable tasks and media and organizational breaks. Alternatively, BPMN

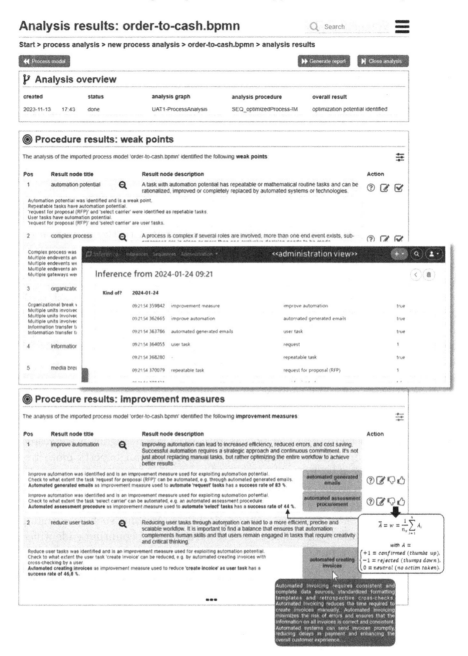

Fig. 2. Process analysis view and excerpt of administration view.

models that have been generated on the basis of previously analyzed event log data by process mining applications can also be uploaded via an API. In this way, a process mining analysis can be refined by our knowledge graph-based approach to explainable process analysis. After uploading our sample process model, the analysis is carried out.

The view of analysis results reflects the core of the XUI, see Fig. 2. It consists of an *Analysis overview* with metadata of process analysis, procedure results on process deficiencies and procedure results on improvement measures. The overall result indicates that optimization potential was identified in the analyzed process model. *Procedure results: weak points* represents an excerpt of identified process deficiencies. The first weakness displayed *automation potential* starts with two sentences with global explanations. The third sentence shows which tasks in the process model have automation potential and for what reason (*repeatable tasks*). The zoom magnifier symbol is used to display descriptions for a global explanation, which provides the domain expert or end user with local explanations of how process deficiencies were identified in the knowledge graph. This involves the traversed paths and activated nodes that contributed to the identification of the result node. A log of all result path runs π_n, including the calculated results and activated nodes (*true*), is documented in the administration view. A log excerpt for identifying the improvement measure *automated generated emails* in relation to the user task *request for proposal (RFP)* as repeating task with automation potential is shown in the little window of Fig. 2. All node pairs of a result path with the result value *true* are transformed into natural language statements, which are displayed as explanation content in the analysis view for domain experts as well as all other end users. *Procedure results: improvement measures* are indicated for each weak point, as shown in Fig. 3 as an example for *automation potential*. In addition to the explanation sentences, two specific improvement measures with a success rate are proposed. The success rate reflects the result weighting w which is calculated through user feedback in the interactive learning procedure [9]. The success rate is therefore higher if suggested improvement measures for a weakness are rated by human experts more frequently as being suitable. Regardless of the user group, analysis results can be filtered according to weak points or searched for terms. Quick-infos on selected terms in the analysis results are displayed via mouse-over, e.g. for the improvement measure *automated creating invoicing* in Fig. 2. Actions, such as changing node labels or calculation formulas, as well as verifying and confirming identified result nodes of improvement measures or rejecting them if they are unsuitable, are executed in the *Action* area by system or domain experts. The edit icon opens an administration window for managing, adapting and expanding the knowledge graph. Within the training phase, domain experts can assess improvement measures according to the identified weaknesses of their result paths by confirming with *thumbs up* (+1), rejecting with *thumbs down* (–1) or taking no action (rated with 0) in order to calculate weightings as success rates [9].

4.3   Evaluating the XUI for KBXAI-PA Through Expert Interviews

The design components implemented in the developed XUI were finally evaluated by means of explorative expert interviews with process analysts and consultants as domain experts. For a first initial evaluation, three consultants from a SAP consultancy as well as three other participants from the fields of IT consulting, project management and logistics were recruited. A broad evaluation with different case studies and a larger survey participation is currently being prepared. After a brief introduction, the XUI was demonstrated and tested by the interviewee using a web-based prototype, followed by a discussion of improvement potential. Interviewees' opinions were summarized in several statements and rated on a five-point Likert scale with strongly agree, rather agree, neither, rather disagree and strongly disagree, see Fig. 3.

Firstly, the relevance of specific design components was assessed. Both visual and textual forms of explanation, local explanations, which refer to a specific process analysis, as well as search functions, filters and sorting are rated as the most relevant by the respondents. Global explanations that provide general descriptions, multiple views of explanations, correcting features and instances as well as accuracy indicators for process analysis results were rated as relevant or rather relevant by all interviewees. 2/3 of participants consider feature relevance to be essential. In the prototype, for example, identified weaknesses are listed according to the time of their identification and improvement measures according to success rate. Quick-infos were assessed with approval by the majority, whereby 33% of interviewees rated a quick-info as neither relevant nor irrelevant.

The willingness to use the XUI of our KBXAI-PA approach is summarized in five statements, see Fig. 3. Over half of respondents disagreed with the statement that they had doubts about the results. The majority of respondents rated the forms of explanation implemented in the XUI (visual, textual, multiple views) as sufficient. Correction functions increase the willingness to use according to a surveyed majority of 83%. The number of explanation forms contained in an XUI does seem to have an positive effect on the explanatory power. Whereas many different design components do not increase the willingness to use the XUI for all respondents. 67% of respondents agree or strongly agree with the statement that many different XUI components increase the willingness to use, 17% neither agree nor disagree and another 17% tend to disagree with this statement.

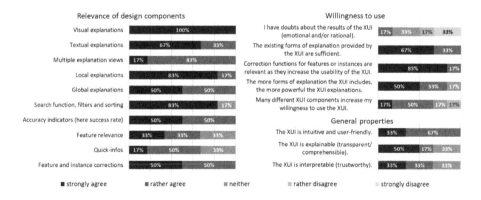

Fig. 3. Overview of expert interview results (n = 6).

In summary, the developed XUI delivers explainable and technically comprehensible results in a user-friendly manner, whereas interpretability and trustworthiness through meaningful results are considered to be less fulfilled. The meaningfulness of generated results is mainly affected by the scope of the knowledge graph which can be extended by domain-specific knowledge. Furthermore, the experts suggested that the analyzed BPMN models be displayed in excerpts in the analysis results. Another wish that was expressed concerns the connection of the analysis tool including XUI to existing source systems or their integration into other (process mining) analysis tools, such as the EMS of Celonis.

5   Key Findings, Research Perspectives and Implications

For hybrid knowledge-based AI systems with intrinsically interpretable models, such as KBXAI-PA, an XUI enables an user-friendly, comprehensible and understandable presentation of analysis results that allows appropriate user interactions for IML. A systematic literature review was used to establish a design catalog of components for the development of XUIs regardless of the explanatory purpose of an XAI system in order to derive suitable requirement specifications.

The demonstration and evaluation of selected design components in an XUI of our KBXAI-PA approach has shown that different forms of explanation can support the explanatory power in terms of comprehensible results. However, the highest possible number of implemented components does not necessarily increase the willingness to use AI systems with an XUI. Users can be overwhelmed by the wide range of explanation components on offer. Interaction functions that contribute to both the explanation and the adaptation of the learning model are rated positively and can increase the willingness to use the system. Interaction and correction elements give the user the feeling of participating in the system's behavior and of being able to continuously improve the analysis knowledge graph through individual domain knowledge, which can increase user acceptance.

The evaluation of design components always refers to the respective XUI implementation, which depends largely on the application domain and the AI system. Usability aspects also influence the assessment of XUIs. In follow-up evaluations, further design components, such as counterfactual or example-based explanations, are to be implemented prototypically and evaluated through various case studies in larger survey rounds. In addition, an XUI should also help to specifically improve interactive learning models, which should be evaluated accordingly. In this way, learning systems can be optimized in a human-centric way and analysis results can be improved transparently and comprehensibly for different application domains.

Self-service applications for AI-based process analysis with user-centric XUIs should be offered on digital platforms not only for consultants, but also for consulting clients to self-analyze their own business processes. A reduction in the required number of consultants for process analysis through automation leads to cost advantages. Moreover, automated and, thus, more cost-effective analysis services, can open up new client segments, who are not able or willing to pay high rates for individualized human consulting services today.

References

1. Amershi, S., Cakmak, M., Knox, W.B., Kulesza, T.: Power to the people: the role of humans in interactive machine learning. AI Mag. **35**(4), 105–120 (2015)
2. Arrieta, A.B., et al.: Explainable artificial intelligence (XAI): concepts, taxonomies, opportunities and challenges toward responsible AI. Inf. Fusion **58**, 82–115 (2020)
3. Chromik, M., Butz, A.: Human-XAI interaction: a review and design principles for explanation user interfaces. In: Ardito, C., et al. (eds.) INTERACT 2021. LNCS, vol. 12933, pp. 619–640. Springer, Cham (2021). https://doi.org/10.1007/978-3-030-85616-8_36
4. Dudley, J.J., Kristensson, P.O.: A review of user interface design for interactive machine learning. ACM TiiS **8**(2), 1–37 (2018)
5. Eiband, M., Schneider, H., Bilandzic, M., Fazekas-Con, J., Haug, M., Hussmann, H.: Bringing transparency design into practice. In: Berkovsky, S. (ed.) 23rd International Conference on Intelligent User Interfaces, pp. 211–223. ACM Conferences (2018)
6. Fails, J.A., Olsen, D.R.: Interactive machine learning. In: Proceedings of the 8th International Conference on Intelligent User Interfaces. ACM Press, New York, USA (2003)
7. Füßl, A., Nissen, V.: Interpretability of knowledge graph-based explainable process analysis. In: IEEE 5th AIKE, pp. 9–17 (2022)
8. Füßl, A., Nissen, V., Dopf, S., Füßl, F.F.: An inferential knowledge model for the digitalisation and automation of business process analysis. In: Gronau, N., Heine, M., Poustcchi, K., Krasnova, H. (eds.) Proceedings of the WI2020, pp. 185–200. GITO (2020)
9. Füßl, A., Nissen, V., Heringklee, S.H.: Interactive machine learning of knowledge graph-based explainable process analysis. In: Ruiz, M., Soffer, P. (eds.) Advanced Information Systems Engineering Workshops. CAiSE 2023. LNBIP, vol. 482, pp. 112–124. Springer, Cham (2023). https://doi.org/10.1007/978-3-031-34985-0_12
10. Ghai, B., Liao, Q.V., Zhang, Y., Bellamy, R., Mueller, K.: Explainable active learning (XAL). In: Proceedings of the ACM on Human-Computer Interaction, vol. 4, no. CSCW, pp. 1–28 (2021)
11. Gunning, D., Aha, D.: Darpa's explainable artificial intelligence (XAI) program. AI Mag. **40**(2), 44–58 (2019)
12. Herlocker, J.L., Konstan, J.A., Riedl, J.: Explaining collaborative filtering recommendations. In: Kellogg, W. (ed.) Proceedings of the ACM conference on Computer Supported Cooperative Work, pp. 241–250. ACM Conferences (2000)
13. Millecamp, M., Htun, N.N., Conati, C., Verbert, K.: To explain or not to explain. In: Fu, W.T. (ed.) Proceedings of the 24th International Conference on Intelligent User Interfaces, pp. 397–407. ACM Conferences, ACM, New York, NY (2019)
14. Moore, J.D., Paris, C.L.: Requirements for an expert system explanation facility. Comput. Intell. **7**(4), 367–370 (1991)

15. Nissen, V., Joksch, N.S., Füßl, A.: Wie die corona-pandemie die unternehmensberatung verändert hat. In: Bruhn, M., Hadwich, K. (eds.) Gestaltung des Wandels im Dienstleistungsmanagement. Forum Dienstleistungsmanagement, pp. 633–670. Springer, Wiesbaden (2023). https://doi.org/10.1007/978-3-658-41813-7_23

16. Peffers, K., Tuunanen, T., Rothenberger, M.A., Chatterjee, S.: A design science research methodology for information systems research. JMIS **24**(3), 45–77 (2007)

17. Shneiderman, B.: Bridging the gap between ethics and practice. ACM Trans. Interact. Intell. Syst. **10**(4), 1–31 (2020)

18. van der Aalst, W.M.P.: Process Mining: Data Science in Action, 2nd edn. Springer, Berlin, Heidelberg (2016). https://doi.org/10.1007/978-3-662-49851-4

19. Webster, J., Watson, R.T.: Analyzing the past to prepare for the future: writing a literature review. MIS Q. **26** (2002)

20. Xu, W.: Toward human-centered AI. Interactions **26**(4), 42–46 (2019)

Enhancing Research Clarity: Ontology-Based Modeling of Argumentation in RPML

Knut Hinkelmann[1,3]([envelope]) [iD], Valeriia Afonina[1] [iD], and Devid Montecchiari[1,2] [iD]

[1] FHNW University of Applied Sciences and Arts Northwestern Switzerland, Olten, Switzerland
{knut.hinkelmann,valeriia.afonina,devid.montecchiari}@fhnw.ch
[2] School of Science and Technology, UNICAM University of Camerino, Camerino, Italy
[3] Department of Informatics, University of Pretoria, Pretoria, South Africa

Abstract. Navigating the research process, from problem identification to argumentation construction, challenges novice researchers. This study introduces RPML (Research Problem Modeling Language), a meta-model and ontology designed to address these challenges by visually representing key aspects of research argumentation. RPML enhances clarity and coherence in research discourse by providing researchers with a visual representation of argumentation for a research problem. RPML is represented as a specialization of the OMG Business Motivation Model and Toulmin's argumentation model approach. This enables researchers to gain a comprehensive overview of their research projects, identify research problems, build robust argumentation, and select suitable research strategies.

Keywords: Motivation Modeling · Argumentation Modeling · Research Design · Ontology-Based Modeling · Problem Identification · Ontology · Metamodel · Ontology-Based Metamodeling

1 Introduction

Research is a complex endeavor that needs careful structuring and management [10]. Argumentation for a "research worthy" problem [6] which leads to the contribution of new knowledge is based on existing knowledge, comparison of different arguments, and a need of the environment in which the research results might make a change. Analysis of various scientific and trusted sources allows for formulating a solid problem statement that demonstrates the significance and relevance of the research problem and guides the research [27,31]. Since not all problems are research-worthy, a problem statement should be supported by evidence from the environment and literature.

© The Author(s), under exclusive license to Springer Nature Switzerland AG 2024
J. P. A. Almeida et al. (Eds.): CAiSE 2024 Workshops, LNBIP 521, pp. 85–96, 2024.
https://doi.org/10.1007/978-3-031-61003-5_8

Conceptual modeling is a technique for representing the structure and relationships of a domain or problem that involves identifying and defining key concepts, their attributes, and the relationships between them [25, 35]. These models are often represented visually using diagrams or graphs. Visualization can also help to structure and understand the argumentation for defining research problems, setting up research goals determining an appropriate research strategy [15, 30]. Representing conceptual models as an ontology allows for automated reasoning over the models.

This paper extends the visual modeling of the argumentation for a research problem and the research design as described in [9] with an ontological representation and definition of the concepts of the modeling language.

2   Literature Review

This section provides a review of the literature on identifying a research problem, visualization of argumentation, and conceptual modeling in the research problem and argumentation visualization.

2.1   Identification of a Research-Worthy Problem

Finding a problem worthy of research is an important first stage in the research process since it establishes the parameters for the entire study. It involves looking for gaps in existing literature or unresolved issues in a specific field. A clear and concise problem statement is essential since it is acknowledged as the foundation of any successful research [6]. When choosing a research problem, researchers must be cautious not to choose a problem that is too broad or too narrow, as this can impact the manageability and significance of the research [6]. It is essential to comprehensively analyze the body of knowledge and its practical applications to have a clear argumentation for the research problem and to identify a research challenge that can effectively handled [29]. Setting up research goals and subgoals and supporting them with thorough methodological explanations enables a more in-depth analysis of the topic [29].

Rigor and relevance are key components of research-worthiness [6]. Balancing rigor and relevance in research problems generates insights that benefit scientific understanding and practical impact [8]. This is reflected in the argumentation about the research-worthiness of a problem, which is based on a review of the scientific literature. Maedche et al.'s conceptual model is a valuable tool for overcoming difficulties in grounding, situating, diagnosing, and resolving research problems when using the Design Science Research approach [20]. The problem space in this model underscores the importance of analysis of the needs, goals, and requirements of the stakeholders. These criteria influence the direction of the research and play an important role in providing effective and significant research outcomes.

When collecting and analyzing statements, it is important to assess their impact on the research problem [6]. Finding contentious arguments-arguments that validate, rebut, or support the stated problem is the main objective of this research step, which enables the development of a compelling argument when identifying a research problem. Research has shown that argumentation and motivation modeling could play significant roles in identifying a research problem [19, 21]. The close connection between modeling and argumentation in the context of scientific knowledge illustrates that modeling naturally supports an argumentative process [21].

2.2   Conceptual Modeling for Visualization of Research Problems

Conceptual modeling is a technique for representing the structure and relationships of a domain or a problem [12, 13, 24]. It involves identifying and defining key concepts, their attributes, and the relationships between them [25, 35]. These models are often represented visually using diagrams or graphs, allowing for a clear and intuitive understanding of the complex relationships within the domain. Conceptual modeling serves as a skeleton, providing a structured framework for understanding and organizing their research ideas. Understanding and using conceptual frameworks are essential tools in scientific problem-solving. Conceptual models are central for analyzing and designing Information Systems (IS) [23, 36] as they support communication and collaboration among stakeholders and understanding of the domain [36].

Conceptual modeling can be applied to research problems. Several approaches exist for conceptual modeling argumentation, motivation and research problem identification.

Zhou et al. [37] developed the Scientific Paper Argumentation Ontology (SAO) to illustrate the interplay between argumentation logic and specific content in scientific papers (Fig. 1). SAO employs an argumentation graph to encapsulate the semantic annotation in forming the argumentative structure within scientific research. This approach facilitates a comprehensive overview of the research and supports researchers in constructing and visualizing arguments.

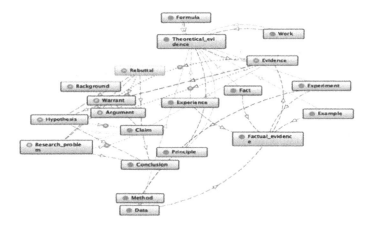

Fig. 1. The structure of SAO [37]

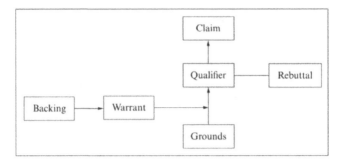

Fig. 2. Toulmin's Model [30]

Toulmin [30] has previously explored systematic representations of argumentation and laid the groundwork for visualizing problem approaches that defy simplistic categorization, documented in notations. Toulmin's model of argumentation provides a framework for analyzing and evaluating arguments and consists of six main components: claim, grounds, warrant, backing, qualifier, and rebuttal (Fig. 2) [2]. This model was essential in communication and composition studies in the late twentieth century [2]. Visualizing argumentation can be a helpful strategy to enhance the understanding and application of Toulmin's argumentation model in research problems and research design [29].

Graphical Issue-Based Information System (gIBIS) [28], is another argumentation system which is a graphical representation of IBIS [16]. The visual framework helps stakeholders to visualize the connections between issues, positions, and arguments, thus facilitating a deeper understanding of the problem at hand [3]. This visualization enhances critical thinking, facilitates the exploration of diverse perspectives, and ultimately supports the resolution of complex problems. In research problem visualization and research design, IBIS notation allows stakeholders to engage in structured discussions and develop a comprehensive understanding by facilitating the systematic exploration of issues and their interconnections [4,5,28].

Business Motivation Model (BMM) is another approach that can be used to visualize argumentation for research problems and research design. The Business Motivation Model provides a holistic framework for visualizing argumentation in research problems and research design (Fig. 3) [2]. It allows stakeholders to identify and analyze the motivations and goals driving a research problem and the resources, constraints, and activities involved. The elements of BMM allow the display of the goal or goals the company wants to achieve, what strategy, tactics, and objectives need to be defined to achieve it, what might influence the results, etc. These elements have similarities with elements of the gIBIS notation, such as issues, positions, and arguments. They might be integrated to provide a comprehensive visualization of the argumentation of research-worthy problems and research design.

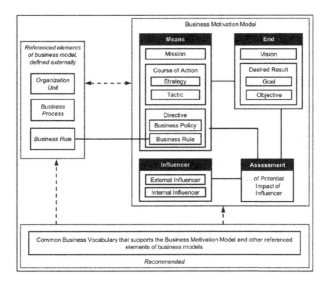

Fig. 3. BMM Overview [26]

While there are conceptual modeling languages for argumentation and motivation, they are not specific for modeling research problems and thus do not provide guidance for the researcher. Combining the existing approaches for modeling argumentation and motivation for visualizing a research problem and research design can enhance the effectiveness and clarity of the research process. It can help researchers to organize and analyze complex information, identify connections between different elements of the research, and make well-informed decisions, proving the research-worthiness of the researched problem and an appropriate research design.

The objective of our research is to develop a conceptual modeling language that specializes the motivation modeling for visualizing the justification for the research problem and extending it with concepts for additionally providing arguments and counter-arguments. The focus is on the specification of the meta-model, which is represented as an ontology.

3   Methodology

This study used the Design Science Research Methodology (DSR). The analysis of research papers and project reports revealed that argumentation for research problem and research design lack clarity and have gaps in their argumentation, particularly concerning the synthesis and evaluation of the findings from literature [18]. Based on that, approaches for visualization of argumentations are identified (see Sect. 2). The artifact of the novel Research Problem Modeling Language (RPML) is the ontology-based metamodel for visualizing argumentation for research problems and research design. It consists of an ontology defining the concepts and a modeling language for the visualization. The visualization helps to facilitate a better understanding and communication of the arguments for the research worthiness of the research problem, and choosing a research design.

Karagiannis and Kühn have proposed a layered approach for metamodeling [11] This research focuses on the metamodel and modeling language to ensure the machine interpretability of models and allow reasoning [1,17,22]. The metamodel is represented as an ontology. Ontologies are conceptual models that enable information exchange inside a specific domain by providing universal user interpretations of terminology and relationships [33]. To set them apart from basic taxonomies, these models contain declarations of object relationships as well as derivation rules and constraints for inferring new facts [7,34]. Keet [14] also emphasizes the role of ontologies in "computer-computer, computer-human, and human-human communication." Ontologies provide a vocabulary of domain-specific concepts with defined machine-interpretable semantics.

We applied Design Science Research with the phases from Vaishnavi and Kuechler [32]. For the problem awareness, we made a literature review (see Sect. 2). In the suggestion phase, we determined appropriate modeling concepts from BMM [26] and Toulmin's argumentation model [30] and then developed the ontology and modeling language. We show the applicability of the artifact by applying it to our own research (see Sect. 5).

4   An Ontological Metamodel for Research

We developed an ontology-based metamodel artifact that defines the core aspects of the Research Problem Modeling Language (RPML). The metamodel establishes a unified approach for visualizing argumentation in research problems and research design. It amalgamates elements from the business motivation modeling, argumentation modeling and concepts specific to the research domain.

The class hierarchy of the ontology for the Business Motivation Model BMM [26] has been extended with elements of Toulmin's argumentation. Figure 4 shows a class diagram of our metamodel and Fig. 5 show an excerpt of the ontology representation. Elements from the research domains are represented as sub-classes of BMM (Fig. 5) and relations are defined as object properties (Fig. 6).

We borrowed the following concepts from the BMM notation [26], specializing them to represent research domain elements: the *Influencer* element expresses the information about the environment and existing knowledge and methods from the body of knowledge that have an influence on the research problem. The *Assessment* element represents the evaluation of the influencers. According to the BMM notation *Assessment* can be *judged* as *Threat*, *Opportunity*, *Strength* or *Weakness*. Concepts of Toulmin's argumentation model can *support* or *contradict* the *Assessments*: *Ground*, *Backing*, and *Rebuttal*. *Assessments* can *lead to* the *Research Problem* which is a specialization of BMM's *Vision*.

The Solution Space in Fig. 4 corresponds to the *Means* for solving the RESEARCH PROBLEM. *Research Contribution* specializes *Mission*. It *contributes*

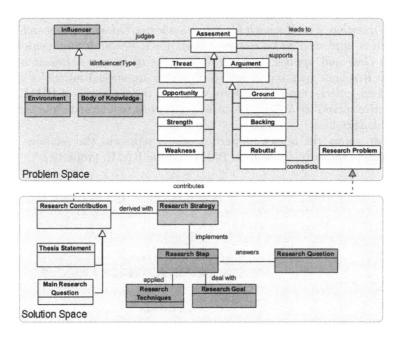

Fig. 4. Metamodel to visualize argumentation for research problem and research design

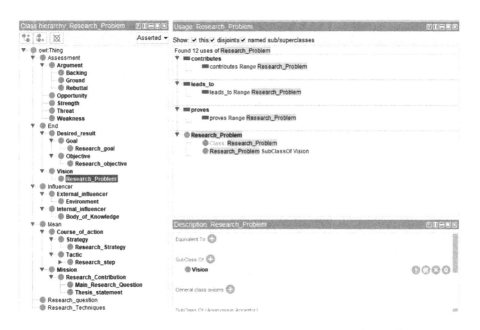

Fig. 5. The structure of Research Problem Modeling Language (RPML) ontology

to the *Research Problem* and can be formulated as a *Thesis Statement* or *Main Research question*. The *Research Contribution* is *derived with* a *Research Strategy* which is *implemented* be *Research Step*. Each *Research Step deals with* a *Research Goal* and *applies Research Techniques* to answer a *Research Question*. The *Research goal* and *Research objective* are specializations of BMM's *Goal* and *Objective*, respectively. Here we follow the semantics of BMM, where an *Objective* quantifies a *Goal*, i.e. a *Research objective* must be phrased with measurable variables.

Figure 6 shows the object properties, which represent the relations of the metamodel. It shows relations from BMM and the RAML properties.

Fig. 6. Research Problem Modeling Language (RPML) ontology object properties

Having those elements defined provides not only a visual representation of the research problem but also a comprehensive overview of the logic and connection between different elements of the research problem and supports the building of a strong argumentation, applying principles of BMM and argumentation modeling within the research problem domain.

5   Application of the Modelling Language

To demonstrate the usability of the visualization and ontology, we applied it to the research problem for visualizing the argumentation for a research problem. Figure 7 shows the visualization of the problem space as described in [9]. There are *Influencers* from the *Environment* and from the *Body of Knowledge*. It was observed that researchers have difficulties identifying a research problem when they make a literature review and that argumentation for research problems often lacks clarity, making it difficult to understand. On the other hand side, the BMM and argumentation modeling methods have been found in the body of knowledge, which allow for tracing decision making and modeling pros and cons in argumentation. These *Assessments* lead to the *Research Problem* of how visualization can support researchers in developing and articulating their research problem and research design.

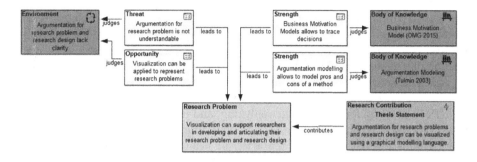

Fig. 7. Visualization of the problem space for this research [9]

The intended *Research Contribution*, here phrased as a *Thesis Statement*, is the connector between problem space and solution space, as it *contributes* to the *Research Problem*.

Figure 8 shows part of the ontology representation of graphical model. For each model element, there exists an individual of the corresponding class. There is a data property *Text* for each element that has as value the full text of the elements. The relations are represented with object properties. Figure 8 shows the object property for the *Thesis Statement*.

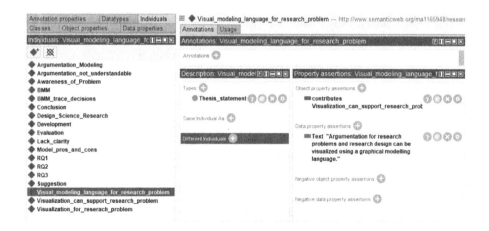

Fig. 8. Visualization of the problem space for this research [9]

6   Conclusion

Our study identified gaps in research problem identification and design argumentation, leading to the development of the Research Problem Modeling Language (RPML) metamodel and ontology. By integrating elements from the Business Motivation Model (BMM), Toulmin's argumentation model, and ontology-based metamodeling, RPML serves as a comprehensive framework for understanding and communicating research structures, assessing problem-worthiness, and guiding design selection while ensuring machine interpretability. This structured approach enhances the clarity, coherence, and effectiveness of research problem articulation and argumentation within diverse domains.

RPML is a tool for visualizing, analyzing, and communicating research argumentation, advancing research endeavors by leveraging ontology-based modeling and rigorous evaluation. The integration of principles from BMM, and argumentation modeling methodologies within RPML provides researchers with a structured framework to navigate complex research landscapes with strategic intent. This framework not only aids in visualizing research problems but also strengthens the coherence and connectivity between different elements, paving the way for robust argumentation and informed decision-making within research endeavors.

Ontological representation of the metamodel enables the automated interpretation of the models. In future research endeavors, we will expand the metamodel with domain concepts which will allow to assess the consistency and coherence of RPML models against predefined syntactic rules and constraints, generating a comprehensive validation report. By embracing methodological rigor, structured modeling approaches, and interdisciplinary integration, researchers can enhance their problem-solving capabilities and contribute to knowledge creation within their respective domains.

While this paper has a focus in the integration of symbolic AI and modelling, in a future research it is planned to exploit large language models and machine learning to identify papers that contradict or support an assessment of argumentation - similar to the scite.ai[1] tool.

References

1. Afonina, V., Hinkelmann, K., Montecchiari, D.: Enriching enterprise architecture models with healthcare domain knowledge. In: Ruiz, M., Soffer, P. (eds.) CAiSE 2023. LNCS, vol. 482, pp. 17–28. Springer, Cham (2023). https://doi.org/10.1007/978-3-031-34985-0_2
2. Andrews, R.: Models of argumentation in educational discourse. Text-Interdisc. J. Study Discourse **25**, 107–127 (2005). https://doi.org/10.1515/text.2005.25.1.107
3. Conklin, J., Begeman, M.L.: gIBIS: a hypertext tool for exploratory policy discussion. ACM Trans. Inf. Syst. (TOIS) **6**(4), 303–331 (1988)
4. Conklin, J., Begeman, M.L.: gIBIS: a tool for all reasons. J. Am. Soc. Inf. Sci. **40**(3), 200–213 (1989)

---

[1]   https://scite.ai/.

5. De Moor, A., Weigand, H.: Effective communication in virtual adversarial collaborative communities. J. Commun. Inform. **2**(2) (2006)
6. Ellis, T.J., Levy, Y.: Framework of problem-based research: a guide for novice researchers on the development of a research-worthy problem. Informing Sci. Int. J. Emerg. Transdiscipl. **11**, 017–033 (2008). https://doi.org/10.28945/438
7. Guizzardi, G.: Conceptualizations, modeling languages, and (meta) models. In: Databases and Information Systems IV: Selected Papers from the Seventh International Baltic Conference, DB&IS'2006 (2007)
8. Hevner, A.R.: A three cycle view of design science research. Scand. J. Inf. Syst. **19**(2), 4 (2007)
9. Hinkelmann, K., Afonina, V., Montecchiari, D.: Visualizing argumentation for research problem and research design. In: 19th International Conference on Design Science Research in Information Systems and Technology (DESRIST 2024). Trollhättan (2024)
10. Horváth, I.: Structuring the process of design research-a necessary step towards ensuring scientific rigor. In: DS 75-2: Proceedings of the 19th International Conference on Engineering Design (ICED13), Design for Harmonies, vol. 2: Design Theory and Research Methodology, Seoul, Korea, 19-22.08. 2013 (2013)
11. Karagiannis, D., Kühn, H., et al.: Metamodelling platforms. In: EC-web, p. 182. Citeseer (2002)
12. Karagiannis, D., Lee, M., Hinkelmann, K., Utz, W. (eds.): Domain-Specific Conceptual Modeling: Concepts, Methods and ADOxx Tools. Springer, Cham (2022). https://doi.org/10.1007/978-3-030-93547-4
13. Karagiannis, D., Mayr, H.C., Mylopoulos, J. (eds.): Domain- Specific Conceptual Modeling. Springer, Cham (2016). https://doi.org/10.1007/978-3-319-39417-6
14. Keet, C.M.: An Introduction to Ontology Engineering. University of Cape Town, Cape Town (2018)
15. Khambete, P.: Adaptation of Toulmin's model of argumentation for establishing Rigour and relevance in design research. In: Chakrabarti, A. (ed.) Research into Design for a Connected World. SIST, vol. 134, pp. 3–13. Springer, Singapore (2019). https://doi.org/10.1007/978-981-13-5974-3_1
16. Kunz, W., Rittel, H.: Issues as elements of information systems. Institute of Urban and Regional Development, University of California, Berkeley, California, Technical report (1970)
17. Laurenzi, E., Hinkelmann, K., Montecchiari, D., Goel, M.: Agile visualization in design thinking. In: Dornberger, R. (ed.) New Trends in Business Information Systems and Technology. SSDC, vol. 294, pp. 31–47. Springer, Cham (2021). https://doi.org/10.1007/978-3-030-48332-6_3
18. Levy, Y., Ellis, T.J.: A systems approach to conduct an effective literature review in support of information systems research. Informing Sci. J. **9** (2006)
19. Lytos, A., Lagkas, T., Sarigiannidis, P., Argyriou, V., Eleftherakis, G.: Modelling argumentation in short text: a case of social media debate. Simul. Model. Pract. Theory **115**, 102446 (2022)
20. Maedche, A., Gregor, S., Morana, S., Feine, J.: Conceptualization of the problem space in design science research. In: Tulu, B., Djamasbi, S., Leroy, G. (eds.) DESRIST 2019. LNCS, vol. 11491, pp. 18–31. Springer, Cham (2019). https://doi.org/10.1007/978-3-030-19504-5_2
21. Mendonça, P.C.C., Justi, R.: The relationships between modelling and argumentation from the perspective of the model of modelling diagram. Int. J. Sci. Educ. **35**(14), 2407–2434 (2013)

22. Montecchiari, D., Hinkelmann, K.: Towards ontology-based validation of EA principles. In: Barn, B.S., Sandkuhl, K. (eds.) The Practice of Enterprise Modeling. LNBI, vol. 456, pp. 66–81. Springer, Cham (2022). https://doi.org/10.1007/978-3-031-21488-2_5

23. Moody, D.L.: Theoretical and practical issues in evaluating the quality of conceptual models: current state and future directions. Data Knowl. Eng. **55**(3), 243–276 (2005)

24. Mylopoulos, J.: Conceptual modelling and telos. Conceptual modelling, databases, and CASE: an integrated view of information system development, pp. 49–68 (1992)

25. Olivé, A.: Conceptual Modeling of Information Systems. Springer, Heidelberg (2007)

26. OMG: Meta object facility (MOF) core specification, version 2.4.2. Technical report, Object Management Group (2015). https://www.omg.org/spec/BMM/1.3/PDF

27. Österle, H., et al.: Memorandum on design-oriented information systems research. Eur. J. Inf. Syst. **20**(1), 7–10 (2011). https://doi.org/10.1057/ejis.2010.55

28. Rittel, H., Noble, D.: Issue-Based Information Systems for Design. Institute of Urban and Regional Development. University of California, Berkeley (1989)

29. Streeb, D., El-Assady, M., Keim, D.A., Chen, M.: Why visualize? arguments for visual support in decision making. IEEE Comput. Graph. Appl. **41**, 17–22 (2021). https://doi.org/10.1109/MCG.2021.3055971

30. Toulmin, S.E.: The Uses of Argument. Cambridge University Press, Cambridge (2003)

31. Tracy, S.J.: Taking the plunge: a contextual approach to problem-based research. Commun. Monogr. **74**(1), 106–111 (2007)

32. Vaishnavi, V.K.: Design Science Research Methods and Patterns: Innovating Information and Communication Technology. Auerbach Publications (2007)

33. Verdonck, M., Gailly, F., Pergl, R., Guizzardi, G., Martins, B., Pastor, O.: Comparing traditional conceptual modeling with ontology-driven conceptual modeling: an empirical study. Inf. Syst. **81**, 92–103 (2019)

34. Veres, C., Sampson, J., Cox, K., Bleistein, S., Verner, J.: An ontology-based approach for supporting business-it alignment. Complex Intell. Syst. Appl. 21–42 (2010)

35. Wand, Y., Weber, R.: An ontological analysis of the relationship construct in conceptual modeling. ACM Trans. Database Syst. **24**, 494–528 (1999)

36. Wand, Y., Weber, R.: Research commentary: information systems and conceptual modeling-a research agenda. Inf. Syst. Res. **13**(4), 363–376 (2002)

37. Zhou, H., Song, N., Chang, W., Wang, X.: Linking the thoughts within scientific papers: Construction and visualization of argumentation graph. In: Proceedings of the Association for Information Science and Technology, vol. 56, no. 1, pp. 757–759 (2019)

Student Performance Prediction Model Based on Course Description and Student Similarity

David Mäder[1], Maja Spahic-Bogdanovic[1,2][✉] ⓘ,
and Hans Friedrich Witschel[1] ⓘ

[1] FHNW University of Applied Sciences and Arts Northwestern Switzerland,
Riggenbachstrasse 16, 4600 Olten, Switzerland
`david.maeder@students.fhnw.ch`,
`{maja.spahic,hansfriedrich.witschel}@fhnw.ch`
[2] University of Camerino, Via Madonna delle Carceri 9, 62032 Camerino, MC, Italy

Abstract. Choosing courses at the beginning of each semester is a complex decision that affects students' future careers and academic performance, especially when given the freedom to choose. Among other factors, the expected grade at the end of the semester and/or the expected ability to successfully complete a course plays an important role in course selection. This paper introduces a prototype for predicting student performance using state-of-the-art natural language processing techniques. The prototype, designed to assist students in course selection, uses historical course enrollment data and current course descriptions to predict possible grades and warn students of possible negative performance. A large language model, BERT, was used to analyse text and create course description embeddings. For this purpose, descriptions of courses a student has attended were considered and formed the basis for the student knowledge profile. In addition, student performance profiles are created by examining grades from the historical enrolment data. This two-pronged analysis is used to identify patterns that lead to negative study results. Although the idea of creating knowledge profiles based on course descriptions is promising, the evaluation showed room for improvement in terms of accuracy and recall.

Keywords: Student's performance · Decision making · Educational data mining · Performance prediction

1 Introduction

Course selection at the start of each semester, especially with the freedom of choice, is a complex decision affecting students' future careers and academic performance. [9] identified, based on a survey with 396 students, five key factors influencing students during course selections: class and lecturer, time-space, ease and comfort, course mate, and commitment factors. Each factor contains several items that influence the decision. In four categories, the grades were mentioned as one of the items; for example, lecturers tend to give marks easily or are lenient

J. P. A. Almeida et al. (Eds.): CAiSE 2024 Workshops, LNBIP 521, pp. 97–108, 2024.
https://doi.org/10.1007/978-3-031-61003-5_9

when grading. The possible grades that students can achieve are important for the course selection. Therefore, helping students in this decision-making process and predicting their grades before enrollment is valuable.

Due to digitisation, curriculum-relevant information becomes available and can be extracted from Academic Information Management Systems (AIMS). The discipline of Educational Data Mining (EDM) [11] uses the data logs retrieved from the AIMS to explore the underlying connections between the educational data and predict students' academic performance. Personal information, student activities, courses attended, grades, and course descriptions can be used to extract important indicators to design a prediction model [11], which, in turn, can help students make well-considered decisions.

Various approaches to predicting grades exist, but only a few consider unstructured data as an attribute. Further, while the focus of prior work has been identifying course-taking patterns that positively impact achievement and developing predictive models to forecast student grades, the impact of negative course-taking patterns is largely unexplored. This paper introduces a new approach to assist students in course selection at the start of the semester, utilising historical data and current course descriptions. This method predicts potential grades by analysing factors and patterns that negatively affect course performance and using these insights to recommend or advise against selected courses. We achieve this by generating individual student knowledge profiles and correlating them with course performance. We employ the Large Language Model (LLM) BERT to analyse course descriptions, utilising averaged vector embeddings based on each student's course history. By only advising against certain courses, our approach otherwise leaves maximum freedom of choice to students.

Enrollment process data from the Business Information Systems (BIS) master's degree program at the FHNW University of Applied Sciences and Arts Northwestern Switzerland (FHNW) was used to develop the approach. The data set, extracted from AIMS, contains information about course registrations, enrollment mutations, and students' final grades per course from the fall semester of 2012 to the fall semester of 2023.

2 Related Work

Several research studies focused on developing methods for predicting student grades. This focus benefits students by detecting potential problems early, improving the overall educational experience and student success.

Existing studies use a wide range of different attributes to describe student backgrounds, interests, performance and living circumstances. Two groups of attributes are very commonly used – with very different success:

- **Demographic attributes** are very widely used [1–4,7,12,15], but have consistently found to be be less predictive of academic achievements.
- On the other hand, **prior academic performance**, also very widely used [2,4,7,15], often in the form of (Cumulative) Grade Point Averages ((C)GPA), has repeatedly been shown to be the best predictor of future success.

Table 1. Frequently used attributes to predict student performance [3]

Attributes	Attribute Domain
Academic performance	GPA, Grade level, High school score, attendance to lessons, number of courses per semester
Demographic	Gender, nationality, place of birth, age
Behavioral	Raised hands, visit resources, school satisfaction, discussion, attend class, answer questions
Psychological	Personality, motivation, learning strategies, approach to learning, contextual influence
Family background	Mother and father Education, family income, location of parents
School environment	School size, medium of instruction, lecturer/teacher behaviour in class

Many other types of attributes have been explored in individual studies. Surveys such as [3,12] give an overview, see Table 1.

For instance, many studies take into account student behaviour, be it in class (e.g. attendance [8] or participation [3]), study-related activities outside class (e.g. course-taking patterns [11], interaction with other students [5], interaction with learning management systems [15]) or unrelated to studies, e.g. whether students have regular meals [5].

Other studies focus on psychological factors [13] – such as dealing with stress, resilience, mindset – or family background [2]. Finally, some studies also investigate the influence of the courses themselves, i.e. they consider e.g. the student feedback given on a course [10], the delivery mode (onsite, on-line or hybrid) [8] or the knowledge acquired through course materials/exercises [6]. Note that from all considered features, students' feedback on courses (see [10] is the only unstructured information used in all previous work.

In summary, existing forecasting models focus on analysing student performance in the current semester and predicting the student's performance after final enrolment. Moreover, these models rely primarily on structured data where GPA or CGPA plays a central role. Unstructured data sources are rather overlooked. Additionally, many authors presuppose a vertically integrated curriculum with restricted student choice. Also, the specifics of the courses, particularly the mix of chosen courses, have not been widely considered.

3   Methodology

Design science research (DSR) [14] was selected as the methodological framework for developing a student performance prediction model due to its focus on generating prescriptive knowledge through designing and assessing artifacts to solve specific real-world problems. Problem awareness was raised through a literature review and a case study about the BIS student's course enrollment process at FHNW. In addition, interviews were conducted with BIS students to understand how students select courses and how important a possible grade is in their choice. During the suggestion phase, exported enrollment data was pre-processed and analysed in order to identify important attributes for the grade prediction. Furthermore, artefact requirements were defined based on the findings from the previous phase. The development phase involved the incremental creation of a prototype. The data was prepared to link the course enrollment data and corresponding course description data. In the evaluation phase, the prototype's reliability was measured by calculating precision and recall. In addition, the confusion matrix was created, and a cost matrix was calculated to obtain an overall impression of the prototype's reliability. In the conclusion, the contribution to the body of knowledge and further research were discussed.

4   Data Set from Student Enrolment Process

The BIS Master's program starts twice a year and can be taken full-time (1.5 years) or part-time (2.5 years). A large proportion of students are employed and study part-time. Students can design their individual study plans and choose from a pool of four compulsory courses and over 20 elective courses. The grades are awarded on a scale of one to six, rounded to the nearest half-grade. Where one is the lowest grade, six is the highest, and at least a four is expected to pass a course. Students register for offered courses before the beginning of the semester and can de-register from the course in the first two weeks of the semester without penalty. Later, de-registrations will be penalised with a grade of one for the respective course. In addition, students who have failed a course can only repeat it once.

The interviews with the students revealed that personal interest in the subject is decisive when choosing a course. In addition, they are careful to take thematically similar courses within the same semester with the intention of getting better grades. Nevertheless, there are various course registrations and de-registrations, especially in the first two weeks of the semester.

The exported dataset includes records from 856 students from the spring semester of 2012 to 2023. The data set includes students' demographic (age, sex) and academic performance (grade per course and semester, current semester) attributes. Figure 1 shows the grade distribution before pre-processing. The data set was cleansed during pre-processing, and outliers were removed, like grades from students who de-registered too late and got a grade of one or sets with course registrations but without grades. Afterwards, the data set showed a higher imbalance in the distribution of grades, as positive performance was more common than negative performance. To overcome this imbalance and to make the learned model more sensitive to potential failures, a straightforward oversampling method was employed: students with at least one negative grade during their academic career, along with their semester records, were replicated three-fold, thereby augmenting the original dataset.

Table 2 shows an example of the data after pre-processing. Each row in the dataset represents a single semester for an individual student. The semesters for

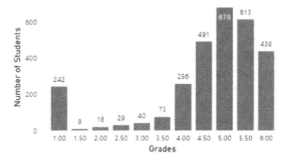

Fig. 1. Grade distribution

each student are sequentially arranged in the order they were undertaken. A separate column represents each course. For every semester of a student, the dataset includes both the grades obtained in that current semester and the cumulative grades from all previous semesters of the same student. The Gender column shows whether the student is a male (0) or female (1). Age is the respective age of the student, where the value in this column has also been normalised. Max_semester indicates the number of semesters the student intends to complete their studies. Embeddings represent the mapping of course descriptions into vector space.

5   Design and Development of the Prototypes

A hybrid performance prediction system is suggested, utilising similarities among students. Based on the insights from student interviews, we equipped our similarity measure with two components: one to capture students' interests in certain subjects and the other to capture their performance in previous courses. The

Table 2. Example of data after pre-processing

ID Person	Semester Nr	Gender	Age	max_semester	Cloud Computing	Aligment of Business and IT	Research Methods in Information Systems	Business Process Management	Strategic Management in the Digital Economy	Emerging Topics for Business Information Systems	Business Intelligence	Supply Chain Management	Compliance Management and Governance of IT	Knowledge Processing and Decision Making	Digitalization of Business Processes	Master Thesis Proposal	Managers Shadow Project	Master Thesis	...	Competitive Strategy in the Information Age	Information Management	User-centered Design and Design Thinking	Artificial Intelligence for Business Processes	Unique Identifier	Embeddings
708299	1	0	0.30769231	5	5.5	5	0	0	0	0	0	0	0	0	0	0	0	0	...	0	0	0	0	708299-1	[-0.02533539 - 0.0201073 -
708299	2	0	0.30769231	5	5.5	5	5	5	5.5	6	0	0	0	0	0	0	0	0	...	0	0	0	0	708299-2	[-0.02170304 - 0.02289635 -
708299	3	0	0.30769231	5	5.5	5	5	5	5.5	6	5	5	5.5	0	0	0	0	0	...	0	0	0	0	708299-3	[-0.02136705 - 0.02271209 -
708299	4	0	0.30769231	5	5.5	5	5	5	5.5	6	5	5	5.5	5.5	5.5	5.5	5.5	0	...	0	0	0	0	708299-4	[-0.02268211 - 0.02359489 -
708299	5	0	0.30769231	5	5.5	5	5	5	5.5	6	5	5	5.5	5.5	5.5	5.5	5.5	6	...	0	0	0	0	708299-5	[-0.02290371 - 0.0235733 -

first component involves comparing students using a 'student knowledge profile,' derived from averaged vector embeddings of the course descriptions from each student's course history. Secondly, the system compares students' course performances through an Euclidean Distance similarity measurement. An overall student similarity score is then computed by integrating these two components, applying a weighted combination of the knowledge profile comparison and the Euclidean Distance measurement. The dataset, not particularly extensive, encompasses students in the Master's program who possess Bachelor's degrees in closely related fields, such as business informatics, computer science, or business administration. However, their professional experiences vary significantly. Post-Bachelor's, these students have pursued diverse career paths. Consequently, their academic and professional histories were not considered in the analysis. Given the dataset's limited size, constructing student profiles based on their academic and professional backgrounds for predictive purposes presents a considerable challenge. Interviews with students indicated that course selections are primarily interest-driven. Therefore, the Large Language Model BERT was employed using course descriptions to identify students with similar course interests.

5.1 Course Description Similarity

Course descriptions were collected from a publicly accessible course description website[1] and from the university administrations. The course descriptions contain information about the competencies to be achieved, content, teaching and learning methods, and assessment. As far as possible, the course descriptions from the respective semesters reflected the reality at the time. Any information available in the course descriptions has been transformed into a vector space using BERT, a transformer-based language model. For each student, the courses they had enrolled in up to the semester preceding the target semester for prediction are analysed. The embeddings of these course descriptions are processed and normalised, and their average is calculated. This average embedding represents the student's knowledge profile, reflecting the content of courses they have already completed. L2 Normalization was applied to normalise the course description embeddings. This process guarantees that each course description embedding vector has a length of one, an essential step for averaging them effectively. Normalising the embeddings ensures that each course contributes equally to the average calculation, thereby maintaining uniformity in weight. Figure 2 shows the procedure.

Once the knowledge profiles for each student were computed, cosine similarity was employed to identify the most similar students. This was done by comparing the averaged vector embeddings constituting the student knowledge profiles. The cosine similarity formula $cos(\theta) = \frac{\sum_{i=1}^{n} E1_i E2_i}{\sqrt{\sum_{i=1}^{n} E1_i^2}\sqrt{\sum_{i=1}^{n} E2_i^2}}$, utilised in this context, facilitates the calculation of similarities between various student knowledge profiles. Whereby, $E1_i$ and $E2_i$ represent the ith components of the vectors E1 and E2.

---

[1] See https://modulbeschreibungen.webapps.fhnw.ch/.

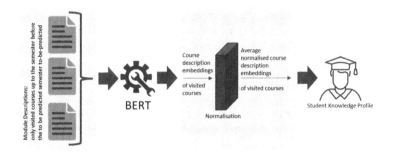

Fig. 2. Calculating students knowledge profile

5.2 Course Performance Similarity

To succinctly represent each student's historical cumulative semester performance, their course performance data was pre-processed into a single row per student in the dataset. The course performance similarity was then calculated by transforming each student's grades to the semester before the one being predicted into a vector space. In this space, each course and its corresponding grade is represented by a distinct vector dimension. Subsequently, the Euclidean Distance was computed between student grade vectors for courses attended by both students, and a normalised similarity measure was derived. The Euclidean Distance calculation underwent a slight modification to accommodate scenarios where courses were attended by only one of the compared students. In these instances, a smoothing factor of 0.1 was added to the Euclidean Distance calculation. The methods involve several key formulas:

- Min-Max Normalization: This process converted each student's grades into a range between 0 and 1.
- Adjusted Euclidean Distance: The normalised grades were inputted into a multi-dimensional vector, encompassing all courses attended and unattended up to the semester preceding the forecasted one. Here, a value of 0 indicates courses not attended. This Adjusted Euclidean Distance was employed to factor in performance in courses not accounted for by the course description similarity. Additionally, it introduced a penalty for courses exclusively attended by one of the two compared students.
- Course Performance Similarity: This metric is based on the calculated Adjusted Euclidean Distance:
  ($CoursePerformanceSimilarity = \frac{1}{1+AdjustedEuclideanDisntace}$). It aims to transform the Adjusted Euclidean Distance into a similarity score ranging from 0 to 1, thus quantifying the likeness in course performance between students.

The final student similarity score was derived by integrating the previously computed similarities from course descriptions and performance:
($FinalStudentSimilarityScore = w_1 * courseDescSim + w_2 * coursePerfSim$).

As these similarities produce values ranging from 0 to 1, a weighted approach was employed for their combination, allowing for a balanced integration of both metrics.

5.3 Performance Prediction

The prototype considers two cases when predicting the grades: (1) Grade prediction for students beyond the first semester and (2) grade prediction for first-semester students.

Grade prediction for students beyond the first semester: The prototype calculates grade predictions by averaging the grades of the five most similar students who have previously taken the same course in the same semester. The number of similar students to be considered for this calculation can be set as a parameter. If fewer students than the parameter have taken the course in the same semester, the prediction uses the actual number of students for averaging. In cases where students have yet to take the course in the same semester, the grade is predicted by averaging the grades of students who completed the program within the same number of semesters. If no students meet this criterion, the average is then based on the grades of all students, regardless of the semester they took the course.

Grade prediction for first-semester students: A different approach is adopted for students who lack an academic record. The predicted grade is determined by averaging students who completed the program within the same number of semesters and took the course in their first semester. If no students meet these criteria, the prediction is based on the average grades of students who finished the program within the same number of semesters. Should this also not be applicable, the grade is predicted by averaging all students' grades across all semesters.

The objective of the prototype is to proactively alert students about potential underperformance while aiding them in choosing their courses with minimal restrictions. To achieve this, the output from the performance prediction Prototype has been simplified into a binary response. This response either warns about the possibility of failing or endorses the student's course selection. A predefined threshold determines the classification of grades as positive or negative. A positive grade is considered when the predicted grade is higher or equal to 4. A warning is issued if the grade is below 4.

6 Evaluation

The Performance Prediction System's effectiveness is assessed by setting a classification threshold: grades below 4 are deemed negative, while those 4 and above are considered positive. This system was evaluated using the dataset prepared in the pre-processing stage, employing Leave-One-Out cross-validation. The evaluation concentrated on comparing two configurations of the prototype, one considering the performance prediction based on five similar students and the other on seven. Various metrics were used to gauge the model's performance:

- Precision: This metric is computed by dividing the number of true positives (correctly predicted negative performances) by the total predicted positives (both correctly and incorrectly predicted negative performances). Precision thus reflects the accuracy of correctly predicted negative performances.
- Recall: Recall is calculated by dividing the number of true positives (correctly predicted negative performances) by the sum of true positives and false negatives (incorrectly predicted positive performances). It indicates the proportion of actual negative performances that were correctly identified.
- Confusion Matrix: This matrix provides a visual and numerical representation of the model's predictions, contrasting them against the actual outcomes. It is segmented into four quadrants: true positives, true negatives, false positives, and false negatives. True positives and negatives represent correctly predicted negative and positive performances, respectively. False positives are instances where negative outcomes are incorrectly predicted, and false negatives are where positive outcomes are incorrectly predicted.
- Cost Matrix: Unlike the confusion matrix, which counts the number of correct and incorrect predictions, the cost matrix assigns a value to the impact of incorrect predictions. For the prototype's evaluation, false positives are assigned a cost of 1 and false negatives a cost of 3, acknowledging that not all incorrect predictions have the same severity. This matrix is crucial for understanding and quantifying the actual impact of these incorrect predictions.

The prototype's main aim is to assist students in course selection, offering freedom in their choices except when performance warnings are raised. A true positive (a correctly predicted negative performance) is valued higher than a true negative, as the cost of over-warning students is less severe than the risk of under-warning, which could lead students into a false sense of security.

The comparative analysis of the performance prediction system, focusing on the impact of considering 5 versus 7 most similar students, revealed that an increase in the number of similar students does not necessarily enhance the prototype's effectiveness. Notably:

- Precision Decrease: The precision dropped from 0.36734 (with 5 similar students) to 0.24 (with 7 similar students), indicating that the prototype's accuracy in correctly identifying negative performances diminished as more similar students were included.
- Recall Decrease: There was also a decline in recall, from 0.45 (with 5 similar students) to 0.2926 (with 7 similar students). This suggests a reduced sensitivity in detecting negative cases, leading to a lower rate of correctly identifying actual negative performances.
- True Positives and False Negatives: The number of true positives declined from 18 to 12 when the count of similar students considered rose from 5 to 7, signifying a reduction in the prototype's effectiveness in correctly identifying negative performances. Concurrently, false negatives increased from 23 to 29, indicating that more negative performances were overlooked.

- False Positives Increase: There was a rise in false positives from 31 to 38, suggesting a higher likelihood of the prototype erroneously categorising positive performances as negative with 7 similar students.
- Slight Decline in True Negatives: The number of true negatives marginally decreased from 1622 to 1615, implying a slight drop in the prototype's ability to accurately recognise positive performances.
- Higher Overall Cost: The total cost of the prototype's predictions rose from 100 to 125. This increment reflects the increased inaccuracy in performance predictions, particularly due to the rise in incorrectly predicted negative performances and a decline in accurately identifying negative performances when a larger group of similar students was considered.

Table 3 summarises the comparative analysis:

Table 3. Comparison of the results

	5 Students	7 Students
Precision	0.36734	0.24
Recall	0.45	0.2926
F1	0.40	0.2637
Cost	100	125

These findings suggest that while expanding the number of similar students considered for predictions, the prototype may lose precision and recall, potentially leading to higher costs due to increased inaccuracies. The results indicate that expanding the number of similar students factored into the performance prediction adversely affects the prototype's accuracy. Specifically, the increase in the considered similar students leads to a decline in the prototype's ability to predict performance outcomes accurately. This finding suggests that the current prototype construction approach requires further refinement, as it fails to identify many negative performances. The implication is that the method of determining similarity among students and how it influences prediction accuracy needs to be re-evaluated and optimised to enhance the prototype's efficacy in predicting student performance.

7   Conclusion

The introduced approach offers promising future development potential. However, the evaluation indicates room for improvement, particularly in precision and recall. A key area for enhancement is the optimisation of the LLM approach to differentiate course descriptions more effectively.

Several potential improvements have been identified:

Adding a feature that allows students to input their interests could personalise the systems. Further, the prototype could be improved by considering known positive and negative course sequences reported by students in its performance prediction calculations.

Additionally, the current method of addressing data imbalance involves oversampling the minority class by duplicating performance data. Future research could explore more sophisticated sampling methods, like the Synthetic Minority Over-sampling Technique (SMOTE) or Generative Adversarial Networks (GAN), which create synthetic samples rather than duplicating existing ones. This approach could offer a more robust solution to the imbalance issue and reduce overfitting risks.

Lastly, the current use of the BERT model for embedding course descriptions faces challenges in differentiating them effectively. Future research efforts could focus on optimising these descriptions to improve embeddings, possibly by applying feature extraction techniques or altering the structure of the course descriptions to better align with the model's learning algorithms. Enhanced differentiation of course description embeddings would significantly improve the prototype's ability to match students based on their interests accurately.

In conclusion, while the prototype marks a significant advancement, the identified improvements offer a roadmap for evolving this tool into a more refined and effective aid for students in their academic journey. Additionally, replicating the described methodology in another university setting, as shown in Fig. 2, could validate the model's effectiveness and scalability across different academic environments.

References

1. Arifin, M., Widowati, W., Farikhin, F., Gudnanto, G.: A regression model and a combination of academic and non-academic features to predict student academic performance. TEM J. **12**(2), 855–864 (2023). https://doi.org/10.18421/TEM122-31 https://doi.org/10.18421/TEM122-31
2. Cheng, B., Liu, Y., Jia, Y.: Evaluation of students' performance during the academic period using the XG-boost classifier-enhanced AEO hybrid model. Expert Syst. Appl. **238**, 122136 (2024). https://doi.org/10.1016/j.eswa.2023.122136
3. Issah, I., Appiah, O., Appiahene, P., Inusah, F.: A systematic review of the literature on machine learning application of determining the attributes influencing academic performance. Decis. Anal. J. **7**(October 2022), 100204 (2023). https://doi.org/10.1016/j.dajour.2023.100204
4. Khudhur, A., Ramaha, N.T.: Students' performance prediction using machine learning based on generative adversarial network. In: 2023 5th International Congress on Human-Computer Interaction, Optimization and Robotic Applications (HORA), pp. 1–6. IEEE (2023). https://doi.org/10.1109/HORA58378.2023.10156733
5. Li, M., Zhang, Y., Li, X., Cai, L., Yin, B.: Multi-view hypergraph neural networks for student academic performance prediction. Eng. Appl. Artif. Intell. **114**(June), 105174 (2022). https://doi.org/10.1016/j.engappai.2022.105174
6. Liu, Q., Huang, Z., Yin, Y., Chen, E., Xiong, H., Su, Y., Hu, G.: EKT: exercise-aware knowledge tracing for student performance prediction. IEEE Trans. Knowl. Data Eng. **33**(1), 100–115 (2021). https://doi.org/10.1109/TKDE.2019.2924374

7. McKenzie, K., Schweitzer, R.: Who succeeds at university? factors predicting academic performance in first year Australian university students. High. Educ. Res. Dev. **20**(1), 21–33 (2001). https://doi.org/10.1080/07924360120043621

8. Nachouki, M., Mohamed, E.A., Mehdi, R., Abou Naaj, M.: Student course grade prediction using the random forest algorithm: analysis of predictors' importance. Trends Neurosci. Educ. **33**, 100214 (2023). https://doi.org/10.1016/j.tine.2023.100214

9. Othman, M.H., Mohamad, N., Barom, M.N.: Students' decision making in class selection and enrolment. Int. J. Educ. Manage. **33**(4), 587–603 (2019). https://doi.org/10.1108/IJEM-06-2017-0143

10. Phan, M., De Caigny, A., Coussement, K.: A decision support framework to incorporate textual data for early student dropout prediction in higher education. Decision Support Syst. **168**, 113940 (2023). https://doi.org/10.1016/j.dss.2023.113940

11. Priyambada, S.A., Usagawa, T., ER, M.: Two-layer ensemble prediction of students' performance using learning behavior and domain knowledge. Comput. Educ. Artif. Intell. **5**(January), 100149 (2023). https://doi.org/10.1016/j.caeai.2023.100149

12. Shahiri, A.M., Husain, W., Rashid, N.A.: A review on predicting student's performance using data mining techniques. Procedia Comput. Sci. **72**, 414–422 (2015). https://doi.org/10.1016/j.procs.2015.12.157

13. Tormon, R., Lindsay, B.L., Paul, R.M., Boyce, M.A., Johnston, K.: Predicting academic performance in first-year engineering students: The role of stress, resiliency, student engagement, and growth mindset. Learn. Individ. Differ. **108**(October), 102383 (2023). https://doi.org/10.1016/j.lindif.2023.102383

14. Vaishnavi, V.K., Kuechler, W.: Design Science Research Methods and Patterns, 2nd edn. CRC Press, Boca Raton (2015)

15. Waheed, H., et al.: Predicting academic performance of students from the assessment submission in virtual learning environment. In: Visvizi, A., Troisi, O., Grimaldi, M. (eds.) RIIFORUM 2022, pp. 417–424. Springer, Cham (2023). https://doi.org/10.1007/978-3-031-19560-0_33

Towards Explainable Public Sector AI: An Exploration of Neuro-Symbolic AI and Enterprise Modeling (Short Paper)

Václav Pechtor[(✉)] [iD]

Prague University of Economics and Business, Prague, Czech Republic
vaclav@pechtor.ch

Abstract. Artificial Intelligence (AI) offers transformative potential for enhancing public sector services. However, the lack of explainability within many AI systems, particularly those relying on opaque 'black box' neural networks, hinders widespread adoption due to concerns about fairness, accountability, and trust. To address this, explainable AI (XAI) has emerged as a vital area of research, aiming to illuminate the reasoning behind AI decisions. Neuro-Symbolic AI (NSAI) provides a powerful technique for XAI, combining the strengths of symbolic reasoning with neural pattern recognition. Enterprise Modeling (EM) offers systematic methodologies to capture multifaceted domain knowledge, including process models, rules, and ontologies. This paper explores the potential synergy between XAI, NSAI, and EM for developing trustworthy and transparent AI solutions tailored to the public sector. While this integration offers exciting possibilities for explainable AI, the field is still nascent.

Keywords: Hybrid AI · Public Sector · Enterprise Modeling Applications

1 Introduction

While the potential of AI for public administration is undeniable, its adoption is often slowed by a lack of trust. This exposes the limitations of 'black box' AI within public administration. Recently, the promise of Big Data [1] and Artificial Intelligence (AI) has spurred new hopes for public sector transformation [2]. AI offers the potential to automate tasks, freeing up administrative resources in an era of potential staff shortages [3]. The current hype around generative AI like ChatGPT further underscores the challenge of understanding and managing complex AI systems [4]. A recent survey found transparency to be the most frequently mentioned principle in global AI ethics guidelines [5].

Large language models (LLMs) illustrate this explainability crisis. While impressive, LLMs can't distinguish fact from fiction and lack true language understanding due to their subsymbolic nature [6]. Further, they can produce confidently incorrect, even harmful, outputs [7]. To address these shortcomings, researchers are working to create symbolic, explainable, and ontologically grounded language models [6].

J. P. A. Almeida et al. (Eds.): CAiSE 2024 Workshops, LNBIP 521, pp. 109–114, 2024.
https://doi.org/10.1007/978-3-031-61003-5_10

2   XAI: The Imperative for Explainability in the Public Sector

The ability to understand the decision-making processes of AI systems is termed "explainability." Explainable AI (XAI) has deep roots in the history of computing, with early expert systems offering rudimentary explanations of their conclusions [8]. Today, as AI permeates high-stakes decision-making in the public sphere, XAI is more critical than ever. However, AI adoption often faces resistance due to a critical lack of trust. Consider the System Risk Identification (SyRI) project in the Netherlands, a fraud detection system fueled by the integration of vast amounts of personal data across government agencies [9]. While intended to improve resource allocation, SyRI's reliance on opaque AI models created deep unease. Entire neighborhoods were labeled as high-risk based on factors like car ownership and income, undermining the presumption of innocence and blurring the line between targeted investigation and mass surveillance. While this might seem anecdotal, the recent rise of LLMs is worsening the situation [10, 11]. XAI can be achieved through various approaches like Pre-modeling methods which are scrutinizing the datasets that train AI models, ensuring they are representative and free from biases, and in-modeling methods which involve designing inherently interpretable AI models, making their decision processes easier to comprehend.

3   Neuro-Symbolic AI (NSAI) for Enhanced Explainability

Neuro-Symbolic AI (NSAI) brings together the strengths of two distinct AI paradigms. Symbolic AI, inspired by how humans reason, uses logic and explicit rules to represent knowledge and solve problems. While the fluency of large language models (LLMs) can be impressive, there are crucial reasons why their role in the public sector must be approached with caution. The "knowledge" LLMs acquire is represented within billions of parameters, hindering the ability to explain their responses or trace errors, a key XAI need [6]. Incorporating background knowledge in the form of logical statements within knowledge bases (KBs) has been shown to significantly improve both the explainability and accuracy of AI systems compared to purely data-driven methods [12]. This hybrid approach offers a crucial advantage: the ability to remain robust even when the training data contains errors. Further, NSAI techniques can enable joint learning and reasoning across symbolic and sub-symbolic representations, allowing for sophisticated probabilistic-logical analysis [13]. One promising area is the integration of graph neural networks with neuro-symbolic AI. This includes advancements in logical neural networks, logic tensor networks, and related approaches [14–16].

4   Enterprise Modeling (EM): Discovering Rules for the Symbolic AI

EM provides a comprehensive approach to understanding and representing an organization's structure, processes, and interconnected web of rules and relationships that govern its decision-making [17]. It involves systematically analyzing and documenting goals, processes, information flows, and the complex web of rules that govern how an organization operates [17]. EM allows us to explicitly capture not only the 'what' of administrative processes but also the 'why': the regulations, policies, and stakeholder considerations that guide decision-making.

Enterprise Modelling focuses on the holistic analysis and documentation of goals, processes, information flows, and the complex decision-making criteria within an organization [18]. This makes it particularly well-suited to provide the structured knowledge that NSAI systems leverage for explainability. Process modeling notations such as BPMN (Business Process Model and Notation) provide a way to visualize workflows, explicitly capturing decision points and the rules or logic that determine how a process proceeds [19]. This structured format can then be directly utilized by the symbolic components of an NSAI system for rule-based reasoning. Ontologies offer a way to formally define concepts and their relationships within a specific domain (e.g., tax regulations, benefits eligibility), providing a knowledge base, grounded in the realities of public sector operations, that an NSAI system can draw upon.

5 Integration: Exploring the Synergy of XAI, NSAI, and EM

While the potential of AI for public administration is undeniable, its successful adoption hinges on building trust. A promising approach lies in the potential synergy between three key elements: Explainable AI (XAI), Neuro-Symbolic AI (NSAI), and Enterprise Modeling (EM). While this specific combination is a nascent area of exploration, it offers rich possibilities for developing trustworthy and transparent AI solutions tailored to the unique demands of public service delivery.

EM provides a systematic methodology for capturing the complex web of rules, processes, and knowledge that forms the bedrock of public service delivery [17]. This translates to a comprehensive understanding of an organization's goals, information flows, and the complex decision-making criteria that govern its operations [20]. Within the public sector, EM is particularly valuable because it allows us to explicitly capture not only the "what" of administrative processes but also the "why." This includes the regulations, policies, and stakeholder considerations that guide decisions [21].

EM techniques such as process modeling (e.g., BPMN - Business Process Model and Notation) and ontologies play a vital role in knowledge capture. Process modeling helps visualize workflows, explicitly capturing decision points and the rules or logic that determine how a process proceeds [32]. Ontologies, on the other hand, provide a way to formally define concepts and their relationships within a specific domain (e.g., tax regulations, benefits eligibility) [33]. This creates a structured knowledge base that reflects the realities of public sector operations.

The knowledge base meticulously constructed through EM serves as a critical bridge to Neuro-Symbolic AI systems. NSAI offers a unique approach by combining the strengths of symbolic and neural AI paradigms [22]. Symbolic AI, inspired by human reasoning, relies on logic and explicit rules to represent knowledge and solve problems. Neural networks, in contrast, excel at pattern recognition within large datasets and learning from experience. NSAI integrates these approaches, enabling systems to handle abstract concepts, reason logically, and adapt to new information. Most importantly, NSAI systems are designed to provide clear explanations for their decisions [18].

The structured knowledge extracted through EM techniques, such as process models and ontologies, can potentially be translated into formats compatible with the symbolic components of an NSAI system. This holds the promise of equipping the NSAI system with a deep understanding of the domain-specific knowledge and decision-making frameworks that govern public sector operations.

The synergy between EM and NSAI paves the way for what could be a significant advancement in Explainable AI. By leveraging both the pattern recognition capabilities of neural networks and the structured knowledge from EM, NSAI systems have the potential to not only arrive at a decision but also explain the reasoning behind it [18]. This explanation can take various forms, depending on the specific XAI technique employed. It could involve tracing the decision back to relevant steps within a process model, highlighting the rules or regulations that were applied, or outlining the logical inferences made by the system. This level of transparency is critical for building trust in public sector AI, as it allows stakeholders to understand the rationale behind decisions and ensures that these decisions align with public values and principles [15] (Fig. 1).

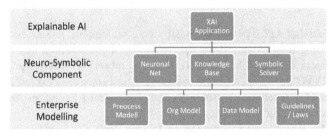

Fig. 1. Interplay of Enterprise Modelling, Neuro-Symbolic AI, and explainable AI as a layered model (source: author)

6   Conclusion and Future Work

The development of trustworthy and explainable AI is vital for realizing the full potential of AI within the public sector. XAI, by making the reasoning behind decisions transparent, fosters accountability, fairness, and ultimately, trust in the institutions that serve us. Neuro-Symbolic AI offers a powerful approach with its ability to combine both symbolic and neural reasoning, enabling systems to make complex decisions while providing clear explanations. Enterprise Modeling provides the critical foundation for this, offering systematic methods to capture the rules, processes, and domain knowledge that underpin real-world public administration. While the integration of EM, NSAI, and XAI holds transformative promise, it's imperative to acknowledge this field is still in its early stages. Proactive and collaborative efforts are needed to navigate the challenges ahead.

References

1. Di Vaio, A., Hassan, R., Alavoine, C.: Data intelligence and analytics: A bibliometric analysis of human–Artificial intelligence in public sector decision-making effectiveness. Technological Forecasting and Social Change. 174, (2022). https://doi.org/10.1016/j.techfore.2021. 121201
2. van Noordt, C., Misuraca, G.: Artificial intelligence for the public sector: results of landscaping the use of AI in government across the European Union. Gov. Inf. Q. **39**, 101714 (2022). https://doi.org/10.1016/j.giq.2022.101714
3. Mehdiyev, N., Houy, C., Gutermuth, O., Mayer, L., Fettke, P.: Explainable Artificial Intelligence (XAI) Supporting Public Administration Processes – On the Potential of XAI in Tax Audit Processes. In: Ahlemann, F., Schütte, R., and Stieglitz, S. (eds.) Innovation Through Information Systems. pp. 413–428. Springer International Publishing, Cham (2021). https://doi.org/10.1007/978-3-030-86790-4_28
4. Leaver, T., Srdarov, S.: ChatGPT Isn't Magic: The Hype and Hypocrisy of Generative Artificial Intelligence (AI) Rhetoric. M/C J. 26, (2023). https://doi.org/10.5204/mcj.3004
5. Jobin, A., Ienca, M., Vayena, E.: The global landscape of AI ethics guidelines. Nat Mach Intell. **1**, 389–399 (2019). https://doi.org/10.1038/s42256-019-0088-2
6. Saba, W.S.: Stochastic LLMs do not Understand Language: Towards Symbolic, Explainable and Ontologically Based LLMs. In: Almeida, J.P.A., Borbinha, J., Guizzardi, G., Link, S., and Zdravkovic, J. (eds.) Conceptual Modeling. pp. 3–19. Springer Nature Switzerland, Cham (2023). https://doi.org/10.1007/978-3-031-47262-6_1
7. Bender, E.M., Gebru, T., McMillan-Major, A., Shmitchell, S.: On the Dangers of Stochastic Parrots: Can Language Models Be Too Big? . In: Proceedings of the 2021 ACM Conference on Fairness, Accountability, and Transparency. pp. 610–623. ACM, Virtual Event Canada (2021). https://doi.org/10.1145/3442188.3445922
8. Xu, F., Uszkoreit, H., Du, Y., Fan, W., Zhao, D., Zhu, J.: Explainable AI: A Brief Survey on History, Research Areas, Approaches and Challenges. In: Tang, J., Kan, M.-Y., Zhao, D., Li, S., and Zan, H. (eds.) Natural Language Processing and Chinese Computing. pp. 563–574. Springer International Publishing, Cham (2019). https://doi.org/10.1007/978-3-030-32236-6_51
9. AlgorithmWatch: How Dutch activists got an invasive fraud detection algorithm banned, https://algorithmwatch.org/en/syri-netherlands-algorithm/, last accessed 2020/04/06
10. Bender, E.M.: Resisting Dehumanization in the Age of "AI." Curr Dir Psychol Sci. 09637214231217286 (2024). https://doi.org/10.1177/09637214231217286
11. Omiye, J.A., Lester, J.C., Spichak, S., Rotemberg, V., Daneshjou, R.: Large language models propagate race-based medicine. npj Digit. Med. 6, 195 (2023). https://doi.org/10.1038/s41 746-023-00939-z
12. Oltramari, A., Francis, J., Henson, C., Ma, K., Wickramarachchi, R.: Neuro-symbolic Architectures for Context Understanding, http://arxiv.org/abs/2003.04707, (2020)
13. Garnelo, M., Shanahan, M.: Reconciling deep learning with symbolic artificial intelligence: representing objects and relations. Curr. Opin. Behav. Sci. **29**, 17–23 (2019). https://doi.org/10.1016/j.cobeha.2018.12.010
14. Garcez, A. d'Avila, Gori, M., Lamb, L.C., Serafini, L., Spranger, M., Tran, S.N.: Neural-Symbolic Computing: An Effective Methodology for Principled Integration of Machine Learning and Reasoning, http://arxiv.org/abs/1905.06088, (2019)
15. Lamb, L.C., Garcez, A., Gori, M., Prates, M., Avelar, P., Vardi, M.: Graph Neural Networks Meet Neural-Symbolic Computing: A Survey and Perspective, http://arxiv.org/abs/2003.00330, (2021)

16. Riegel, R., Gray, A., Luus, F., Khan, N., Makondo, N., Akhalwaya, I.Y., Qian, H., Fagin, R., Barahona, F., Sharma, U., Ikbal, S., Karanam, H., Neelam, S., Likhyani, A., Srivastava, S.: Logical Neural Networks, http://arxiv.org/abs/2006.13155, (2020)
17. Stirna, J., Persson, A.: Enterprise Modeling: Facilitating the Process and the People. Springer International Publishing, Cham (2018). https://doi.org/10.1007/978-3-319-94857-7
18. Vernadat, F.: Enterprise modelling: Research review and outlook. Comput. Ind. **122**, 103265 (2020). https://doi.org/10.1016/j.compind.2020.103265
19. Bazhenova, E., Zerbato, F., Weske, M.: Data-Centric Extraction of DMN Decision Models from BPMN Process Models. In: Teniente, E. and Weidlich, M. (eds.) Business Process Management Workshops. pp. 542–555. Springer International Publishing, Cham (2018). https://doi.org/10.1007/978-3-319-74030-0_43
20. Fallmyr, T.: INNOVATION IN THE PUBLIC SECTOR USING IN-HOUSE COMPETENCE IN ENTERPRISE MODELLING. (2020)
21. Van Der Voet, J., Kuipers, B., Groeneveld, S.: Held back and pushed forward: leading change in a complex public sector environment. J. Organ. Chang. Manag. **28**, 290–300 (2015). https://doi.org/10.1108/JOCM-09-2013-0182
22. Sheth, A., Roy, K., Gaur, M.: Neurosymbolic Artificial Intelligence (Why, What, and How). IEEE Intell. Syst. **38**, 56–62 (2023). https://doi.org/10.1109/MIS.2023.3268724

A Survey to Evaluate the Completeness and Correctness of a Morphological Box for AI Solutions

Jack Daniel Rittelmeyer[1]([⊠]) [iD] and Kurt Sandkuhl[1,2] [iD]

[1] Institute of Computer Science, University of Rostock, Albert-Einstein-Str. 22, 18057 Rostock, Germany
{jack.rittelmeyer,kurt.sandkuhl}@uni-rostock.de,
kurt.sandkuhl@ju.se
[2] School of Engineering, Jönköping University, Jönköping, Sweden

Abstract. Artificial Intelligence (AI) is a key technology driving digital transformation in enterprises worldwide. However, the implementation of AI projects often faces hurdles, primarily due to misconceptions about AI's capabilities and suitable applications. This research represents a step in a broader research process aimed at creating an artifact to help companies, particularly those outside the IT sector, navigate these challenges. We present an evaluation of a morphological box that outlines critical factors for successful AI integration. The evaluation was carried out by conducting and analyzing a survey in which participants rated the individual features and values, as well as their structure. We also conducted the Kaiser-Meyer-Olkin and Bartlett tests and created a correlation matrix as statistical measures to identify overlap between the elements of the box. After analyzing the data, we found some further room for improvement but that the box seems to include the generally most important aspects. Overall, the participants' ratings for the individual elements were also satisfactory.

Keywords: Artificial Intelligence · Morphological Box · Survey · AI Solution Development

1 Introduction

The integration of Artificial Intelligence (AI) in businesses presents numerous opportunities and potential benefits. However, the successful implementation of AI projects often encounters challenges. A 2019 survey revealed that less than 6% of companies are utilizing AI [1]. Several reasons were cited for this hesitant adoption of AI, including data security and privacy concerns, difficulties in funding AI projects, the absence of customized solutions, and most importantly, a lack of skills and knowledge within the company despite their actual growing interest in AI [2]. Still, the biggest obstacle for them is to decide what kind of AI solution is suitable for them and how they should introduce it in their company successfully [3]. Especially, because an organizational problem can be solved or goal can be reached arguably in various ways with different AI technologies like component analysis [4], machine learning (ML), deep learning (DL) [6] or support vector machines [7].

J. P. A. Almeida et al. (Eds.): CAiSE 2024 Workshops, LNBIP 521, pp. 115–129, 2024.
https://doi.org/10.1007/978-3-031-61003-5_11

We argue, that the systemization of features of AI can help with understanding this complex field. Those features break down the complex areas into smaller parts that are easier to understand. A morphological box, a tool from product development, can help address this knowledge gap exactly by breaking down the complex problem of AI implementation and understanding AI in general, into smaller, more manageable problems [8]. In this paper, we aim to evaluate a morphological box for AI solutions that was developed to address this issue. The background and the box will be explained in Sect. 2. We initially conducted a survey to assess its completeness and correctness by having participants rate the features and values of the box. We also aimed to identify any missing or unnecessary features and values. The planning and preparation of the survey will be explained in Sect. 3. In the subsequent chapter, we analyze the data and present the results of the survey (Sect. 4). Sect. 5 discusses the results and findings and their potential impact on the morphological box. The final chapter summarizes this research, outlines its limitations and depicts potential future work.

2   Theoretical Background

In this chapter, the theoretical basics of the paper and the previous development steps of the morphological box for AI solutions as well as the box itself will be explained.

2.1   Morphological Box for AI Solutions

A morphological box is a systematic tool used in problem-solving and product development processes, particularly in the fields of engineering and design. It aids in exploring and analyzing the different components or features of a system or product and their potential combinations. It simplifies problem-solving by dividing larger problems into smaller, more manageable ones [8]. The chart is a matrix consisting of rows and columns. Each row represents a different component or aspect of the system or product, while each column corresponds to the various options or alternatives for each component. The goal is to systematically combine the different options from each row to generate a range of potential solutions. In the case of the morphological box for AI solutions, the smaller problems are represented by the features, which form the rows, and the values, which are the possible forms each feature can take and are organized in columns. The morphological box has already undergone several evaluation cycles, and Fig. 1 shows the current version of the box. The morphological box comprises 17 features that represent different aspects of AI that need to be considered before implementing AI in enterprises. Each feature consists of three to seven values. Detailed definitions of each feature and its values can be found in [9, 10]. In the last evaluation period, we conducted expert interviews and applied a taxonomy development method to our approach [11]. So far, only qualitative evaluations have been conducted to analyze the morphological box for AI solutions. Therefore, a quantitative approach was chosen for the next evaluation step. Furthermore, the box can be used in the AI context modelling method developed by Sandkuhl that helps to plan AI introduction in companies by (1) modelling the organizational context of planned AI applications (e.g. processes, roles, applications), (2) elicit AI requirements, (3) analyze the context model with requirements for each enterprise architecture layer, (4) decide on feasibility and (5) finally design the future enterprise architecture [12]. The morphological box can be applied especially in steps (3), (4) and (5) of the context modelling method [9].

Feature	Values						
AI Focus	Processing input	Generating output		Computing task			
End-User	IT-Expert	IT-Savvy		No IT-Knowledge			
Computing Source	Cloud	Local computing center	End-Device	Hybrid			
Time to Decision	Real-time	Near Real-Time	Several Hours	Later			
Special Hardware Required	Computing	Data Capture	Data Visualization	Data Output			
Reliability and Precision of Results	~ 99,9 % Required	Defined by Enterprise	Defined by Domain	Defined by Competitors			
Point in Time of AI Use in Solution Development	Design-Time	Runtime	Accompanying runtime	Hybrid			
Primary Purpose	Assistance	Decision Making	Forecasting	Classification	Anomaly Detection		
Data Source	Own Data	Augmented Data	Open Data	Commercial Collection	Synthetic Data		
Data Quantity	Very High	High	Moderate	Low	Very Low		
Maturity	COTS	Commercial Components	Open Source Components	Prototype	Individual		
Data and Model Update Frequency	Continuously	In Case of Changes in Regulation	In Case of New Documents/Data	In case of Changes in Customer Behavior	In Case of Quality Problems		
Extent of Effect on Enterprise	Isolated Solution	Single Process	Workflow	Work System	Business Model		
Communication	Frequent & detailed, active collaboration	Regular, some collaboration	Minimal, min. collaboration	Specific moments	None		
Primary Data Type	Audio	Video	Raster Image	Vector Image	Transaction Records	Time Series Data	
Data Quality	Inconsistent	Duplicate	Incomplete	Outdated	Biased	Noisy	Corrupted
Data Security	Compliance	Data Encryption	Access Control	Data Integrity	Data Privacy	Incident Management	Audit & Monitoring

Fig. 1. The morphological box for AI solutions by Rittelmeyer & Sandkuhl [11].

2.2 Taxonomy Development

Nickerson, Varshney, and Muntermann proposed a method for developing taxonomies for information systems [13]. We used this method for the development of the morphological box because we argue that a morphological box is similar to a taxonomy. A detailed explanation how we applied the box can be found in [11]. In summary, the method begins with the identification of a meta-characteristic, which is based on the taxonomy's purpose, potential users, target audience, and projected use. The second step involves determining the ending conditions for the taxonomy development process, differentiating between subjective and objective conditions. A useful taxonomy should be concise, robust, comprehensive, extendible, and explanatory. They also present eight general objective ending conditions that we have adopted. The actual development of the taxonomy starts after these two preparation phases. The approach for the first iteration of the process can be either empirical-to-conceptual or conceptual-to-empirical, depending on whether the researcher has more data or domain knowledge. The last step is to check if the ending conditions are met. If they are, the taxonomy is finished. If not, the process returns to the third step and the empirical-to-conceptual or conceptual-to-empirical approach is repeated until the ending conditions are met [13].

Because we have not yet met all ending criteria for our artefact, we chose to conduct a survey and thereby follow the empirical-to-conceptual approach to collect more data. The criteria we particularly want to address are the objective ending conditions that "no object was merged with a similar object or split into multiple objects" and that "no new dimensions or characteristics were added in the last iteration" as well as the subjective ending condition "comprehensiveness" which means to make sure that the taxonomy includes "all dimensions of objects of interest" [13].

3   Research and Survey Design

In quantitative evaluation, responses are converted into numerical data and statistically analyzed. Quantitative research methods, such as surveys or systematic observations, aim to provide a reliable overview of a defined section of reality by focusing on the quantity of the results. Surveys are a crucial method in scientific research for collecting data from a group of people. They can be conducted in various forms, including online, by post, by telephone, or in person. The questions can be either closed or open, and the responses can be analyzed quantitatively or qualitatively [14].

The questionnaire designed for this research project primarily consisted of closed questions. However, at the beginning of each group of questions, we implemented an open question that allowed respondents to express their own opinions. The individual questions were developed based on the morphological box and its features and values. The questionnaire will be explained in detail in the following section.

The survey was conducted among master's students in the Business Information Systems course at the University of Rostock. The survey lasted approximately 3.5 weeks, starting on June 20, 2023, and ending on July 14, 2023.

The structure of the survey is based on the structure of the morphological box. The survey begins with an introductory text that explains the topic, goal, and structure of the survey to the participants. After the participants have read this text, the survey continues with the collection of demographic data to gain an overview of the participants. The following data was collected in this step: Level of IT experience (expert, experienced, starter, no IT knowledge, no answer), level of AI experience (expert, experienced, starter, no AI knowledge), employment status, employment sector, level of education, current job title, duration of work in the current role, in case of work experience with AI: duration of work with AI. The demographic questions are followed by an open question asking for the respondent's personal opinion on the topic of the survey and to share their own knowledge or suggestions. Specifically, the participant is asked what they believe is important for successfully introducing and integrating an AI solution in a company. Are there, for example, any factors that could potentially influence a successful integration of an AI solution? This question is deliberately asked before the main part of the survey begins to get an uninfluenced answer from the participants. The main part of the survey has the goal to evaluate whether the features and their associated values are correct or whether any aspects are missing. In the entire survey, the respondent can only give one answer per question, unless it is an open question. The main part consists of 17 groups of questions. These 17 question groups represent the 17 features of the box. Each of these 17 question groups is structured identically.

Each feature is first introduced to the respondent with a short information text. The purpose of this text is to ensure comprehensibility. Despite making the survey significantly longer, it is the only way to ensure that the respondent can answer the questions meaningfully. Furthermore, if someone were to work with the box, they would also read the explanation of each feature first to ensure they understand it correctly.

After the introduction, it is asked whether the values belonging to the respective feature are meaningful or not. The evaluation system is based on the following five possibilities: Not at all meaningful; Less meaningful; Partly/partly (neutral); Partly meaningful; Very meaningful. This is followed by two open questions to give the participant the opportunity to express their own opinion on the respective feature. First, it is asked whether they can see other possible values for the feature and second, whether the subdivision of the respective characteristic makes sense to them or if they would divide them differently. The last question of each group of questions is again an assessment. This time the question refers to the feature in general. It explicitly asks whether the overall feature itself is a relevant factor for the introduction of AI according to the participant. The answer options were: Yes; Partly; No; No answer.

After the participant has answered all the questions, the survey is closed with an ending text. This text thanks the participant for their participation once again.

4 Analysis of the Survey Results

This chapter presents descriptive statistics about the survey participants and the data collected. It is divided into four sections: Section one summarizes information about the participants of the survey, their experience and background. Section 4.2 describes the statistical analysis conducted with the collected data. After that follows an analysis of the descriptive statistics created from the questions about the features of the morphological box (Sect. 4.3). In the final section, the ratings for all values will be compared.

4.1 Participants

We received 14 complete and eight incomplete surveys. Two of the eight incomplete surveys were completely conducted despite the personal information. After data cleansing, we ended up with 16 useful surveys for data analysis. However, for the analysis of the participants, only 14 surveys could be used. The participants were students of the University of Rostock. All but two had a bachelor's degree; the remaining two had a master's degree. Most of the participants work in the telecommunications and information technology industries, with a few also working in the services or business/political sectors. This suggests that most of our participants are likely to be IT savvy, i.e., interested or knowledgeable about IT and likely to be interested in the progress and development of AI, machine learning, and similar emerging technologies.

Out of 14 complete responses, two identified themselves as IT experts, eight as IT experienced, and four as IT novices. The AI experience measures paint a different picture: only one person claimed to be an expert in artificial intelligence. In addition, only two were AI-experienced and the vast majority, 11, described themselves as AI-beginners. But on the other hand, no one stated to have no IT or AI knowledge. We choose the students from the business IT masters course, because we could be sure that they have at least some knowledge about AI because of courses in their curriculum.

4.2 Statistical Evaluation

To verify the constructs measured in the survey, we performed two tests using the survey data. The first was a correlation matrix, which is a table showing correlation coefficients between variables. Each cell in the table shows the correlation between two variables. A correlation matrix is used to summarize data, as an input into a more advanced analysis, and as a diagnostic for advanced analyses [15]. In our case, it was used to check for any dependencies between features. An excerpt of this is presented in Fig. 2. Some features showed a high correlation with one another (0.7 +, red cells), indicating potential dependencies between the features "Primary Datatype", "Communication", "Data Security", "Extent of Effect on Enterprise", "Maturity", and "Data Source.

	Eindruckar	KIFokus	Rechenquelle	Antwortzeit	Spezielle_Hardware	Zuverlässig	Primäere Aufgabe	Datenquelle	Datenmenge	Reifegrad	Auswirkungen	Kommunikation	Primäere Datentyp	Datenqualität	Datensicherheit
Eindruckar		0,716	0,481	0,609	0,396	0,208	0,307	0,219	-0,230	0,595	0,664	0,323	0,579	0,632	0,433
KIFokus	0,716		0,012	0,115	0,124	-0,202	0,006	0,024	-0,261	0,031	0,361	0,102	0,168	0,275	0,213
Rechenquelle	0,481	0,012		0,512	0,499	0,590	0,831	0,465	0,081	0,861	0,709	0,776	0,863	0,543	0,629
Antwortzeit	0,609	0,115	0,512		0,167	0,531	0,330	0,602	0,124	0,759	0,614	0,473	0,664	0,348	0,513
Spezielle_Hardware	0,396	0,124	0,499	0,167		0,362	0,584	0,313	0,158	0,603	0,553	0,376	0,610	0,646	0,481
Zuverlässig	0,209	-0,202	0,590	0,531	0,362		0,630	0,620	0,636	0,686	0,369	0,464	0,685	0,477	0,391
Primäereaufgabe	0,307	0,006	0,831	0,330	0,584	0,630		0,580	0,246	0,750	0,804	0,693	0,866	0,515	0,552
Datenquelle	0,219	0,024	0,465	0,602	0,313	0,620	0,580		0,322	0,659	0,569	0,724	0,744	0,506	0,607
Datenmenge	-0,230	-0,261	0,081	0,134	0,158	0,636	0,246	0,322		0,210	-0,009	0,151	0,202	0,053	0,221
Reifegrad	0,595	0,031	0,881	0,759	0,603	0,686	0,750	0,659	0,210		0,791	0,742	0,941	0,668	0,728
Auswirkungen	0,664	0,361	0,709	0,614	0,553	0,369	0,804	0,569	-0,009	0,791		0,711	0,834	0,605	0,921
Kommunikation	0,323	0,102	0,776	0,473	0,376	0,464	0,693	0,724	0,151	0,742	0,711		0,786	0,532	0,746
Primäeredatentyp	0,579	0,168	0,863	0,664	0,610	0,685	0,889	0,744	0,202	0,941	0,834	0,786		0,653	0,765
Datenqualität	0,632	0,275	0,543	0,346	0,646	0,477	0,515	0,506	0,053	0,668	0,605	0,532	0,653		0,507
Datensicherheit	0,433	0,213	0,629	0,513	0,481	0,391	0,552	0,607	0,221	0,728	0,921	0,746	0,765	0,507	

Fig. 2. Excerpt of the correlation matrix for the survey results.

Secondly, we conducted the Kaiser-Meyer-Olkin (KMO) and Bartlett Test. The KMO measure of sampling adequacy is a statistic that indicates the proportion of variance in your variables that might be caused by underlying factors. High values (close to 1.0) generally indicate that a factor analysis may be useful with your data. If the value is less than 0.50, the results of the factor analysis probably won't be very useful. Bartlett's test of sphericity tests the hypothesis that your correlation matrix is an identity matrix, which would indicate that your variables are unrelated and therefore not suitable for structure detection. Small values (below 0.05) of the significance level indicate that factor analysis may be useful for your data [15].

The tests for each question block in our survey show that the factors are independent of each other and can be used in further calculations because most of the features of our survey deliver a result of 0.6 to 0.8. As an example, Fig. 3 shows the KMO measure of sampling adequacy for the values of the feature "Extent and Effect on Enterprise" to determine if the values are independent of each other. This gives us an indication of whether calculating averages of them provides any meaningful insights. The example delivers a result of 0.8. The next step would be factorial analysis, but due to not measuring any regression relationships, this is not necessary in this case.

Communalities

	Initial	Extraction
Auswirkungen_Unterneh men_1_1	1,000	,741
Auswirkungen_Unterneh men_1_2	1,000	,734
Auswirkungen_Unterneh men_1_3	1,000	,545
Auswirkungen_Unterneh men_1_4	1,000	,622
Auswirkungen_Unterneh men_1_5	1,000	,847

Extraction Method: Principal Component Analysis.

KMO and Bartlett's Test

Kaiser-Meyer-Olkin Measure of Sampling Adequacy.		,800
Bartlett's Test of Sphericity	Approx. Chi-Square	39,607
	df	10
	Sig.	<,001

Total Variance Explained

Component	Initial Eigenvalues			Extraction Sums of Squared Loadings		
	Total	% of Variance	Cumulative %	Total	% of Variance	Cumulative %
1	3,488	69,761	69,761	3,488	69,761	69,761
2	,595	11,908	81,669			
3	,505	10,104	91,773			
4	,253	5,054	96,827			
5	,159	3,173	100,000			

Extraction Method: Principal Component Analysis.

Fig. 3. KMO & Bartels test results for the feature "Extent of Effect on Enterprise".

4.3 Feature Analysis

One of the primary objectives of this research was to determine if all the existing features were indeed relevant for the implementation of AI solutions. To answer this question, we asked participants to rate each feature on a three-point Likert scale with three possible responses: Yes (5), No (1), and Partly (3). Figure 4 provides an overview of the responses to this question for each of the features presented.

The first notable observation from this figure is the range of responses. For the following features, no participant chose 'no': End User, AI Focus, Hardware, Reliability and Accuracy, Primary Purpose, Data Source, Maturity, Update Frequency, and Data Security. This strongly supports the relevance of these features. Regarding the average rating of the features, "Primary Purpose", "Data Quality", and "Data Security", highlighted in yellow, ranked highest with an average score of 4.62 out of 5. As you can see, the majority of features (12 out of 16) achieved a score of four or higher. This high score on a scale of one to five suggests that for most respondents, these characteristics are important factors for the implementation of AI in enterprises and should be included in the morphological box. On the other hand, even the three lowest-performing features, highlighted in red, still achieved scores above 3.50, which corresponds to an average neutral to positive rating. This indicates that participants still believed that these features fit into the context of AI implementation but that they may have potential for further improvement. The feature "Maturity" is particularly interesting because it has one of the lowest average performances without anyone choosing "does not fit", which means that for this particular feature, participants were uncertain and mostly chose "partly" (3). To further evaluate these features should be part of future research. Overall, the sentiment towards these features was very positive, with an average score of 4.2/5 across all features, supporting the combination of features in the box.

Descriptive Statistics

	N	Minimum	Maximum	Mean	Std. Deviation
Endnutzer_4	16	3	5	4,50	,894
KI-Fokus_4	16	3	5	4,25	1,000
Rechenquelle_4	16	1	5	4,25	1,238
Antwort-/Reaktionszeit_4	16	1	5	4,38	1,204
Spezielle_Hardware_Anf orderung_4	16	3	5	4,13	1,025
Zuverlässigkeit/Genauigk eit_Ergebnisse_4	16	3	5	4,13	1,025
Zeitpunkt_der_KI-Nutzung_4	16	1	5	3,50	1,155
Primaere_Aufgabe_4	16	3	5	4,63	,806
Datenquelle_4	16	3	5	4,37	,957
Reifegrad_4	16	3	5	3,75	1,000
Haeufigkeit_der_Daten-und_Modellaktualisierun g_4	16	3	5	4,13	1,025
Auswirkungen_Unterneh men_4	16	1	5	3,88	1,258
Kommunikation_4	16	1	5	3,69	1,302
Primaerer_Datentyp_4	16	1	5	4,37	1,204
Datenqualitaet_4	16	1	5	4,63	1,088
Datensicherheit_4	16	3	5	4,62	,806
Valid N (listwise)	16				

Fig. 4. Minimum and maximum ratings, mean and standard deviation for all features.

4.4 Value Analysis

The next part of our report focuses on another crucial part of the morphological box, the values. Each feature has certain potential values. The second major goal of the survey was to assess how participants evaluate the existing values and to discover if any values are missing. The latter will be discussed in the following chapter, where we will discuss all the free-text answers that participants provided during the survey. For the assessment of the values for each feature, we used a 5-point Likert scale with the following possible responses to calculate the meaningfulness of these values: very meaningful (5), partially meaningful (4), neutral (3), less meaningful (2), and not meaningful at all (1). It's important to note that meaningfulness always refers to the trait itself. This means that when we find outliers, we need to compare them with values in the same group to determine if they are redundant or outdated. Figure 5 presents the average performance results of all values, grouped by feature. The evaluation here is similar to the evaluation of the features in the previous section. All value groups achieved rounded scores around four. Even the lowest value groups, "End-user" and "AI Focus", reached scores of 3.6875/5 and 3.7292/5 respectively, indicating that most of the values were perceived as meaningful and appropriate. This is quantified by the average value meaningfulness of 3.96/5. The best-performing value groups were "Primary Purpose", "Primary Data Type", and "Data Security", each with an average perceived importance of more than 4.2/5. However, how to improve the lower-rated value groups, especially those below 4.0, should be part of future research.

Most of the values reach an average perception of 4 or higher, while the values of the "End-User" only reach averages of 3.5, 3.69, 3.94, and 3.63. The same applies to the "AI Focus", with averages of 3.88, 3.81, and 3.5. The first two values of the "Computing

Descriptive Statistics

	N	Minimum	Maximum	Mean	Std. Deviation
MEAN_Endnutzer	16	1,75	5,00	3,6875	,98531
MEAN_KIFokus	16	1,67	5,00	3,7292	,98296
MEAN_Rechenquelle	16	3,00	5,00	4,0156	,82900
MEAN_Antwortzeit	16	2,50	5,00	3,7500	,73598
MEAN_Spezielle_Hardware	16	3,00	5,00	4,1563	,50724
MEAN_Zuverlaessig	16	3,00	5,00	3,8438	,61830
MEAN_PrimaereAufgabe	16	3,00	5,00	4,2750	,70000
MEAN_Datenquelle	16	2,60	5,00	3,8625	,77535
MEAN_Datenmenge	16	3,00	5,00	3,7375	,71075
MEAN_Reifegrad	16	3,00	5,00	4,1750	,77589
MEAN_Auswirkungen	16	1,80	5,00	3,9125	,94366
MEAN_Kommunikation	16	2,60	5,00	3,7375	,92871
MEAN_PrimaererDatentyp	16	3,00	5,00	4,2292	,69355
MEAN_Datenqualitaet	16	2,14	5,00	4,0000	1,01015
MEAN_Datensicherheit	16	2,86	5,00	4,3036	,66163
MEAN_ALL	16	3,01	4,86	3,9610	,56230
Valid N (listwise)	16				

Fig. 5. Mean statistics of all values for each feature.

Source" were rated above the average of 3.96 (Cloud, Local Computing Center), whereas the last two were rated below average (End-Device, Hybrid). For the "Time to Decision", only "Real-time" was rated above average, with "Several Hours" and "Later" having comparably low ratings of 3.31 each. The "Special Hardware Required" values all score above average, except for "Data Output", which reaches a score just below the average (3.88). For "Reliability and Precision of Results", "99.9% Required" and "Defined by Competitor" scored below average. For the "Point in Time of AI Use" all values are rated above the average. The same goes for "Primary Purpose" with "Assistance" and "Anomaly Detection" reaching some of the highest scores overall with 4.56. Regarding the "Data Source" only "Open Data" fell shortly below the average and "Synthetic Data" reached the lowest score overall with 3.0. For the "Data Quantity" required for an AI solution only the values from "Very High" to "Moderate" were rated above average. Not surprisingly, a "Low" or "Very Low" amount of data were deemed below average, opening the question of those values are necessary at all as most AI applications need data to work. For the features "Maturity" and "Data and Model Update Frequency" all values were rated above average with just "In Case of Changes in Customer Behavior" falling 0.02 points short. The values for "Extent of Effect on Enterprise" reaches mixed scores with "Isolated Solution" and "Work System" being above average, the whole "Business Modell" just −0.02 below average and "Single Process" and "Workflow" being below average. It seems like the participants assume that an AI solution mostly either functions as a small isolated solution or directly as one that has a huge impact on a company. For "Communication" the first two values representing that a regular collaboration is required are rated the best with the remaining three values scoring below average. All of the "Primary Datatype" values easily score above average. The same goes for "Data Security" where "Data Integrity" scores the highest overall rating. For "Data Quality" all values besides "Noisy" (−0.02) and "Biased" (−0.17) were rated above average. Even the lowest value overall, the data source value "Synthetic Data", has a neutral rating. The fact that no value is perceived negatively, and that the average perceived meaningfulness is 3.96/5, further supports the current status of the values of the morphological box. However, 3.0 is still no good rating and that the average is below 4.0 still shows room for improvement. Therefore, future research should focus on the lowest rated values. The next chapter will focus on all the improvements to the morphological box suggested by the participants in the survey and indicated areas for possible improvement that can be deduced from the low ratings discussed in this chapter.

5 Discussion

This chapter discusses possible changes of the morphological box that were either directly suggested by the survey participants or can be deduced from the analyzed data (Sect. 4). The first section concentrates on possible new features, whereas the second section focuses on possible new values. The final section discusses possible changes in the allocation of the values within each feature.

5.1 Possible New Features

At the start of the survey, we asked participants about key factors for successfully implementing and integrating an AI solution in a company. This question aimed to stimulate thinking about AI and potentially uncover new features or values for the box. We systematized the answers by labeling and grouping them into general topic areas, resulting in the graph shown in Fig. 6.

We identified 11 areas deemed important for successful AI introduction. Most frequently mentioned were "Purpose", "Knowledge", "Data", and a "Legal Framework". Other areas included "Cultural Factors", "Technological Resources", "Measuring Success of AI Implementation", "Ethics", "Change Management", and "Flexibility". The term "Knowledge" had many variations, indicating the need for someone knowledgeable about AI implementation in the company. This aligns with the purpose of the morphological box, which is to aid those in smaller and medium-sized companies who may lack an AI expert. The "Purpose" category elicited a range of responses, but all agreed that AI needs a clear reason for use, linked to business goals, and an AI strategy.

This is currently represented by the "Extent of Effect on Enterprise" feature, which includes potential automation or business model changes, and the "Primary Purpose" feature from a technological perspective. The same goes for the need for "Data" which is considered by the several data related features. No indications for further required data-related information was found. "Cultural Factors" primarily involve fostering acceptance of AI among employees and customers. Key to this is alleviating employee fears of being replaced by AI. This can be addressed by identifying the "End-User", planning their preparation, and considering the "Extent of Effect" on processes and organizational structures. The communication aspect, originally focused on developers and users, could also encompass communication with company employees. The "Measuring Success of AI Implementation" category includes testing the AI against common metrics such as accuracy or precision before implementation. Some participants suggested measuring success by Return on Investment (ROI). However, the box's goal is to aid successful AI implementation and introduction, not to guarantee financial profit.

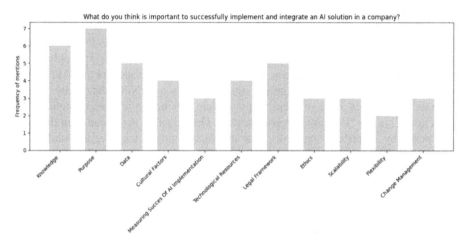

Fig. 6. Systematized answers for factors influencing AI introduction.

The 'Reliability and Precision of Results' feature fulfills the technical measurement aspect. The "Technological Resources" area is represented by the "Special Hardware Required". The "Legal Framework" and "Ethics" areas depend on the country where the AI solution is used, industry and type of AI application. These areas are not represented in the box so far and could be objective of future iterations. It should be analyzed if they fit the scope of the box and if so, what values they could have. For "Ethics" universally applicable ethical aspects for the usage of AI could be collected while for a "Legal Framework" some examples like the GDPR and European AI Act could be provided. One step further would be to extract the most important regulations from such documents, but this could potentially be out of the scope of the box. "Scalability" and "Flexibility", like measuring financial success of an AI solution, are not part of the box's scope as they are not necessary for successful implementation. The "Change Management" area can be covered by a combination of several features like "Extent of Effect", "End-User" and "Communication".

In summary, we argue that the box provides most necessary areas important for introducing AI solutions as mentioned by the participants. However, the "Ethics" and "Legal Framework" could be added as new features but require further investigation first. The "Communication" feature could be extended to include communication with a company's employees.

5.2 Possible New Values

For each feature, we posed an open-ended question to identify any potential missing values. The responses were generally less detailed than those in the previous section, with fewer answers and not every feature having proposed new values. Table 1 groups all suggested values by their features. Any additional comments from participants that don't suggest new values but could still be relevant to the research are included in the comment column. As highlighted in Sect. 4, all feature values are generally accepted as none received a negative rating. However, some values were rated higher or lower than average. The features with the lowest average ratings were "End-User", "AI Focus", "Time to Decision", "Data Quantity", and "Communication". This is reflected in the free-text responses and the suggestions for additional values in Table 1 as only those received ideas for possible new values. Most additions were suggested for the "AI Focus". Suggestions included prediction, optimization, autonomous driving, data analysis, and automation. However, none of these fit the feature. Prediction is already included as "Forecasting" in the "Primary Purpose" feature. Optimization is a broad term that can be achieved by all primary purposes. Autonomous driving is too specific, while data analysis is too broad. Automation could potentially be added as an additional value to the primary purposes, but it would overlap with other values like "Assistance" or "Decision Making", which also offer a form of automation. Therefore, we decided not to add automation as a new value. For the "End-User", a suggestion was made to add a user who only knows "AI as ChatGPT". However, this is irrelevant for determining the knowledge level of the end user, as this feature should help design the AI solution. It was further noted that applications should be user-friendly and usable without technical prerequisites. In the case of "Computing Source", there was a suggestion to expand the values to include 'as a service' components such as "Software as a Service (SaaS)", "Platform as a Service (PaaS)", and "Infrastructure as a Service (IaaS)". While generally correct, these suggestions are merely specifications of 'Cloud' as a computing source or "Commercial of the Shelf" (COTS) as a "Maturity" if a company would buy the entire solution externally. In this case, it could also be an "AIaaS" solution. For "Time to Decision", a value 'on request' was submitted. However, if a solution only delivers results on request, it still needs to be determined if the results have to be shown immediately (requiring processing before the request or very fast) or if it's sufficient to deliver the results after a specific time. The most significant comment from the question about further values per feature is the desire for concrete values for the amount of data required ("Data Quantity"). This was desired by several survey participants, with 18.75% explicitly stating they would like a measurable specification, for example in gigabytes. This should be investigated further. The main question will be, how we can group the required amount of data. Could it be grouped according to specific AI technologies like how much data is recommended for machine learning, deep learning, or others? The final proposal was to add values for complete and uncorrupted data for the "Data Quality" feature. Although these are two important qualities that data should fulfill, our approach for this feature was to mention all qualities in their negative forms, hence what should be avoided. Here we already included negative forms of the suggested values in "Incomplete" and "Corrupted" data.

5.3 Possible Reorganization of the Values

In the final open-ended question, we asked participants if they would organize the values for each feature differently. The aim was to uncover potentially new and improved ways to structure the features, stimulate open thinking among participants, and identify any

Table 1. Suggested new values grouped by features.

Feature	Values	Comments
AI-Focus	Prediction | Optimization | Autonomous driving | Data analysis | Automation	No additional comments.
End-User	Users, who only know ChatGPT as AI.	Applications should be as user-friendly as possible without technical prerequisites.
Computing Source	SaaS | IaaS | PaaS	No additional comments.
Time to Decision	On request	No additional comments.
Data Quantity	No proposed values.	Specific values would be helpful.
Data Quality	Complete | Uncorrupted	No additional comments.

undiscovered overlap between values. We categorized the responses into 'New Value Structure' for suggestions on reorganizing the values, and 'Comments' for more general feedback relevant to the topic. The findings are displayed in Table 2.

The limited number of suggestions could indicate satisfaction with the current distribution of values. However, it's important to note potential bias, as participants were first introduced to the distribution established by the box. Two comments indicated that the values 'Computing Task' for 'AI Focus' and 'Data Output' and 'Data Visualization' for 'Special Hardware Required' were unclear. For future research, the descriptions of those values should be reworked and made clearer. There was a suggestion to further distinguish the 'End-User' according to the degree of software application, but the participant's intent was not entirely clear. The only concrete proposal was to divide the maturity level of the application into the classic make, take, or buy levels. However, this is already represented by the current values.

Table 2. Suggested new value structure for features.

Feature	New Value Structure	Comments
AI-Focus		Meaning of *Computing Task* unclear.
End-User	Level of application of the software.	
Special Hardware Required		*Data Output* and *Data Visualization* unclear.
Maturity	Make | Take | Buy	

6 Summary and Future Research

In this paper, we conducted a survey aimed at evaluating the current iteration of our morphological box for AI solutions. We began by outlining the rationale and objectives of the box, followed by a detailed description of the survey's structure and its application. Subsequently, we delved into an explanation and analysis of the survey results, which paved the way for a discussion on potential adjustments to the features, values, and structure of the box based on the survey findings.

The data analysis, coupled with the open-ended responses, indicated that the features and values of the box appear to be accurate. For the features, the two new areas "Ethics" and "Legal Framework" were discovered. The quantitative results were satisfactory overall, but also showed some room for improvement for the features and values that performed below average (especially the ones rated below 4.0). Additionally, dependencies between features may exist and should be investigated further.

The survey has strong limitations, including the number of participants and the fact that all participants were students from the same university that mostly learned about AI from their university courses. The survey should be revised and conducted again with "real" AI experts from a diverse and international background. However, rather than a measurement of the completeness of the box, the answers of the students and this survey could be seen as a test of understandability for the box and its features and values as the students might be on a similar level of IT knowledge as possible general users of the box in companies.

References

1. Stowasser, S.: Erfolgreiche Einführung von KI im Unternehmen. In: Knappertsbusch, I., Gondlach, K. (eds.) Arbeitswelt und KI 2030. Herausforderungen und Strategien für die Arbeit von morgen. Research, pp. 145–153. Springer Gabler, Wiesbaden, Heidelberg (2021). https://doi.org/10.1007/978-3-658-35779-5_15
2. Mikalef, P., et al.: Examining how AI capabilities can foster organizational performance in public organizations. 0740-624X, **40**, 101797 (2023). https://doi.org/10.1016/j.giq.2022.101797
3. Hansen, E.B., Bøgh, S.: Artificial intelligence and internet of things in small and medium-sized enterprises: a survey. J. Manuf. Syst. **58**, 362–372 (2021). https://doi.org/10.1016/j.jmsy.2020.08.009
4. Bro, R., Smilde, A.K.: Principal component analysis. Anal. Methods **6**, 2812–2831 (2014). https://doi.org/10.1039/C3AY41907J
5. Machine learning algorithms-a review (2020)
6. Pouyanfar, S., et al.: A survey on deep learning. ACM Comput. Surv. **51**, 1–36 (2019). https://doi.org/10.1145/3234150
7. Suthaharan, S.: Support vector machine. Mach. Learn. Models Algorithms Big Data Classif. **36**, 207–235 (2016). https://doi.org/10.1007/978-1-4899-7641-3_9
8. Zwicky, F.: Discovery, invention, research through the morphological approach, vol. (1969)
9. Rittelmeyer, J.D., Sandkuhl, K.: Features of AI solutions and their use in AI context modeling. Gesellschaft für Informatik e.V (2022)
10. Rittelmeyer, J.D., Sandkuhl, K.: A Morphological Box for AI Solutions: Evaluation, Refinement and Application Potentials. In: Ruiz, M., Soffer, P. (eds.) CAiSE 2023. LNBIP, vol. 482, pp. 5–16. Springer, Cham (2023). https://doi.org/10.1007/978-3-031-34985-0_1

11. Rittelmeyer, J.D., Sandkuhl, K.: Morphological box for AI solutions: evaluation and refinement with a taxonomy development method. In: Hinkelmann, K., López-Pellicer, F.J., Polini, A. (eds.) BIR 2023. LNBIP, vol. 493, pp. 145–157. Springer, Cham (2023)

12. Sandkuhl, K., Rittelmeyer, J.D.: Use of EA models in organizational AI solution development. In: Aveiro, D., Proper, H.A., Guerreiro, S., de Vries, M. (eds.) EEWC 2021. LNBIP, vol. 441, pp. 149–166. Springer, Cham (2022). https://doi.org/10.1007/978-3-031-11520-2_10

13. Nickerson, R.C., Varshney, U., Muntermann, J.: A method for taxonomy development and its application in information systems. Eur. J. Inf. Syst. **22**, 336–359 (2013). https://doi.org/10.1057/ejis.2012.26

14. Jamsen, J., Corley, K.: E-survey methodology. In: Reynolds, R.A., Woods, R., Baker, J.D. (eds.) Handbook of research on electronic surveys and measurements, pp. 1–8. Idea Group Reference, Hershey, Pa (2007). https://doi.org/10.4018/978-1-59140-792-8.ch001

15. Velicer, W.F., Jackson, D.N.: Component analysis versus common factor analysis: some issues in selecting an appropriate procedure. Multivar. Behav. Res. **25**, 1–28 (1990). https://doi.org/10.1207/s15327906mbr2501_1

KG4SDSE

Preface: 2nd Workshop on Knowledge Graphs for Semantics-Driven Systems Engineering (KG4SDSE 2024)

Robert Buchmann[1], Dimitris Karagiannis[2], and Dimitris Plexousakis[3]

[1] Babeș-Bolyai University, Cluj-Napoca, Romania
[2] University of Vienna, Austria
[3] Institute of Computer Science, FORTH and University of Crete, Greece

The 2nd Workshop on **Knowledge Graphs for Semantics-Driven Systems Engineering** (KG4SDSE) followed the successful launch of the workshop in 2023 with a desire to create a focus point for CAiSE community members who are engaged in projects relying on Knowledge Graphs and their associated technologies (e.g. graph databases) and paradigms (e.g. knowledge engineering, conceptual modeling). The workshop aimed to highlight the role of semantics in information systems engineering. Emerging tools and methods - originating in research on the Semantic Web or Conceptual Modeling - can be operationalized for engineering or artifact-building research. We believe that Knowledge Graphs (KG) will become a key ingredient for an emerging semantics-driven engineering paradigm and as a symbolic complement to Large Language Model (LLM) services, making this workshop a timely event that will grow as ecosystems focused on machine-readable semantics diversify.

This year the workshop received 12 submissions in total, from 5 countries. Based on the constructive evaluations from the Program Committee, we accepted 5 full papers and 2 short papers, covering diverse research in various stages of refinement - from advanced results to visions of early-stage projects that will benefit from the workshop discussions:

- Abgrall and Franconi's paper presents a semantic layering approach over legacy databases, in rich technical and formal detail;
- Iga and Silaghi reported preliminary experiments with prompt engineering as an early step towards further work on task-oriented dialogue systems relying on LLM-KG integration;
- Iga and Ghiran presented a domain-specific modeling tool that exposes diagrammatic service designs to a Knowledge Graphs treatment;
- Kumarasinghe and Kirikova reported work on the development of a Knowledge Graph for describing a portfolio of analytics projects descriptions;
- Laurenzi et al. also reported on a domain-specific application hybridizing Knowledge Graphs with a diagrammatic approach to building management systems;
- The short paper of Kondylakis et al. is a position paper formulating a research roadmap regarding property graphs beyond the state of the art;
- The short paper of Bianchini et al. introduced an architectural vision integrating LLMs and Knowledge Graphs for the legal domain.

We are thankful to the contributing authors who helped turning this workshop into a recurring event, and we are grateful that the CAiSE workshop chairs committed to hosting it during the Workshops Days of CAiSE 2024.

This event could not have taken place without the sponsorship of OMiLAB NPO, Germany, and FORTH-CS, Greece, as well as the efforts of our Web presence chair, Iulia Vaidian (University of Vienna).

Organization

Workshop Chairs

Robert Buchmann	Babeş-Bolyai University, Romania
Dimitris Karagiannis	University of Vienna, Austria
Dimitris Plexousakis	Institute of Computer Science, FORTH and University of Crete, Greece

Web Chair

Iulia Vaidian	University of Vienna, Austria

Program Committee

Nick Bassiliades	Aristotle University of Thessaloniki, Greece
Sjaak Brinkkemper	Utrecht University, The Netherlands
Michael Fellmann	University of Rostock, Germany
Hans-Georg Fill	University of Fribourg, Switzerland
Aurona Gerber	University of Pretoria, South Africa
Ana-Maria Ghiran	Babeş-Bolyai University, Romania
Adrian Groza	Technical University of Cluj-Napoca, Romania
Marite Kirikova	Riga Technical University, Latvia
Manolis Koubarakis	National and Kapodistrian University of Athens, Greece
Ana León	Universitat Politècnica de València, Spain
Andreas Opdahl	University of Bergen, Norway
Andrea Polini	University of Camerino, Italy
Achim Reiz	University of Rostock, Germany
Ben Roelens	Open University, The Netherlands
Anisa Rula	University of Brescia, Italy
Maribel Yasmina Santos	University of Minho, Portugal
Alberto Rodrigues da Silva	University of Lisbon, Portugal
Takahira Yamaguchi	Keio University, Japan

Understanding the Semantic SQL Transducer

Théo Abgrall and Enrico Franconi[(✉)] [iD]

KRDB Research Centre for Knowledge-driven Artificial Intelligence,
Free University of Bozen-Bolzano, Bolzano, Italy
`theo.abgrall@student.unibz.it, franconi@inf.unibz.it`

Abstract. Nowadays we observe an evolving landscape of data management and analytics, emphasising the significance of meticulous data management practices, semantic modelling, and bridging business-technical
divides, to optimise data utilisation and enhance value from datasets
in modern data environments. In this paper we introduce and explain
the basic formalisation of the Semantic SQL Transducer, a well-founded
but practical tool providing the materialised lossless conceptual view of
an arbitrary relational source data, contributing to a knowledge-centric
data stack.

1 Introduction

The landscape of data management and analytics is undergoing continuous evolution, aiming to optimise data utilisation, ensure governance, and enhance the
value derived from the datasets. Several pivotal concepts shape an enhanced
modern data environment, emphasising the significance of robust data preparation, semantic modelling, and bridging the gap between technical and business
perspectives. In [3] we present a thorough analysis of the current trends in data
management. Key aspects of these directions include the increasing significance
of metadata management for data governance, the necessity of comprehensive
semantic enrichment in data contracts and data preparation, the importance of
bridging the divide between business problem models and data domains through
the integration of semantic mediation, the adoption of a semantic-based declarative transformation process, and the facilitation of seamless data integration
and improved interoperability through shared semantic understanding.

Given this context, we believe a contribution to support proper semantic
modelling within a data preparation pipeline is badly needed. In this paper we
introduce and explain the basic formalisation of the *Semantic SQL Transducer*, a
well-founded but practical tool providing the materialised *lossless* and possibly
conceptual view of an arbitrary relational data, contributing to a knowledge-
centric data stack. The Semantic SQL Transducer can be seen as a seamless
semantic wrapper around arbitrary relational data at any stage of the data stack,
independently on its architecture. The advantage of this technology is that it can
be seen as a replacement of the data it models, providing a restructuring of the

J. P. A. Almeida et al. (Eds.): CAiSE 2024 Workshops, LNBIP 521, pp. 135–146, 2024.
https://doi.org/10.1007/978-3-031-61003-5_12

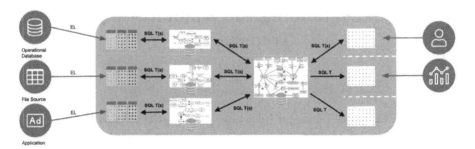

Fig. 1. A Semantic Data Stack

data according to its restructured (and possibly conceptual) model as a standard SQL database, which can be therefore queried, updated, transformed. It can be used also to replace procedural data transformation tasks with semantic-based declarative executable specification of the transformation task, guaranteeing the losslessness of the transformation itself. By restructuring the relational data directly in its conceptual model, the transducer provides a conceptual access to the data, providing to business users and data analysts the right understanding of the available data.

2   The Role of a Semantic SQL Transducer

Our contribution to a knowledge-centric data stack consists in a SQL-based tool (supported by a design methodology) providing the materialised *lossless* conceptual view of an arbitrary relational source data. Such materialised conceptual view can be queried and updated using the knowledge vocabulary, with virtually no overhead with respect to the original source data. Updates to the materialised conceptual view are replicated instantaneously to the source data (e.g., to push a semantic-conscious data cleaning update to the source), and updates to the source data are replicated instantaneously to the materialised conceptual view providing always a fresh view of the source. The materialised view is the conceptual lossless mirror of the source data, and it acts as a mediator by providing the conceptual API for a complete access and change to the source data.

Our *Semantic SQL Transducer* is based completely on standard SQL technology, it can be deployed on any SQL platform, and it does not require any additional tool or code to work. The transducer can exactly translate legacy SQL queries and updates over the source schema to SQL queries and updates over the conceptual schema, and it can exactly translate analytical SQL queries and updates over the conceptual schema to SQL queries and updates over the source schema. By using semantic SQL transducers within a data prep process as semantic wrappers around the data sources (e.g., see Fig. 1), the "transform" part of the ETL process can operate over semantically well defined entities and relationships. The transducer supports transactions, to systematically guarantee semantic integrity and consistency of both the source and its conceptual model.

In order to represent the exact semantics of the source data, the Semantic SQL Transducer supports several popular conceptual data models: ERD, ORM, UML Class Diagrams, Property Graphs Schemas, Knowledge Graphs. It is based on several years of theoretical research by us on the formalisation of the connection between conceptual data models and relational databases, and on the formalisation of core SQL [1,2,7,9,18]. A rigorous methodology to properly design a semantic SQL transducer given the data sources has been studied and experimented [23,24]; we are developing several tools to support it, which are not yet publicly available.

We believe that our pragmatic approach to semantic enrichment provides a useful knowledge-based core element which can be embedded within many different data architectures, improving on the issues emphasised above in the direction of making the boring data stack more exciting: auditing and data governance now are based on a clear semantic view of the data, supporting a more transparent environment to exploit business literacy; during data preparation, semantic integrity checks can be defined over the conceptual structures, and data cleaning can be enforced at the level of the conceptual view; data integration and entity recognition are now semantic-based, and the presence of a unified conceptual model exactly capturing the diverse data sources supports the harmonisation of the disparate data elements within the enterprise; the gap between data management and data analysis is reduced, being mediated by the transducers, reducing therefore the risk of a technical debt; data scientists operate over high-quality data, contributing to a more robust and efficient data warehouse.

Note that there are many semantic-based approaches that introduce an intermediate layer between the data layer and the business layer, which should be compared the proposal, such as enterprise data fabrics, data meshes, data lakes, etc. It is important to observe that the proposed Semantic SQL Transducer is orthogonal to any of such architectural choices. The suggested semantic data stack in Fig. 1 above had the only purpose how the Semantic SQL Transducer could support semantic enrichment in a modern data stack. The unicity of our proposal lies in the fact that it can losslessly "present" the data in a restructured way, possibly according to its conceptual schema, always using SQL as the foundational formalism.

3   Inside the Semantic SQL Transducer

The abstract internal architecture of the Semantic SQL Transducer is shown in Fig. 2. It is a generic architecture, implementing the lossless bidirectional interoperation between two databases, called S (source) and T (target). The SQL code guarantees that the two databases are always automatically synchronised after any update (wrapped within a transaction) to any of the two databases. The two databases maintain their original constraints and indexes, maximising therefore the efficiency of querying. The updates to a database are recasted directly as actual updates to the other database, maximising therefore the efficiency of updates. Some attention has to be paid to avoid infinite looping of the triggers.

```
Source S:
create table S1 ...    (with source constraints)
...
create table Sm ...    (with source constraints)

Target T:
create table T1 ...    (with target constraints)
...
create table Tn ...    (with target constraints)

Insert S ⇒ T:
create table S1_INSERT ...    (same schema as S1)
...
create table Sm_INSERT ...    (same schema as Sm)

create trigger S1_INSERT after insert on S1 ...  (updates S1_INSERT)
...
create trigger Sm_INSERT after insert on Sm ...  (updates Sm_INSERT)

create table T1_INSERT as select ... from S1_INSERT,...,Sm_INSERT ...   (same schema as T1)
...
create table Tn_INSERT as select ... from S1_INSERT,...,Sm_INSERT ...   (same schema as Tn)

create trigger T1_INSERT after insert on T1_INSERT ...  (updates T1)
...
create trigger Tn_INSERT after insert on Tn_INSERT ...  (updates Tn)

Insert T ⇒ S:
create table T1_INSERT ...    (same schema as T1)
...
create table Tn_INSERT ...    (same schema as Tn)

create trigger T1_INSERT after insert on T1 ...  (updates T1_INSERT)
...
create trigger Tn_INSERT after insert on Tn ...  (updates Tn_INSERT)

create table S1_INSERT as select ... from T1_INSERT,...,Tn_INSERT ...   (same schema as S1)
...
create table Sm_INSERT as select ... from T1_INSERT,...,Tn_INSERT ...   (same schema as Sm)

create trigger S1_INSERT after insert on S1_INSERT ...  (updates S1)
...
create trigger Sm_INSERT after insert on Sm_INSERT ...  (updates Sm)

Similarly: Delete S ⇒ T, Delete T ⇒ S.
```

Fig. 2. The Semantic SQL Transducer abstract architecture

The real complexity comes in defining both the lossless mappings from S to T and from T to S (appearing in the SQL code as `create table X as select ...`) and the constraints of the two databases S and T. Those mappings and constraints are provided by our theory of *lossless transformations* [1,2,18,23,24], based on the original works on *information capacity* [15,16,20,22,25,26].

When the transducer is used to provide the semantic enrichment as a conceptual view of a data source within an ETL pipeline, the database S is indeed the source database, and the database T is the dynamic restructuring of S according to its conceptual schema. The involved mappings and constraints are a generalisation of classical mappings studied in the reverse engineering literature [4,5,8,17,21,27], started by the seminal papers by Hainaut [12–14].

We can show that any source database has associated a unique *canonical abstract relational model* [19], which is the lossless materialisation of the database in its conceptual schema in 6th normal form. The canonical abstract relational model has a direct correspondence with the most popular conceptual modelling languages such as ERD, ORM, UML Class Diagrams, Property Graphs Schemas, RDF-based models. We provide a rigorous methodology to properly design the conceptual schema in the form of a canonical abstract relational model, given the data sources [1,2]; we are developing several tools to support it. In the next

Section we will define the notion of losslessness in database restructuring, and we will explain all the basic transformation steps of the design methodology through a completely worked out example.

In conclusion, the Semantic SQL Transducer provides a seamless access to databases through their conceptual schemas, and it contributes to a knowledge-centric data stack adding a declarative semantic layer to databases.

4   Designing the Semantic SQL Transducer

In order to formalise the SQL transducer, we introduce first the notion of a *first-order database schema*. A first-order database schema DB is a pair $\langle \mathbb{A}_{DB}, \mathbb{C}_{DB} \rangle$ where $\mathbb{A}_{DB}$ is a set of database predicates with their attributes $R(a_1, a_2, \cdots, a_n)$ – for simplicity we do not consider here the domains of the attributes – and $\mathbb{C}_{DB}$ is a set of first order constraints (aka dependencies) over the predicates. In order to capture exactly SQL, we restrict constraints to be in the domain-independent fragment of first-order logic: all interesting kinds of constraints can be represented, ranging from functional and multivalued dependencies (including keys), to inclusion dependencies (including foreign keys), to constraints on domain values. We will use a standard notation for classical database dependencies, most notably, $a_1, \cdots, a_n \rightarrow b_1, \cdots, b_m$ for functional dependencies, $a_1, \cdots, a_n \twoheadrightarrow b_1, \cdots, b_m$ for multivalued dependencies, $a_1, \cdots, a_n \subseteq b_1, \cdots, b_n$ for inclusion dependencies, and $a \subseteq \{\text{"}k_1\text{"}, \cdots, \text{"}k_n\text{"}\}$ for domain constraints. We will write general dependencies using relational algebra.

Lossless Transformations. Suppose that $I(S)$ and $I(T)$ are the sets of legal database instances (or models) for schemas S and T respectively: following [15, 22] a *schema transformation* from S to T is a total mapping function $f_{S \rightarrow T} : I(S) \rightarrow I(T)$. In order to define a *lossless* transformation, we need to introduce first the notion of schema dominance [15, 22].

Given two schemas S and T, T *dominates* S if there is a total and injective mapping function $f_{S \rightarrow T} : I(S) \rightarrow I(T)$ which maps legal database instances in S to legal database instances in T. Equivalently, we can say that T *dominates* S if there are two mapping functions $f_{S \rightarrow T} : I(S) \rightarrow I(T)$ and $f_{T \rightarrow S} : I(T) \rightarrow I(S)$ exist, such that their composition, $f_{T \rightarrow S} \circ f_{S \rightarrow T}$ (the result of applying $f_{T \rightarrow S}$ after applying $f_{S \rightarrow T}$), is the identity on $I(S)$.

Two schemas S and T are equivalent, written $S \equiv T$, if and only if T dominates S and S dominates T. When two schemas S and T are equivalent, the mappings $f_{S \rightarrow T}$ and $f_{T \rightarrow S}$ are bijective, and we say that both schemas have the same *information capacity* and that the transformation is *lossless*.

In our setting, we consider mappings as first-order *views* establishing the relation between two database schemas. More precisely, given two schemas S and T, a first-order mapping from S to T, written $M_{S \rightarrow T}$, is a set of first-order views $R_T = e_S^{R_T}$ for each predicate R_T of arity n in $\mathbb{A}_T$, with $e_S^{R_T}$ a relational algebra expression of arity n over the alphabet $\mathbb{A}_S$.

In the first-order setting, it can be proved that the definition of equivalence (or lossless transformation) between S and T corresponds to the following condition over the schemas and mappings: $(\mathbb{C}_S \cup M_{S \to T}) \equiv (\mathbb{C}_T \cup M_{T \to S})$, which really means $I(\langle \mathbb{A}_S \cup \mathbb{A}_T, \mathbb{C}_S \cup M_{S \to T} \rangle) = I(\langle \mathbb{A}_S \cup \mathbb{A}_T, \mathbb{C}_T \cup M_{T \to S} \rangle)$; see [23,24].

Transformation Patterns. *Transformation patterns* are crafted templates describing a specific structure of schema transformation with the constraints necessary to ensure its losslessness [2]. The two basic lossless transformation patterns are *vertical decomposition* and *horizontal decomposition*. We introduce them via two basic examples.

Given two schemas S and T as follows:

$$S = \langle \{p(a,b,c)\}, (p.b \to p.c) \} \rangle$$
$$T = \langle \{q(a,b), r(b,c)\}, (r.b \to r.c), (q.b = r.b) \} \rangle$$

The schemas S and T have the same information capacity since there is a lossless transformation through the following mappings – characterising the vertical decomposition in the classical database literature:

$$M_{S \to T} = \{(q = \pi_{ab}\ p), (r = \pi_{bc}\ p)\}$$
$$M_{T \to S} = \{(p = q \bowtie r)\}$$

The vertical decomposition transformation pattern maps a schema with a join dependency (i.e., a key dependency, or a functional dependency, or a multivalued dependency) to its vertical decomposition, with all the appropriate dependencies in both schemas to guarantee losslessness.

As an example of a lossless horizontal decomposition transformation, consider the schema U:

$$U = \langle \{q(a,b), r_1(b,c), r_2(b,c)\}, \{(r_1.b \to r_1.c), (r_2.b \to r_2.c),$$
$$(r_1.c = \{\text{"}k\text{"}\}), (r_2.c \not\subseteq \{\text{"}k\text{"}\}),$$
$$(\pi_b\ q = \pi_b\ r_1 \cup \pi_b\ r_2), (\pi_b\ r_1 \cap \pi_b\ r_2 = \emptyset)\} \rangle$$

The schemas T and U have the same information capacity since there is a lossless transformation through the following mappings – characterising the horizontal decomposition via the condition $\sigma_c = \text{"}k\text{"}\ r$:

$$M_{T \to U} = \{(r_1 = \sigma_{c=\text{"}k\text{"}}\ r), (r_2 = \sigma_{c \neq \text{"}k\text{"}}\ r)\}$$
$$M_{U \to T} = \{(r = r_1 \cup r_2)\}$$

The horizontal decomposition transformation pattern maps a schema to a horizontally decomposed one via a selection condition, with all the appropriate dependencies in both schemas to guarantee losslessness.

We can also observe that also S and U have the same information capacity, since they are related by a sequence of lossless transformations.

A special case of horizontal decomposition is the lossless transformation leading to a SQL NULL-free schema. According to the logic theory of SQL NULL values [10,11], a schema has the same information capacity as an horizontally decomposed one via a NULLABLE condition over some attribute. Whenever there is a NULLABLE constraint over an attribute, a table can be losslessy decomposed into two tables, one having all the attributes but not the NULLABLE one, and the other having all the attributes but with a NOT NULL constraint replacing the NULLABLE constraint.

We have identified several lossless transformation patterns [2, 24], which can be used to design a Semantic SQL Transducer allowing for arbitrary data restructuring processes, whenever we want to guarantee that no information is lost during the restructuring process. The transformation patterns identify the lossless mappings from S to T and from T to S and the constraints of the two databases S and T, needed to design a correctly working Semantic SQL Transducer, as described in Sect. 3.

A very special data restructuring process is the *reverse engineering* process, which looks for the lossless transformation from a source database schema to the schema corresponding to its conceptual schema – see [13] for a survey. This is the scenario we have presented in Sect. 2: we want to expose the source data with a vocabulary that corresponds to its conceptual schema, useful for the business perspective. If the transformation is lossless, we have the guarantee that no information is lost, and that high-level users can query and update freely the transformed database, in this case the database organised in a meaningful structure. More specifically, we want to losslessly transform a source schema into a schema in 6th normal form with explicit *Object Identifiers* (OIDs) to identify "entities", namely instances of entity types. Object identifiers can be implemented by surrogate keys, URIs, or UUIDs. This form is called an Abstract Relational Model (ARM) [6]. We can show that (a) given an arbitrary database schema, there exists a unique *Canonical Abstract Relational Model* (CARM) for that schema, based on the 5th or 6th normal forms, which plays the role of the *Core Conceptual Schema* of the original database, and (b) the CARM schema corresponds to a unique conceptual schema directly expressible in conceptual modelling languages such as ORM, EER, UML class diagrams, or in RDF-based modelling languages.

In order to understand how to losslessly transform a database schema into an equivalent one (the CARM) which includes OIDs, let's consider the following basic example. Assume we have a schema in 5th normal form, so that the only constraints within a table are key constraints, and the constraints across tables are foreign keys or inverse foreign keys, for example:

Employee(ssn,name), works-in(ssn,depname), Department(depname,address)
Employee.ssn → Employee.name
works-in.ssn → Employee.ssn
works-in.depname → Department.depname
Department.depname → Department.address

A domain expert should recognise that Employee and Department are *entity types*, while works-in is a *relationship type*. As a rule of thumb, we can recognise entity types since they should be the target of at least a foreign key with a relationship type as source, while a relationship type should have at least one attribute as the source of a foreign key with an entity type as target. A new attribute with domain OID (disjoint from STRING and INTEGER) is added as a surrogate key to each entity type table, and coherently a new OID attribute replaces the attributes involved in a foreign key path from the entity type. The foreign key and inverse foreign key constraints holding across tables are duplicated to hold between the added OID attributes. Following our example, the lossless transformation of the above schema with added OIDs is:

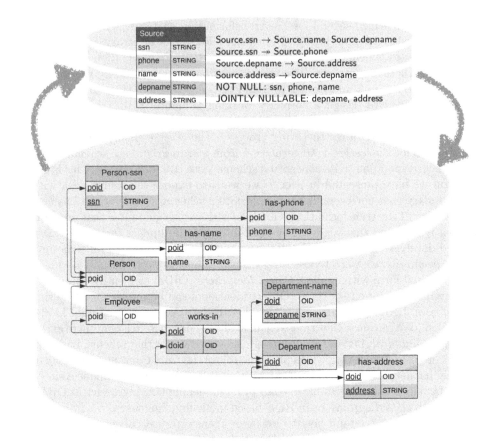

Fig. 3. The Semantic SQL Transducer of the example

Employee(eoid,ssn,name), works-in(eoid,doid), Department(doid,depname,address)
Employee.eoid ⇄ Employee.ssn
Employee.ssn → Employee.name
works-in.eoid → Employee.eoid
works-in.doid → Department.doid
Department.doid ⇄ Department.depname
Department.depname → Department.address

The schema above is the logical representation of the diagrammatic conceptual schema below, expressed here as an Entity-Relationship Diagram:

A Complete Example. Suppose we have a source database schema as described at the top of Fig. 3. The schema is composed by a single table Source and a set of constraints. As humans, we can tell that the schema is about people,

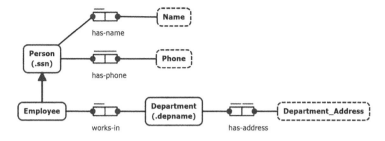

Fig. 4. The conceptual schema of the example (in the ORM notation)

identified by their social security number, having one or more phone numbers, and possibly working in some department, identified by its name, having an address, which also uniquely identifies the department at that address.

Clearly, a lot of the information we just described about this database is hidden in the schema, and we may wonder which could be its explicit conceptual schema to have a more direct understanding of the data. By jumping a little ahead, let's have a glance at the conceptual schema, expressed in the ORM notation, in Fig. 4. That schema describes precisely, non-ambiguously, and formally the data as we were saying above. But how can we get this conceptual schema from the original source schema? First we notice that this conceptual schema has a direct representation as a logical schema in the relational setting: this is described at the bottom of Fig. 3. The relational version of the conceptual schema denotes exactly the same legal databases as the ORM schema of Fig. 4, but now in a pure relational setting. Note that the constraints of this schema are only key constraints and unary inclusion dependencies among OID datatypes – this property holds for all core conceptual schemas derivable from arbitrary source schemas.

The core conceptual schema is obtained by the application of a sequence of lossless transformation patterns, of the type we have briefly introduced in the previous Section. Since any lossless transformation step is accompanied by the mappings in the two directions, we get from the transformation process also the views from the source data to the conceptual data *and* the views from the conceptual data to the source data. In our example, these mappings are shown in Fig. 5. We have devised a methodology driving the design of the correct sequence of lossless transformation patterns leading to a core conceptual schema from a source schema.

So now we have all the ingredients (the two sets of constraints and the two mappings) to finalise the implementation of a Semantic SQL Transducer for the source schema as explained in Sect. 4. Many things can be done once we have the transducer in place. We can understand what the source data is about. We can query the source database with SQL queries using only the core conceptual schema table names, bridging therefore the gap between business models and available data sources. Along these lines, business users can directly update the source data using just the conceptual vocabulary. In the other direction, legacy

$$\text{Person} = \varrho_{[\text{ssn}/\text{poid}]}(\pi_{\text{ssn}}(\text{Source}))$$
$$\text{Person-ssn} = \varrho_{[\text{ssn}_1/\text{poid},\text{ssn}_2/\text{ssn}]}(\sigma_{\text{ssn}_1=\text{ssn}_2}(\pi_{\text{ssn}_1,\text{ssn}_2}(\text{Source} \times \text{Source})))$$
$$\text{has-name} = \varrho_{[\text{ssn}/\text{poid}]}(\pi_{\text{ssn},\text{name}}(\text{Source}))$$
$$\text{has-phone} = \varrho_{[\text{ssn}/\text{poid}]}(\pi_{\text{ssn},\text{phone}}(\text{Source}))$$
$$\text{Employee} = \varrho_{[\text{ssn}/\text{poid}]}(\pi_{\text{ssn}}(\sigma_{\text{depname}}\text{ NOT NULL}\,\text{Source}))$$
$$\text{works-in} = \varrho_{[\text{ssn}/\text{poid}]}(\pi_{\text{ssn},\text{depname}}(\sigma_{\text{depname}}\text{ NOT NULL}\,\text{Source}))$$
$$\text{Department} = \varrho_{[\text{depname}/\text{doid}]}(\pi_{\text{depname}}(\sigma_{\text{depname}}\text{ NOT NULL}\,\text{Source}))$$
$$\text{Department-name} = \varrho_{[\text{depname}_1/\text{doid},\text{depname}_2/\text{depname}]}$$
$$\left(\sigma_{\text{depname}_1=\text{depname}_2}\left(\pi_{\text{depname}_1,\text{depname}_2}\right.\right.$$
$$\left.\left(\left(\sigma_{\text{depname}}\text{ NOT NULL}\,\text{Source}\right) \times \left(\sigma_{\text{depname}}\text{ NOT NULL}\,\text{Source}\right)\right)\right)$$
$$\text{has-address} = \varrho_{[\text{depname}/\text{doid}]}(\pi_{\text{depname},\text{address}}(\sigma_{\text{depname}}\text{ NOT NULL}\,\text{Source}))$$

$$\text{Source} = \pi_{\text{ssn},\text{phone},\text{name},\text{depname},\text{address}}$$
$$\bowtie (\text{Person, Employee, has-phone, has-name,}$$
$$\text{works-in, has-address, Person-ssn, Department-name})$$

Fig. 5. The lossless mappings from source to CARM and viceversa

queries over the source database can be explained by looking at their expansion in terms of the conceptual schema. The Semantic SQL Transducer provides a well-founded semantic layer for data catalogues. Source data structured according its core conceptual schema makes data analysis much more effective, since the correlations, the classifications, and the similarities of the data elements are much more meaningful when done in business terms.

5 Conclusions

We have introduced in this paper a tool to losslessly restructure relational data, allowing for seamless views of the data, which can be queried and updated at both ends maintaining consistency and integrity. A special kind of transformation is when a database is restructured according to its conceptual schema, providing therefore a materialised copy of the data, always in sync with it, using the actual vocabulary understood by the business.

Acknowledgments. This long-standing work has been realised through collaborations and discussions with Nicola Pedot, Nonyelum Ndefo, Francesco Sportelli, Sergio Tessaris, Volha Kerhet, Nhung Ngo, Paolo Guagliardo, David Toman, Grant Weddell, Alex Borgida, Terry Halpin, Jan Hidders, Sebastian Link. The activity has been partly funded by the Confucius project of the Free University of Bozen-Bolzano.

References

1. Abgrall, T.: Formalization of data integration transformations. In: Chiusano, S., et al. (eds.) ADBIS 2022. CCIS, vol. 1652, pp. 615–622. Springer, Cham (2022). https://doi.org/10.1007/978-3-031-15743-1_56
2. Abgrall, T.: Schema decomposition via transformation patterns (2024, submitted)

3. Abgrall, T., Franconi, E., Pedot, N.: Enhancing data management and value creation through a knowledge-centric data stack (2024, submitted)
4. Andersson, M.: Extracting an entity relationship schema from a relational database through reverse engineering. In: Loucopoulos, P. (ed.) ER 1994. LNCS, vol. 881, pp. 403–419. Springer, Heidelberg (1994). https://doi.org/10.1007/3-540-58786-1_93
5. Astrova, I.: Reverse engineering of relational databases to ontologies. In: Bussler, C.J., Davies, J., Fensel, D., Studer, R. (eds.) ESWS 2004. LNCS, vol. 3053, pp. 327–341. Springer, Heidelberg (2004). https://doi.org/10.1007/978-3-540-25956-5_23
6. Borgida, A., Toman, D., Weddell, G.: On referring expressions in information systems derived from conceptual modelling. In: Comyn-Wattiau, I., Tanaka, K., Song, I.-Y., Yamamoto, S., Saeki, M. (eds.) ER 2016. LNCS, vol. 9974, pp. 183–197. Springer, Cham (2016). https://doi.org/10.1007/978-3-319-46397-1_14
7. Calvanese, D., Franconi, E.: First-order ontology mediated database querying via query reformulation. In: Flesca, S., Greco, S., Masciari, E., Saccà, D. (eds.) A Comprehensive Guide Through the Italian Database Research Over the Last 25 Years. SBD, vol. 31, pp. 169–185. Springer, Cham (2018). https://doi.org/10.1007/978-3-319-61893-7_10
8. Chiang, R.H., Barron, T.M., Storey, V.C.: Reverse engineering of relational databases: extraction of an EER model from a relational database. Data Knowl. Eng. **12**(2), 107–142 (1994)
9. Franconi, E., Sattler, U.: A data warehouse conceptual data model for multidimensional aggregation. In: International Workshop on Design and Management of Data Warehouses, DMDW 1999 (1999)
10. Franconi, E., Tessaris, S.: On the logic of SQL nulls. In: 6th Alberto Mendelzon International Workshop on Foundations of Data Management, pp. 114–128. CEUR Workshop Proceedings (2012)
11. Franconi, E., Tessaris, S.: Relational algebra and calculus with SQL null values. CoRR abs/2202.10898 (2022)
12. Hainaut, J.L., Chandelon, M., Tonneau, C., Joris, M.: Contribution to a theory of database reverse engineering. In: 1993 Proceedings Working Conference on Reverse Engineering, pp. 161–170. IEEE (1993)
13. Hainaut, J.L.: Introduction to Database Reverse Engineering. LIBD Lecture Notes (2002)
14. Hainaut, J.-L., Tonneau, C., Joris, M., Chandelon, M.: Schema transformation techniques for database reverse engineering. In: Elmasri, R.A., Kouramajian, V., Thalheim, B. (eds.) 12th International Conference on the Entity-Relationship Approach. ER 1993. LNCS, vol. 823, pp. 364–375. Springer, Heidelberg (1993). https://doi.org/10.1007/BFb0024380
15. Hull, R.: Relative information capacity of simple relational database schemata. SIAM J. Comput. **15**(3), 856–886 (1986)
16. Kobayashi, I.: Losslessness and semantic correctness of database schema transformation: another look of schema equivalence. Inf. Syst. **11**(1), 41–59 (1986)
17. Lammari, N., Comyn-Wattiau, I., Akoka, J.: Extracting generalization hierarchies from relational databases: a reverse engineering approach. Data Knowl. Eng. **63**(2), 568–589 (2007)
18. Lubyte, L., Tessaris, S.: Automatic extraction of ontologies wrapping relational data sources. In: Bhowmick, S.S., Küng, J., Wagner, R. (eds.) DEXA 2009. LNCS, vol. 5690, pp. 128–142. Springer, Heidelberg (2009). https://doi.org/10.1007/978-3-642-03573-9_10

19. Ma, W., Keet, C.M., Oldford, W., Toman, D., Weddell, G.: The utility of the abstract relational model and attribute paths in SQL. In: Faron Zucker, C., Ghidini, C., Napoli, A., Toussaint, Y. (eds.) EKAW 2018. LNCS (LNAI), vol. 11313, pp. 195–211. Springer, Cham (2018). https://doi.org/10.1007/978-3-030-03667-6_13

20. McBrien, P., Poulovassilis, A.: Data integration by bi-directional schema transformation rules. In: Proceedings 19th International Conference on Data Engineering (ICDE-03), pp. 227–238 (2003)

21. Mian, N.A., Khan, S.A., Zafar, N.A.: Database reverse engineering methods: what is missing? Res. J. Recent Sci. **2**(5), 49–58 (2013)

22. Miller, R.J., Ioannidis, Y.E., Ramakrishnan, R.: The use of information capacity in schema integration and translation. In: 19th International Conference on Very Large Data Bases (VLDB-1993), pp. 120–133 (1993)

23. Ndefo, N., Franconi, E.: On preserving information in schema transformations: a constructive perspective. In: 2nd IEEE International Conference on Artificial Intelligence and Knowledge Engineering, AIKE 2019, pp. 57–64 (2019)

24. Ndefo, N., Franconi, E.: A study on information-preserving schema transformations. Int. J. Semant. Comput. **14**(1), 27–53 (2020)

25. Poulovassilis, A., McBrien, P.: A general formal framework for schema transformation. Data Knowl. Eng. **28**(1), 47–71 (1998)

26. Qian, X.: Correct schema transformations. In: Apers, P., Bouzeghoub, M., Gardarin, G. (eds.) EDBT 1996. LNCS, vol. 1057, pp. 114–128. Springer, Heidelberg (1996). https://doi.org/10.1007/BFb0014146

27. Soutou, C.: Relational database reverse engineering: algorithms to extract cardinality constraints. Data Knowl. Eng. **28**(2), 161–207 (1998)

Enhancing Complex Linguistic Tasks Resolution Through Fine-Tuning LLMs, RAG and Knowledge Graphs (Short Paper)

Filippo Bianchini[ID], Marco Calamo[ID], Francesca De Luzi[(✉)][ID],
Mattia Macrì[ID], and Massimo Mecella[(✉)][ID]

Dipartimento Ingegneria informatica, automatica e gestionale Antonio Ruberti,
Sapienza Università di Roma, Rome, Italy
{bianchini,calamo,deluzi,macri,mecella}@diag.uniroma1.it

Abstract. Given the synergy between Large Language Models (LLMs) and Knowledge Graphs (KGs), we introduce a pipeline to tackle complex linguistic tasks, which we are experimenting in the legal domain. While LLMs offer unprecedented generative capabilities, their reliance on sub-symbolic processing can lead to fallacious outcomes. Our methodology introduces an advanced Retrieval Augmented Generation (RAG) pipeline, enriched with two KGs and optimized LLMs, promising to enhance the resolution of complex linguistic tasks. Through KG construction based on prompt engineering techniques and iterative fine-tuning, we transcend the limitations of conventional LLMs.

Keywords: Large Language Models · Knowledge Graphs · Complex linguistic tasks

1 Introduction

Potential applications of Artificial Intelligence (AI) in the judicial field pose several challenges, such as extracting information from legacy information systems and analyzing legal documents [2]. Modern information systems increasingly rely on AI to support automated procedures emphasizing new methods to assist specific legal user categories. In this context, the development of knowledge guided by *sub-symbolic* approaches is undergoing an unprecedented transformation with recent large-scale LLMs. These models acquire knowledge from raw data, solving tasks like recognizing words or faces in images and showcasing remarkable flexibility in task performance. However, despite the promises they offer, carrying out complex tasks through the exclusive use of the aforementioned approaches still presents plentiful challenges, as well as results that tend to be unsatisfactory. The fundamental differences between symbolic and sub-symbolic approaches have not

J. P. A. Almeida et al. (Eds.): CAiSE 2024 Workshops, LNBIP 521, pp. 147–155, 2024.
https://doi.org/10.1007/978-3-031-61003-5_13

restrained recent literature, which increasingly demonstrates an effective connection between them through the exploration of intermediate methods [12]. This article follows this research direction, proposing an intermediate methodology that leverages symbolic approaches through the integration of KGs above sub-symbolic approaches using LLMs.

We define a *complex linguistic task* as a linguistic task that requires specific domain information and knowledge and reasoning abilities to be correctly fulfilled. The linguistic task's complexity increases in domains such as legal, where a merely sub-symbolic approach could give rise to logical errors like the *post hoc*[1] fallacy. The post hoc fallacy, rooted in the assumption that temporal succession implies causation, draws a striking parallel to the behavior of LLMs. Similar to how the fallacy confuses temporal sequence with causal connection, LLMs often fail to discern causality from correlation. Indeed, the post hoc fallacy neglects other factors that help to exclude the relationship. Thus the LLM can draw seemingly valid conclusions, neglecting crucial contextual information. There is therefore a clear need for nuanced approaches to reasoning and inference in artificial intelligence systems. In the legal domain, understanding *reply memorandum*[2] is a complex task. They must detail the "reconstruction of legal facts", but grasping the logical or temporal sequence can be challenging. For example, a sentence like "the appeal was previously rejected, therefore the court's decision was erroneous" might lead to misinterpretation by LLMs. They may infer causation where none exists, highlighting the challenge of avoiding logical fallacies without full context comprehension.

An essential requirement for solving complex linguistic tasks involves the continuous refinement of domain knowledge. Moreover, establishing causal connections among domain information would empower LLMs to yield better outputs, both in terms of response accuracy and in terms of the lexicon used for its generation. Already proficient in generating coherent and high-quality outputs, LLMs benefit greatly from *prompt engineering*. Indeed, an effective prompt formulation is increasingly essential for achieving good outcomes. However, adopting a prompt engineering strategy does not eliminate the possibility that the model may suffer from so-called *hallucinations*, which are inevitable and independent of the model architecture, learning algorithms, prompting techniques, or training data [27]. The first step in this direction is document retrieval to provide relevant information through RAG. However, an additional step is needed to meet the aforementioned requirements, namely to seek the integration of a structured knowledge representation through KGs. As shown in Table 1, with the first step we can improve the coherence of the output, while with an additional effort, we ensure the domain knowledge retrieval. Ultimately, to achieve effective improvement in generation, it's necessary to specialize the LLM with a

---

[1] **Post hoc ergo propter hoc** (Latin: 'after this, therefore because of this') is a logical fallacy in which one event seems to be the cause of a later event because it occurred earlier. It is often shortened simply to **post hoc fallacy**.

[2] A reply memorandum is a legal document responding to arguments presented by the opposing party.

fine-tuning process that customizes it to solve complex tasks. Therefore, in this paper, we propose a pipeline to improve the effectiveness of results in contexts requiring reasoning abilities, such as legal ones, by combining document retrieval, knowledge integration through KGs, and the development of specialized LLMs through a well-defined pipeline.

The rest of the paper is organized as follows. In Sect. 2 we discuss the related work on integrating symbolic and sub-symbolic approaches. Section 3 outlines our pipeline, merging KGs with LLMs and RAG techniques to enhance the coherence and accuracy of generated responses. In Sect. 4 we explores future research and implications of our approach in advancing AI within the judicial domain.

Table 1. Research directions to enable *complex linguistic tasks* resolution.

Direction	Coherence	Knowledge Retrieval	Complex Tasks
LLMs	X	X	X
LLMs & RAG	✓	X	X
LLMs & RAG & KG	✓	✓	X
Specialized LLMs & RAG & KG	✓	✓	✓

2   Related Work

Large Language Models with RAG. LLMs, such as GPT-4 [20] or LLama2 [23], represent a transformative advancement in NLP. However, the intricate nature of LLMs may occasionally result in hallucinatory outputs [28], prompting the proposal of various mitigation techniques [22]. To address this challenge and enhance the credibility of content, RAG techniques have been introduced [14]. RAG integrates retrieval mechanisms with generative models, allowing LLMs to access and incorporate external knowledge sources during text generation [8]. By leveraging RAG, AI systems produce outputs grounded in factual information retrieved from external and heterogeneous sources [30], thus mitigating concerns regarding the reliability of LLM-generated content.

KGs Construction with LLM Prompting. According to [10], a KG is a *graph of data intended to accumulate and convey knowledge of the real world, whose nodes represent entities of interest and whose edges represent potentially different relations between these entities.* On the other hand, mastering prompt engineering has become essential for adeptly communicating and interacting with advanced AI models [18,19]. This practice involves crafting precise input queries, known as *prompts*, to effectively harness LLMs. Recent studies have investigated methods for constructing KGs using LLM [25] or prompt engineering techniques [4,7,21]. These approaches leverage the generative capabilities of LLMs to automate KG construction tasks, reducing the need for manual curation [31].

RAG with KGs. By combining the generative power of LLMs with the knowledge retrieval mechanisms of RAG and the structured information representation of KGs, researchers aim to develop comprehensive methodologies for addressing complex linguistic challenges [11,29]. One of the early examples is KGLM [17]. It retrieves facts from a knowledge graph based on the current context to generate factual sentences. REALM [9] introduces an innovative knowledge retriever to aid the model in retrieving and attending to documents from a vast corpus during the pre-training phase, resulting in significant performance enhancements for open-domain QA. Furthermore, [16] proposes a collaborative training-free reasoning scheme that involves LLMs iteratively exploring KGs and selectively retrieving task-relevant knowledge subgraphs to support reasoning, while [33] integrates LLM-driven RAG to enhance multimodal EHR[3] representations, extracting task-relevant medical entities from a KG (PrimeKG) and integrating them with EHR data, yielding superior clinical predictive performance on MIMIC-III dataset[4]. [1] presents a methodology for guiding the fine-tuning of LLMs through ontological reasoning on Enterprise Knowledge Graphs (EKGs) to augment their effectiveness in financial contexts.

3   Proposed Pipeline

While LLMs demonstrate excellent results in executing general linguistic tasks, there is still room for improvement in tasks that require specific domain knowledge and reasoning capabilities. It has been acknowledged [24] that LLMs still exhibit certain limitations in coherence and reasoning. In this paper, we outlined a pipeline that we envision to implement in the next works. Our pipeline aims to enhance the Large Language Models' performance in complex linguistic tasks by introducing an improved RAG pipeline that integrates various elements. The enhanced RAG pipeline builds upon the generic one by incorporating support from two different KGs and a fine-tuned LLM.

3.1   Enhancing LLMs with RAG and KGs

Our research aims to enable LLMs to solve complex language tasks through the support of RAGs and KGs. RAG enhances LLMs by integrating knowledge retrieved from external sources during text generation, thereby improving accuracy and relevance. However, RAG still encounters limitations in real-world applications when it comes to linguistic complex tasks. Among the challenges that RAG presents are: *(i)* retrieving the necessary information to complete the task and *(ii)* ensuring compliance of the output with the request and domain rules. To address these challenges we will introduce, in the generic RAG architecture the *Domain-specific KG* and the *Constraints KG*, a conceptual Knowledge Graph. Figure 1 shows where the two KGs are introduced in the generic RAG architecture.

---

[3] Electronic Health Record.

[4] The Medical Information Mart for Intensive Care III.

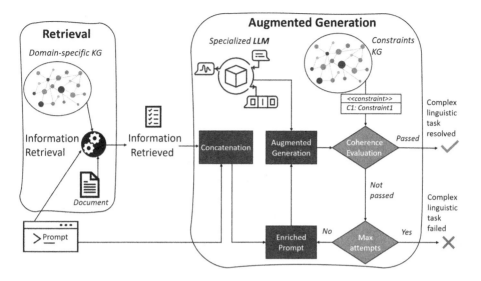

Fig. 1. Pipeline

Domain-Specific Knowledge Graph. In the retrieval phase, *Domain-specific KG* allows to handle limitation *(i)*. Modern RAG paradigms [8] are already capable of using LLMs to query a KG to solve conventional graph tasks. However, the community has not yet identified definitive implementation solutions for applying KG in the information retrieval process for certain pieces of information [27].

Certain types of information may be stored only in structured data rather than unstructured ones, hence in our architecture the Domain-specific KGs is used in synergy with unstructured documents to improve the RAG information retrieval process. The combination of unstructured documents and Domain-specific KG for the information retrieval provides contextual information relevant to the complex linguistic task and domain-specific knowledge to fulfill it.

A Domain-specific KG is built from specific instances of domain documents. In our application domain, we intend to perform complex linguistic tasks such as *drafting or analyzing citation acts*; therefore, the related Domain-specific KG will be built by extracting information from instances of citation acts. A KG is extracted for each domain document, and the extracted KGs are automatically merged into the final Domain-specific KG. Each KG of a domain document will contain information from the simplest to be individuated to logical relationships and consecutio. Regarding the citation acts example[5]:

- Identifications of the petitioner, the accused, and the representing lawyers;
- Subject of the citation act;
- Description of the legal fact;
- Presentation of juridical elements;

---

[5] Note that the list is not exhaustive of all the elements that will be extracted but is purely for example purposes.

- List of mentioned laws and the reason why each law was mentioned;
- Connection between the legal fact and the damage caused to the petitioner.

The final Domain-specific KG will be built by automatically establishing connections between similar nodes from different KGs. For instance, it may link two citation acts with similar legal facts or two citation acts mentioning the same laws for identical reasons. Constructing the Domain-specific KG requires minimal human supervision to validate its accuracy.

Constraints Knowledge Graph. Regarding limitation *(ii)*, we use the *Constraints KG*. In the standard RAG procedure, once the enriched prompt is created, it's given to the LLM as input for generating a response. However, the accuracy or relevance of the response is not assessed using external tools. In cases of complex language tasks, generating the expected response may not be straightforward. That's why the Constraints KG is used to check iteratively the correctness of the final output. In our proposed architecture, in the augmented generation phase, the specialized LLM generates a proposed output based on the enriched prompt. This output then undergoes an automatic sanity check using the Constraints KG. To achieve this, the output is parsed and validated over reasoning on the Constraints KG, using the methodologies suggested by [13,32]. If the output shows any fallacy or does not comply with the structure described in the Constraints KG, the previous enriched prompt is refined by incorporating the violated constraints at its end, and a new proposed output is generated. If the maximum number of retries is reached, the task is considered failed. If the Coherence Evaluation part is satisfied, the *final* output will be shown to the user.

The Constraints KG contains all the semantics necessary – both from the domain point of view and the task – to validate a domain complex linguistic task's generation. In the context of the *drafting citation acts* application, for instance, a Constraints KG should encompass legal administrative information and knowledge (which extends beyond citation acts) to draft well-structured citation acts and also provide guidance on performing the task correctly. For example, the Constraints KG should include information such as:

- the mandatory elements required in each type of citation act, such as "the subject of the citation act must be written at the beginning of the document and separately from the description of the facts";
- summarized content of the laws in the Italian Code of Administrative Procedure, enabling verification of whether a law has been cited appropriately in the draft citation act such as "article 21 of the Italian Code of Administrative Procedure discusses the timeframe for issuing administrative decisions";
- the indications to follow for drafting citation acts correctly, such as "to ensure accuracy in domain-specific document writing, it is essential to employ the most fitting lexical terms available".

The generation of the Constraints KG can be partially automated, but some specific parts still require an expert in the field, and heavy human supervision is necessary in any case for validation.

3.2   KGs Construction via Prompt Engineering

Our methodology involves the construction of ad-hoc KGs from unstructured textual data. However, standard tools for automatically extracting relations are not suitable for our needs because we require extracting highly specific domain-related information, as well as logical and structural relationships. Given that state-of-the-art LLMs are showing promising results in Information Extraction [15], especially with prompt engineering approaches for zero-shot and few-shot scenarios [5,26], we have decided to develop tailored prompting methods to extract RDF relations from unstructured textual documents. To validate these methods, we plan to conduct a human evaluation involving experts in the domain in which our research focuses. Once we have created, validated, and applied these new prompting methods in our research domain, we anticipate they can be broadly applied across different domains.

3.3   Guide Complex Tasks Resolution via Fine-Tuning

Fine-tuning involves retraining some parameters of a pre-trained LLM using a dataset containing domain-specific text. We plan to implement a two-step fine-tuning process for a selected base LLM:

1. **To learn the specific lexicon.** Learning specific vocabulary through fine-tuning requires a corpus of domain documents from which to extract domain-specific phrases. These domain documents can be automatically preprocessed and used to construct the dataset. For this type of fine-tuning, domain experts' supervision is not needed;
2. **To enable the LLM to leverage the information contained in the enriched prompt.** Compared to the previous fine-tuning process, this one presents a more complex challenge. We will need to construct an instructional dataset that enables the pre-trained LLM to learn how to perform complex linguistic tasks based on the retrieved information. In this case, the creation and validation process will be conducted collaboratively with the research's domain experts.

For both fine-tunings, we will follow the pipeline developed in [6] and validate results through a two-step evaluation process [3]. Both works were made by our research group, and the domain application is still Italian juridical, hence both the pipeline and the evaluation process will be easily reused in this research.

4   Conclusions and Future Work

In this paper, we envision a new pipeline for resolving complex linguistic tasks by enhancing the generic RAG pipeline with KGs. We have shown how to build Domain-specific KGs exploiting prompt engineering from documents with limited human supervision. We proposed a high-level architecture that takes advantage of the reasoning and fact-checking capabilities of KGs to produce accurate results from specialized LLM. We are currently working on implementing our methodology in an Italian legal field, exploring with human experts how far we can push the complexity of the LLM's generated output without compromising on the quality of the results from a professional standpoint.

Acknowledgements. The work of Mattia Macrì has been supported by the PhD fellowship Pubblica Amministrazione DM118 - CUP B83C22003460006. The work of Marco Calamo and Filippo Bianchini has been supported by the Next-Generation EU (Italian PNRR - M4 C2, Invest 1.3 - D.D. 1551.11-10-2022), named PE4 - MICS (Made in Italy - Circular and Sustainable).

References

1. Baldazzi, T., Bellomarini, L., Ceri, S., Colombo, A., Gentili, A., Sallinger, E.: Fine-tuning large language models for financial markets via ontological reasoning. Technical report, Bank of Italy, Directorate General for Markets and Payment System (2024)
2. Bianchini, D., Ceri, S., De Luzi, F., Mecella, M., Pernici, B., et al.: Challenges in AI-supported process analysis in the Italian judicial system: what after digitalization? Digit. Govern.: Res. Pract. **5**, 1–10 (2024)
3. Calamo, M., De Luzi, F., Macrì, M., Mencattini, T., Mecella, M.: CICERO: a GPT2-based writing assistant to investigate the effectiveness of specialized LLMs' applications in e-justice. Front. Artif. Intell. Appl. (2023)
4. Carta, S., Giuliani, A., Piano, L.: Iterative zero-shot LLM prompting for knowledge graph construction. arXiv preprint arXiv:2307.01128 (2023)
5. Catalano, N., Matteucci, M.: Few shot semantic segmentation: a review of methodologies and open challenges. arXiv preprint arXiv:2304.05832 (2023)
6. De Luzi, F., Macrì, M., Mecella, M., Mencattini, T.: Cicero: an AI-based writing assistant for legal users. In: Cabanillas, C., Pérez, F. (eds.) CAiSE 2023. LNBIP, vol. 477, pp. 103–111. Springer, Cham (2023). https://doi.org/10.1007/978-3-031-34674-3_13
7. Fang, Y., Zhang, Q.: Knowledge graph-enhanced molecular contrastive learning with functional prompt. Nat. Mach. Intell. 1–12 (2023)
8. Gao, Y., et al.: Retrieval-augmented generation for large language models: a survey (2024)
9. Guu, K., Lee, K., Tung, Z., Pasupat, P., Chang, M.W.: REALM: retrieval-augmented language model pre-training (2020)
10. Hogan, A., Blomqvist, E.: Knowledge graphs. ACM Comput. Surv. (CSUR) **54**(4), 1–37 (2021)
11. Hu, L., Liu, Z., Zhao, Z., Hou, L., Nie, L., Li, J.: A survey of knowledge enhanced pre-trained language models (2023)
12. Ilkou, E., Koutraki, M.: Symbolic vs sub-symbolic AI methods: friends or enemies? In: Proceedings of the CIKM 2020 Workshops Co-located with 29th ACM International Conference on Information and Knowledge Management (CIKM 2020). CEUR Workshop Proceedings, vol. 2699. CEUR-WS.org (2020)
13. Kim, J., Park, S., Kwon, Y., Jo, Y., Thorne, J., Choi, E.: FactKG: fact verification via reasoning on knowledge graphs. arXiv preprint arXiv:2305.06590 (2023)
14. Lewis, P., Perez, E.: Retrieval-augmented generation for knowledge-intensive NLP tasks. Adv. Neural. Inf. Process. Syst. **33**, 9459–9474 (2020)

15. Li, B., Fang, G.: Evaluating ChatGPT's information extraction capabilities: an assessment of performance, explainability, calibration, and faithfulness. arXiv preprint arXiv:2304.11633 (2023)
16. Li, Y., Zhang, R..: An enhanced prompt-based LLM reasoning scheme via knowledge graph-integrated collaboration. arXiv preprint arXiv:2402.04978 (2024)
17. Logan, R., Nelson, L., Peters, M.: Barack's wife hillary: using knowledge graphs for fact-aware language modeling. In: Proceedings of the 57th Conference of the Association for Computational Linguistics, ACL 2019, pp. 5962–5971 (2019)
18. Marvin, G., Hellen, N.: Prompt engineering in large language models. In: Data Intelligence and Cognitive Informatics, pp. 387–402 (2024)
19. Narayanan, N.: The era of generative AI: transforming academic libraries, education, and research, pp. 282–293. St. Agnes College, Mangaluru (2024)
20. OpenAI: GPT-4 technical report (2023)
21. Tianyi, L., Nikos, P.: Task-specific pre-training and prompt decomposition for knowledge graph population with language models (2022)
22. Tonmoy, S.M.T.I., Zaman, S.M.M., Jain, V.: A comprehensive survey of hallucination mitigation techniques in large language models (2024)
23. Touvron, H., et al.: Llama 2: open foundation and fine-tuned chat models (2023)
24. Valmeekam, K., Olmo, A., Sreedharan, S., Kambhampati, S.: Large language models still can't plan (a benchmark for LLMs on planning and reasoning about change). arXiv preprint arXiv:2206.10498 (2022)
25. Wang, C., Liu, X., Song, D.: Language models are open knowledge graphs (2020)
26. Wei, X., Cui, X., Cheng, N.: Zero-shot information extraction via chatting with ChatGPT. arXiv preprint arXiv:2302.10205 (2023)
27. Xu, Z., Jain, S., Kankanhalli, M.: Hallucination is inevitable: an innate limitation of large language models. arXiv preprint arXiv:2401.11817 (2024)
28. Yao, J.Y., Ning, K.P., Liu, Z.H., Ning, M.N., Yuan, L.: LLM lies: hallucinations are not bugs, but features as adversarial examples (2023)
29. Yin, D., Dong, L., Cheng, H., Liu, X., Chang, K.W., Wei, F., Gao, J.: A survey of knowledge-intensive NLP with pre-trained language models (2022)
30. Yu, W.: Retrieval-augmented generation across heterogeneous knowledge. In: Proceedings of the 2022 Conference of the North American Chapter of the Association for Computational Linguistics: Human Language Technologies: Student Research Workshop (2022)
31. Zhong, L., Wu, J., Li, Q., Peng, H., Wu, X.: A comprehensive survey on automatic knowledge graph construction. arXiv preprint arXiv:2302.05019 (2023)
32. Zhou, J., Han, X.: GEAR: graph-based evidence aggregating and reasoning for fact verification. In: Proceedings of the 57th Annual Meeting of the Association for Computational Linguistics, pp. 892–901 (2019)
33. Zhu, Y., Ren, C., Xie, S., Liu, S.: REALM: RAG-driven enhancement of multimodal electronic health records analysis via large language models (2024)

Improving the Service Quality in Fitness Industry by Using a Knowledge Graph Based Modeling Toolkit

Vasile Ionut Remus Iga🆔 and Ana-Maria Ghiran$^{(\boxtimes)}$ 🆔

Babeş-Bolyai University, Cluj-Napoca, Romania
anamaria.ghiran@econ.ubbcluj.ro

Abstract. In recent years, the vibrant growth in the fitness industry sector generated a significant increase in the number of available services, such as personal trainers or online training programs, or facilities, like indoor or outdoor gyms. However, the lack of an overview of all provided services and their contribution to the business' profit translates into an inability in managing the effectiveness of the business and identifying the reasons why clients are giving up on them after a relatively short period. To overcome this, we designed a modeling toolkit for the fitness industry using the ADOxx fast prototyping platform, to assess the quality of the delivered services, evaluate risks and seek automation possibilities enabled by a knowledge graph that backs up the visual representations. The toolkit can be used by the managers of fitness facilities to obtain a perceived service quality from the customers' perspective. Capturing the customers' perceptions is more likely to improve the service creation for fitness and sport activities.

Keywords: Conceptual modeling · service quality · fitness · design thinking

1 Introduction

As people began to understand the benefits of sport activities and the need of them for a good health, so the business initiatives for setting up fitness centers or gym studios were gradually growing. Nowadays, the fitness industry is facing an increased competitive environment. Various alternatives can be encountered: from physical gym studios, online training platforms and applications, home workout options to other outdoor activities that exceed each other. Considering this abundance of choices, the customers for fitness services are now more demanding and meeting their expectations becomes a challenge.

There is an intensified need to capture the preferences of the customers in order to deliver a service that transforms a customer into a loyal one (i.e. retain the existing customers) or attract new ones. Especially in sport and fitness industry a customer represents, most of the time, a membership in admission or subscription based services and memberships are very important as they generate advance revenue and can provide a certain stability regarding income forecasts for the organization.

Many studies show there is a relationship between service quality and the customer satisfaction and their loyalty [1–3]. Consequently, the focus of organizations has shifted

J. P. A. Almeida et al. (Eds.): CAiSE 2024 Workshops, LNBIP 521, pp. 156–167, 2024.
https://doi.org/10.1007/978-3-031-61003-5_14

from creating brands to building customer relationships and creating compelling customer experiences [4]. Positive customer experience is a better way to become noticeable among the other brands than other traditional marketing efforts. This is a key principle in *inbound marketing campaigns*, which are attracting potential customers through targeted campaigns rather than relying on mass advertising, as it is the case with *outbound marketing* [5].

By leveraging modeling tools, marketers can acquire awareness of the effectiveness of their campaigns during all customers lifecycle stages. In these cases, marketers are capturing in diagrammatic views the stages their customers undergo through. There are studies that considered developing domain specific modeling methods to obtain a description of the customers' journeys. However, they are limited in regarding the analysis capabilities as they do not include a reasoning engine.

This paper explores the possibilities of capturing the customers' preferences of a fitness center by using a modeling based approach. Conceptual models transcend mere visual representations as they can assist the modeler in analysis and spur creativity in the design phase. This is enabled by the underlying meaningful structure that can be extracted from the models. Our conceptual models translate into a graph representation – each element in the model is a node and the connections between them serve as pathways for in-depth analysis. By organizing information in a graph structure, it becomes easier to identify how different pieces of information relate to each other or identify hidden relationships.

The remainder of the paper is structured as follows: Sect. 2 presents some key benefits of using modeling tools in designing innovative scenarios that business executives and marketing teams can employ before an actual implementation. The stress is on showcasing how modeling tools can enhance creativity in the service design phase. Then in Sect. 3, based on the problem description, we introduce our approach taking a systematic method. Last section concludes the paper.

2   Storytelling with Modeling Tools

Using a modeling tool, we can evaluate multiple scenarios regarding the delivered business value by comparing which of the personalized experiences are more appealing to a specific target audience. Moreover, models conceived with modern modeling tools are not anymore simple drawings but are powerful means to capture a representation of the envisioned scenario in a digital format. In this way, models enable their externalization towards other actors that did not participate in identifying the business solution. Furthermore, they can provide an integration with other parts or components of the enterprise system given by the possibility to capture various semantic expressivity in the designed innovation artefact. Nevertheless, analyzing and reasoning capabilities are enabled if conceptual models are stored on a graph based structure besides the visual representation.

Our modelling toolkit introduces the possibility of designing storyboards about fitness gyms that, supplementary to traditional services, aim to include technology in their environment to support various activities, from personized training programs to automated methods for accessing the center's resources (e.g. pass cards). Combining products and multiple services into a bundle is considered a distinguished offer that companies can provide to increase their advantage over competitors [6]. In some industries like the travel industry for instance, bundling is common and well known and was perceived as a value-add practice to satisfy complex customer needs that otherwise cannot be met by just one service. Therefore, we assume that the modern fitness center embraces technology and we can model smart devices like wearable devices or tracking apps which are indispensable to cater the demands in the current context. Research regarding the integration of wearable fitness technology by health and fitness clubs [7] reports that technology innovations provide opportunities "to further engage with customers beyond the physical confines of the service environment".

The designing of various bundle services for the fitness gym stored as storyboards is valuable as they enable an easy comparison of various scenarios. Knowledge graphs play a crucial role in supporting the analysis of storyboards. For instance, one can explore scenarios like changing equipment layout, modifying trainer schedules or introducing new fitness classes to analyze their impact on member engagement and overall gym performance.

Our modeling toolkit offers personalized concepts, including customer and trainer characters, smart or standard gym equipment and membership cards, training or nutritional plans, gym-related places, or even some abstract concepts like motivation that can be attached to customers. With the help of the mentioned concepts, one can describe business processes that include customers who want to keep in shape, lose weight, or fulfill medical advice. Products and services may be outlined, such as personalized or assisted training sessions, monitored sessions via a mobile application, nutritional plans designed for each individual, and smart gym access using different technologies, QR codes, cards, or the app itself.

3   Research Problem

The overall research can be position according to the Design Science methodological frame [8] which considers the proposal of new artifacts in context. We formulate the problem statement by framing our proposal within the Design Science Research template [8]:

> *Improve* **the service experience in the fitness industry currently facing an increase in the competition from various other service experience providers** *(including technology solutions designed for individual use like wrist based wearable devices) (problem context)*
>
> *... by treating it with* **a knowledge graph based modeling method customised to the domain of fitness industry** *(artifact)*
>
> *... to satisfy* **the need for analyzing various scenarios identified during the innovation sessions/workshops** *(requirements)*
>
> *... in order to* **enable managers to come up with the right innovative solutions for service experience to gain or retain customers and thus reaching business goals** *(goals).*

In order to capture various customer centric business offers, we need a structured approach that will guarantee that the problem under study is analyzed from all the possible perspectives. 6W is an approach that asks questions like What, Why, Where, Who, When, Which to cover all possible angles of a problem. The initial methodology was called 5W and 1 H (What, Why, When, Where, Who and How) and it originated in a poem written by Rudyard Kipling. 5W1H might be more popular than its successor being used mainly by journalists in interviewing and creating information threads [9]. It applies a stepwise interrogation that helps in breaking the problem into manageable pieces and identifying as much as possible about the application domain.

Although knowing as much as possible about the domain and about the multiple stakeholders can help in business initiatives, being innovative and finding the right balance between meeting users' needs and the goals of the business owners is regarded as a "wicked problem" [10] and it often requires a unique solution in a given environment.

That is, the next step in tackling the problem is to apply *design thinking*, which employs different methods to design the solution or components of the innovative idea. Such methods are presented in [11] and most of them are applied in workshops, making use of sticky notes, flipcharts, paper figures, etc. Presenting the scenario in such working groups and discussing about the idea can foster the creativity among the participants and can lead in generating an innovative artefact [11].

However, until recently, exchanging knowledge with shareholders that did not participate in the workshop about the resulted artefact had limited support, using pictures of the scenes accompanied by optional textual explanations.

Scene2Model [12] has been proposed as an alternative to capture the created artefacts as digital models. Although the modeling tool employs a domain specific modeling language that includes concepts from SAP Scenes [13], it still maintains a general point of view and does not focus on a specific area of activity.

Applying Scene2Model for the fitness industry requires other adaptations regarding the concepts included in the modeling language to better grasp the particularities of the domain. Furthermore, it should enable a semantic description of the proposed business innovation idea by attaching various properties and relationships to the concepts in the models. In the same time, having this digital representation of the proposed business scenario, it will provide an integration opportunity with other digital components representing the actual enterprise and operational contexts.

In this paper, we present the customizations of classes from the Scene2Model modeling method [12]. For this, we employ ADOxx [14], which is a metamodeling platform that enables adaptation of a modeling method to serve a certain purpose through a metamodeling approach. Based on the defined metamodel, the platform generates a modeling tool that accommodates any changes made to the modeling language or include any new defined concepts.

In the following, we describe the changes added to the Scene2Model modeling method. We grouped them into the dimensions of the 6W (Who, What, Why, Where, When, How) excluding the Time dimension which was not customized.

3.1 Who

The Who dimension highlights the actors involved in a business process. Usually, these actors can be understood as the stakeholders that have an interest in the described process (in our case, the employees and customers of the fitness clubs).

To better represent the actors taking part in fitness industry processes, we designed two new concepts to the Character concept, namely Customer and Trainer. Both concepts have two visual choices, man and woman. The Trainer has an additional attribute that refers to the list of possible clients, where Customer instances may be added. Both of them (Customers and Trainers) are used with two personalized relationships, *owns* and *trainOn*. The first one connects a Character to an owned Device, such as their personal phone or smartwatch, while the second one points to the gym equipment used for training (the gym equipment is another example of a concept created for extending the Scene2Model tool, which is described in the next section, the "What" dimension).

In Fig. 1, examples of the mentioned concepts and relationships are shown; *owns* relationship is depicted in yellow, while *trainOn* is in green.

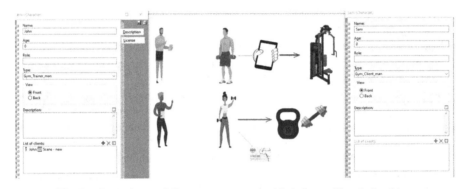

Fig. 1. The Trainer and Customer concepts, with their specific relationships.

As we already mentioned, our tool benefits from the exploration of the graph structure that can be extracted from the models. The mapping between diagrammatic models and RDF graph structures has been described in [15], while in [16] transformation patterns intended to provide guidance for implementations were presented.

Figure 2 exemplifies the conversion mechanism from diagrammatic models to RDF, (sample of the triples that are generated from visual models).

To evaluate the utility of our graph based modeling method we formulate a sample of competency questions [17]. Competency questions are considered a powerful way to assess if an ontology is an appropriate representation for a domain [17]. Usually, ontology engineers use them as semantic queries or reasoning obtained from a set of requirements or inquiries over the specific domain and applied to its formalization in order to check the correct and complete representation. This approach is likewise applicable to our exported content from diagram-to-RDF, allowing for the evaluation of results generated by knowledge-driven systems.

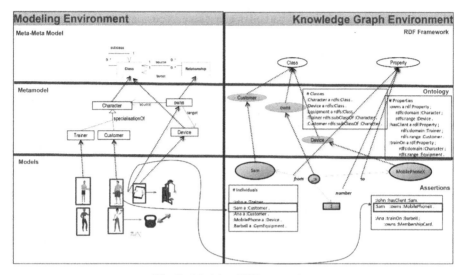

Fig. 2. Model to RDF conversion

Competency Question 1: *Count the number of clients assigned on each trainer. This can be used to evaluate whether an equilibrium is maintained on the workload for each employee.* Prefix declarations have been omitted.

```
SELECT ?trainer (COUNT(DISTINCT ?client) AS ?clientCount)
    WHERE {
        ?trainer a :Trainer .
        ?trainer :hasClient ?client .
    }
    GROUP BY ?trainer
```

Competency Question 2: *Count the number of the customers that belong to a certain age group. Here we used 2 groups: people below 45 are considered young while those above are considered old.*

```
SELECT ?ageGroup (COUNT(?client) AS ?clientCount)
WHERE {
    ?client a :Customer.
    ?client :age ?age .
    BIND( IF (?age < 45, "Young", "Old") AS ?ageGroup)
}
GROUP BY ?ageGroup
```

3.2   What

The What dimension focuses on things that are required throughout the execution of a process, whether they are artifacts, assets, or documents. They help accomplish a desired task (e.g. in SAP Scenes these are represented as Accessories and Devices).

In our case, to adapt the concepts to the fitness industry, we added two concepts: Equipment and Membership Card. The Equipment is attached to the Accessory concept, with two possible visual choices: a barbell or a machine. A custom relationship, *connectedTo* was created in order to link a Device to an Equipment, to capture the connection between a device, for example, a smartphone, with physical equipment, to control its behavior and store statistics about the training session. The Membership Card emulates the physical or online subscription a customer must have to access the services of a gym. It has two attributes, its type (bronze, silver, or gold) and the acquiring date. It is connected to a character (a person) via the *owns* relationship.

Figure 3 presents a Membership Card and its attributes. Based on the visual description, the following RDF triples are generated:

```
:MobilePhoneX :connectedTo :Machine1, :Barbell1.
:Machine1 a :Equipment.
:Barbell1 a :Equipment_Barbell.
:Ana :owns :Membership-49232 .
:Membership-49232 a :MembershipCard ;
                  :cardType :BronzeSubscription ;
                  :acquiringDate "2023-01-01T12:00:00"^^xsd:dateTime .
```

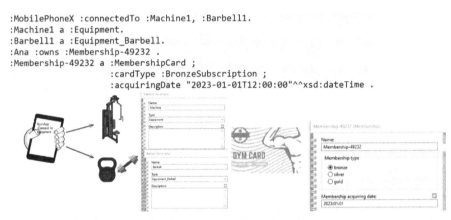

Fig. 3. Example of a) connection between a Device and multiple pieces of Equipment. b) a Membership Card concept

The following competency question evaluates whether the described scenario can answer to management needs in finding the new customers in relation with a specific event.

Competency Question: *List all the customers who acquired a Membership Card after a specific date*

```
SELECT ?person ?membershipCard ?acquiringDate
WHERE {
  ?person a :Customer .
  ?person :owns ?membershipCard .
  ?membershipCard a :MembershipCard .
  ?membershipCard :acquiringDate ?acquiringDate .
  FILTER (?acquiringDate > "2023-01-01T00:00:00"^^xsd:dateTime)
}
```

3.3 Why

The Why dimension focuses on the motivations that lead to the execution of a business process.

To underline specific motivations a person might have to take up fitness services, a new concept is created, called Motivation. It has three visual representations, corresponding to three different incentives: building muscles, losing weight, and following medical advice. The Lose_Weight subtype has an additional attribute, named Target_Weight, to denote the goal of the customer. The Medical_Advice subtype also enables another attribute called Detailed_Advice, to include a better description of the prescription plan to follow for the medical problem. A custom relationship is created, *motivatedBy*, to connect customers to Motivation instances, highlighting each one's objective.

Figure 4 presents the concepts and the relationship depicted with pink color. Here are the RDF triples generated based on the description:

```
:Sam :motivatedBy :SamBuildMuscleMotivation.
:SamBuildMuscleMotivation a :Build_Muscle_Motivation.
:Build_MuscleMotivation a :Motivation.

:Ana :motivatedBy :AnaLoseWeightMotivation.
:AnaLoseWeightMotivation a :Lose_Weight_Motivation.
:Lose_Weight_Motivation a :Motivation.

:Peter :motivatedBy :PeterMedicalAdviceMotivation.
:PeterMedicalAdviceMotivation a :Medical_Advice_Motivation.
:Medical_Advice_Motivation a :Motivation.
```

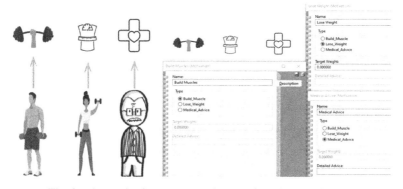

Fig. 4. The Motivation concept and the motivatedBy relationship.

An example of a **competency question** to test here is: *List all the customers that have a different motivation than the Medical_Advice_Motivation.*

```
SELECT ?customer ?motivation
WHERE {
  ?customer rdf:type :Customer .
  ?customer :motivatedBy ?motivation .
  FILTER (?motivation != :Medical_Advice_Motivation)
}
```

3.4 How

The How dimension describes the execution of a business process. It includes specific steps that should be taken to solve a task.

We added a new concept called Plan, which is meant to represent two schedules: a training plan to respect when executing different fitness exercises, a nutritional plan to set what to eat. A specific plan is included by checking the labeled box. The training plan attribute can point to an entire BPMN model that describes the schedule to follow. The nutritional plan attribute is a complex attribute, with three columns for mapping the food's name (String), quantity to eat (Double), and the unit of measurement (String). A Plan instance is attached to a customer via the assignedTo relationship, colored in purple.

Figure 5 presents a plan assigned to a customer, where both plans are included.

The following RDF triples correspond to the description in the figure:

```
:Jane a :Customer.
:PlanforJane :assignedTo :Jane.
:PlanforJane :hasPlan :TrainingPlan1, :NutritionalPlan1.
:TrainingPlan1 a :TrainingPlan.
:NutritionalPlan1 a :NutritionalPlan.
:NutritionalPlan1 :includes [:food :Rice; :quantity 200; :um :grams],
                            [:food :Chicken_Breast; :quantity 100; :um :grams].
```

Fig. 5. An example of a Plan instance and the assignedTo relationship.

Information about the training and nutritional plans empowers fitness employees to have a holistic approach about health and fitness of their customers, beyond exercises alone. Hence, the **competency question** is to retrieve the *list of customers and their plans. We use OPTIONAL clause to handle cases where a customer might not have associated a nutritional plan.*

```
SELECT distinct ?customer ?plan ?trainingPlan ?nutritionalPlan ?food ?quantity
WHERE {
  ?customer a :Customer .
  ?plan :assignedTo ?customer.
  OPTIONAL {
        ?plan :hasPlan ?trainingPlan .
        ?trainingPlan a :TrainingPlan.
  }
  OPTIONAL {
        ?plan :hasPlan/:includes ?nutritionalPlan .
        ?nutritionalPlan :food ?food.
        ?nutritionalPlan :quantity ?quantity.
  }
}
```

3.5 Where

The Where dimension refers to the place where the business process happens.

Our toolkit includes two concepts for this dimension: Gym Related Places (added to the Background concept from SAP Scenes) and the Gym (added to the Building concept available in the SAP Scenes). The first one is employed to provide a more appropriate background to the location in the gym where the action takes place. It has three visual representations: Gym_Inside, Gym_Locker, and Gym_Reception. The second one shows the image of a gym from the outside, and makes use of a relationship named *trainAt* to depicts the connection between a customer and the gym where they train.

In Fig. 6, the Gym Related Places are presented, while in Fig. 7, the connection between a Customer and a Gym can be seen with a green dotted arrow.

Fig. 6. Gym related places (Gym_Inside, first row, first picture, Gym_Locker, first row, second picture, and Gym_Reception, last row).

Location data is a valuable asset for fitness businesses, providing insights that contribute to strategic decision making. Understanding the distribution of employees and customers helps in allocating resources more effectively.

:Jane :trainsAt :GymFSEGA.

Fig. 7. A Customer instance that trains at a Gym instance.

The following is an example of a **competency question** that retrieves information about the popularity of fitness locations.

```
SELECT ?location (COUNT(?customer) AS ?attendance)
WHERE {
  ?customer a :Customer .
  ?customer :trainsAt ?location.
}
GROUP BY ?location
ORDER BY DESC(?attendance)
```

4 Conclusions

In an increasingly competitive landscape, to attract and retain customers fitness centers must adapt their services by differentiating their offerings, creating unique experiences and embracing technological advancements. The fitness industry is currently facing high customer churn rates as suggested by [7] and understanding the consumer's involvement and loyalty in this context might prove a viable solution for other situations, opening up generalization potential.

In this paper, we presented a possible implementation of a modeling toolkit for describing business processes and resources from the fitness industry, that can capture various customer centric perspectives. As an alternative to the tangible design thinking techniques that are traditionally used in workshops when searching for innovative business offerings, we stress over the need to employ an approach that captures the design idea into a digital format which can be further semantically enriched and linked with other components from the enterprise system. The digital representation could also enable further evaluations and simulations of the proposed business solution. Starting from the Scene2Model toolkit that provides means to transform the tangible objects from SAP Scenes into digital representations in a modeling tool, we propose several customizations to adapt it to the fitness domain. With the help of the ADOxx platform, we added new concepts and relationships to better emulate specific tasks, and the possibilities of integrating technologies within gym's services or machines.

References

1. Alexandris, K., Zahariadis, P., Tsorbatzoudis, C., Grouios, G.: An empirical investigation of the relationships among service quality, customer satisfaction and psychological commitment in a health club context. Eur. Sport Manag. Q. **4**(1), 36–52 (2004)
2. Tsitskari, E., Antoniadis, C.H., Costa, G.: Investigating the relationship among service quality, customer satisfaction and psychological commitment in Cyprian fitness centres. J. Phys. Educ. Sport **14**(4), 514 (2014)
3. Nuviala, A., Grao-Cruces, A., Pérez-Turpin, J.A., Nuviala, R.: Perceived service quality, perceived value and satisfaction in groups of users of sports organizations in Spain. Kinesiology **44**(1), 94–103 (2012)
4. Maklan, S., Klaus, P.: Customer experience: are we measuring the right things? Int. J. Mark. Res. **53**(6), 771–772 (2011)
5. Mehmet, B.A.Ş., Tarakçi, İ.E., Aslan, R. (eds.): The Essentials of Today's Marketing-3. Efe Akademi Yayınları (2023)
6. Lawless, M.W.: Commodity bundling for competitive advantage: strategic implications. J. Manage. Stud. **28**(3), 267–280 (1991)
7. Pizzo, A.D., Baker, B.J., Jones, G.J., Funk, D.C.: Sport experience design: wearable fitness technology in the health and fitness industry. J. Sport Manag. **35**(2), 130–143 (2020)
8. Wieringa, R.J.: Design Science Methodology for Information Systems and Software Engineering. Springer, Heidelberg (2014). https://doi.org/10.1007/978-3-662-43839-8
9. Narvala, H., McDonald, G., Ounis, I.: Identifying chronological and coherent information threads using 5W1H questions and temporal relationships. Inf. Process. Manage. **60**(3), 103274 (2023)
10. Buchanan, R.: Wicked problems in design thinking. Des. Issues **8**(2), 5–21 (1992)
11. Chasanidou, D., Gasparini, A.A., Lee, E.: Design thinking methods and tools for innovation. In: Marcus, A. (ed.) DUXU 2015. LNCS, vol. 9186, pp. 12–23. Springer, Cham (2015). https://doi.org/10.1007/978-3-319-20886-2_2
12. Muck, C., Miron, E.T., Karagiannis, D., Moonkun, L.: Supporting service design with storyboards and diagrammatic models: the scene2model tool. In: Joint International Conference of Service Science and Innovation (ICSSI 2018) and Serviceology (ICServ 2018) (2018)
13. SAP-AppHaus: Every great experience starts with a great story - scenes. https://apphaus.sap.com/resource/scenes. Accessed 13 Nov 2023
14. BOC Group. The ADOxx Metamodeling platform (2023). https://www.adoxx.org/live/home. Accessed 01 Jan 2024
15. Buchmann, R.A., Karagiannis, D.: Enriching linked data with semantics from domain-specific diagrammatic models. Bus. Inf. Syst. Eng. **58**, 341–353 (2016)
16. Buchmann, R.A., Karagiannis, D.: Pattern-based transformation of diagrammatic conceptual models for semantic enrichment in the web of data. Procedia Comput. Sci. **60**, 150–159 (2015)
17. Bezerra, C., Freitas, F., Santana, F.: Evaluating ontologies with competency questions. In: 2013 IEEE/WIC/ACM International Joint Conferences on Web Intelligence (WI) and Intelligent Agent Technologies (IAT), vol. 3, pp. 284–285. IEEE (2013)

LLMs for Knowledge-Graphs Enhanced Task-Oriented Dialogue Systems: Challenges and Opportunities

Vasile Ionut Remus Iga$^{(\boxtimes)}$ (ID) and Gheorghe Cosmin Silaghi (ID)

Business Informatics Research Center, Babeş-Bolyai University,
Cluj-Napoca, Romania
{vasile.iga,gheorghe.silaghi}@ubbcluj.ro

Abstract. Large Language Models are a great tool for solving diverse tasks formulated in natural language. Recent work has demonstrated their capacity of solving tasks related to Knowledge Graphs, such as Knowledge Graph Completion or Knowledge Graph Reasoning, even in Zero- or Few-Shot paradigms. However, given a particular input, they do not always produce the same output, and sometimes point to intermediate reasoning steps that are not valid, even if they produce a satisfactorily answer. Moreover, the use of LLMs is mostly studied for static knowledge graphs, while temporal ones are overlooked. To highlight opportunities and challenges in knowledge graph related tasks, we experiment with ChatGPT on graph completion and reasoning for both static and temporal facets, using three different prompting techniques in Zero- and One-Shot contexts, on a Task-Oriented Dialogue system use case. Our results show that ChatGPT can solve given tasks, but mostly in a non-deterministic way.

Keywords: Large Language Models · Knowledge Graph · Knowledge Graph Completion · Knowledge Graph Reasoning · Task-Oriented Dialogue System

1 Introduction

Knowledge Graphs (KG) can be defined as graphs of data intended to accumulate and convey knowledge of the real world, whose nodes represent entities of interest and edges represent potentially different relations between these entities [3]. Two main categories of KGs are of our interest: static and temporal. The former captures the information valid at a certain moment in time, similar to a snapshot, while the latter is more dynamic, adding the temporal context to each fact [6] i.e. duration for the knowledge validity. To keep the KG consistent and valid and to perform inference on the stored knowledge base, two tasks are especially important: Knowledge Graph Completion (KGC) and Knowledge Graph Reasoning (KGR). KGC aims to infer missing facts in a given KG [9].

J. P. A. Almeida et al. (Eds.): CAiSE 2024 Workshops, LNBIP 521, pp. 168–179, 2024.
https://doi.org/10.1007/978-3-031-61003-5_15

It can done be either from input text or from already existing knowledge. KGR focuses on generating an answer that is grounded with facts stored in KG.

In the last years, chatbots and task-oriented dialogue systems (TODs) gained an incredible popularity, all culminating with the well-known ChatGPT[1], as the latest expression of the Artificial Intelligence advances. While chatbots are mostly used for simple chatting without a specific goal in mind, TODs aim to solve the user's specific tasks within certain domains

In our previous work [5] we developed an ontology-enhanced TOD that uses a static KG to map the context of the discussion and store relevant information. This innovation leads to important advantages, such as the possibility of having multiple threads of discussion in the same conversation, and the KG acting as a proxy for data validation. Eventually, the system can help the company to construct and manage its specific knowledge base and perform several tasks on it, such as the Create-Retrieve-Update-Delete (CRUD) operations. With the help of our TOD system, we are able to perform the tasks of KGC to construct the KG, and KGR to solve the CRUD operations.

However, our system based its abilities on text template-matching rules, which limited the naturalness of dialogues, and the possibility of adapting to new concepts that are outside the provided ontology. Therefore, in a subsequent work [4], we trained neural networks to detect the intent of the user and relevant related entities from the input text. Although it has shown promising results, this approach didn't fully solve the aforementioned shortcomings. Another limitation is the use of static KGs, which cannot capture time-related validity of facts, as opposed to temporal KGs.

Therefore, in our current work, we study the usage of Large Language Models (LLMs) to solve the KGC and KGR tasks, in the context of the our TOD system. KGs and LLMs have shown possible integration, as KGs can enhance LLMs by providing external knowledge for inference and interpretability, while LLMs can solve KG-related tasks using natural language prompts [9].

Our experiments explore LLMs for KGC and KGR in both static and temporal contexts. Through the use of ChatGPT, we test its capabilities of solving the mentioned tasks using three different prompting techniques, in two contexts: Zero-Shot (ZS) Direct Prompting (DP) and Chain of Thought (COT), and One-Shot (OS) In-Context Learning (ICL) and Chain of Thought. To highlight a proper use case for LLMs to KG tasks, example phrases are extracted from the training phase of the TOD System. In this way, we not only test whether the LLM can solve KG-specific tasks, but we also explore its integration with our dialogue system.

The initial experiments run in the current paper aim to test the water about the interconnection between the mentioned technologies, thus paving the way for further, more robust experiments. Therefore, as stated in [1,10], positive feedback from initial testing may show that LLMs can be used as a new type of interface for humans to interact with any kind of systems through natural

---

[1] https://openai.com/blog/chatgpt.

language. LLMs may enhance a TOD system that helps any subject-matter experts in fulfilling their roles.

Our research brings in the following contributions: (i) We evaluate ChatGPT for the KGC and KGR tasks, in both static and temporal KGs, using three different prompting techniques (DP, ICL, COT) in two data contexts (Zero- and One-Shot), revealing insights on how a powerful LLM perform such tasks. (ii) We test whether such models can be integrated in a domain-specific ontology-enhanced TOD system, by extracting and using test phrases specific to its training.

The paper evolves as following: in Sect. 2 we describe recent works about solving the KGC and KGR tasks using general and LLM-based approaches, on both static and temporal KGs. Next, Sect. 3 presents our methodology, describing each steps of our experiments, the used examples, ontology, and prompts. Section 4 discusses the obtained results, while Sect. 5 concludes the paper.

2   Related Work

Ji et al. [6] present solutions for the KGC task on static KGs using embedding-based models (ex. TransE), relation path reasoning (ex. Path-Ranking Algorithm), reinforcement-learning path finding (ex. path-finding between entity pairs as a Markov Decision Process), rule-based reasoning (ex. KALE), or meta relational learning (ex. using R-GCN or LSTM). For KGR, neural network approaches are presented, for single and multi-hop question answering. Similar findings are presented by Zhang et al. [12] while classifying them as neural, symbolic and neural-symbolic.

Temporal KGs require more sophisticated systems, therefore new or refinement ones were further engineered. Wang et al. [10] present solutions for temporal KGC, including interpolation methods (i.e. estimating missing values from known ones) such as timestamps dependent-based, timestamps specific functions-based, or deep learning-based, and extrapolation methods (i.e. predicting future facts based on known ones) such as rule-based, graph neural network-based, meta-learning-based, or reinforcement learning based. Liang et al. [7] distinguish between RNN-based (using RNNs, LSTMs or GRU networks) or RNN-agnostic models (time-vector guided or time-operation guided) for Temporal KG.

All of the previous presented works emphasize the use of neural networks, logic networks, logic rules or mathematical operations to solve KGC and KGR in static and temporal KGs, but none of them actually focus on using LLMs. Pan et al. [9] studies the synergy between LLMs and KGs, proposing a unified roadmap, where KGC and KGR are also tackled. Zhu et al. [14] experimented with ChatGPT and GPT4 for KGC and KGR, concluding that they are below state-of-the-art (SOTA) fine-tuned Pre-Trained Language Models (PLMs) for KGC in a zero/one shot paradigm, but their reasoning capabilities are either close or above SOTA models. Still, the usage of an LLM and its efficiency compared to a specialized PLM is unclear. Han et al. [2] propose PiVE, a prompting technique, where an LLM (ChatGPT) extracts facts from input texts while a smaller fine-tuned PLM checks and completes its responses in an iterative manner. In a somewhat similar fashion, Wei et al. [11] proposes a multi-stage dialogue with ChatGPT to extract relevant information from input texts, given a certain schema.

Similar to Wei et al. [11], we test the capacity of a LLMs (ChatGPT) on KGC and KGR tasks. We depart from them as we extend the analysis from static to temporal KGs. Moreover, we also test the possibility of integrating the LLM with an ontology-enhanced TOD system, to sharpen its natural language processing and KG-related capabilities, by using example phrases from its training schedule.

3 Methodology

In this section, we describe how we assess that ChatGPT is fit for the study at hand using preliminary questions, the ontology used to anchor's the LLMs knowledge, setup format for the static/temporal KGC and KGR tasks, and prompting techniques with examples. The ontology and extracted triples are described in RDF, using the Turtle syntax. ChatGPT 3.5 is used, while prompts are manually designed. Each individual prompt with each example is fed three times to ChatGPT in the same conversation, for three different sessions. In this way, we test the inter- and intra-conversation determinism of the LLM. All prompts are available at https://github.com/IonutIga/ChatGPT-KGC-KGR/tree/main.

3.1 Preliminary Questions for ChatGPT

Before experimenting with ChatGPT, we decided to question its knowledge to assess if it is fit to solve our intended KG-related tasks. First, we design six questions related to the tasks at hand, such as:

1. Do you know what a Knowledge Graph is?
2. Do you know what a Temporal Knowledge Graph is?
3. Do you know what an ontology is, in the context of Knowledge Graphs?
4. Do you know what Turtle syntax is, in the context of Knowledge Graphs?
5. Do you know what a triple is, in the context of Knowledge Graphs?
6. Do you know how to extract triples from a natural language phrase, given a provided ontology in the Turtle syntax?

ChatGPT responded in an organized, clear, and factual manner to each of the above questions, demonstrating its understanding of KGs, Temporal KGs, Turtle syntax, ontologies and tasks at hand. Two additional questions were asked, related to time:

7. Do you know today's date?
8. Do you know today's time?

Today's date was not a problem to ChatGPT, also being able to respond to subsequent questions regarding yesterday or tomorrow's date, given a certain one. However, it couldn't respond to time-related questions, stating "*I don't have real-time capabilities, including the ability to provide the current time in specific time zones*".

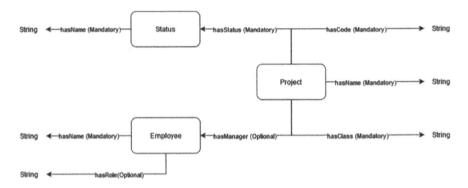

Fig. 1. The ontology used throughout the experiments. It contains three classes and six relationships

3.2 Ontology

We use the ontology from our previous work [5] (see Fig. 1). It contains three classes (i.e. concepts): *Project, Employee,* and *Status,* and six relationships between them (*hasManager, hasStatus*) or classes and literal values (*hasName, hasRole, hasClass, hasCode*).

3.3 Setup Format

The ontology is written using the Turtle syntax, where each fact has the form of a triple (subject, relationship, object), therefore each of the extracted facts are aligned to the same format.

For the Temporal KGs, inspired by the work of Nguyen et al. [8], each relationship becomes an instance of its actual type, while two new temporal relationships are added to it: *startDate* and *endDate*. The start date is either today (when the input text is encountered) or a provided date. The end date is either "*Now*" - highlighting the continuous knowledge validity, or a provided date. For example, suppose we have the triple :Employee1 :hasName :John. The relationship :hasName will be instantiated as :hasName1 rdf:instanceOf :hasName. Then, the two temporal relationships are defined, as :hasName1 :startDate "20-02-2024", :hasName1 :endDate "Now", meaning the fact where :hasName1 is valid from 20-02-2024 until further notice.

For KGR, ChatGPT has to use the provided KG to answer the input question, ensuring its time validity. For example, given the above example, a question such as "*Is there an employee named John?*" requires ChatGPT to find any employee named "*John*" and compare its start date and end date with today's date.

3.4 Prompting Techniques and Examples

Three prompting techniques are used to communicate with ChatGPT, namely Direct Prompting, In-Context Learning, and Chain of Thought. All three follow

You are an expert in Knowledge Graphs. Turtle is used as the syntax language. An ontology is provided to you. It contains classes and relationships between classes or classes and literals (strings, numbers, dates etc.). A natural language phrase is the input to you.
It may or may not contain references to an instance of a class provided in the ontology, together with specific relationships.
Your task is to extract information from the input phrase about the instance of a class using the provided ontology, in the form of a triple (subject,relationship, object), using the Turtle syntax.
Each instance should be identified by an ID, using the format Class + DDMMYYYY + R, where class is the detected class, + is concatenation, DDMMYYYY is the format for today's date, and R is a random number between 0-100.
The first triple you always create is between the ID and the class type, using the rdf:type relationship. Next, each extracted information that is related to the detected instance should use the ID as the subject.
Make sure each triple is in line with the ontology, meaning each class type and relationship that is detected should be present in the ontology.
The ontology:
The input phrase:

Fig. 2. The standard prompt template used among all techniques

the guidelines of Zhao et al. [13], where a prompt must be detailed enough, but straightforward, with no negative directives (i.e. only telling what to do), adding relevant examples to the task and input phrase when needed. Direct Prompting assumes no further information than the task description, context information, ontology, and input phrase are fed to ChatGPT. In-Context Learning adds one relevant example to the prompt, while Chain-Of-Thought requires the model to think step by step about the solution to the task at hand, theoretically enhancing its focus on it. As the aim of our study is Zero- and One-Shot paradigms, we obtain four possible combinations:

- Zero-Shot Direct Prompting
- Zero-Shot Chain of Thought, by only adding *"Let's think step by step"* to the prompt
- One-Shot In-Context Learning, adding one relevant example to the prompt
- One-Shot Chain of Thought, adding one relevant example, together with reasoning steps to the prompt.

Each technique uses a standard prompt, depicted in Fig. 2. It starts by saying *"You are an expert in Knowledge Graphs"*, that should guide ChatGPT to use adequate knowledge. Next, we supply ChatGPT with details about the ontology and the format, together with the task description. In our previous work [5], each instance's ID in the KG had a similar format to "Class name + DDMMYYY + R", where we concatenate the name of instance's type, today's date - when the input phrase is encountered using the DDMMYYYY format, and R i.e. a random number between 0–100. Lastly, some verification guidelines are provided.

For KGC on temporal KGs, additional text is added to guide ChatGPT in constructing proper temporal-enhanced triples, as presented in Subsect. 3.3. First, it becomes *"an expert in Temporal Knowledge Graphs"*. Then, we guide ChatGPT how to construct each relationship instance's ID, by concatenating the name of the relationship type with the random number between 0-100, similarly to class instances' IDs.

Table 1. Input phrase examples and their types

Input phrase example	Input phrase type
Insert an employee with name as Michael and role as CEO	explicit Information
It seems I cannot find Michael as an employee, therefore you should add him. Remember, he's our CEO	implicit Information
Michael is not on the list of employees, but it should, as it is our CEO	misleading information
Michael is a very good boy, doing a good job as a guide dog	misleading information
Assuming today's date is 01-01-2010, what is Michael's role?	before validity time
Assuming today's date is 01-01-2030, what is Michael's role?	after validity time

For KGR, the prompt is straightforward: *"You are an expert in Temporal Knowledge Graphs. Your task is to answer the input question based on the provided knowledge graph. Knowledge Graph: ... Input question:"*.

Table 1 presents each input phrase used throughout experimenting. As mentioned before, all the input phrases are extracted from the training schedule of our TOD System. Three input phrases types are tested: explicit information, implicit information, and misleading information. Each aims to reveal ChatGPT's capacity of dealing with explicit phrases where the instances and relationships are easy to spot, implicit ones that need some additional reasoning, and misleading examples where either mistakes or out-of-ontology class types are used.

For temporal KGs, we use the same input phrase example as the one for explicit information. For KGR, we asked ChatGPT two additional questions, to test its reasoning capabilities on Temporal KGs, where we assumed the date of questioning it is outside or inside the validity time interval specified in the provided KG.

4   Results and Discussion

In this section, we discuss the overall conclusions extracted from our experiments. Each of them are grouped based on the task at hand.

4.1   ChatGPT on the Static KGC Task

We analyze the results of ChatGPT on the Static KGC task, by breaking down to each input phrase type and technique.

Explicit Information
Regarding explicit information phrase type with Zero-Shot Direct Prompting, ChatGPT was able to extract the target triples from the input phrase, and was

consistent on output and explanations through each conversation. However, it had difficulties in generating a random number R and concatenate it to the instance's ID.

On Zero-Shot Chain of Thought, ChatGPT had no problems extracting the triples, providing detailed explanations of the reasoning process. Results were consistent intra- and inter-conversations, having the same problem with the random number R concatenation.

The model followed the provided example when prompted with One-Shot In-Context Learning technique, having as output only the triples (one conversation added short explanations for each fact). The ID is correctly formulated, while results were consistent throughout conversations.

One-Shot Chain of Thought paradigm provided the most complete answers, in terms of explanations and output triples. As expected, ChatGPT followed the detailed step-by-step reasoning process given in the prompt. Results were consistent inter- and intra-conversations.

Overall, the explicit information type phrase was easy to work with for Chat-GPT, mostly following the provided guidelines. Some problems regarding the number R concatenation were faced with ZS DP and COT, which is surprising, as it was the simple tasks of all. Consistency between chats and conversations was mostly kept, making ChatGPT reliable for such task.

Implicit Information
With Zero-Shot Direct Prompting, ChatGPT faced the first problems in outputting a correct set of triples. As a result, in two out of three conversations, it added one more fact stating that the instance is also of type owl:Class, giving a wrong explanation. Thus, is not consistent inter-conversation, only in the same dialogue session. It has the same aforementioned problems with the number R concatenation.

Zero-Shot Chain of Thought raised some interesting problems. First, Chat-GPT missed the name fact two out of three conversations. Next, it didn't generate neither correct date or R in any conversation. Therefore, the results were not consistent at all.

One-Shot In-Context Learning fixed the issues from above, outputting correct sets of triples, following the provided examples. However, we assume the model made no fundamental changes in the reasoning process, it just perfectly followed the example. Results were consistent in all conversations.

Finally, One-Shot Chain-of-Thought raised again some of the same problems as in the ZS paradigm. Although conversations were more intra-consistent, between them the name fact was missed, while the date was also not correctly generated throughout one conversation. Finally, explanations were more in-lined with the given prompt.

Overall, the implicit information phrase type has created problems for Chat-GPT. Although OS ICL managed to generate proper triples, the other techniques shown the limitations of the reasoning aspect from ChatGPT.

Misleading Information – First Example

In practice, some input phrases may contain misspelled words that should still give enough information to generate correct triples. Therefore, we tested Chat-GPT with an implicit information phrase type regarding an employee, where the word *"employee"* is misspelled.

ChatGPT shows its limitations from the first set of tests. With Zero-Shot Direct Prompting, the model is able to find some of the right triples, but either misses the others, or adds statements that are not consistent with the ontology. Moreover, it provides ambiguous explanations regarding the detection of some relationships. Additionally, it doesn't generate the right ID for the instances, by confusing today's date and not being able to concatenate the random number.

Surprisingly, Zero-Shot Chain of Thought has similar results with the above technique. Some new problems appear, for example, it suggests that the *"CEO"* role found in the input phrase is just a placeholder for another one. Moreover, results are not consistent throughout conversations. Literature suggests COT should enhance its reasoning process, but it seems it does not work for the task at hand.

In line with other results, One-Shot ICL works best for ChatGPT, as it extracted the right facts, following the provided example. Lastly, One-Shot Chain of Thought alleviates most of the problems from its ZS counterpart. Results become more consistent, while facts are mostly in line with the ontology.

Overall, the main concern is that ChatGPT has encountered more problems by only providing one misspelled word, compared to the implicit information tests. In practice, such use cases would certainly be faced, while ChatGPT fails to display the right behavior.

Misleading Information – Second Example

To test whether ChatGPT follows the provided ontology and prompts, while also being able to handle Out-Of-Distribution cases, we design an implicit information input phrase where the instance is of type *"Dog"*, that is outside the ontology, and we expect ChatGPT to output such response.

We summarize the results of Zero-Shot Direct Prompting, Zero-Shot Chain of Thought, and One-Shot In-Context Learning, as they are very similar. Chat-GPT fails to follow one simple instruction from the prompt, to adhere to the given ontology, and outputs triples that are not factually correct. Some of them borrow relationships from existing classes, while others contain made-up ones by ChatGPT. Explanations are also ambiguous, as it assigns the `hasRole` relationship to an instance because *"it is a guide dog"*. Conversations are not consistent, only by being wrong, while failing to concatenate the R number.

In contrary with the above results, One-Shot Chain of Thought was able to guide ChatGPT into outputting the right explanation (i.e. that no triples were extracted based on the ontology) almost each time. Only one chat of a conversation resulted in wrong triples being extracted.

Overall, ChatGPT was not able to follow basic instructions about dealing with Out-Of-Distribution instances, continued to do some of the same mistakes regarding the generated ID, while being inconsistent in answers. Only OS COT produced relevant results that can be considered correct.

4.2   ChatGPT on the Temporal KGC Task

The above section analyzes the results on the static KGC task, while this section takes into consideration the temporal component of Knowledge Graphs. The input phrase is the explicit information type one, as ChatGPT displayed some issues with more complex ones. The time should be the moment when our examples were run, specifically on February 28, 2024.

Zero-Shot Direct Prompting generated some interesting results. ChatGPT managed to follow the rules of instantiating each relationship and assigning proper time related values, but it was not able to generate correct IDs either for the class or relationship instances. Also, it did not use the `rdf:instanceOf` relationship, as mentioned in the prompt, for the relationship instance fact, but the `rdf:type` one. This mistake is not huge, but it shows that ChatGPT may not follow the guidelines. Moreover, one conversation revealed wrong triples, where a `hasRole` relationship instance was considered as a *Status* class type. Finally, conversations were intra-consistent, but not between sessions.

In accordance with some of the above findings, Zero-Shot Chain of Thought did not improve ChatGPT's output. Moreover, they were inconsistent among conversations, missing triples or adding unnecessary statements. In one occasion, the IDs of relationship instances were far from the provided template. However, time-related relationships were still correctly extracted.

One-Shot In-Context Learning once again highlighted ChatGPT's underlying nature of being a statistical model. The output follows the provided example, by even copying the date in some conversations (although it has explicit guidelines to use the current date). Even the random R numbers assigned to IDs are the same. Although the output is correct, it is doubtful that it is the result of an underlying reasoning process.

One-Shot Chain of Thought successfully reduced the error from the ZS counterpart, by providing a running example with explicit intermediate reasoning steps. Although this achievement, ChatGPT again copied the current date from the example, without following the prompt on using today's date.

Overall, ChatGPT had no problems with time-related relationships. It successfully anchored each relationship instance in time. However, instantiating each relationship raised problems to the model. The generation of the IDs, together with following the ontology and provided guidelines were the main problems.

4.3   ChatGPT on the KGR Task

In this section, we discuss ChatGPT's performance on the KGR task. We analyze two situations, when the time of discussion is assumed to be beyond the knowledge scope of the provided KG, and the other is known.

When the time of discussion is assumed to be beyond the knowledge scope of the provided KG, all techniques managed to lead ChatGPT to valid answers.

Each time, all conversations were intra- and inter-consistent, leading to same responses, differing only in formulation. Therefore, ChatGPT could reason correctly about the time validity of certain facts.

When the time of discussion falls in the valid interval of time stated in the KG, ChatGPT faces a few problems with the format of time labeling. We chose *"Now"* to be the value of the endDate relationship when the fact is continuously valid to the current date. Because of that, for Zero-Shot Direct Prompting and, surprisingly, for One-Shot In-Context Learning, the model generated responses where it states that it cannot infer the answer because *"Now"* is not a fixed date and it does not know its meaning. ChatGPT is not entirely wrong, as *"Now"* may be ambiguous, but it is confusing how it could determine it in all other cases, especially during Zero- and One-Shot Chain of Thought.

In conclusion, ChatGPT may be used for temporal reasoning, with additional information for the labeling schema.

5   Conclusion

In line with the findings of Zhu et al. [14], we find that ChatGPT is better at reasoning than extracting facts from input text. The KGR task raised almost no difficulties, as the model was only confused by the definition of the *"Now"* label.

The Static and Temporal KGC tasks brought to surface the limitations of LLMs when it comes to real reasoning. ChatGPT had almost no problems handling explicit type of phrases, but could not follow the provided guidelines and ontology when handling the implicit and temporal ones. Moreover, only ICL was able to generate consistent answers most of the time, but it seems it does not enhance the model's reasoning abilities, only guiding it to follow exactly the provided example. Surprisingly, COT did not help most of the times, which underlines the difficulty of KGC. The temporal aspect did not raise problems to ChatGPT, showcasing its possible use in temporal KGs.

ChatGPT has shown weaknesses when dealing with simple concatenation tasks. Most of the times, it could not generate a random number and concatenate it to the ID, leaving the letter *"R"* as provided in the template. Although it stated in the preliminary questions that it knows today's date, when asked to use it in building the IDs, ChatGPT was easily misguided by provided examples and copied their dates, instead of the current one. Unfortunately, ChatGPT cannot be trusted yet, as for the same input, we may get quite different outputs, therefore being non-deterministic.

Regarding its usage in TOD Systems, based on the above conclusions, Chat-GPT cannot be directly integrated with no further fine-tuning.

Future work may consider more detailed prompts with diverse use cases, an extended ontology, and other LLMs. In this way, we can truly test LLMs capabilities on the KGC and KGR tasks, on both Static and Temporal KGs, and their possible integration with Task-Oriented Dialogue Systems.

In conclusion, our work has highlighted the advantages and disadvantages of using LLMs (here, ChatGPT) for the Static and, most importantly, Temporal

KGC and KGR tasks. Our results show prominent use cases, while underlying the necessity of carefully monitoring them.

References

1. Fill, H., Fettke, P., Köpke, J.: Conceptual modeling and large language models: impressions from first experiments with ChatGPT. Enterp. Model. Inf. Syst. Archit. Int. J. Concept. Model. **18**, 3 (2023). https://doi.org/10.18417/EMISA.18.3
2. Han, J., Collier, N., Buntine, W.L., Shareghi, E.: PiVe: prompting with iterative verification improving graph-based generative capability of LLMs. CoRR abs/2305.12392 (2023). https://doi.org/10.48550/ARXIV.2305.12392
3. Hogan, A., et al.: Knowledge Graphs. Synthesis Lectures on Data, Semantics, and Knowledge. Morgan & Claypool Publishers (2021). https://doi.org/10.2200/S01125ED1V01Y202109DSK022
4. Iga, V.I., Silaghi, G.C.: Leveraging BERT for natural language understanding of domain-specific knowledge. In: 25th International Symposium on Symbolic and Numeric Algorithms for Scientific Computing, SYNASC 2023, Nancy, France. IEEE (2023, to appear)
5. Iga, V.I., Silaghi, G.C.: Ontology-based dialogue system for domain-specific knowledge acquisition. In: da Silva, A.R., et al. (ed.) ISD2023 Proceedings, Lisbon, Portugal. AIS (2023). https://doi.org/10.62036/ISD.2023.46
6. Ji, S., Pan, S., Cambria, E., Marttinen, P., Yu, P.S.: A survey on knowledge graphs: representation, acquisition, and applications. IEEE Trans. Neural Netw. Learn. Syst. **33**(2), 494–514 (2022). https://doi.org/10.1109/TNNLS.2021.3070843
7. Liang, K., et al.: A survey of knowledge graph reasoning on graph types: static, dynamic, and multimodal. CoRR abs/2212.05767 (2022). https://doi.org/10.48550/arXiv.2212.05767
8. Nguyen, V., Bodenreider, O., Sheth, A.P.: Don't like RDF reification?: making statements about statements using singleton property. In: Chung, C.-W., et al. (ed.) 23rd International WWW Conference, Seoul, Republic of Korea, pp. 759–770. ACM (2014). https://doi.org/10.1145/2566486.2567973
9. Pan, S., Luo, L., Wang, Y., Chen, C., Wang, J., Wu, X.: Unifying large language models and knowledge graphs: A roadmap. CoRR abs/2306.08302 (2023). https://doi.org/10.48550/ARXIV.2306.08302
10. Wang, J., et al.: A survey on temporal knowledge graph completion: taxonomy, progress, and prospects. CoRR abs/2308.02457 (2023). https://doi.org/10.48550/ARXIV.2308.02457
11. Wei, X., et al.: Zero-shot information extraction via chatting with chatgpt. CoRR abs/2302.10205 (2023). https://doi.org/10.48550/ARXIV.2302.10205
12. Zhang, J., Chen, B., Zhang, L., Ke, X., Ding, H.: Neural, symbolic and neural-symbolic reasoning on knowledge graphs. AI Open **2**, 14–35 (2021). https://doi.org/10.1016/J.AIOPEN.2021.03.001
13. Zhao, W.X., et al.: A survey of large language models. CoRR abs/2303.18223 (2023). https://doi.org/10.48550/ARXIV.2303.18223
14. Zhu, Y., et al.: LLMs for knowledge graph construction and reasoning: recent capabilities and future opportunities. CoRR abs/2305.13168 (2023). https://doi.org/10.48550/ARXIV.2305.13168

Property Graphs at Scale: A Roadmap and Vision for the Future (Short Paper)

Haridimos Kondylakis[1]([✉]), Vassilis Efthymiou[1,2], Georgia Troullinou[1], Elisjana Ymeralli[1], and Dimitris Plexousakis[1]

[1] FORTH-ICS, N. Plastira 100, 70013 Heraklion, Crete, Greece
{kondylak,vefthym,troulin,ymeralli,dp}@ics.forth.gr
[2] Harokopio University of Athens, Omirou 9, 17778 Tavros, Athens, Greece

Abstract. The prevalence and the rapid growth of interconnected data have sparked the rise of graph models and systems focusing on the management of large graphs now available both in research and industry. The property graph model allows the representation of information through multigraphs where nodes and edges can have labels and properties (i.e., key-value pairs). The model is becoming very popular and widespread, however related data management technology still faces many challenges, limiting the wide adoption of the model. In this vision paper, we present directions for future work in the domain focusing on the availability of a single declarative graph language, data integration, and scalable data processing. In our view, these areas represent key challenges for advancing research and practical solutions in the domain.

Keywords: Property Graphs · Graph Query Languages · Schema Discovery · Data Integration · Scalable Data Processing

1 Introduction

Graphs serve as a versatile and dynamic data model, adept at representing intricate network-structured data across various application domains. These domains include social networks, biological networks, bioinformatics, cheminformatics, medical data, and knowledge management. Graphs, by their inherent nature, act as 'unifying abstractions,' harnessing interconnectedness to depict, explore, predict, and elucidate phenomena in both the real and digital worlds.

In our current landscape, we are witnessing an unprecedented surge in interconnected data, emphasizing the critical role of graph processing in our society. A recent article in CACM [1] highlights that "the future is big graphs". Instead of one single, compelling ("killer") application, we see big graph processing systems underpinning many emerging, but already complex and diverse data management ecosystems in many areas of societal interest [2]. The impact of this growth is evident, with sophisticated graph data management tasks already benefiting from big data processing systems.

To address the increasing prevalence of graphs, academia, start-ups, and major tech companies like Google, Facebook, and Microsoft have introduced diverse systems for

© The Author(s), under exclusive license to Springer Nature Switzerland AG 2024
J. P. A. Almeida et al. (Eds.): CAiSE 2024 Workshops, LNBIP 521, pp. 180–185, 2024.
https://doi.org/10.1007/978-3-031-61003-5_16

managing and processing large-scale graphs. However, the current landscape remains fragmented, lacking a clear direction for the community. According to the same CACM paper, the Resource Description Framework (RDF) and Property Graph (PG) stand out as the most prominent data models for graph data management. RDF, a W3C recommendation, facilitates data sharing and interoperability scenarios, playing a central role in initiatives like Linked Data and FAIR data within the Semantic Web community. On the other hand, PG, on which we focus here, emerged in the context of enterprise data management. To merge these gaps RDF* [3] has been proposed, extending RDF with a convenient way to make statements about other statements, and practical approaches are pushed (e.g., neosemantics by RDF4J) [4], however yet they have not been highly adopted and extensively supported by commercial vendors.

Property graphs are multigraphs where nodes and edges can have labels and properties (i.e., key-value pairs). The model is becoming very popular and widespread: PG solutions now serve 75% of Fortune 500 companies [5] and Gartner predicted that by 2025, graph technologies will be used in 80% of data and analytics innovations [6]. Note that, at the foundational level, all the models underlying graph database systems are subsumed by the PG model. The popularity of PG in the industrial community is justified by the fact that its development was picked by the main international standards body, namely ISO (International Organisation for Standardisation). However, diverse languages and systems for PG processing and analysis populate a fragmented market, thus causing a lack of clear direction for the research and industrial communities.

As such, a holistic view of data management technologies for property graphs is currently missing. In the following, we present our vision focusing on three distinct areas, i.e., a) the availability of a declarative graph language; b) the integration of disparate graph data, and finally c) how to enable PG data processing at scale, highlighting our vision for future work in the domain.

2   Roadmap to the Future

2.1   Establishing a Declarative Query Language for PGs

There are already well accepted languages for RDF graphs, such as the SPARQL language [7], whereas graph databases that adopt property graphs, e.g., Amazon Neptune, Neo4j, Oracle, SAP, TigerGraph, enable graph access via non-declarative APIs, such as Gremlin or, in the style of traditional relational databases, declarative languages, such as Cypher [8], PGQL [9], and GSQL [10]. An upcoming graph query language standard from ISO, called GQL [11], aims to unify these declarative languages, in a way SQL did for relational databases. For example, GQL is expected to be composable like Cypher, to fully support regular path queries like PGQL, and to eventually offer an expressivity as close as possible to Gremlin and GSQL, which are Turing-complete. The first version of the GQL Standard is scheduled to appear in early 2024, but it will have a number of important omissions. The two most notable omissions are support for sophisticated graph schemas and a complete lack of support for graph-to-graph transformations. Indeed, GQL currently allows writing only graph-to-relational queries, which are adequate for many scenarios, though not all. For example, in data analytics tasks that require extensive data exploration, a user expects to see graphs as query answers [12].

To cater to these needs, existing PG solutions provide various ad-hoc tools (basic visualization, library functions for limited graph projection, etc.). However, a proper graph query language must treat graphs as first-class citizens, and support, among others query compositionality – i.e., the result of a query should be a graph itself allowing further queries on it. In fact, treating graphs as first-class citizens is a stated goal of GQL design [13]. However, compositionality has been dropped from the first version of GQL for a simple reason: there is no underlying research telling us how to add such facilities to the language.

Moving Beyond the State of the Art. Graphs constantly need to be transformed, to be updated with new information, and to be moved between applications. Our state of understanding of such transformations is very preliminary (as is indicated, for example, by multiple issues existing in the updating facilities of the leading graph query language Cypher). Crucially, we completely lack the framework for checking the correctness of such transformations, such as adherence to the typing information or being compatible with the requirements of an application that uses the output of a graph query.

The lack of research underpinnings for a proper graph-to-graph language is currently limiting the development of essential features like views, subqueries, and updates in graph query languages. Indeed, the first specification of the GQL industrial standard, which will appear in the first half of 2024, will still be a graphs-to-relations language borrowing its engine - pattern matching - from its purely relational counterpart SQL/PGQ. As such, a concentrated effort is required in order to understand and ultimately unlock the aforementioned features. In particular, more research is required on sophisticated types of graph modifications that we currently do not know how to perform safely and how to incorporate schemas into querying, which is yet another aspect of relational databases that is well understood and commonly used that requires much new foundational research for graphs. Future research could benefit from experience in formalizing languages for graphs (e.g., ICS-FORTH RDFSuite [14] and RQL [15]).

2.2 Data Integration

Data Integration is a well-established research area with tangible results for relational databases. However, the PG data model significantly differs from the relational one especially due to the fact that graph instances can be defined without a priori schema. While entity alignment has been studied for knowledge graphs in other data models (e.g., RDF) by leveraging ontologies and RDF types, schema-based PG integration is largely unexplored, due to the lack of definitions of schemas and constraints for this data model. In this direction, methods for schema discovery [16], which are necessary for establishing mappings [17] and transformation rules between multiple PGs, are currently underway. Property graph schemas [18] are being defined as part of the LDBC standardization activities and these definitions are expected to be adopted by graph database vendors. Schema inference methods can be used to extract standard schemas from PGs and use them to specify mappings across different PGs. Similarly, an appropriate mapping language for data exchange and transformation [19] is still not present and should be defined on top of standard graph query languages. The correctness and the validity of the generated mappings are critical for processing tasks and, thus, there is a need for methods to ensure that the available mappings represent the intended transformations appropriately. Finally, the integration of PG with other graph data models (e.g., from/to RDF) is relevant, with appropriate characterization of cases where loss of information might occur.

Moving Beyond the State of the Art. Graphs provide a very flexible data model that makes it appropriate for integrating data from multiple disparate sources. Inspired by the work done for relational databases, future research in the domain should tackle several foundational issues for integrating PGs, starting by adapting to PGs the well-known three-layered architecture of relational data integration systems, i.e., sources to be integrated, the target providing an integrated view over the sources, and the mappings establishing the relationship between the sources and the target. In this direction, future research should carry both a thorough investigation of the complexity of basic foundational services of graph data integration; it should investigate the definition of a mapping language based on existing standards, capitalizing experience accumulated over the years for mapping languages (i.e., X3ML [20]), establishing the formal underpinnings of graph data integration and exchange. Future work should consider both schema-based and schema-less mappings: for the former, methods should be explored for discovering the schema of PGs that will be used for establishing mappings and transformations. For the latter different techniques will have to be devised. Finally, mappings between other data models (i.e. RDF) should be explored, both for the sources and the target, with appropriate characterization of cases where loss of information might occur.

2.3   Scalable Data Processing

Graph data management and processing systems have been adopted by many companies and organizations, but the gap in their adoption for business intelligence use cases and analytical tasks is still substantial. Indeed, practitioners are missing guidelines and best practices that can help them identify non-trivial applications of graph analytics tools and approaches beyond one-shot operations. Moreover, we have only recently witnessed the creation of data management tools that are able to map, within themselves, data imported from multiple sources and models. Thus, their performance, capabilities, and limitations when trying to address hybrid transactional and analytical workflows are still largely unexplored [21, 22]. Further, as schema on top of graph data sources is not available, methods for schema-based data partitioning and query optimization are still missing.

Moving Beyond the State of the Art. State-of-the-art research is already focusing on schema discovery [16, 23] schema-based data partitioning using big data infrastructures [24, 25] and analytical tasks through materialized views [26] for knowledge graphs. Such approaches can fuel the development of similar solutions for PGs. Future research in the domain should focus on partitioning for big graph data, exploring summary-based partitioning and hierarchical schemas for improving query answering efficiency. Further, summaries will be exploited as materialized views for further speeding up query answering, whereas there is room for focusing not only on exact but also on approximate answers.

3 Conclusions

The property graph data model has emerged as a versatile and powerful paradigm for data management and its penetration in the industry is constantly increasing. However, in order to enable effective and efficient management of the data, a set of problems should be first tackled starting from establishing a powerful declarative query language, defining and discovering schemas for property graphs, and enabling data integration. Further techniques for data processing at scale, such as data partitioning, should also be devised in order to facilitate efficient querying. Already, the first steps in all these domains exist, however, a holistic solution in the domain is still missing.

Acknowledgments. The work reported in this paper is implemented in the framework of H.F.R.I call "Basic research Financing (Horizontal support of all Sciences)" under the National Recovery and Resilience Plan "Greece 2.0" funded by the European Union – NextGenerationEU (H.F.R.I. Project Number: 16819).

References

1. Sakr, S., et al.: The future is big graphs: a community view on graph processing systems. Commun. ACM **64**(9), 62–71 (2021)
2. Hegeman, T., Iosup, A.: Survey of graph analysis applications. arXiv preprint arXiv:1807. 00382 (2018)
3. RDF-star and SPARQL-star. Draft Community Group Report. https://w3c.github.io/rdf-star/cg-spec/editors_draft.html. Accessed Apr 2024
4. NeoSemantics, Neo4j RDF & Semantics toolkit. https://neo4j.com/labs/neosemantics/. Accessed Apr 2024
5. Record investment in Neo4j suggests, maybe it IS all about relationships. https://www.hfs research.com/research/record-investment-in-neo4j-suggests-maybe-it-is-all-about-relations hips/. Accessed 26 Feb 2024
6. Gartner Identifies Top 10 Data and Analytics Technologies Trends. https://www.gartner.com/en/newsroom/press-releases/2021-03-16-gartner-identifies-top-10-data-and-analytics-technologies-trends-for-2021
7. SPARQL 1.1 Query Language, W3C Recommendation. https://www.w3.org/TR/sparql11-query/. Accessed Mar 2024
8. Nadime, F., et al.: Cypher: an evolving query language for property graphs. In: Proceedings of the 2018 International Conference on Management of Data (SIGMOD 2018), pp. 1433–1445. Association for Computing Machinery, New York (2018). https://doi.org/10.1145/3183713. 3190657
9. van Rest, O., Hong, S., Kim, J., Meng, X., Chafi, H.: PGQL: a property graph query language. In: Proceedings of the Fourth International Workshop on Graph Data Management Experiences and Systems (2016)
10. Deutsch, A.: Querying graph databases with the GSQL query language. SBBD **313** (2018)
11. GQL Standards. https://www.gqlstandards.org/. Accessed 26 Feb 2024
12. Lissandrini, M., Mottin, D., Palpanas, T., Velegrakis, Y.: Graph-query suggestions for knowledge graph exploration. In: Proceedings of the Web Conference 2020 (WWW 2020), pp. 2549–2555. Association for Computing Machinery, New York (2020). https://doi.org/10.1145/336 6423.3380005

13. Deutsch, A., et al.: Graph pattern matching in GQL and SQL/PGQ. In: Proceedings of the 2022 International Conference on Management of Data (SIGMOD 2022), pp. 2246–2258. Association for Computing Machinery, New York (2022). https://doi.org/10.1145/3514221.3526057

14. Alexaki, S., Christophides, V., Karvounarakis, G., Plexousakis, D., Tolle, K.: The ICS-FORTH RDFSuite: managing voluminous RDF description bases. In: SemWeb 2001 (2001)

15. Karvounarakis, G., Alexaki, S., Christophides, V., Plexousakis, D., Scholl, M.: RQL: a declarative query language for RDF. In: WWW, pp. 592–603 (2002)

16. Kellou-Menouer, K., Kardoulakis, N., Troullinou, G., et al.: A survey on semantic schema discovery. VLDB J. **31**, 675–710 (2022)

17. Rahm, E., Bellahsene, Z., Bonifati, A. (eds.): Schema Matching and Mapping. Springer, Cham (2011)

18. Renzo, A., et al.: PG-keys: keys for property graphs. In: Proceedings of the 2021 International Conference on Management of Data (SIGMOD 2021), pp. 2423–2436. Association for Computing Machinery, New York (2021). https://doi.org/10.1145/3448016.3457561

19. Boneva, I., Bonifati, A., Ciucanu, R.: Graph data exchange with target constraints. In: EDBT/ICDT Workshops, pp. 171–176 (2015)

20. X3ML Toolkit. https://www.ics.forth.gr/isl/x3ml-toolkit. Accessed 26 Feb 2024

21. Mhedhbi, A., Lissandrini, M., Kuiper, L., Waudby, J., Szárnyas, G.: LSQB: a large-scale subgraph query benchmark. In: Proceedings of the 4th ACM SIGMOD Joint International Workshop on Graph Data Management Experiences & Systems (GRADES) and Network Data Analytics (NDA) (GRADES-NDA 2021), Article no. 8, pp. 1–11. Association for Computing Machinery, New York (2021)

22. Lissandrini, M., Mottin, D., Hose, K., Pedersen, T.B.: Knowledge graph exploration systems: are we lost? In: CIDR (2022)

23. Kardoulakis, N., et al.: HInT: hybrid and incremental type discovery for large RDF data sources. In: SSDBM, pp. 97–108 (2021)

24. Troullinou, G., Agathangelos, G., Kondylakis, H., Stefanidis, K., Plexousakis, D.: DIAERESIS: RDF data partitioning and query processing on SPARK. Semant. Web J. (2024)

25. Bonifati, A., Dumbrava, S., Kondylakis, H., Troullinou, G., Vassiliou, G: PING: progressive querying on RDF graphs. In: ISWC (Posters/Demos/Industry) (2023)

26. Troullinou, G., Kondylakis, H., Lissandrini, M., Mottin, D.: SOFOS: demonstrating the challenges of materialized view selection on knowledge graphs. In: SIGMOD Conference (2021)

Knowledge Graph for Reusing Research Knowledge on Related Work in Data Analytics

Aritha Kumarasinghe$^{(\boxtimes)}$ ⓘ and Marite Kirikova ⓘ

Institute of Applied Computer Systems, Riga Technical University, 6A Kipsalas Street, Riga 1048, Latvia

{balasuriyage-aritha-dewnith.kumarasinghe, marite.kirikova}@rtu.lv

Abstract. Data analytics projects encompass a multitude of facets, including the types of analytics employed, algorithms utilized, and data sources scrutinized. Despite this wealth of information, there remains a challenge in effectively leveraging previous related work for future projects. Traditional approaches often lack mechanisms for preserving and repurposing the knowledge gained from the analysis of related works. In response, this paper introduces a novel method leveraging RDF triples to encapsulate attributes of analytics projects. These RDF triples are then integrated into a web-based knowledge graph, facilitating the exploration of related work within specific data analytics domains. By harnessing this method, researchers and practitioners can identify valuable resources, including data sources, tools, and algorithms, for future endeavors. To demonstrate its efficacy, we apply this method to the domain of real estate analytics, showcasing its potential to enhance project efficiency and innovation.

Keywords: Knowledge Reuse · Analytics · Knowledge Graphs

1 Introduction

Data analytics is the field of study that relates to systematically analyzing a real-world system by using mathematical and statistical techniques on data that represents the system in question [1]. With data analytics projects generating valuable insights regularly, the collective knowledge they offer holds immense potential for informing future endeavors. However, each project concerns multiple attributes, i.e., data sources, and analytics algorithms that depend on various factors such as the problem domain and the type of analytics being carried out, which makes having an overview of related works concerning the single attributes and their combinations a time and labor-consuming process. Therefore, once the analysis of related work has been conducted, the reuse of knowledge gained is low.

The goal of this paper is to solve the above-mentioned problem with the knowledge graphs which would amalgamate the knowledge gained in the analysis of related work thus making it easier to reuse this knowledge about data analytics projects.

© The Author(s), under exclusive license to Springer Nature Switzerland AG 2024
J. P. A. Almeida et al. (Eds.): CAiSE 2024 Workshops, LNBIP 521, pp. 186–199, 2024.
https://doi.org/10.1007/978-3-031-61003-5_17

While knowledge graphs have found various applications in the realm of data analytics [2, 3], our proposed approach resides on a meta-level and introduces an ontology grounded in analytics project attributes. This ontology forms the backbone of a knowledge graph that enables exploration of related work within the analytics domain from diverse perspectives, such as project context (e.g., Biomedical [4]) or data types (e.g., numerical [5]).

In the subsequent sections, we outline the research methodology employed (Sect. 2) and present the analytics project ontology (Sect. 3). Section 4 delves into the creation of the knowledge graph, exemplified through the representation of real estate analytics project data. The utility and efficacy of the resulting knowledge graph are demonstrated in Sect. 5, followed by a concise conclusion in Sect. 6.

2   Research Method

In this paper, the following research method was used:

Step 1. To create the ontology for building the knowledge graph, the analytics project attributes were defined based on research articles that explicitly stated analytics project attributes, e.g., data sources [6] or research articles from which analytics project attributes could be derived, e.g., data sets in [7], where the attribute of data sets was concluded from mentioned training and test data sets of the analytics project. All the defined analytics project attributes, with some examples of their potential values which these attributes can have, are amalgamated in Table 1 alongside the sources (references to the research articles) from which the attributes were identified.

Step 2. Relationship types linking each attribute to the analytics project were established, adhering to principles of clarity and unambiguity. These relationship types provided the structure necessary for effectively organizing and navigating the knowledge graph.

Step 3. The analytics project attributes and relationship types obtained in the previous two steps were used to create a star-like ontology for the knowledge graph where all attributes are of one link distance from the central node "Analytics Project". The triple underlying the structure of the ontology is shown in Fig. 1 with a subject (Analytics Project) representing considered analytics projects and the predicate (definesDataset) relating to a specific attribute (Dataset used), which represents the type of respective object being the value(s) of the analytics project attribute (e.g. Training Dataset).

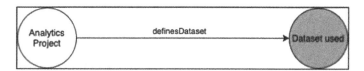

Fig. 1. Single triple for the data analytics project ontology.

Step 4. The established ontology was used to create a knowledge graph for real estate analytics. This involved mapping project-specific data to the defined ontology and encapsulating the project's characteristics within the knowledge graph.

Step 5. The utility of the created knowledge graph was showcased through a web application, allowing for interactive exploration and visualization of project attributes and their relationships based on specific use cases.

The approach used in this paper can be considered as a semi-automatic construction of a knowledge graph with a predefined set of elements on an ontology level [8]. Thus, it combines features of manually created knowledge graphs which reflect human-interpreted content [9], and the features of automatically created knowledge graphs [10–12]. The approach differs from [10–12] in (1) the method for choosing the attributes for the top level of the knowledge graph and (2) the manual processing of the related work about a specific analytics domain (which can be considered as higher quality of interpretation than by artificial intelligence tools). The purpose of the created knowledge graph is to facilitate more effective use and reuse of acquired knowledge.

3 Analytics Project Ontology

The analytics project attributes are accumulated in Table 1, alongside their descriptions and examples of the potential values that the attributes can take referring to the sources from which the analytics project attribute values were acquired.

Table 1. Analytics project attributes.

Analytics Project Attribute	Comments on the Attribute
Project Context/ Field [13]	This attribute of the analytics project refers to the problem domain within which the data analytics project is being carried out, for instance, Business, or Biomedical
Object/ System/ Measure of interest [4, 14]	This attribute defines what object(s) or system(s) the analytics project is concerned with, for instance, such as healthcare or geothermal energy operations
Analytics Type [1]	Defining the type of analytics that is being carried out within the project is very important, especially for the analysis phase of the project since the goal of the project is very dependent on the type of analytics. The types of analytics considered in this paper are descriptive, predictive, and prescriptive
Project Documentation [15]	The documentation that is provided can change the amount of detail an analyst provides on things that relate to data (data dictionaries), available resources, and expected results

(continued)

Table 1. (*continued*)

Analytics Project Attribute	Comments on the Attribute
Data Type(s) Used [5, 16]	The types of data that are used with any analytics project can be placed into one of the categories (numerical, textual, etc.), regardless of the format. The type of data used within a project can affect other factors, e.g., the type of analytics method that will be used and the possible visualization methods
Dataset(s) Used [7]	Whether or not the datasets used in the analytics project are already present. In the context of machine learning models, the definition of training and test data sets needs to be defined
Data Source(s) [6]	The sources from which the data can be acquired need to be specified for the data analytics project. Corporate websites and social networking sites are some commonly used web data sources
Data Extraction Technique [16]	The technique used to extract data is dependent on the form of data that is extracted and where it is extracted from. For instance, when extracting web-based data, web wrapper-based data extraction techniques can be used
Data Integration [17]	If there are multiple sources of data, then data integration might be necessary to combine them into a singular format. For instance, record linkage is a data integration method based on non-unique identifiers
Analysis Method [13]	The applied methods of analysis impact most aspects of the analytics project and vice versa. Therefore, the selection of the techniques used in the project and the definition of the method(s) used are essential for the success of the project. Some examples of analytics methods used are correlation analysis and regression analysis

(*continued*)

Table 1. (*continued*)

Analytics Project Attribute	Comments on the Attribute
Analysis Software [18]	The tools that are used to carry out the analysis change the nature of the analytics project similarly to the selected analysis technique. A good demonstration of this is how the software will affect "Data Types Used" because different tools have different inbuilt data types, as well as rules regarding how those data types can be manipulated. A commonly used tool for data analysis is Python and its libraries such as Pandas
Model(s) Used for Analysis [19]	This attribute relates to the preexisting models and mathematical or statistical methods that will be used to carry out the analytics. The models represent real-world entities/events and can be used to analyze these entities/events. An example of a model is the 'WaterGap' model
Algorithm(s) Used for Analysis [20]	Many algorithms can be utilized in analytics such as SVM and random forests. These algorithms can be used to analyze or to create analytics models
Report Specification [21]	The results of a data analytics project can be put into a report. Different analytics projects can have various reports, e.g., a data summary
Graphical Results [22]	Data visualizations can be used for the analysis of data and to present the results of the analysis. Box plots and bar charts are some of the data visualizations used with the box plot showing variability of data, and bar charts being used to show data trends
Interactive Results [23]	Using various software applications (e.g., Tableau), interactive tools such as dashboards can be produced as a result of the analytics project
Created Model(s) [24]	Some analytics projects result in the creation of models that have been trained using data. Different analytics projects result in models that have different functionality, for instance, a predictive analytics model for power consumption in manufacturing

(*continued*)

Table 1. (*continued*)

Analytics Project Attribute	Comments on the Attribute
Method Used for Verification/validation of Results [25]	Once the result of the analytics project is created there may be a need to test it. For instance, a method to verify the resulting predictive model is k-fold cross-validation

The list of attributes was defined when identifying generic requirements for the analytics projects [26]. Concerning one attribute – the analytics type – only one of the possible classifications was chosen [1] which prescribe the following four types of analytics: (1) Descriptive analytics: it uses data to present information regarding the previous states of a system or an object; (2) Diagnostic analytics: it deals with the (close to) real-time data to explore the current state of a system or an object; (3) Predictive analytics: it tries to forecast the future state of a system or objects predicting what events might take place; and (4) Prescriptive analytics: it is based on future events and seeks to use data to determine the course of action for the future.

If the Analytics Project is considered the subject of a Resource Description Framework (RDF) triple, then the predicates would refer to the relationship between the project and a project attribute (attributes value) thus making the attribute the object of the triple. Table 2 shows the analytics project attributes (the same as in Table 1) and their corresponding relationships to the subject Analytics Project. The attribute and relationship names shown in this paper are preliminary versions and have not yet been tuned to the fully elaborate naming, which is expected to emerge during the regular use of the graph in scientific and educational settings.

Table 2. Analytics project attributes and the corresponding relationships.

Analytics Project Attribute	Attributes relationship to the analytics project (Predicate)
Project Context/Field	inContext
Object/System/Measure of interest	concernsSystemOrObjectOrMeasureOfInterest
Analytics Type	carriesOutAnalyticsOfType
Project Documentation	utilizesProjectDocumentation
Data Types Used	utilizesDataOfType
Datasets Used	definesDataset
Data Source	utilizesDataSource
Data Extraction Technique	extractsDataUsing
Data Integration	integratesDataThrough
Analysis Method	utilizesAnalysisMethod

(*continued*)

Table 2. (*continued*)

Analytics Project Attribute	Attributes relationship to the analytics project (Predicate)
Analysis Software	utilizesSoftwareForAnalysis
The Model Used for Analysis	utilizesModelForAnalysis
Algorithm Used for Analysis	utilizesAlgorithmForAnalysis
Report Specification	resultsInReport
Graphical Result	resultsInGraphicalResult
Interactive Result	resultsInInteractiveResult
Created Model	resultsInModel
The Method Used for Verification/validation of Results	verifiesResultsUsing

Based on these analytics project attributes and relationships, an analytics project ontology was created (Fig. 2). This ontology can be used to define any analytics project and there is also the possibility to define additional attributes for the analytics project or to leave some attributes not represented in case information about their values is not available.

4   Real Estate Analytics Knowledge Graph

Referencing the ontology discussed in Sect. 3, a knowledge graph was created to represent real estate analytics projects. The analytics project attribute values were defined for the 20 real estate analytics projects through the review of research articles reporting on these projects. The obtained information was then converted into RDF triples using the RDFlib available in Python.

The created RDF triples were then utilized to create a web application that would allow users to query the RDF triples to generate knowledge (sub)graphs that present the relationship between different analytics project attributes that the user is interested in. This application can be used by data analytics professionals to explore the research domain of real estate data analytics.

Table 3 shows an example of some of the defined real estate analytics project attribute values that were used in the creation of the knowledge graph. In the left column, the name of the analytics project attribute as a part of the predicate is shown except for Reference which is an addition to the knowledge graph to allow users to access the research article when needed. The right column consists of the values for the analytics project attributes, and the objects (instances) in the RDF triple.

These defined analytics project attribute values were parsed to create a Pandas data frame which was then converted into a knowledge graph using the RDFlib (a Python library made for working with RDF data) by using the class Graph to create nodes, based on research articles, and edges, based on various values for the data analytics attributes.

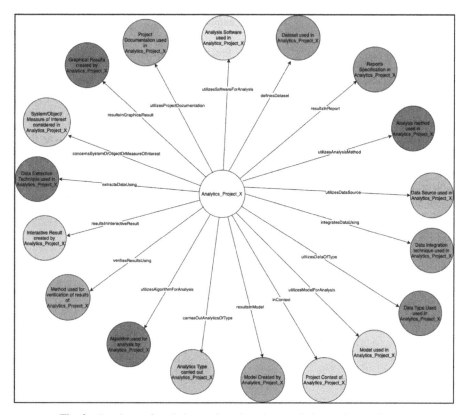

Fig. 2. Ontology of analytics projects based on analytics project attributes.

Table 3. Example of a real estate analytics project attribute values.

Predicate	Project 1 attribute values
Reference	Li, M., Bao, Z., Sellis, T., Yan, S. and Zhang, R., 2018. HomeSeeker: A visual analytics system of real estate data. Journal of Visual Languages & Computing, 45, pp.1–16
inContext	Real Estate
concernsSystemOrObjectOrMeasureOfInterest	Real estate properties from the buyers' perspective
carriesOutAnalyticsOfType	Descriptive
definesDataset	Location-centric real estate dataset
utilizesAnalysisMethod	Data characteristic analysis

(*continued*)

Table 3. (*continued*)

Predicate	Project 1 attribute values
	Data visualizations
verifiesResultsUsing	Domain expert interaction with demo system

The created knowledge graph was then serialized into a Turtle file that was then visualized using RDF Grapher, a web-based tool that can be utilized to parse RDF data to visualize knowledge graphs. Figure 3 shows a fragment of the resulting knowledge graph consisting of 13 triples with the real estate analytics project (indexed 1) being the subject and analytics project attribute values being the objects.

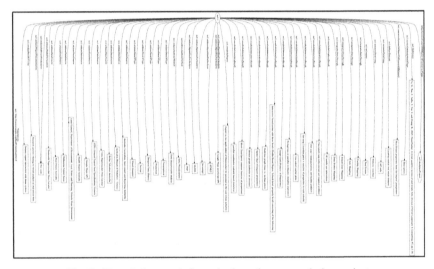

Fig. 3. Knowledge graph for a single real estate analytics project.

From this fragment of the knowledge graph, the methods and results related to descriptive real estate analytics projects can be deduced, however, this fragment is sufficient for just one analytics project. If 20 projects were to be represented in this manner the results would be very difficult to read and understand.

Therefore, it was decided to develop a web-based application that could enable the querying of RDF triples and create a more understandable visualization that would allow users to easily understand the presented knowledge.

5   Using Knowledge Graph Based Web Application

The generated knowledge graph was first verified by running several SPARQL queries on it. An example of a SPARQL query for the use case of finding data sources that were used by real estate analytics research projects that utilized Visual (Image) data is shown in Fig. 4. The obtained results are shown in Fig. 5.

```
PREFIX ns1: <http://www.example.org/RealEstateAnalytics#>
SELECT ?reference (GROUP_CONCAT(?dataSource; SEPARATOR=", ") as ?dataSources)
WHERE {
    ?project a ns1:AnalyticsProject ;
             ns1:Reference ?reference ;
             ns1:utilizesDataOfType "Visual (Images)" ;
             ns1:utilizesDataSource ?dataSource ;
             ns1:inContext "Real Estate" .
}
GROUP BY ?reference
```

Fig. 4. SPARQL query for finding data sources that were used by real estate analytics research projects that utilized Visual (Image) data.

```
Project Reference and Data Sources for Visual (Images) Data:
Project Reference: Li, M., Bao, Z., Sellis, T., Yan, S. and Zhang, R., 2018. HomeSeeker: A visual analytics system of real estate data. Journal of Visual
Languages & Computing, 45, pp.1-16.
Data Sources: Australia Curriculum, Assessment and Reporting Authority, Australian Bureau of Statistics – Census, Better Eduation Australia, Coles Superm
arket Store Locator, GTFS (General Transit Feed Specification) Victoria, Google Maps API, Health Engine Australia, Land Channel, Department of Environmen
t, Land, Water and Planning, Victoria State Government, Melbourne School Zones, Real Estate Australia, Woolworth Supermarket Store Locator

Project Reference: Eduard Hromada,
Mapping of Real Estate Prices Using Data Mining Techniques,
Procedia Engineering,
Volume 123,
2015,
Pages 233-240,
ISSN 1877-7058,
https://doi.org/10.1016/j.proeng.2015.10.083.
(https://www.sciencedirect.com/science/article/pii/S1877705815031847)
Data Sources: Servers of real estate companies, Webpages of real estate companies

Project Reference: M. De Nadai and B. Lepri, "The Economic Value of Neighborhoods: Predicting Real Estate Prices from the Urban Environment," 2018 IEEE 5
th International Conference on Data Science and Advanced Analytics (DSAA), Turin, Italy, 2018, pp. 323-330, doi: 10.1109/DSAA.2018.00043
Data Sources: Google Street View API , Italian National Institute for Statistics (ISTAT) , OpenStreetMap , Real estate website Immobiliare.it, Urban Atla
s 2012
```

Fig. 5. Results of the SPARQL query for finding data sources that were used by real estate analytics research projects that utilized Visual (Image) data.

After the verification, the generated RDF data was utilized in a web application that would allow users to query the triples to generate desired knowledge sub-graphs consisting of nodes and edges. The web application was developed using Python with RDFlib being used to parse the RDF data and Dash Cytoscape being used to generate the web-based interactive knowledge graph (the source code and data for which can be viewed on GitHub [27]).

Figure 6 shows one of the resulting visualizations for the project which was used as an example in Table 3 in Sect. 4. The edges in the graph are labeled and colored based on the predicate (analytics project attributes) to which they relate, the square nodes in the graph represent the analytics projects (subjects). The grey nodes represent the objects (project attribute values). The user can move the nodes within this graph to improve the visibility of the text.

Further querying of the graph is possible based on the predicates. If the user is interested in seeing the relationship between the type of analytics being carried out in the projects and the algorithms used for analysis, the resulting graph (Fig. 7) would allow the users to understand what algorithms have been used in previous projects and to deduce what algorithms have not yet been tested/used (the room for innovation). This also allows users to find research articles that compare the algorithms such as Project 12 and Project 2 which use 6 and 16 algorithms respectively.

Another use case for this web-based visualization tool is to see the relationship between the system, object, or measure of interest and the data sources that have been utilized in previous analytics projects (Fig. 8). With this knowledge graph, the users can see what data sources they can access to carry out their projects. For instance, if the user

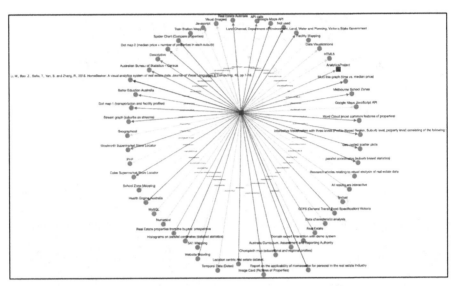

Fig. 6. Knowledge graph visualization for a single real estate analytics project as produced by the web-based visualization tool.

is interested in Real Estate Valuations, they can see the data sources used by 10 different analytics projects.

Similarly, a user can visualize any combination of data analytics project attributes to see which issues previous projects have addressed in terms of data sources, algorithms, models, etc. This would allow users to explore the data analytics domain from many different perspectives and, also, would allow for the reuse of knowledge acquired from previous analytics projects without the need to scour again research databases.

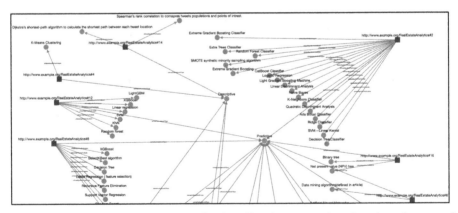

Fig. 7. (Section of) knowledge graph reflecting all real estate projects based on the type of analytics being conducted and the algorithms used for analysis.

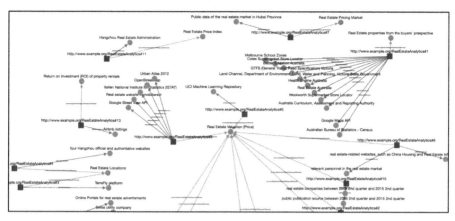

Fig. 8. (Section of) knowledge graph reflecting all real estate projects based on the system, object, or measure of interest and the data sources being utilized.

6 Conclusion

This work proposes a method by which the knowledge gained in previous analytics projects reported in research papers can be preserved in the form of a knowledge graph and thereby be reused in subsequent projects. Using this method, a knowledge graph was created for the domain of real estate analytics based on the defined set of analytics project attributes. The values of these attributes were defined through the analysis of research articles relating to 20 different real estate analytics projects. The obtained knowledge was amalgamated in RDF triples that were then deployed in a web-based interactive knowledge graph application that allows users to query the triples based on the users' attributes of interest.

The created knowledge graph allows users to effectively explore the related work in the real estate analytics research domain and to reuse the captured knowledge for new analytics projects.

Regarding the technical representation, it is possible to improve the web application's user interface to make it more accessible, for instance, through the combination of multiple subjects (real estate analytics projects) that relate to the same object (analytics entity, e.g., Python) into a single node in the graph that can be clicked to expand the node to show all related analytics projects. There is also the possibility to extend the scope of the analytics project attributes to represent an analytics project from more perspectives or in more detail.

Similar knowledge graphs can be created for other domains of data analytics.

Acknowledgment. The choice of real estate analytics to demonstrate the knowledge graph for the reuse of research knowledge on related work in data analytics was inspired by the cooperation with Ltd Lursoft IT and Ltd Hagberg, Latvia.

References

1. Balali, F., Nouri, J., Nasiri, A., Zhao, T.: Data analytics. In: Balali, F., Nouri, J., Nasiri, A., Zhao, T. (eds.) Data Intensive Industrial Asset Management: IoT-based Algorithms and Implementation, pp. 105–113. Springer, Cham (2020). https://doi.org/10.1007/978-3-030-35930-0_7

2. Duan, W., Chiang, Y.Y.: Building knowledge graph from public data for predictive analysis: a case study on predicting technology future in space and time. In: Proceedings of the 5th ACM SIGSPATIAL International Workshop on Analytics for Big Geospatial Data, pp. 7–13 (2016)

3. Hasan, S.S., Rivera, D., Wu, X.C., Durbin, E.B., Christian, J.B., Tourassi, G.: Knowledge graph-enabled cancer data analytics. IEEE J. Biomed. Health Inform. **24**(7), 1952–1967 (2020)

4. Mehta, N., Pandit, A.: Concurrence of big data analytics and healthcare: a systematic review. Int. J. Med. Inform. **114**, 57–65 (2018)

5. Gidea, M., Katz, Y.: Topological data analysis of financial time series: landscapes of crashes. Physica A **491**, 820–834 (2018)

6. Blazquez, D., Domenech, J.: Big Data sources and methods for social and economic analyses. Technol. Forecast. Soc. Chang. **130**, 99–113 (2018)

7. Huang, F., Teng, Z., Guo, Z., Catani, F., Huang, J.: Uncertainties of landslide susceptibility prediction: Influences of different spatial resolutions, machine learning models and proportions of training and testing dataset. Rock Mech. Bull. **2**(1), 100028 (2023)

8. IEEE Standard for Framework of Knowledge Graphs. In IEEE Std 2807-2022, pp. 1–52 (2022). https://doi.org/10.1109/IEEESTD.2022.10017167

9. Graudone, J., Kirikova, M.: A weighted knowledge graph for representing the results of a systematic literature review. In: Ruiz, M., Soffer, P. (eds.) CAiSE 2023 LNBIP, vol. 482, pp. 125–131. Springer, Cham (2023)

10. Masoud, M., Pereira, B., McCrae, J., Buitelaar, P.: Automatic construction of knowledge graphs from text and structured data: a preliminary literature review. In: 3rd Conference on Language, Data and Knowledge (LDK 2021). Schloss Dagstuhl-Leibniz-Zentrum für Informatik (2021)

11. Vincent, N.: Automatic Creation of Knowledge Graphs from Scientific Literature. Kairntech. https://kairntech.com/blog/articles/automatic-creation-of-knowledge-graphs-from-scientific-literature/. Accessed 03 Mar 2024

12. Sahlab, N., Kahoul, H., Jazdi, N., Weyrich, M.: A knowledge graph-based method for automating systematic literature reviews. Procedia Comput. Sci. **207**, 2814–2822 (2022)

13. Runkler, T.A.: Data Analytics. Springer Fachmedien Wiesbaden, Wiesbaden (2020)

14. Abrasaldo, P.M.B., Zarrouk, S.J., Kempa-Liehr, A.W.: A systematic review of data analytics applications in above-ground geothermal energy operations. Renew. Sustain. Energy Rev. **189**, 113998 (2024)

15. Rashid, S.M., et al.: The semantic data dictionary–an approach for describing and annotating data. Data Intell. **2**(4), 443–486 (2020)

16. Pichiyan, V., Muthulingam, S., Sathar, G., Nalajala, S., Ch, A., Das, M.N.: Web scraping using natural language processing: exploiting unstructured text for data extraction and analysis. Procedia Comput. Sci. **230**, 193–202 (2023)

17. Dong, X.L., Srivastava, D.: Big data integration. In: 2013 IEEE 29th International Conference on Data Engineering (ICDE), pp. 1245–1248. IEEE (2013)

18. Unpingco, J.: Python Programming for Data Analysis. Springer, Heidelberg (2021)

19. Lehner, B., Czisch, G., Vassolo, S.: The impact of global change on the hydropower potential of Europe: a model-based analysis. Energy Policy **33**(7), 839–855 (2005)

20. Adadi, A.: A survey on data-efficient algorithms in big data era. J. Big Data **8**(1), 24 (2021)
21. Edwards, J.R., et al.: National Healthcare Safety Network (NHSN) report: data summary for 2006 through 2008, issued December 2009. Am. J. Infect. Control **37**(10), 783–805 (2009)
22. Streit, M., Gehlenborg, N.: Bar charts and box plots: creating a simple yet effective plot requires an understanding of data and tasks. Nat. Methods **11**(2), 117–118 (2014)
23. Hoelscher, J., Mortimer, A.: Using Tableau to visualize data and drive decision-making. J. Account. Educ. **44**, 49–59 (2018)
24. Shin, S.J., Woo, J., Rachuri, S.: Predictive analytics model for power consumption in manufacturing. Procedia CIRP **15**, 153–158 (2014)
25. Rodriguez, J.D., Perez, A., Lozano, J.A.: Sensitivity analysis of k-fold cross validation in prediction error estimation. IEEE Trans. Pattern Anal. Mach. Intell. **32**(3), 569–575 (2009)
26. Kumarasinghe, A., Kirikova, M.: Generic requirements template for data analytics. In: BIR 2023 Workshops and Doctoral Consortium, 22nd International Conference on Preceptive in Business Informatics Research (BIR 2023), Ascoli Piceno, Italy, 13–15 September 2023 (2023)
27. Kumarasinghe, A.: Knowledge Graph for Reusing Research Knowledge on Related Works in Data Analytics (Version 2.0.4) [Computer software] (2023). https://github.com/Aritha RTU/Knowledge-Graph-for-Reusing-Research-Knowledge-on-Related-Works-in-Data-Ana lytics.git

An Ontology-Based Meta-modelling Approach for Semantic-Driven Building Management Systems

Emanuele Laurenzi[1]([⊠]) [ID], James Allan[2] [ID], Nathalie Campos[1], and Sascha Stoller[2]

[1] FHNW – University of Applied Sciences Northwestern Switzerland, Riggenbachstrasse 16, 4600 Olten, Switzerland
emanuele.laurenzi@fhnw.ch, nathalie.campos@students.fhnw.ch
[2] Urban Energy Systems Laboratory, Empa, Überlandstrasse 129, 8600 Dübendorf, Switzerland
{james-allan,sascha.stoller}@empa.ch

Abstract. The increase in smart buildings has led to an increase in data produced and consumed by buildings. Despite growing digitalisation trends, data interoperability, data quality, and a lack of transparency hinder the development of scalable energy applications. Knowledge graphs alleviate some of these challenges through their ability to integrate and analyse diverse data sources. Despite these benefits, knowledge graphs require specific skills typically uncommon in building and energy system engineers. This work tackles this challenge by enabling system engineers to create and maintain knowledge graphs about BMS by dealing with visual diagrammatical models they are familiar with. For this, we built on the ontology-based meta-modelling approach and created a proof-of-concept AOAME4BMS, in which we implemented a BMS and used it for evaluation purposes.

Keywords: ontology-based meta-modeling · semantic-driven building management systems · AOAME4BMS

1 Introduction

Building operation is responsible for 28% of the global energy-related CO_2 Emissions [1]. Digitalisation and the increase of interconnected devices are considered key technologies to improve energy efficiency and reduce emissions across the energy sector in Switzerland [2] and globally [3]. In smart buildings, energy consumption can be reduced by controlling loads in a responsive, adaptive and intelligent manner, taking into account local environmental conditions and occupant needs [3]. However, despite increased interconnectivity and data availability, there is a lack of semantic interoperability hindering the development of scalable energy applications in buildings [4]. The application of semantic web technologies to link and formalise can overcome these challenges. Firstly, they provide an integrated information model that bridges the information gap between different building phases and stakeholders, enabling the exchange and application of information in a holistic way [5]. Secondly, they provide a foundation for advanced

J. P. A. Almeida et al. (Eds.): CAiSE 2024 Workshops, LNBIP 521, pp. 200–211, 2024.
https://doi.org/10.1007/978-3-031-61003-5_18

analysis and automation across domains relevant to the function of smart cities and buildings [6]. The use of ontology-based architectures within a semantic layer supports shareable domain models, enables information exchange and logical inference. This leads to the promotion of data consistency, interoperability, and automated reasoning capabilities [7].

In this work we prove the adequacy of the ontology-based meta-modeling [8] as an architecture to pursue in the creation of semantic-driven building management systems by non-ontology experts such as system engineers. For this, we propose an ontology-based meta-model reflecting concepts, relations and graphical notations that are used by system engineers to create schemas of building management systems. As diagrammatical models are created, knowledge graphs are automatically and consistently produced. The latter are linked with the domain ontology standard Brick [9, 10], which adds semantics about building management systems.

This paper is structured as follows. Section 2 describes the related work. Section 3 elaborates on the methodology. Section 4 presents the solution, including the prototype AOAME4BMS (i.e., AOAME for Building Management Systems), which implemented the new proposed ontology-based meta-model. The evaluation is described in Sect. 5, and finally Sect. 7 concludes the paper.

2   Related Work

Utilising knowledge graphs and ontologies can help address interoperability challenges in the domain of smart buildings, leading to improved energy flexibility, environmental comfort, operational efficiency and reduced energy expenses [3]. Indeed, in the context of building management systems, the more frequent application of ontologies in real-life buildings could enhance their practical utility [11]. However, research indicates that the development and maintenance of knowledge graphs require considerable time and effort [12–14]. Engineers and architects are familiar with Computer Aided Design (CAD) and Building Information Modelling (BIM) but they are unfamiliar with knowledge graphs. Developing, maintaining and utilising semantic models and ontologies is work-intensive and costly [4]. It would be unreasonable and impractical to train system engineers with computer and data engineering skills to build, maintain and query knowledge graphs to support building operations. Nevertheless, it is essential to capture the expert knowledge of engineers when making knowledge graphs of energy systems. Converters for BIM data schemas, such as Industry Foundation Classes (IFC), have been converted into linked data as a starting point for knowledge graphs [5, 15]. This is not always possible, as BIM models are not always available, and their schema can be complex and inconsistent [16]. It has been shown that there is a need to combine knowledge science with BIM to support the Architecture, Engineering and Construction (AEC) industry [17]. The uptake of BIM across the industry is also relatively slow [18] and requires additional expertise and training [19].

This highlights the need for more practical and efficient approaches to creating and maintaining knowledge graphs, as well as the importance of incorporating ontologies in real-world scenarios.

One promising strategy for addressing these challenges is the application of ontology-based conceptual modelling for semantic-driven systems engineering [20]. This approach has been successfully tested in various domains, such as information systems architecture, business process management and genomic science [21–23]. In particular, the ontology-based meta-modeling in [8] involves the integration of domain-specific modelling languages and domain ontologies, enabling domain experts to create visual models enriched with machine-interpretable meta-data. This data is valuable for generating knowledge graphs, allowing for a more efficient and accurate representation of domain knowledge while also facilitating improved communication and understanding among various stakeholders. While ontology-based conceptual modelling has shown promise in various fields, it is not yet well-established in the realm of cyber-physical modelling. In the smart building domain, building models and schemas are widely employed to help humans interpret complex building management systems and calculate physical behaviour. However, according to the literature review, there is currently no existing domain modelling language that inherently integrates domain ontologies directly into graphical model elements and gives the possibility for domain experts to create ontology-based building models that can improve the communication between the different stakeholders and overcome system barriers.

3 Methodology

This research followed the five phases of the Design Science Research methodology [24]: problem awareness, suggestion, development, evaluation and conclusion.

The problem understanding has been deepened by supplementing findings from the literature with a focus group with relevant stakeholders around the creation and maintenance of building management systems from Empa NEST [25] such as knowledge engineers, model designers, architects. Results from the focus group led to the selection and detailed of a real-world use case scenario, which is presented in Sub-sect. 3.1. The latter was, thus, analysed to create a list of design-requirements for the artefact. The following design problem was framed based on the template described in [26]: *improve the status quo regarding the creation and maintenance of knowledge graphs about building management systems by adopting an ontology-based meta-modelling approach such that the elicited design-requirements are addressed in order to include system engineers in the creation and maintenance of the knowledge graphs.*

The requirements were addressed to suggest a solution concept, that consisted of an ontology-based meta-model and a graphical notation.

In the third phase, the designed artefact was implemented in a functioning modelling tool that we call AOAME4BMS. This builds on the principles of the agile and ontology-based meta-modelling environment [8], where a user interface allows for modelling, a web service implements methods to keep the modelling language and related models consistent with the ontology and knowledge graph stored in a Jena Fuseky triple store.

The approach was evaluated with respect to its correctness. For the correctness we looked at the results in terms of (1) the designed visual model and (2) the respective knowledge graph post-modelling.

In the conclusion, the relevant findings are discussed, and future work is pointed out.

3.1 Focus Group Findings

The focus group involved two knowledge engineers and three system designers, all senior experts in building management systems (BMS) at Empa NEST. The focus group lasted 3 h, where an introductory phase was followed by a discussion on common activities for the creation and maintenance of BMS. Finally, a real-world use case scenario was identified and explained, where the modelling and maintenance activities are required. In the following, we report the main findings from the focus group, grouped by four main requirements (R1 to R4).

R1: Accommodate Representational Requirements of Use Case UMAR

The NEST is an experimental facility comprised of interconnected modular units. Energy is produced on-site using integrated renewable technologies or supplied through energy networks. Piping and Instrumentation Diagrams (PID) are a type of schematic to show the interconnection of process equipment and instrumentation to control the process. Figure 1 shows the PID of the Heating, Ventilation and Air Conditioning (HVAC) system of the Urban Mining and Recycling (UMAR) building unit in the NEST building. This diagram was created using sPlan7.0 software, ABACOM, Germany. The system comprises two temperature networks connected to a heat exchanger and a series of radiant ceiling panels that provide either heating or cooling to the rooms, depending on the season.

Engineers use graphic symbols to prepare system schematics. Several standardisation organisations such as CIBSE, ISO and DIN publish libraries of these symbols to standardise the creation of schematics of energy systems. There is often overlap between many universal components, such as pumps; however, there is sometimes some discrepancy between components. In this study, standardised graphical symbols were obtained from the ISO Online Browsing Platform and then mapped to PID components. Any symbols not identified from the platform were taken directly from the schematic shown in Fig. 1.

R2: Enable Non-ontology Experts to Consistently Produce Knowledge Graphs

The engineers raised concerns about how the flexibility of the mapping process between BMS schemata and knowledge graphs could lead to inconsistencies in the resulting knowledge graph from different engineers. Focus meetings with the engineer revealed a need for a tool to streamline existing procedures while ensuring consistency in the resulting knowledge graph. Engineers are rather familiar with CAD-based, 2-dimensional schematics of energy systems.

R3: Link the Knowledge Graph to the Brick Ontology

The knowledge graph provides a flexible yet formal approach to representing metadata about the buildings and its systems. There are several advantages including standardisation, improved quality and consistency and the ability to perform semantic queries based on inference. Conformance to the Brick ontology provides an understanding of the underlying mechanics of the system to enable applications such as portable analytics [9]. It has also been used to train expected performance from a physical model to identify and diagnose deviations this during operation [27]. An example query on the NEST

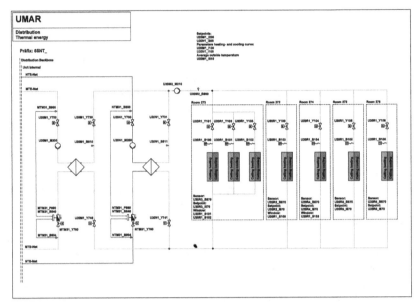

Fig. 1. The Piping and Instrumentation Diagram of the UMAR unit at the NEST Building, Empa, Switzerland

knowledge graph using the SPARQL's property paths feature is shown in Fig. 2. This enables all valves downstream of heat exchangers to be queried. The operational state of valve has an influence on the state of the downstream sensors, therefore being able to represent this information in the graph is useful for operational diagnostics. However, the process of linking sensors manually using tabular structures is meticulous and error prone as it requires a flow relation to either the upstream or downstream components. This is particularly problematic if there are multiple components connected. The ability to represent this information efficiently and quickly during PID creation is highly desirable.

```
PREFIX brick: <https://brickschema.org/schema/Brick#>
PREFIX nest: <https://www.empa.ch/digital-twin/>
select * where {
    ?exchanger a brick:Heat_Exchanger.
    ?exchanger brick:feeds* ?equipment .
    ?equipment brick:isPartOf ?loop;
        brick:hasPoint ?point.
    ?point a brick:Position_Command.
}
```

Fig. 2. An example query enabled by the Brick ontology to learn the status of the system.

R4: Facilitate Mapping Physical Assets to the Brick Ontology

Across the NEST, approximately 10,000 sensor measurements are recorded every minute and stored in a time-series database. These include internal conditions, e.g. temperature, the state of actuators, e.g. valves and energy consumption, e.g. electricity. A knowledge graph is used parallel to the time series database to store knowledge about the building and its systems according to ontologies. Ontologies formally define the types of entities and possible relationships in the relevant domains to facilitate accurate data integration, querying, and analysis. The HVAC system, shown in Fig. 1, was mapped to version 1.3 of the Brick ontology. The Brick ontology provides semantic descriptions of physical, logical and virtual assets of building energy systems and their relationships [28]. The mapping of the physical assets of Fig. 1 to the Brick ontology required knowledge from the system engineer to map the system components to their relevant classes in the ontology. Mapping the ontologies to the physical assets was found to be the most time-consuming step, requiring considerable input from the system engineer. The first stage in the mapping process was to create intermediate csv tables. In these structured tables, each unique asset is a row, and the columns provide details of the relationships to other assets. SPARQL Generate [29] is a tool to generate triples from structured data such as csvs. Input scripts for SPARQL Generate were used to iterate over the intermediate files and create the triples of the knowledge graph as.ttl files. The process of generating the input files is stored in a GitHub repository[1]. This knowledge graph was implemented using GraphDB from Ontotext, which can be queried through an endpoint[2].

4   The Ontology-Based Meta-modelling Approach for Building Management Systems

This section describes the developed artefact, which includes the ontology-based meta-modelling architecture, the integrated Pipe and Instrument Diagram (PID) Language, its graphical notation and the implementation in AOAME for creating visual diagrammatical models.

4.1   The Ontology Architecture

Figure 3 depicts the architecture of the ontology-based meta-modelling, comprehensively described in [8]. This contains three main ontologies in the meta-layer: (1) the Meta-Model Ontology, containing concepts and relations of PID, (2) the Palette Ontology, containing the graphical notation properties of PID, (3) the Domain Ontology, which maps concepts from the PID to the Brick Ontology. The model instantiates the ontology-based PID meta-model.

As models are designed, instances of the ontology-based metamodel are created, thus enabling engineers to create knowledge graphs by dealing only with PID models. This addressed **R2**. Given the inheritance principle in RDF(S) [30], the instances inherit the mapping to the Brick Ontology, thus covering **R4** and **R5**.

---

[1] https://github.com/Ja98/nest_knowledge_graph [05/03/2024].
[2] https://graphdb.nestcloud.ch/login [05/03/2024].

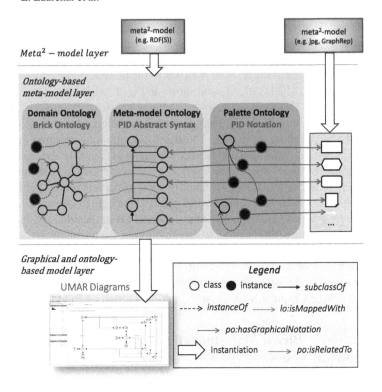

Fig. 3. The Ontology-based Meta-Modelling Architecture. Adapted from [8].

4.2 The Ontology-Based PID Language

The ontology-based meta-model for the PID Language was conceptualised to address **R1** (accommodate representational requirements of use case UMAR). Thus, the abstract syntax is based on the existing PID language. The abstract syntax was integrated with the three ontologies in the meta layer of the above-described architecture.

The parent classes of the Palette Ontology, highlighted in blue in Fig. 4, represent the elements and connectors used in the model layer to depict model elements. These classes are related to the abstract syntax, highlighted in green, which illustrates the meta-model of PID. Each element corresponds to a class, and these classes are connected to other classes either as subclasses or through an object property. Every class possesses attributes that provide additional information about the element, which can be utilised for incorporation into a knowledge graph.

Ultimately, the classes from the abstract syntax are connected to the Domain Ontology, highlighted in orange, representing the Brick classes.

Graphical Symbols

Table 1 shows an excerpt of the graphical notations for the ontology-based PID Language and related properties.

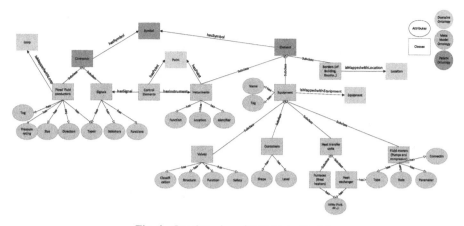

Fig. 4. Ontology-based PID Meta-Model

Table 1. Graphical Notation for the Ontology-based PID Language

Meta-Model-Ontology (pid)	Symbol	is mapped with Domain Ontology (do)	Subclass of Pallete Ontology (po)	Subclass of Language Ontology (lo)
pid:Pipe		brick:feeds	po:PaletteConnector	lo:ModellingRelation
pid:Container		brick:Boiler	po:PaletteElement	lo:ModellingElement
pid:FluidMovers (PC)		brick:HVAC_Equipment	po:PaletteElement	lo:ModellingElement

5 Evaluation

The evaluation of the artifact focused on (1) the correct design model and (2) the correct creation of the knowledge graph, i.e., its consistency with the related visual models. For both evaluation criteria, we modeled the use case scenario UMAR in the modelling tool AOAME4BMS and analysed the respective knowledge graphs. AOAME4BMS extends the prototypical open-source software AOAME [8] (available on the Internet[3]) with the ontology-based PID language. The upper part of Fig. 5 shows the user interface of AOAME4BMS, containing the visual model of the UMAR scenario, which is translated into a knowledge graph (bottom of Fig. 5). The figure contains numbers (from 1 to 5)

---

[3] https://aoame.herokuapp.com/.

to show the 1:1 correspondence among visual elements and instances in the knowledge graph. Finally, both criteria were successfully evaluated as (1) the UMAR scenario could be modelled and (2) the corresponding knowledge graph was produced respectively.

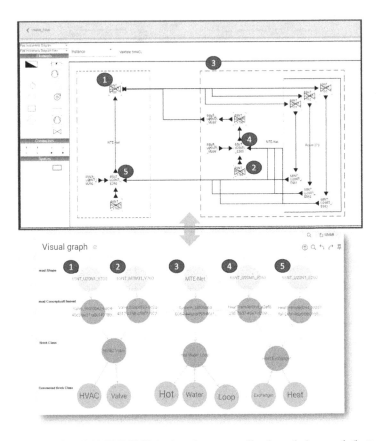

Fig. 5. Model in AOAME4BPMS (top) and corresponding knowledge graph (bottom)

6 Findings and Discussion

Overall, the research approach of extending the AOAME architecture for the building management system domain proved to be feasible, allowing for the generation of ontology-based building models. Domain experts can create these models and map the elements to a domain ontology. Simultaneously, they can produce a human-interpretable model and a machine-interpretable data file, which can be used to feed other systems. This approach promotes inclusion of stakeholders that understand the diagrammatical models but not necessarily the ontologies or knowledge graphs. The latter are used by data scientists for operations on building management systems which, e.g., aim to reduce energy consumption in buildings.

The approach enables the inclusion of multiple domain ontologies, allowing elements of the DSML to be mapped to one or more classes from different ontologies, including concepts from the domain ontology standard Brick. This promotes interoperability and adaptability of the underlying knowledge base within the dynamic field of building management systems, thus overcoming semantic issues and bridge system barriers.

The approach and the PID-language offer flexibility and ease of expansion. Adding more PID classes for model elements or connectors is relatively straightforward, allowing the incorporation of additional requirements and giving the possibility of modelling other units of the NEST building.

7 Conclusion

This work aimed to prove the adequacy of using an ontology-based meta-modelling for the creation of semantic-driven building management systems. An ontology-based domain-specific modelling language (i.e. the PID-Language) has been created for system engineers to create and maintain knowledge graphs. By leveraging the Agile and Ontology-Based Modelling Environment (AOAME) and integrating the Brick ontology, the approach facilitates the visual representation of building elements and their relationships. The correctness of the approach was tested by modelling a real-world scenario about a building management system, i.e., UMAR heating and cooling system within the NEST building. The evaluation proved that a system engineer without ontology expertise can create and maintain knowledge graphs through the use of the visual PID-language. Such knowledge graphs are linked with the domain ontology standard BRICK to foster interoperability among systems and interpretability across experts.

Future work revolves around the integration of a visualization of the constraint language SHACL in AOAME4BMS to validate the created ontology-based model.

References

1. UNEP: 2020 Global Status Report for Buildings and Construction: Towards a Zero-emissions, Efficient and Resilient Buildings and Construction Sector - Executive Summary (2020)
2. BFS: Digital Switzerland Strategy. https://www.bakom.admin.ch/dam/bakom/en/dokumente/informationsgesellschaft/strategie/strategie_digitale_schweiz.pdf.download.pdf/Strategie-DS-2020-EN.pdf
3. De Andrade Pereira, F., et al.: Towards semantic interoperability for demand-side management: a review of BIM and BAS ontologies. Presented at the 2022 European Conference on Computing in Construction (2022). https://doi.org/10.35490/EC3.2022.154
4. Pritoni, M., et al.: Metadata schemas and ontologies for building energy applications: a critical review and use case analysis. Energies 14, 2024 (2021). https://doi.org/10.3390/en14072024
5. Dibowski, H., Massa Gray, F.: Applying knowledge graphs as integrated semantic information model for the computerized engineering of building automation systems. In: Harth, A., et al. (eds.) ESWC 2020. LNCS, vol. 12123, pp. 616–631. Springer, Cham (2020). https://doi.org/10.1007/978-3-030-49461-2_36
6. Fensel, A.: Keynote: building smart cities with knowledge graphs. In: 2019 International Conference on Computer, Control, Informatics and its Applications (IC3INA), p. 1 (2019). https://doi.org/10.1109/IC3INA48034.2019.8949613

7. Pauwels, P., Zhang, S., Lee, Y.-C.: Semantic web technologies in AEC industry: a literature overview. Autom. Constr. **73**, 145–165 (2017)

8. Laurenzi, E.: An agile and ontology-based meta-modelling approach for the creation and maintenance of enterprise knowledge graph schemas. Enterprise Model. Inf. Syst. Architect. (EMISAJ) **19** (2023). https://doi.org/10.18417/EMISA.19.6

9. Balaji, B., et al.: Brick: metadata schema for portable smart building applications. Appl. Energy **226**, 1273–1292 (2018)

10. Brick: Brick v1.3 – BrickSchema. https://brickschema.org/ontology/1.3/#Shapes. Accessed 24 Sept 2023

11. Lygerakis, F., Kampelis, N., Kolokotsa, D.: Knowledge graphs' ontologies and applications for energy efficiency in buildings: a review. Energies **15**, 7520 (2022). https://doi.org/10.3390/en15207520

12. Abu-Salih, B.: Domain-specific knowledge graphs: a survey. J. Netw. Comput. Appl. **185**, 103076 (2021). https://doi.org/10.1016/j.jnca.2021.103076

13. Kejriwal, M.: Knowledge graphs: a practical review of the research landscape. Information **13**, 161 (2022). https://doi.org/10.3390/info13040161

14. Zou, X.: A survey on application of knowledge graph. In: Journal of Physics: Conference Series, vol. 1487, p. 012016 (2020). https://doi.org/10.1088/1742-6596/1487/1/012016

15. Schneider, G.F., Rasmussen, M.H., Bonsma, P., Oraskari, J., Pauwels, P.: Linked building data for modular building information modelling of a smart home. In: eWork and eBusiness in Architecture, Engineering and Construction. CRC Press (2018)

16. Pazlar, T., Turk, Ž: Interoperability in practice: geometric data exchange using the IFC standard. J. Inf. Technol. Constr. ITcon. **13**, 362–380 (2008)

17. Hu, Z.-Z., Leng, S., Lin, J.-R., Li, S.-W., Xiao, Y.-Q.: Knowledge extraction and discovery based on BIM: a critical review and future directions. Arch. Comput. Methods Eng. **29**, 335–356 (2022). https://doi.org/10.1007/s11831-021-09576-9

18. Andersson, R., Eidenskog, M.: Beyond barriers–exploring resistance towards BIM through a knowledge infrastructure framework. Constr. Manag. Econ. 1–16 (2023)

19. Shojaei, R.S., Oti-Sarpong, K., Burgess, G.: Leading UK construction companies' strategies to tackle BIM training and skills challenges. Int. J. Constr. Educ. Res. **19**, 383–404 (2023). https://doi.org/10.1080/15578771.2022.2123071

20. Buchmann, R., et al.: Large Language Models: Expectations for Semantics-Driven Systems Engineering (2023). https://doi.org/10.2139/ssrn.4633719. https://papers.ssrn.com/abstract=4633719

21. Guarino, N., Guizzardi, G., Mylopoulosc, J.: On the philosophical foundations of conceptual models. Front. Artif. Intell. Appl. **321**, 1–15 (2020). https://doi.org/10.3233/FAIA200002

22. Bernasconi, A., Canakoglu, A., Ceri, S.: From a conceptual model to a knowledge graph for genomic datasets. In: Laender, A.H.F., Pernici, B., Lim, E.-P., de Oliveira, J.P.M. (eds.) ER 2019. LNCS, vol. 11788, pp. 352–360. Springer, Cham (2019). https://doi.org/10.1007/978-3-030-33223-5_29

23. Thomas, O., Fellmann, M.: Semantic EPC: enhancing process modeling using ontology languages. Presented at the CEUR Workshop Proceedings (2007)

24. Vaishnavi, V., Kuechler, B.: Design science research in information systems. Assoc. Inf. Syst. (2004)

25. EMPA: Empa – NEST. https://www.empa.ch/web/nest/overview. Accessed 30 Oct 2023

26. Wieringa, R.J.: Design Science Methodology for Information Systems and Software Engineering. Springer, Heidelberg (2014)

27. Ploennigs, J., Maghella, M., Schumann, A., Chen, B.: Semantic diagnosis approach for buildings. IEEE Trans. Ind. Inform. **13**, 3399–3410 (2017). https://doi.org/10.1109/TII.2017.2726001

28. Balaji, B., et al.: Brick: towards a unified metadata schema for buildings. In: Proceedings of the 3rd ACM International Conference on Systems for Energy-Efficient Built Environments, pp. 41–50. Association for Computing Machinery, New York (2016). https://doi.org/10.1145/2993422.2993577
29. Lefrançois, M., Zimmermann, A., Bakerally, N.: A SPARQL extension for generating RDF from heterogeneous formats. In: Blomqvist, E., Maynard, D., Gangemi, A., Hoekstra, R., Hitzler, P., Hartig, O. (eds.) ESWC 2017. LNCS, vol. 10249, pp. 35–50. Springer, Cham (2017). https://doi.org/10.1007/978-3-319-58068-5_3
30. W3C: RDF Vocabulary Description Language 1.0: RDF Schema (RDFS) - Semantic Web Standards. https://www.w3.org/2001/sw/wiki/RDFS. Accessed 22 Apr 2023

EOMAS

20 years of the EOMAS workshop

When we, led by Professor Joseph Barjis, founded SIGMAS (Special Interest Group on Modeling And Simulation) at the Association for Information Systems and its EOMAS (Enterprise Organization Modeling And Simulation) workshop 20 years ago, this was the time of the final penetration of the object-oriented paradigm into the area of building large software applications. Indeed, software analysis and design methods at that time had still assumed that software engineering processes begin with the description of requirements, but finding, verifying, and validating these requirements was considered as something that did not belong to software engineering techniques because the software engineer must receive it ready-made from other specialists. However, we have learned from experience that this is not an accurate statement, and that requirements engineering must be an inevitable part of the software engineering process. Specifically, software development intersects with business engineering and management consulting. Over two decades, the importance of this kind of conceptual analysis and information system prototyping has grown compared to writing program code.

We take pride in the EOMAS workshop, a breeding ground for various innovative approaches that have gained recognition at large conferences. However, at the time of their inception, these ideas might only have the opportunity to be accepted in the EOMAS community. We are committed to maintaining this unique feature of our workshop, ensuring it remains a platform for communication, inspiration, and collaboration on new ideas. In many countries, including mine, publications in peer-reviewed journals are more highly regarded than those at conferences of our type. This poses a significant challenge for young scientists, who often need prior contact with the expert community to start writing journal articles. Our workshop addresses this need and provides a stepping stone for their academic journey.

Dear colleagues, we also went through the COVID period and experimented with changing our workshop's name to MOBA (Modelling Of Business Agility). This year, we are returning to the original name, EOMAS, with which we started 20 years ago. There is a future ahead of us with new challenges. Java's dominance has been declining. New programming languages like Python, graph databases, the massive rise of artificial intelligence, and the strengthening of the functional paradigm are coming to the scene. The creative spirit of the old, nearly forgotten technologies is returning. Artificial intelligence and non-imperative programming styles are no longer just exciting toys but are becoming practical technologies thanks to the growing performance of today's computers. We are much more interested in conceptual modelling and lifting software engineering to higher spheres of abstraction, which are closer to classical philosophical thinking. The whole of human society is changing. Today's requirements engineers and business consultants use various software tools for modelling and simulation. This fact confirms the need for our workshop and brings new inspiration. Thank you for 20 years of EOMAS (and MOBA) workshops. Let us look to the future with great hope.

June 2024

Vojtěch Merunka
Martin Molhanec

Organization

Martin Molhanec — Czech Technical University in Prague, Czech Republic

Joseph Barjis — San Jose State University, USA

Eduard Babkin — HSE University, Russia

Steering Committee

Vojtěch Merunka — Czech University of Life Sciences Prague, Czech Republic

Petra Pavlíčková — Czech Technical University in Prague, Czech Republic

Pavel Malyzhenkov — HSE University, Russia

Simona Colucci — Politecnico di Bari, Italy

Konstantinos Tsilionis — Eindhoven University of Technology, The Netherlands

Russell Lock — Loughborough University, UK

Anna Bobkowska — Gdynia Maritime University, Poland

Yves Wautelet — KU Leuven, Belgium

Customizing a Generic Digital Transformation Objectives Model onto a Telecommunication Company

Ghazaleh Aghakhani[1], Ke Xu[2], Yves Wautelet[2(✉)] [iD], Konstantinos Tsilionis[3] [iD], and Manuel Kolp[1] [iD]

[1] Université catholique de Louvain, Louvain-la-Neuve, Belgium
{ghazaleh.aghakhani,manuel.kolp}@uclouvain.be
[2] KULeuven, Leuven, Belgium
{ke.xu,yves.wautelet}@kuleuven.be
[3] Eindhoven University of Technology, Eindhoven, The Netherlands
k.tsilionis@tue.nl

Abstract. Setting-up a Digital Transformation (DT) strategy appears to be challenging for a lot of organizations. Indeed, C-level managers often do not know how to coordinate and align each individual initiative towards a well established long-term vision. Previous work allowed to build-up a set of DT strategic objectives out of literature, validate and extend them through expert opinions. The refined representation was then customized/instantiated onto a case in the healthcare sector. Further validation is nevertheless needed in order to understand the applicability of the generic DT strategic objectives onto cases in various sectors and, very importantly, determine the pros and the cons of such an approach. This paper is part of this effort. It depicts the application of the generic DT strategic objectives model onto the case of a telecommunication company and the validation of the instance. Information collection and validation are performed through domain experts interviews. We discovered that the instantiated strategic DT objectives representation helps to clearly identify the priorities that should be considered by the company in formulating the organization's DT strategy. These prioritized objectives entail the analysis of the government policies and the adjustment of human resources management. The most frequent critics from the three interviewees consist in the generic model's failure in recognizing the vital stake that the government has in the management of a state-owned company. Finally, some objectives were not fully comprehended by the managers despite our detailed explanation, such as the financial allocation ability which, to a certain extent, entails the meaning of assessment of impacts on current core businesses.

Keywords: Digital Transformation · Digital Transformation Strategy · Digital Transformation Objectives

1 Introduction

Many organizations approach their Digital Transformation (DT) in an ad-hoc manner. In order to evaluate each technological initiative alignment within the context of the

J. P. A. Almeida et al. (Eds.): CAiSE 2024 Workshops, LNBIP 521, pp. 217–228, 2024.
https://doi.org/10.1007/978-3-031-61003-5_19

organization's DT, a clear DT Strategy (DTS) should nevertheless be set-up at governance level. Within the range of initiatives destined to help in this process, Aghakhani et al. [1] have proposed to assemble all of the classical DT strategic objectives found in literature, unify them into a generic set of DT strategic objectives later evaluated through expert opinions. This model is aimed to be instantiated onto a specific organization in order to support its DTS formulation. The model is presented using the NFR framework [2] using a decomposition of elements which allows to see them and their hierarchy in an exhaustive manner. This provides an understanding of the scope of action of an organization that seeks digitalization. The latter is composed of 4 main branches, each being a strategic objective that is refined into sub objectives: The first branch is focused on *developing a digital roadmap*; the second branch is focused on *evaluating financial ability*; *identifying structural changes* is what the third branch is focused on; finally, branch four focuses on *identifying possible changes in value creation and operational efficiency*. Once instantiated to a case, the model can be used for Business and DT alignment of to be developed Business IT Services [3] using the MoDrIGo [4] framework. This generic set of DT strategic objectives is here applied onto a telecom company. The latter is state-owned so directed by the national government; this specificity deeply impacts the governance. The DTS and its alignment with individual initiatives is explored using the specified model; data is collected through domain expert interviews before and after the instantiation of the generic model.

2   Research Approach and Method

Being in the paradigm of Design Science Research (DSR) [5] and following-up on the previous study of Aghakhani et al. [1], this research has the aim to further validate the results through the use of a case study. To this end, we address the following Research Question (RQ): *What are the strengths and weaknesses of the use of the generic DT strategic objectives model proposed in Aghakhani et al. [1] to support a telecommunication company in formulating its DTS?*.

Figure 1 situates the research described in the current paper within its broader context. It indeed extends previous research through a new custom Design Cycle (DC). The research activities in the light grey zone of the figure have been performed and published previously and the ones in the white one constitute the contribution of the present paper. As said in the background section, Aghakhani et al. [1] have built up a generic set of DT strategic objectives out of literature (see DC1 in Fig. 1). Then, they validated this first representation through expert opinions leading to an enhanced version of the DT strategic objectives (see DC2 in Fig. 1). Also, still in DC2, the proposal was applied on the case of a hospital going through its DT. The latter case can nevertheless not be considered as a full case study so there is more space for application to extend the validation process and learn more lessons from application; this is the purpose of this paper. Indeed, we introduce here the so-called DC3.

Within DC3, **which is the contribution of the present paper**, the latest (generic) DT strategic objectives representation, outputted from DC2, is applied onto the case of a telecom company going through its DT. The overall approach firstly consisted in the collection of domain knowledge (through interviews) in order to determine the objectives that were relevant for the organization and tune them to this business context.

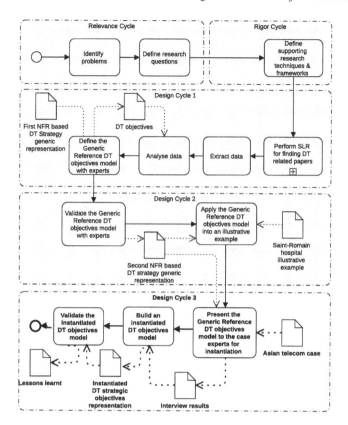

Fig. 1. Research methodology updated by adding a new Design Cycle for validation objectives

Out of these interviews, an instantiated version of the DT strategic objectives representation was built. The latter representation was then presented to the interviewees and explained. These domain experts were then asked to evaluate the applicability and completeness of the model as well as possible implementation flows. Out of the application and instantiation process new lessons were learned and highlighted.

We followed a structured process for conducting the interviews. We indeed conducted in-depth semi-structured interviews with three C-level senior managers of the company. These interviews were conducted between April and May 2022 via online platforms such as Skype and Wechat. All three managers were interviewed twice. Table 1 presents the age, the highest degree, the role, and the seniority years of each of the three interviewees. The first set of interviews was focused on the information regarding the interviewees and their knowledge regarding DT. This allowed us to gather information about the background and the expertise of each of them as well as gathering the necessary inputs for the instantiation of the generic conceptual model respectively. Based on the discussion of this first set, an instantiated representation was built. The latter was then presented to the interviewees during the second set of interviews. Subsequently, the interviewees were asked to describe the implementation of each of the branches of the model within their company, and validate the relevance of the generic objectives to their case, and find out the completeness and potential improvements of the instantiated generic representation model with regards to their case. The first set of the interview took 54 to 69 min, while the second set took 16 to 24 min. The analysis and discussion of the result is then done with the help of Nvivo, a software aimed to analyze qualitative research results.

Table 1. Interviewee Profile

	Age	Highest degree	Position	Seniority (years)
Interviewee 1 (I1)	46	Master	Manager of the DICIT department	17
interviewee 2 (I2)	37	Bachelor	Manager of the B-end department	14
Interviewee 3 (I3)	53	EMBA	Vice general manager	20

3   Results

3.1   Preliminary Interview Round: Domain Knowledge Collection

The interviews began by a brief description of the in place DT implementation and DTS at the telecom company. According to the interviewees, the company has divided its business into four ends: 1) C(customer)-end grouping individual customers who purchase traditional services such as mobile devices and mobile subscriptions; 2) B(business)-end grouping offerings destated for businesses and governments and including digital-enabled services such as smart city, cloud- based system, IoT-related products, etc.; 3) H(home)-end with 5G-enabled offerings for families such as Wi-Fi 6 and smart TV; 4) N(New)-end combining services such as videos, gaming, sports streaming, etc. The C-end being the most traditional part for a telecom firm, the company's ambition in the digital era is to increase the proportion of the other three ends in its overall income. According to I3, *"Currently, the C-end and H-end count for about 70% of our revenue and the B-end counts for merely 20%. Our ambition is, in the coming three years, the B-end and H-end will count for above 60% of our revenue, with C-end being stably developed. This requires us to reconfigure our resources including humans, infrastructure, structure, processing, in order to tackle the challenges brought by the digital transformation."* I1 added an example of such reconfiguration: *"Our change in recruitment policies is an example. In the past, we brought in the graduates mainly as salespersons or customer service operators. Now, the majority come in as IT engineers."* I2 also added: *"At the telecom company, we talk about 'digitally intelligent transformation'. This means we'll be transformed from a pure telecom company to a digital service provider, from resource-driven to innovation-driven development, from traditional to cloud-enabled production processing."*

Branch One: Perform Financial Investment Analytics. According to I1, *"The first thing to consider in financial aspect is the financial increase that digital transformation* will potentially bring us. We need to consider when the B-end and H-end will reach the break-even point and it's based on this analysis that we plan the allocation of financial and other resources." He validated the two sub-objectives and added "the impact of digital transformation on our current core business, which is the C-end businesses, is definitely taken into account when performing financial analytics." Interviewees 2 also confirmed the two sub-objectives, however, believed that "the financial ability isn't a barrier: our financial performance and potentials are excellent and we're in the right time to do the right thing.". I3 approved this and added "from one side, the government has pointed us as the leader of the digital economy and we receive very strong support from the state; from the other, our company is among the most profitable in the world and we have strong confidence on our financial ability."

Branch Two: Develop a Digital Roadmap. According to all three interviewees, the *social-economic environment* is the very first thing to be considered, which is not included in the model as a sub-objective. As mentioned by I1 "*We firstly analysed our external environment. It's important to know that the whole society is being transformed digitally and if you don't follow you'll fail behind. The DT is a consequence of the nation's economic development. As a state-owned company, we ought to respond to the nation's advocacy and we have the responsibility to act as a leader.*" Finally, I2 added "*the digital roadmap of the telecom company is closely tied with the five-year plan of the government.*" The sub-objective "*Prioritize digital ideas*" was mentioned by I1 during his description of digital roadmap development. Other interviewees also agreed on this sub-objective. I2 added that to achieve such objective, they engaged external partners from Europe in this process to optimize the evaluation and prioritisation of digital ideas. The three interviewees emphasized the importance of the sub-objective "*Align stakeholders' objectives*". I1 said that "*our biggest shareholder is the state and it's our mission to safeguard the state's assets.*". Regarding the customers and employees, I2 said that "*the quality of service is one important aspect of our DT strategies and we constantly communicate the values we may bring to our clients to get their satisfaction towards what we're doing. Besides, motivation of our employees' enthusiasm and support is also important to consider.*". Finally, I3 said that: "*what the individual shareholders care most is the value of their stock. We gained their support because our stock is upvalued during the past years.*"

Concerning the *assessment of digital maturity*, all managers emphasized its importance when setting a digital roadmap. According to I3 "*The telecom company has very strong R&D capacity and agile mindset. Since this century, it's constantly recombined its resources into new offerings to adapt to changing environment. R&D is part of our gene.*". I2 added "*it's important to know where you're right now to set the objective you want to achieve by digital transformation. We've certainly assessed the gap between our current situation and the objective stated by the government*". Moreover, he suggested that this should be considered as a separate branch, as "*that's where we analyse the most when we formulate our strategies*" and because "*it makes the whole branch too complicated because the point related to digital maturity alone has 4 layers! If one objective has too many underlying dimensions, it's too difficult to be comprehended and implemented.*" Finally, I1 explained that "*the digital roadmap we developed is closely related to the assessment of our digital maturity. We're currently working on three core digital activities: 'connection, algorithm and empowerment'. These three aspects were proposed based on our digital maturity: we have 90 million customers, making us the largest telecom operator in the world. Our huge customer base allows us to build a gigantic connection network, which is the foundation stone of the 'algorithm' and 'empowerment'.*" When discussing the assessment of risk appetite, the opinions differed. For I1, assessing risk appetite is a valid point. According to him, the telecom company has different risk appetite as a function of the business ends: "*we can accept more risks for N-end businesses because these are the domains that we were not familiar with and thus we need more experiences. However, we expect more stability at C, H, and B-ends businesses because they are where most of our revenue comes from.*" Interviewees 3 held opposite opinion by saying that: "*risks are not something considered by us. As a state-owned company, we must follow what's ordered by the government, who in turn provides us with the support we need and bears all the risks. We are totally different from private companies: we ought to be the pioneer in the digital economy and provide all the necessities for the digital transformation of the whole society.*"

Regarding *develop and increase dynamic capability*, all interviewees confirmed that such objective is crucial when assessing digital maturity and when the fostering of dynamic capability requires the improvement of people agility. Interviewees 1 and 2 confirmed that within the company, there is this regular formation of digital knowledge that is given to the entire company, from high-level leaders to employees. According to I2: "*we have an established formation system across the company. For the employees, everyone is expected to follow online courses on digital technologies such as cloud, big data and IoT. After the courses, you need to take a test and obtain a certificate in digital transformation knowledge. For the high-level leaders, we need to follow one week's formation at our partner university, during which professors and experts from reputed universities and institutions are invited to give us courses.*" For I3, the fostering of dynamic capability asks for intensive competition among employees and leaders. He added "*at our branch, hundreds of people are eliminated each year due to their lack of skills necessary for the digital transformation and even high-level leaders are included. At the same time, a great number of young graduates specialising in IT and management are recruited to replace less-skilled employees. The competition is fierce: if you cannot follow the path, then you are out.*" When it came to the evaluation of the organizational context and environment, all managers confirmed its importance when developing a digital roadmap and also the relevance of the refinement including "*Sense disruption and change*" and "*Seize upon trends and emerging technologies*". Concerning the Market disruption, I1 claimed that the core activities of "*connection, algorithm and empowerment*" is a disruptive ideology and it is also served as their strategic direction. Regarding the emerging technologies, I2 pointed that 5G and other digital technologies fit into this category and should certainly be taken into account in their DTS formulation. As for the development of vision and strategic direction, all interviewees pointed this objective as important to achieve in the development of the digital roadmap. Regarding the "*Organisation-wide communication*", the three interviewees confirmed that the implementation of digital technologies requires communication but the flow of the communication is mainly top-down, meaning that it's the high-level leaders who mandate their decisions. Finally, for I3 this objective was ambiguous and less important at a state-owned company: "*the employees and local branches are expected to follow what's mandated by high-level organisations and there is no room for negotiation.*"

Branch Three: Identify Structural Changes. All interviewees approved the importance of the structural changes in setting DT strategies and the first thing they pointed out was the *establishment of a DT unit*. I1 mentioned *"the department that I'm in charge of is an example of the structural change because it's established to aid digital transformation"*. I2 shared the opinion and added *"we're working on improving the proportion of employees with IT background in the organisation. On the internal side, we're training employees to improve their digital knowledge. Externally, we're adjusting our recruitment policy to bring in graduates of this field."*

As for the reconfiguration of business and IT resources, all the interviewees confirmed that such objective is part of the structural changes. According to I1, they are reconfiguring these resources to support B and H-ends businesses, which is the direction of their DT. I3 added that the resources are also reconfigured into other industries such as agriculture, medical service and aeronautics which were traditionally not part of the telecom company's expertise.

Regarding the *new source of revenue* and *replacing traditional business models with digital-enabled ones*, all interviewees confirmed the importance of these objectives. However, they all pointed out that the idea that these two objectives do not contribute to refining the objective of *identifying structural changes* but rather to the objective *identify possible changes in value creation and operational efficiency* located in the fifth branch of the representation. As for the *replacement of the traditional business model*, I1 mentioned that: *"we start proposing many kinds of cloud- based services to the C-end users as a substitute for traditional services such as instant messages, voice-callings, etc. This is a shift of our business model"*. I2 added *"in the past, we provided business customers with physical equipment. What we're offering more and more is integrated ICT solutions rather than materials alone."*

Branch Four: Identify Possible Changes in Value Creation and Operational Efficiency. According to I1: *"in the past, customers needed to go to sales points to purchase services or recharge their accounts. But with the digital technologies, they're able to do everything online and that brings them convenience."* I2 added *"the integrated cloud-based solutions help B-end customers reduce their cost and makes system update easier for them."* In response to *how the identification of new methods of value creation was satisfied*, I2 confirmed the objective of *"Follow, analyse and anticipate customer behaviour"*, while I1 added *"the customer needs should also be guided as sometimes their needs would never be created without intentional guidance"*. I3 added *"as a state-owned company, government policy is the priority we should consider. To identify what values we should create, the government report is important because it says where the state investments will go and that's the direction we should follow."*

Regarding the objective *establishing synergy between digital and traditional processes and offerings*, all interviewees agreed that it should be considered at this branch. I1 mentioned that *"we gave customers the choice between on-line web site and off-line sales points to compensate the disadvantages of each side. I think that's a kind of synergy."* I3 added *"we call it 'scale-based value creation': we benefit from the loyalty of our customer base thanks to the traditional businesses to propose our digital services that will create more values for them. The synergy can at the same time benefit current traditional core businesses: "when we get in contact with a company, we not only propose the digital offerings that we're famous for but the traditional ones such as internet and mobile devices."* I2 emphasised that same applies for H-end businesses: *"when a customer orders family-related products such as WiFi and broadband internet or simply calls for a repair, we'd at the same time propose them digital smart offerings."*

Branch Five: Assess the Level of Organisational Technology Comfort and Acceptance. All interviewees confirmed the importance of the assessment of capability and compatibility of infrastructure and IS. However, I3 emphasized that *"the assessments of technology comfort or acceptance are not relevant because the cloud-based technologies facilitate in a great deal the digital transformation of all levels"* and also because *"when your hierarchy or the government mandates it and gives all the support you need, you have no choice but to transform, despite your comfort or acceptance."* I1 added *"concerning the infrastructures, we evaluate its capability to be cloud-enabled. The same thing for IS: we evaluate its capability to be 'smart' thanks to digital technologies.".* According to I2, *"before developing 5G services, we surely assessed its compatibility and its impact on 4G, which is our current cure businesses."*

Regarding the assessment of IT department, all interviewees confirmed this objective. I3 mentioned: *"based on our assessment, we adjust our recruitment direction to make sure that the IT department has sufficient ability.".* I2 and 3 had the same opinion. Regarding the *prototyping*, interviewees 1 and 2 emphasized the importance of the objective. I1 explained *"one example is the family gateway that we designed for our H-end business. It's a digital- enabled new product that connects all the home appliances. With all the digital technologies in hand, we made a lot of efforts in prototyping in order to improve its performance."* I3 held a different opinion regarding B-end businesses, *"it's difficult to prototype when you deal with businesses and governments because all we offer is based on their customized needs. As the products are highly customized, all we can do is to improve our core technologies."* Finally, I2 described what should be modified in this branch: *"first, you need to know if your infrastructures and IS can be cloud-enabled; then, the assessment of IT department is done to know if we have enough ability; finally, we prototype the products with all the digital technologies."*

3.2 Instantiated DT Strategic Objectives Representation

As described in Sect. 2, the first set of interviews resulted in an instantiated representation of the DT strategic objectives; the latter is depicted in Fig. 2. In this representation, modified and added objectives are highlighted in different colors. As can be seen, most of the objectives are relevant and can be directly instantiated onto the case, e.g. *"Recognize new sources of revenue through digitalisation"* was instantiated into *"Identify new sources of revenue enabled by B, H, and N-ends businesses.".*

The blue clouds represent the objectives that have been modified after the examination of the interview results in Sect. 3.1. The objective *"Assess and develop digital maturity"* was refined as one main branch of the highest level objective; this modification was made due to two aspects: a) as mentioned by I1 and 2, the assessment of digital maturity is one of the priorities at the telecom company in DTS formulation; b) the separation of this objective from the objective "Determine digital roadmap" reduces the layers of the model and facilitates its comprehensibility and application. *"Align stakeholders' objectives"* was instantiated into *"Align stakeholders' interests"*, as when speaking of this point, most of the interviewees referred to the upvaluation of the stock price and the improved service provided for customers, instead of their objectives. Furthermore, as suggested, the objectives *"Replace traditional business models with new digitally enabled ones"* and *"Recognize new sources of revenue through digitalisation"* were refined as sub-objectives of *"Identify possible changes in value creation & operational efficiency"*. Moreover, the objective *"Follow, analyse & anticipate customer behaviour"* was modified into *"Analyse, anticipate and guide customer needs"*, as I1 suggested that some of the customers would never come true without a proposed guidance. Finally, the objective *"Assess the level of organisational technology comfort & acceptance"* was replaced with *"Assess technology compatibility"* as I3 rejected the idea that the acceptance should be evaluated because *"it is mandated by high-level organisations and you have to follow it despite your comfort or acceptance"*.

The red clouds stand for objectives that did not exist in the generic model but were relevant in the case of the telecom company. The objective of *"Analyse social-economic environment"* was added as the prioritised sub-objective of *"Determine digital roadmap"*. This objective was indeed mentioned by all the interviewees as the first dimension to consider when setting digital objectives. The objective was refined into *"Analyse strategic direction on the national level"* and *"Analyse macro-economic situation"*. The former is prioritized in this refinement as the company's vision is closely tied to the vision of the country. The objective *"Evaluate financial increase potentials"* was suggested by I1 and I2 as one crucial aspect of *"Perform financial analytics"*. The objective *"Analyse government investment directions"* was added as a refinement of the objective *"Identify new methods of value creation"* according to the suggestion of I3 that the telecom company's value should be created where state investments on DT go. Finally, the objective *"Assess IT department capability"* was refined into *"Evaluate recruitment policy"*, which reflects the idea of the interviewees that workers with expertise in digital domains are valued and unskilled workers will gradually be eliminated.

3.3 Post Interview Round: Evaluation and Validation of the Instantiated DT Objectives Representation

Content of the Model. Interviewees 1 and 2 approved the completeness and conformity of the model to the actual company situation. I3, however, did not consider the assessment of digital maturity as a separate branch. He says *"you can consider it, but it's not equally important as other aspects. Mature or not, every industry and company will finally follow the digital path, as it's a strategy at the national level. Even if you aren't mature enough now, you'll finally get used to it."* Regarding the analysis of the social-economic environment, I1 added *"even though it is refined into two aspects: the analysis of the macro-economic situation and the strategic direction on the national level, it's important to notice that the national strategic vision, especially the 'Five-year Plans', is closely tied with the macro-economic situation of the country. They can't be done separately because the two are complementary."*. Concerning the point of analysing government investment directions, I3 added *"what we analyse in particular is the white books who clearly state the industries that will be invested and supported, and that's the direction we should go."*

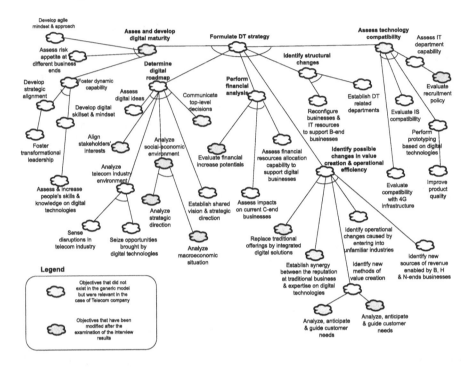

Fig. 2. Adapted DTS NFR Decomposition Representation (Color figure online)

Applicability, Advantages, and Shortcomings. Here, we asked the interviewees to evaluate the model's ease of use and its usefulness in formulating a DTS. I1 approved the applicability of the model and thought that the model follows the right logic that should follow a DTS decision-maker and thus can be used as a checklist. According to I2 the reality is much more complicated and challenging than what the model encompasses, but the usage of this model definitely eases the tasks and makes everything clear and sorted. Moreover, he adds that it is necessary to understand, beyond what the model explains and which specific measures should be taken to achieve each goal. However, for I3 the model is too complicated and *"at the telecom company, DT is more straightforward than what the model shows: we follow the direction of the country and we adjust the strategy whenever it's inappropriate. What's more, it's difficult to say that if this model works for a company like the telecom company, it'll work for other companies: the scale and the financial ability are totally different."*

As for the advantages of the model, all managers referred to its completeness. I2 explained that *"for those companies who have little knowledge of DT, this model is very useful as it tells you all the aspects you should consider when formulating your DTS."* He added *"how? If the model is destinated for providing a methodology, then it should be clearer what should exactly be done regarding each point."* According to I1, the model failed to show its internal logic between different points and the flow of the structure is still unclear. He suggested that *"perhaps you can give each point a weight and use this model to score a company's DTS completeness"*. I3 had the same opinion by saying that: *"I can't see from the clouds what's important and what's not. For me, a model is clear only when is straightforward and tells where the focus should be."*

Steps for the Implementation. Each interviewee was asked to propose an order within the six branches of Fig. 2. I1 suggested the following order: *assessing the digital maturity, developing a digital roadmap, identifying structural changes, identifying changes in value creation and operational efficiency, performing financial analytics*, and *assessing technology comfort and acceptance*. I2 proposed the order as: *performing financial analytics, assessing digital maturity, developing a digital roadmap, identifying changes in value creation and operational efficiency, assessing technology comfort and acceptance*, and *ending up with identifying structural changes*. Finally, I3 gave his order based on the 5 branches excluding the assessment of digital maturity: *"the first is to develop a digital roadmap. The second is to perform financial analytics. The last one is the structural changes. The rest two aspects are in-between and equally important."*

4   Discussion

The instantiated DT strategic objectives representation helps to clearly identify the priorities that should be considered by the company in formulating the organization's DTS. These prioritized objectives entail the analysis of the government policies and the adjustment of human resources management. The digital-enabled offerings of the telecom company encompass cloud-based services and solutions, 5G networks, family smart technologies, etc. Also, it has proposed innovative ideologies that are disruptive to the whole industry. The positions of these offerings and ideologies about DTS formulations and their relationships are illustrated by the decomposition. Besides, the conceptual model suggests that the formulation of DTS entails top-level decision-makers carefully evaluating the resources and taking into account the stakeholders' interests.

According to the interview results, some aspects of the model are criticized by the interviewees. The most frequent critics from the three interviewees consist in the generic model's failure in recognizing the vital stake that the government has in the management of a state-owned company. Our findings suggest that, due to the nature of the company, the formulation of the telecom company's DTS has a close relationship with what is stated by the government. Although confirmed by the interviewees as pertinent, some objectives were suggested to be less crucial than what was shown in previous studies. From the financial aspect, the telecom company has excellent financial performance and is among the most profitable companies on the planet. Meanwhile, the strong support from the government constitutes a significant part of its financial resources. These factors led to the fact that the assessment of its financial allocation was judged as less important by the managers when implementing the DT. Meanwhile, the strong financial capability improved the company's risk tolerance and thus the assessment of the risk appetite was also suggested as less important.

Despite the positive appraisal of the interviewees regarding the completeness and accuracy of the instantiated model, its practicality and the clarity were still questioned. Some objectives were not fully comprehended despite our detailed explanation, such as the financial allocation ability which, to a certain extent, entails the meaning of assessment of impacts on current core businesses. Moreover, there was an overlap within the interviewees' understanding of different objectives whose differences are still ambiguous, such as the notion of *evaluating people ability* and *assessing IT department* which all refer to people's skillset. Also, during the interactions with the interviewees, we also realised that sometimes the model is limited in accurately describing the DTS formulation of a large corporation which deals with diversified businesses. For example, "Perform prototyping" was proved to be relevant in the C-end but not the B-end business due to the different level of customisation. It appeared that the lack of clarification on the horizontal relationships between objectives within the same refinement jeopardized the interviewees' appraisal of the model's applicability. It was also stated that the weight of each objective should be carefully evaluated, which is essential for its application in a real organisational context, because that will facilitate the comprehension of managers and clarify where the focus should be. Furthermore, our findings suggest that the clarification on the specific measures that should be taken regarding each objective appeared to help improve the applicability of the model. In addition, we can conclude that, although stated differently by the three managers, the evaluation of financial ability, the assessment of the digital maturity, and the development of a digital roadmap remain the priorities within the telecom company's DTS formulation.

5   Conclusion

Within the present paper we customized a previously proposed generic DT strategic objectives model to the case of a telecom company. This case study strongly differs from the previous ones in the sense that the organization is state-owned so that the government has a large stake in its governance. The generic DT strategic objectives model encompasses many different aspects that need to be pursued in DTS formulation. Its objectives decomposition classification helps top-level managers identify the internal dependency between different objectives. Moreover, the instantiated representation helps organizations have a long-term overview of the goals they have to achieve through DT and address the challenges caused by the ongoing development of digital technologies. For instance, the telecom industry is subject to constant disruptions. Managers prioritized the analysis of the government policies and the adjustment of human resources management as priority objectives.

References

1. Aghakhani, G., Wautelet, Y., Dijkmans, D., Heng, S., Poelmans, S., Kolp, M.: Supporting digital transformation strategy formulation through a customisable set of objectives: conceptual model and expert opinions. Enterprise Inf. Syst. **18**(3), 2300089 (2024)
2. Chung, L., Nixon, B.A., Yu, E., Mylopoulos, J.: Non-functional Requirements in Software Engineering, vol. 5. Springer, Cham (2012). https://doi.org/10.1007/978-1-4615-5269-7
3. Wautelet, Y., Kolp, M.: Business and model-driven development of BDI multi-agent systems. Neurocomputing **182**, 304–321 (2016)
4. Wautelet, Y.: A model-driven it governance process based on the strategic impact evaluation of services. J. Syst. Softw. **149**, 462–475 (2019)
5. Hevner, A., Chatterjee, S.: Design science research in information systems. In: Hevner, A., Chatterjee, S. (eds.) Design Research in Information Systems. ISIS, vol. 22, pp. 9–22. Springer, Boston (2010). https://doi.org/10.1007/978-1-4419-5653-8_2

Analyzing Customer Sentiments:
A Comparative Evaluation of Large Language
Models for Enhanced Business Intelligence

Pavel Beránek[1,2]([⊠]) [iD] and Vojtěch Merunka[3,4] [iD]

[1] Department of Information Engineering, Faculty of Economics and Management, Czech
University of Life Sciences, Prague, Czech Republic
pavel.beranek@ujep.cz
[2] Department of Informatics, Scientific Faculty, Jan Evangelista Purkyně University in Ústí Nad
Labem, Ústí nad Labem, Czech Republic
[3] Department of Information Engineering, Faculty of Economics and Management, Czech
University of Life Sciences Prague, Prague, Czech Republic
merunka@pef.czu.cz
[4] Department of Software Engineering, Faculty of Nuclear Sciences and Physical Engineering,
Czech Technical University in Prague, Prague, Czech Republic

Abstract. This paper presents a comparative evaluation of Large Language Models (LLMs) against established sentiment analysis tools, focusing on their efficiency in parsing complex customer reviews for sentiment and emotion. Our research reveals that LLMs are capable of detecting a wide range of emotions, offering granular insights that transcend traditional analysis capabilities. However, the study also highlights a notable discrepancy in reproducibility and reliability among smaller LLMs (SLMs) when compared to the VADER model, a stalwart in sentiment analysis. These findings elucidate the potential and limitations of employing SLMs for business intelligence purposes, particularly in automating sentiment analysis of customer feedback. We discuss the implications of these outcomes for businesses looking to leverage AI for customer insights, emphasizing the importance of model selection based on the specific requirements of reproducibility and depth of analysis.

Keywords: Large Language Models · Small Language Models · Sentiment Analysis · Granular Sentiment Analysis · Emotion Detection

1 Introduction

Large Language Models (LLMs) have become pivotal in shaping the future of customer-business interactions. These models facilitate the automation of critical customer relationship processes, such as deriving insights from reviews, engaging in social media interactions, and generating public relations reports. Following the groundbreaking introduction of GPT-3 by OpenAI, the field has witnessed a surge in the development of open-source LLMs. A notable trend is the emergence of smaller models designed for efficient

J. P. A. Almeida et al. (Eds.): CAiSE 2024 Workshops, LNBIP 521, pp. 229–240, 2024.
https://doi.org/10.1007/978-3-031-61003-5_20

integration into applications, capable of performing a wide range of Natural Language Processing (NLP) tasks. Hosted primarily on platforms like HuggingFace, these models excel in tasks such as text classification, sentiment analysis, and text generation, albeit with varying degrees of efficacy.

Despite their advantages, these smaller variants of Large Language Models, referred to as Small Language Models (SLMs), demands significant computational resources, limiting their deployment on low-cost servers, desktops, or mobile devices. This raises a critical question: Can open-source SLMs deliver the quality required for customer satisfaction in diverse NLP tasks? Furthermore, the research will focus on evaluating the impact of model size on sentiment analysis and emotion analysis performance. The comparative analysis will involve assessing the correlation between predictions made by traditional models, SLMs, and LLMs. The importance of sentiment analysis cannot be understated in contexts such as parsing customer reviews or managing conversational interfaces, where understanding the emotional tone is crucial to prevent potential damage to public relations.

This research aims to conduct a comparison of various models, ranging from SLMs with 1.5 to 3 billion parameters, through middle-sized models with 7 to 13 billion parameters, to sentiment-analysis optimized models and GPT-4, which boasts 1.78 trillion parameters. The study also includes traditional models like VADER, TextBlob and (Distil)BERT, considered the gold standard in sentiment analysis. Evaluations are conducted using public domain dataset from Kaggle with tweets to determine the most effective approaches for sentiment analysis in real-world applications.

2 Related Work

2.1 Customer Sentiment Analysis

Customer sentiment analysis is a valuable tool in business intelligence, providing insights into customer opinions, emotions, and satisfaction levels. By analyzing sentiments and emotions expressed in customer reviews and feedback, businesses can better understand customer preferences, identify areas for improvement, make data-driven decisions to improve products, services and marketing strategies [1–3].

Sentiment analysis impacts various aspects of business operations, including customer service dialogue, service satisfaction analysis, and intelligent agent applications [4]. It allows companies to measure customer satisfaction, analyze user feedback, and improve service quality, ultimately leading to increased revenue [5].

Through sentiment analysis, businesses can detect positive or negative attitudes towards their products or services, enabling them to tailor strategies to effectively meet customer needs [3]. This process helps optimize decisions based on customer opinions, enhance customer retention, and refine business processes [6]. Furthermore, sentiment analysis assists in predicting customer behavior, improving purchase patterns, and promoting environmental sustainability [7].

Overall, sentiment analysis is a powerful tool in business intelligence, allowing companies to assess customer satisfaction, make informed decisions, and enhance the overall customer experience. It serves as a valuable mechanism for businesses to stay attuned to customer sentiments, adapt to changing preferences, and drive continuous improvement in their offerings [2, 8].

2.2 Methods for Sentiment Analysis

Various methods are employed in sentiment analysis, including lexicon-based methods, machine learning approaches, and linguistic analysis [9]. Lexicon-based methods involve using sentiment lexicons and rules to determine sentiment [10]. These lexicon-based methods can be further classified into dictionary-based and corpus-based approaches [11]. Machine learning techniques, such as support vector machines and naive Bayes classifiers, are also commonly used in sentiment analysis [12].

Additionally, sentiment analysis can be performed at different levels, including document level, sentence level, and aspect level [13]. Aspect-category based sentiment analysis focuses on joint aspect category detection and category-oriented sentiment classification [14]. Furthermore, sentiment analysis can be applied to various domains, such as social media, healthcare, and e-commerce, to understand customer opinions and emotions [15].

Researchers have also explored new avenues in sentiment analysis, aiming for content-, concept-, and context-based analysis of natural language text [16]. Transfer learning has been investigated as a method to improve sentiment analysis techniques, especially in handling large and unstructured data from social media platforms like Twitter [17].

2.3 Using Large Language Models for Sentiment Analysis

Large language models like BERT, a deep bidirectional transformer model, has been designed to pretrain representations from unlabeled text by considering both left and right context in all layers [18]. With over 300 million model parameters, BERT has been effectively utilized for sentiment analysis tasks, including analyzing sentiments expressed in text data such as positive, negative, and neutral sentiments [19]. Researchers have developed BERT-based pipelines specifically for sentiment analysis on platforms like Twitter, showcasing the model's effectiveness in analyzing sentiments from social media data [20].

Moreover, BERT has been integrated with deep learning techniques for sentiment analysis in various domains, such as analyzing sentiments in Weibo text and Malaysian Airlines data [21, 22]. The model has also been fine-tuned for sentiment analysis on specific topics like the Black Lives Matter movement and Amazon reviews, demonstrating its adaptability to different domains [23, 24]. Additionally, BERT has been used in target-dependent sentiment classification and aspect-based sentiment analysis, showcasing its versatility in handling nuanced sentiment analysis tasks [25, 26]. The model's effectiveness in sentiment analysis tasks has been acknowledged in various studies, highlighting its superiority over traditional methods in extracting sentiments from textual data [27, 28].

Furthermore, pre-trained language models like GPT have been effectively utilized in sentiment analysis tasks, achieving state-of-the-art performance. Research has shown that utilizing GPT embeddings in conjunction with machine learning algorithms can improve sentiment analysis performance [29, 30].

In conclusion, language models like BERT, GPT-3 and GPT-4 have advanced capacity for sentiment analysis on customer data by providing robust tools for extracting sentiments from textual data across various domains and platforms. The model's pretraining and fine-tuning mechanisms have empowered researchers to attain superior results in sentiment analysis tasks, establishing it as a valuable asset in understanding and analyzing customer sentiments from textual data.

Our research uncovered a gap in existing studies regarding the comparison of SLMs in sentiment analysis, especially concerning customer-generated data like Twitter tweets, which are among the most significant data types for comprehending and enhancing public relations.

3 Methodology

3.1 Research Question Statement

Our methodology begins with the formulation of research questions designed to clarify the objectives of our study. The primary goal is to determine whether SLMs can effectively perform sentiment analysis on social media posts on Twitter platform. We have subdivided our investigation into several key research questions:

- RQ1: *Can SLMs analyze sentiment from unstructured preprocessed text?*
- RQ2: *What impact does the size of a language model (measured in parameters) have on its sentiment analysis performance?*
- RQ3: *To what extent do prompt engineering techniques and fine-tuning of langue models affect capabilities in sentiment analysis?*
- RQ4: *How trustworthy are the sentiment analysis predictions made by various language models? Can decision-makers trust the outputs?*
- RQ5: *Can language models detect subtle textual cues indicating specific emotions like sadness, joy, or surprise?*

3.2 Selection of Large Language Models

We have chosen a diverse array of language models for our sentiment analysis efficacy exploration. This range includes compact SLMs such as Phi-1.5 (1.3 billion parameters) and Phi-2 (2.7 billion parameters), providing insights into the effectiveness of smaller language models. Additionally, the mid-sized Falcon-7B (7 bilion parameters) model offer perspectives on scaling benefits and possible drawbacks. GPT-4, with its 1.8 trillion parameters, allows us to examine the extremes of performance scalability.

We encountered technical issues when attempting to operate larger language models, ranging from 13 billion to 40 billion parameters, on the Google Colab computing platform, leading us to exclude these larger models from our experiments. For comparison, we also assess specialized sentiment analysis models, including TextBlob and VADER, as well as the DistilBERT-base-uncased-emotion model for emotion analysis to thoroughly understand the strengths and weaknesses of each model in addressing customer sentiment analysis complexities.

3.3 Dataset Preparation

For our experiments, we chose the Sentiment140 dataset where we randomly selected 5,000 tweets for sentiment analysis and 4,000 tweets for emotion analysis. We then carried out a thorough preprocessing routine to ensure the data was clean and standardized. This process included converting all text to lowercase, transforming hashtags into readable words, and removing links, special characters, extra spaces, punctuation, and numbers. Further refinement through lemmatization and the removal of stop-words made the datasets more suitable for sentiment analysis. These steps are standard for sentiment analysis using traditional models. However, they can make sentiment and emotion analysis more challenging for language models by removing a significant amount of contextual information.

3.4 Exploratory Phase

The initial experimental phase was exploratory, serving as a proof of concept for SLMs' ability to analyze datasets. We utilized the LM Studio application to experiment with SLMs through a GUI interface. This phase enabled preliminary assessments of our capability to address the research questions.

3.5 Focused Experiments

Building on the exploratory experiments, we conducted focused experiments on SLMs and LLMs using a Python scripts that interfaces with the HuggingFace repository via the transformers library and GPT-4 by using OpenAI API. Experiments were conducted on the Google Colab platform, utilizing a Google Colab Pro + subscription to ensure sufficient RAM for running the models.

3.6 Observations Analysis

From focused experiments based on our scripts in Python programming language we have gathered a set of observations. We analyzed the results, systematically addressing and discussing our research questions based on the observations.

4 Observation Analysis

O1. Language models with parameters ranging from 1.3 billion to 1.78 trillion can classify text into sentiment categories.

We utilized the official HuggingFace website's recommended prompt:

Classify the text into neutral, negative or positive.\nText: {{tweet_text}}\nSentiment:

O2. Instruction-based fine-tuning a prompt engineering was not necessary for sentiment classification on twitter data.

Base generative models from the HuggingFace repository were capable of following instructions, with the exception of Phi-1.5, which after a short period started producing answers in a peculiar format.

Classify the text into neutral, negative or positive.\nText: ugh cant stop sneezing wonder pollen level like today\nSentiment: Negative

Example of an answer with a deviated format from Phi-1.5:

```
```python
from nlt
Classify the text into neutral, negative or positive.
Text: change twitter background
Sentiment: positive
Answer: Neutral
```

Due to the minimal difference in computational resource requirements when using Phi-2, which could follow instructions without any issues, we decided against fine-tuning and prompt engineering Phi-1.5. For comparison, we analyzed the performance of Falcon7B base against Falcon7B-instruct in sentiment analysis classification tasks and observed no significant differences.

O3. The sentiment analysis results of all HuggingFace models differ from those obtained using TextBlob and VADER.

When comparing the polarity results from each model, we observe that TextBlob demonstrates a higher correlation with VADER than with other models. VADER exhibits the same level of correlation across models, with the exception of Phi-2. Small models show a greater correlation with each other than with the larger model, GPT-4 (Table 1).

Table 1. The correlation among sentiment polarities is not very high, despite performing the same NLP task of sentiment analysis.

	text_blob_polarity	vader_polarity	phi2	falcon7B	gpt4
text_blob_polarity	1.000000	0.516035	0.400676	0.426881	0.455103
vader_polarity	0.516035	1.000000	0.450544	0.513287	0.521865
phi2	0.400676	0.450544	1.000000	0.689437	0.620900
falcon7B	0.426881	0.513287	0.689437	1.000000	0.639392
gpt4	0.455103	0.521865	0.620900	0.639392	1.000000

In instances where all models concurred on the sentiment, it is evident that even humans would easily categorize such texts into the appropriate sentiment categories (Table 2).

In cases where all language models agreed on the sentiment but differed from VADER and TextBlob, it appears that these texts would be classified by humans in the same manner as by the language models. This suggests that TextBlob and VADER may have misclassified these texts due to a lack of deeper text understanding (Table 3).

Looking at examples where language models disagreed with each other, we find that these texts present a challenge for classification even to human judges (Table 4).
```

Table 2. Randomly selected tweets where sentiment matches across all models.

Text	TextBlob	Vader	Phi2	Falcon7B	GPT4
glad puppy going ok cute rambunctious ever love much	positive	positive	positive	positive	positive
im excited love since youve gone miracle man cant wait hear youve done	positive	positive	positive	positive	positive
ahh got early football today lol early nice day though	positive	positive	positive	positive	positive
omg wow thats amazing beautiful	positive	positive	positive	positive	positive
ugh cant handle one power saw poor car cant handle construction mess feel helpless fml	negative	negative	negative	negative	negative

Table 3. Randomly selected tweets where sentiment differs from TextBlob and VADER.

Text	TextBlob	Vader	Phi2	Falcon7B	GPT4
ugh cant stop sneezing wonder pollen level like today	neutral	positive	negative	negative	negative
oh yeah know made nicholas feel bad let go rip heart like lol	positive	positive	negative	negative	negative
demanding haha cant leave house sorryyy ive gots dough	positive	positive	negative	negative	neutral
possibly sod though ill wait megan fox	negative	negative	neutral	neutral	neutral
watch cocktail dont actually like tom cruise little creepy know ment good	positive	positive	negative	negative	negative

Table 4. Randomly selected tweets where sentiment doesn't match across language models.

Text	TextBlob	Vader	Phi2	Falcon7B	GPT4
good evenin steph kim hope yall havin good evening even though guy workin weekend bummer	positive	positive	neutral	negative	positive
mood show right right quotmeghan musicalquot almost finished least music l	positive	positive	negative	positive	neutral
life fiona know	neutral	neutral	positive	negative	neutral
listening spice girl go watch hehe	neutral	neutral	negative	positive	neutral
got sneaky peek hd icon	neutral	negative	negative	positive	neutral

O4. SLMs results are unstable when changing a prompt a little.

A subtle change in the prompt, despite having the same meaning, has resulted in different classifications in some instances. The results are not stable when selecting different prompts, even though the correlation remains high (Table 5).

Table 5. Correlation of model responses to different prompts with the same meaning.

	phi2	phi2_again	falcon7B	falcon7B_again
phi2	1.000000	0.786768	0.689437	0.680210
phi2_again	0.786768	1.000000	0.695539	0.727329
falcon7B	0.689437	0.695539	1.000000	0.747753
falcon7B_again	0.680210	0.727329	0.747753	1.000000

O5. *Language models can classify text by emotions.*

We employed only Phi-2 and GPT-4 for emotion classification, in conjunction with the optimized model distibert-base-uncased-emotion, which was fine-tuned on the Emotion dataset from the Kaggle repository for emotion recognition tasks. This dataset was annotated with six basic emotions: sadness, joy, love, anger, fear, and surprise, using a semi-supervised graph-based algorithm. The prompt as follows:

Classify the overall emotion of text into one of these categories that suits the best: sadness, joy, love, anger, fear, surprise.\nText: {{tweet_text}}\nEmotion:

O6. Prompt engineering was not necessary for emotion classification. With a sufficiently high-quality dataset, fine-tuning would be the optimal solution.

Although both models were capable of classifying text into emotions, there were instances where emotions were classified into different categories than those specified in the prompt. GPT-4 occasionally indicated that it did not have enough information for reliable classification, while Phi-2 frequently used multiple words to describe the same emotion, such as "sad" and "sadness" or "satisfaction" and "satisfied," which would need to be grouped in practical applications. These issues could be addressed through fine-tuning or improved prompting. However, occurrences of these cases was statistically negligible (under 0.1%).

Phi-2 spectrum of emotions and feelings: sadness, joy, love, anger, fear, surprise, neutral, disappointment, disgust, confusion, pain, jealousy, hope, gratitude, boredom, patience, satisfaction, relief, pride, frustration, excitement, hunger. Some of the identified emotions and feelings were not actually emotions or feelings at all (we did not find them in any list of emotions or feelings): work, relaxed, peace, tired, mellow.

GPT-4 spectrum of classified emotions and feelings: sadness, joy, love, anger, fear, surprise, neutral, disappointment, disgust, confusion, pain, jealousy, regret, hope.

O7. *Language models yield varying results in emotion analysis.*

Conducting a correlation analysis of emotion categories reveals that the correlation is insignificant. Language models classify emotions differently (Table 6).

Table 6. Correlation analysis of emotion classifications by models.

	distilbert_emotions	phi2_emotions	gpt4_emotions
distilbert_emotions	1.000000	0.010500	0.101257
phi2_emotions	0.010500	1.000000	0.004525
gpt4_emotions	0.101257	0.004525	1.000000

Calculating the number of emotion classifications reveals that DistilBERT and GPT-4 have a similar count of identical classifications. The primary discrepancy that skews the statistics is the "surprise" emotion, which GPT-4 identifies frequently in the dataset. In contrast, Phi-2's results are significantly different, with a large portion of the text being classified as "sadness" (Table 7, 8 and 9).

Table 7. Comparison of model classifications for each emotion, expressed as a percentage.

	distilbert_emotions	phi2_emotions	gpt4_emotions
anger	29.29%	3.55%	13.32%
joy	50.24%	16.9%	39.19%
love	1.72%	3.62%	1.57%
sadness	12.35%	53.66%	13.22%
fear	5.82%	3.87%	3.97%
surprise	0.57%	13.1%	23.42%
neutral	0.0%	0.22%	3.75%
other	0.0%	5.07%	1.55%

Table 8. Randomly selected tweets where emotion matches across language models.

text	distilbert_emotions	phi2_emotions	gpt4_emotions
every thats true one might shining star thats take anyways	joy	joy	joy
trying figure feeling old	sadness	sadness	sadness
lol oh oki know look sad tell bye working long everyday final ignored	sadness	sadness	sadness
woohoo work four day goodnight michelle	joy	joy	joy
youre cute like smile	joy	joy	joy

Table 9. Randomly selected tweets where emotions does not match across language models.

text	distilbert_emotions	phi2_emotions	gpt4_emotions
ugh cant stop sneezing wonder pollen level like today	joy	sadness	surprise
oh snap forgot today payday	sadness	hope	surprise
whiskey breakfast nice	anger	fear	joy
goodmorning everybody raining pouring outside dont think umbrella walk	joy	sadness	surprise
party tonight	anger	work	joy

5 Discussion

RQ1. *Can SLMs analyze sentiment from unstructured preprocessed text?*

Based on observation **O1**, we can conclude that they indeed can. The results differ from those of traditional models used in sentiment analysis, such as VADER and TextBlob, as observed in **O3**. In straightforward examples, the results are the same. We can see that SLMs are a potent tool that should be considered for sentiment analysis as an alternative to traditional models and perhaps even as a replacement.

RQ2. *What impact does the size of a language model (measured in parameters) have on its sentiment analysis performance?*

Based on observation **O3**, we observed that Phi-2, achieved classification results nearly identical to those of Falcon-7B, though it required significantly fewer resources. This finding suggests a potential for utilizing SLMs in sentiment analysis not only on server-based web services but also on office computers, mobile phones, and even wearable electronics.

RQ3. *To what extent do prompt engineering techniques and fine-tuning of langue models affect capabilities in sentiment analysis?*

Based on observations **O1**, **O2**, and **O3**, we can conclude that for models with 3 billion parameters, such as Phi-2, prompt engineering and fine-tuning are not necessary, at least for text that resembles Twitter tweets. Models with a smaller number of parameters, such as Microsoft's Phi-1.5, require fine-tuning or prompt engineering because the format of their responses diverged from our basic template. For effective fine-tuning, human-annotated datasets are essential if the research is to be transparent.Because many datasets we encountered were annotated by machine learning algorithms we have reconsidered measuring statistics like accuracy, recall, f1-score.

RQ4. *How trustworthy are the sentiment analysis predictions made by various language models? Can decision-makers trust the outputs?*

Based on observations **O2**, **O3**, **O4**, **O6**, and **O7**, it is evident that language models can classify sentiment and emotions in text effectively when the text is easily interpretable. Furthermore, an issue arises with SLMs sometimes diverging from the prompt template. These observations indicate that SLMs are stable in their classification behavior but require thorough prompt engineering with well-designed templates.

RQ5. *Can language models detect subtle textual cues indicating specific emotions like sadness, joy, or surprise?*

Based on observations **O5**, **O6**, and **O7**, we can conclude that language models are capable of detecting specific emotions, although there is a significant discrepancy between the results of different models. Generally, models do not agree on emotions as consistently as they do in sentiment analysis. When comparing GPT-4 with the fine-tuned DistilBERT, the models yield similar results, except GPT-4 often classifies many emotions as surprise. Phi-2 frequently classifies tweets as sadness, which is clearly flawed upon reviewing the tweet content. Additional experiments on emotion recognition are needed. As with **RQ3**, manually labeled datasets are needed.

6 Conclusions and Future Work

This research explored the capabilities of SLMs in sentiment and emotion analysis, contrasting their performance with both traditional models like VADER and TextBlob and LLMs. Our findings indicate that SLMs can effectively analyze sentiment from unstructured, preprocessed text, challenging the dominance of traditional sentiment analysis tools. The size of a model, measured in parameters, was found to have a minimal impact on sentiment analysis performance, suggesting the feasibility of deploying SLMs in resource-constrained environments. Our investigation into the influence of prompt engineering and fine-tuning revealed that for texts resembling Twitter tweets, such adjustments are not essential for models with around 3 billion parameters. The research also uncovered that discrepancies exist among models, necessitating further refinement through prompt engineering and fine-tuning.

Future research should replicate our study without preprocessing the text to determine if SLMs' efficiency varies significantly when provided with the full context of sentences rather than just lemmas. Other areas to explore include the impact of fine-tuning SLMs in specific domain contexts to improve their precision and applicability across various fields, investigating more advanced prompt engineering techniques using a clear emotion ontology to enhance the consistency of language models in emotion classification, conducting cross-model comparisons between different sizes and types of language models for various NLP tasks, and creating manually annotated datasets for model evaluation. By pursuing these avenues for future work, we can further enhance our understanding of the capabilities and limitations of language models, paving the way for their broader and more effective application in sentiment and emotion analysis.

References

1. Ghasemaghaei, M., Eslami, S., Deal, K., Hassanein, K.: Reviews' length and sentiment as correlates of online reviews' ratings. Internet Res. **28**(3), 544–563 (2018). https://doi.org/10.1108/INTR-12-2016-0394
2. Prananda, A., Thalib, I.: Sentiment analysis for customer review: case study of go-jek expansion. J. Inf. Syst. Eng. Bus. Intell. **6**(1), 1–8 (2020). https://doi.org/10.20473/jisebi.6.1.1-8
3. Khamket, T., Polpinij, J.: Automatically correcting noisy labels for improving quality of training set in domain-specific sentiment classification. Curr. Appl. Sci. Technol. **23**(2) (2022). https://doi.org/10.55003/cast.2022.02.23.006
4. Wang, J., et al.: Sentiment classification in customer service dialogue with topic-aware multi-task learning. In: Proceedings of the AAAI Conference on Artificial Intelligence, vol. 34, no. 05, pp. 9177–9184. AAAI Press (2020). https://doi.org/10.1609/aaai.v34i05.6454
5. Asghar, M., et al.: Senti-eSystem: a sentiment-based eSystem using hybridized fuzzy and deep neural network for measuring customer satisfaction. Softw. Pract. Exp. **51**(3), 571–594 (2020). https://doi.org/10.1002/spe.2853
6. Govindaraj, S., Gopalakrishnan, K.: Intensified sentiment analysis of customer care audio using acoustic and textual features. ETRI J. (2016). https://doi.org/10.4218/etrij.16.0115.0684
7. Rao, N., et al.: Business intelligence appraisal based on customer behaviour profile by using hobby-based opinion mining in India: a case study. Econ. Res. Ekonomska Istraživanja **33**(1), 1889–1908 (2020). https://doi.org/10.1080/1331677X.2020.1763822
8. Chen, H., Li, S., Wu, P., Nian, Y., Li, S., Huang, X.: Fine-grained sentiment analysis of Chinese reviews using LSTM network. J. Eng. Sci. Technol. Rev. **11**(1), 174–179 (2018). https://doi.org/10.25103/jestr.111.21
9. Thelwall, M., Buckley, K., Paltoglou, G.: Sentiment in Twitter events. J. Am. Soc. Inf. Sci. Technol. **62**(2), 406–418 (2010). https://doi.org/10.1002/asi.21462
10. Loukachevitch, N.: Automatic sentiment analysis of texts: the case of Russian. In: pp. 501–516 (2020). https://doi.org/10.1007/978-3-030-42855-6_28
11. Daniel, D., Meena, M.: A novel sentiment analysis for Amazon data with TSA based feature selection. Scalable Comput. Pract. Exp. **22**(1), 53–66 (2021). https://doi.org/10.12694/scpe.v22i1.1839
12. Steven, C., Wella, W.: The right sentiment analysis method of Indonesian tourism in social media Twitter. IJNMT (Int. J. New Media Technol.) **7**(2), 102–110 (2020). https://doi.org/10.31937/ijnmt.v7i2.1732
13. Behdenna, S., Barigou, F., Belalem, G.: Document level sentiment analysis: a survey. EAI Endorsed Trans. Context-Aware Syst. Appl. **4**(13), e154339 (2018). https://doi.org/10.4108/eai.14-3-2018.154339
14. Cai, H., Tu, Y., Zhou, X., Yu, J., Xia, R.: Aspect-category based sentiment analysis with hierarchical graph convolutional network. In: Proceedings of the 28th International Conference on Computational Linguistics (COLING 2020), pp. 833–843. (2020). https://doi.org/10.18653/v1/2020.coling-main.72

15. Liu, S., Lee, I.: Extracting features with medical sentiment lexicon and position encoding for drug reviews. Health Inf. Sci. Syst. **7**(1) (2019). https://doi.org/10.1007/s13755-019-0072-6
16. Wang, Z., Schuller, B., Xia, Y., Havasi, C.: New avenues in opinion mining and sentiment analysis. In: IEEE Intell. Syst. **28**(2), 15–21 (2013). https://doi.org/10.1109/MIS.2013.30
17. Liu, R., Shi, Y., Ji, C., Jia, M.: A survey of sentiment analysis based on transfer learning. IEEE Access **7**, 85401–85412 (2019). https://doi.org/10.1109/access.2019.2925059
18. Devlin, J.: BERT: pre-training of deep bidirectional transformers for language understanding (2018). https://doi.org/10.48550/arxiv.1810.04805
19. Chandra, R., Saini, R.: Biden vs Trump: modeling US general elections using BERT language model. IEEE Access **9**, 128494–128505 (2021). https://doi.org/10.1109/ACCESS.2021.311 1035
20. Pota, M., Ventura, M., Catelli, R., Esposito, M.: An effective BERT-based pipeline for Twitter sentiment analysis: a case study in Italian. Sensors **21**(1), 133 (2020). https://doi.org/10.3390/s21010133
21. Li, H., Ma, Y., Ma, Z., Zhu, H.: Weibo text sentiment analysis based on BERT and deep learning. Appl. Sci. **11**(22), 10774 (2021). https://doi.org/10.3390/app112210774
22. Kang, H., Chye, K., Ong, Z., Tan, C.: Sentiment analysis on Malaysian airlines with BERT. J. Inst. Eng. Malaysia **82**(3) (2022). https://doi.org/10.54552/v82i3.98
23. Peng, J., et al.: A sentiment analysis of the black lives matter movement using Twitter. STEM Fellow. J. **8**(1), 56–66 (2022). https://doi.org/10.17975/sfj-2022-015
24. Mostafa, G., AlSaeed, A.: Sentiment analysis based on BERT for Amazon reviewer. J. ACS Adv. Comput. Sci. **13**(1), 1–10 (2022). https://doi.org/10.21608/asc.2023.171559.1007
25. Gao, Z., Feng, A., Song, X., Wu, X.: Target-dependent sentiment classification with BERT. IEEE Access **7**, 154290–154299 (2019). https://doi.org/10.1109/ACCESS.2019.2946594
26. Tang, T., Tang, X., Yuan, T.: Fine-tuning BERT for multi-label sentiment analysis in unbalanced code-switching text. IEEE Access **8**, 193248–193256 (2020). https://doi.org/10.1109/ACCESS.2020.3030468
27. Fraihat, S.: Telecom big data: social media sentiment analysis. Int. J. Adv. Trends Comput. Sci. Eng. **9**(4), 4322–4327 (2020). https://doi.org/10.30534/ijatcse/2020/22942020
28. Körner, E., Hakimi, A., Heyer, G., Potthast, M.: Casting the same sentiment classification problem. In: Findings of EMNLP (Conference on Empirical Methods in Natural Language Processing), vol. 2021, pp. 584–590. Association for Computational Linguistics (2021). https://doi.org/10.18653/v1/2021.findings-emnlp.53
29. Sathvik, M.: Enhancing machine learning algorithms using GPT embeddings for binary classification. TechRxiv. (2023). https://doi.org/10.36227/techrxiv.22331053.v1
30. Hou, W., Ji, Z.: Geneturing tests GPT models in genomics. Biorxiv (2023). https://doi.org/10.1101/2023.03.11.532238

Conceptual Data Normalisation from the Practical View of Using Graph Databases

Vojtěch Merunka[1,2]([⊠]), Himesha Wijekoon[1], and Pavel Beránek[3]

[1] Department of Information Engineering, Faculty of Economics and Management, Czech University of Life Sciences Prague, Prague, Czech Republic
{merunka,wijekoon}@pef.czu.cz, vojtech.merunka@fjfi.cvut.cz
[2] Department of Software Engineering, Faculty of Nuclear Sciences and Engineering, Czech Technical University in Prague, Prague, Czech Republic
[3] Department of Informatics, Faculty of Science, Jan Evangelista Purkyně University in Ústí Nad Labem, Ústí nad Labem, Czech Republic
pavel.beranek@ujep.cz

Abstract. This article deals with a practical and synthetic view of conceptual modelling. It suggests four graph database normal forms organised into two levels of conceptual modelling: data and metadata, with room for yet one conceivable graph normal form based on old approaches, such as object-oriented class normalisation and the idea of conceptual symmetry. Attention is also paid to bridging the semantic gap between a database on the server side and a programming language on the client side, which argues for using graph databases as better data sources for business intelligence systems and working with machine learning language models. The authors applied their practical experience in teaching database modelling at a university and many years of experience in software development in Smalltalk, Python, Java, and C#.

Keywords: Graph database normal forms · graph databases · conceptual modelling · large language models · business intelligence

1 Introduction

As stated in [3], software engineers and practitioners increasingly use graph databases. It is also evidenced by the activity FDIS 39075 [11] of the ISO/IEC consortium. The professional community agrees that these databases do not require such complex query programming for business intelligence applications, and their data model is more advantageous for machine learning large language models. These databases work differently because, unlike relational databases, they allow more helpful work with paths between individual data records; it is even possible to search for unknown paths in queries and work with the found paths as data objects. [15].

Robinson et al. in [17] say that graph databases offer a powerful platform for representing and analysing interconnected data entities, providing businesses with the tools

© The Author(s), under exclusive license to Springer Nature Switzerland AG 2024
J. P. A. Almeida et al. (Eds.): CAiSE 2024 Workshops, LNBIP 521, pp. 241–252, 2024.
https://doi.org/10.1007/978-3-031-61003-5_21

to gain comprehensive insights into their data landscape and drive informed decision-making because they can capture complex relationships, graph databases are well-suited for various business intelligence tasks, including relationship analysis, network analysis, real-time analytics, fraud detection, and risk management.

Moreover, graph databases can serve as the foundation for implementing dynamic knowledge graphs, as Chen and Xing [5] highlighted. This capability holds a good potential for supporting Large Language Model (LLM) based applications, as demonstrated by recent studies by Huang et al. in [10] and Zhou et. al in [18] which argue leveraging graph databases to build and query knowledge graphs, businesses can enhance the semantic understanding of their data, enabling more accurate and contextually rich language processing and generation within LLM frameworks.

However, followed by [9] and [13], these advantageous properties do not appear automatically and depend on the design. Therefore, software developers are confronted with the question, "How to design the best database structure?" In the past, thanks to the enthusiasm for the new technology of graph databases, it was spread that graph databases do not need many formal techniques and that only importing the data from the original relational tables into the new database engine was enough.

In this article, *four graph normal forms* will be shown, which the authors practically use in their work at the university, as well as software projects in practice. Their connections to a similar technique for designing object class structures by Scott W. Ambler [1] will be discussed as well.

2 Motivation

If a new idea is grounded in analogies or inspiration from various seemingly unrelated sources, it is not necessarily a negative; rather, it may serve as a positive indicator that we are on the right path of understanding. Indeed, this was the approach of ancient thinkers, and, regrettably, it is somewhat forgotten in today's era.

In the history of computer science, there has often been a tendency to forget and rediscover tools and methods under new names. In a way, *graph databases* serve as a prime example of this phenomenon, as they can be viewed as network databases from the 1960s, yet finely adapted to contemporary computer technology. Therefore, this is not a journey into the past but rather a significant advancement, where the original term "network database" might undermine its progress.

The concept of *symmetry* has a rich history. One of the earliest thinkers to systematically engage with symmetry was the ancient Greek philosopher Pythagoras. His school developed the concept of symmetry concerning geometry and harmony, believing it to be a fundamental principle in the physical world and cosmic order. Moreover, in the realm of the physical world, symmetry emerges as an observable mathematical attribute inherent to real systems, remaining invariant under specific transformations. Analogy operates as a mechanism whereby one subsystem's structural attributes are mapped onto another's, elucidating fundamental principles akin to those by which the divine constructs the universe, thus meriting our careful consideration. Drawing parallels to historical examples, such as the Russian chemist Dmitri Mendeleev's work in 1869 reveals symmetry and analogy's power in scientific endeavours by creation of the first widely recognised periodic table of chemical elements exemplifies this, as he ingeniously organised known elements based on recurring properties while also predicting the existence and properties of yet-to-be-discovered elements. Remarkably, subsequent discoveries validated all of Mendeleev's predictions. Similarly, our aspiration for systematising graph database normalisation rules echoes Mendeleev's method, and we anticipate some benefit in enhancing the efficiency and effectiveness of the database designs.

3   Attempts to Overcome the Limitations of Relational Databases

In the past, several interesting object-oriented databases and the ODMG-93 standard [4] have also appeared and are still used in practice. So, it will be interesting to see if graph databases will evolve to support inheritance and composition in the future. Even in this case, today there is no single universal database programming and query language available as it is said in [15].

The survey [2] says that graph databases are not just slightly different from relational databases. Indeed, there are significant qualitative differences compared to relational databases that have great practical use, for example, in language models for machine learning or business intelligence systems.

For all reasons, getting serious about graph databases makes sense. Because graph databases are different from relational databases even on a conceptual level, it would be a mistake to import data structures from existing relational databases or design new structures using procedures from the design of relational databases. The various new and advantageous features would not be reflected, and we would have just the old relational database structure embedded in the graph database engine. However, there is no agreement on the conceptual design methods of a graph database, and we still need to have a generally accepted standard. However, we can be inspired by the procedures described later in this article.

4   Object Class Normalisation - Ambler's Approach

Researchers have been interested in the normalisation of object-oriented structures since the early 1990s. Initially, this research emphasised improving relational techniques to be effectively used in object-oriented systems. With the advent of object-oriented databases, the focus has also moved towards object-oriented class normalisation. Object-oriented database normalisation was introduced as class normalisation by Ambler [1] inspired by Coad and Yourdon from [6]. Hence, Ambler has proposed notable initial ideas regarding object-oriented normalisation.

In a very recent paper, Lo et al. developed seven steps for object-oriented normalisation. [Lo] Their approach was based on both Ambler's class normalisation and relational database normalisation concepts. They took Ambler's approach until the third object-oriented normal form (3OONF) and came up with 4OONF, like the 4th relational database normal form. However, in contrast to Ambler's steps, they suggest generalisation to eliminate homogenous operations between classes. A similar approach to Ambler can also be found by Molhanec in [16].

There has been also few research to normalise object-oriented design not analogically to relational database normalisation. Falleri et al. have proposed a methodology to remove duplicate attributes by introducing general classes. [8] Their approach is based on relational concept analysis (RCA) and supports model-driven engineering (MDE) by automating the discovery of new classes and attributes when normalising. Ubaid et al. have developed the Class Hierarchy Normal Form Pattern (CHNFP) to maintain class schema in an object-oriented database. [14] CHNFP helps to manage objects and their network of objects in a memory-efficient manner by optimising the object graph loaded into the memory and controlling the inheritance hierarchy.

S. W. Ambler is also a pioneer of the agile approach in programming. He has published three object-oriented normal forms for object-oriented application development using agile methods. [1] These normal forms are like the first, second and third relational normal forms but use a different theoretical apparatus than relational normal forms. The relational normalisation is based on the functional dependencies between separate attributes, but Ambler's rules are based on various relationships of different subsets of attributes of objects. Ambler also talks about three object-oriented normal forms as a tool for class structure design complementary to the technique of design patterns.

5   Frisendal's Approach to the Graph Normalisation

Frisendal's approach to the Graph Normal Forms [9] extends the classical relational normal forms without the distinction between the 3rd NF and Boyce-Codd NF and is expressed in a more "programmers-friendly" way but using the ISO/IEC 24707 standard [12]. The first five normal forms are more-or-less identical with the relational normal forms, and the 6th relational normal form is declared as the specific *Graph Normal Form*. The whole approach is based on two software engineering concepts, *primary key* and a *functional dependency*. Frisendal argues that functional dependencies, well known from relational database modelling, are also the basic construction element for graph database modelling if extended. Frisendal's (reformulated classical relational normal forms for the graph database modelling purpose) are and added a specific Graph Normal Form as follows:

- NF1: Eliminate Repeating Groups.
- NF2: Eliminate Redundant Data.
- NF3: Eliminate Columns Not Dependent on Key.
- NF4: Isolate Independent Multiple Relationships.
- GNF: Remaining Functional Dependencies Rule

GNF: Remaining Functional Dependencies Rule
This rule solves the identity and uniqueness of data in detail. Frisendal argues that identity and uniqueness are not the same concepts as it is in a relational database where there is no other concept of identity than (based on the old Codd's rules [7]) to use one or more column values as the unique identification of the whole record stored in a row of the table. However, based on Frisendal's experience, graph database systems (such as Neo4j and Memgraph, for example) have a strong built-in mechanism for system-level generated UUIDs independent of user-defined attributes. Frisendal explains that there must be recognised two levels of identities and uniqueness in graph databases:

1. Business level keys for identities and concatenation of business keys for uniqueness and
2. The database system automatically generates unique physical-level keys (possibly generated UUIDs or other surrogate keys).

Therefore, Frisendal in [9] proposes the following method for finding and resolving possible hidden functional dependencies as defined in NF6:

Make sure that you have business-level identities on everything – no single attribute concept should be independent of business-level identities, and make sure that you also have business-level uniqueness for every object you create. Check the newly created attributes according to all previous rules.

6 Our Approach to the Graph Database Normalisation

Our approach is based on Ambler's three normal forms of object-oriented design, modified in the spirit of Frisendal's proposals. We view data objects as *nodes* in a graph database, and relationships between data objects are *edges* in a graph database.

We worked with the concept of *identity* in the original way; according to our practical experience, data nodes in a graph database (e.g., in the Neo4j system with which we work the most) have a system identity independent of business data values. It is even possible to have two different nodes with the same internal values, but they still be two different nodes. This is because different edges can connect them to other nodes in the database. For this reason, we work with the abstract concept of node identity independently of business data values.

Furthermore, we built one more *level of data types* (or metadata) above the basic *level of data values*. We arranged it symmetrically, following the ideas of Mendeleev's table of chemical elements. Our table has an interesting solution; the first normal form is so specific that its definition directly covers both levels. Of course, Mendeleev's periodic table is also not purely symmetrical but has clear evidence from practice. Our result can be seen in Fig. 1.

data types (metadata level)	**1ˢᵗ GNF** no repeating	**4ᵗʰ GNF** no sharing datatypes (inheritance)	**5ᵗʰ GNF** no independent datatypes (???)
data values (data level)		**2ⁿᵈ GNF** no sharing data	**3ʳᵈ GNF** no independent data

Fig. 1. Graph normal forms.

Now, we proceed with a detailed interpretation of our rules for normalising the graph database. We have also chosen a practical example of *car owners' registration*, which we will use to demonstrate the benefit of our solution. This example model is only a little simplified compared to reality.

First Graph Normal Form - no Repeating Data

Rule 1. *A node is in the first graph normal form (1st GNF) when it does not contain a group of repeating values. Groups of repeating values must be extracted into new nodes and linked to the original node by the edges. A database schema is in the 1st GNF when all nodes are in the 1st GNF.*

Definition 1. Let us have a node a, where for $k \geq 1$ (k is the length of the group of repeating data) and $n > 1$ (n is the number of repetitions of the group of repeating data) as $data(a) = \{\ldots, x_1^1, \ldots, x_1^k, \ldots, x_n^1, \ldots, x_n^k, \ldots\}$, having $\forall i \in (1, \ldots, k): type(x_1^i) = type(x_2^i) = \ldots = type(x_n^i)$. Then, it is required to extract these repeating data groups from the node a and store them in new nodes b_j for $j \in (1, \ldots, n)$ as $data(b_j) = \{x_j^1, \ldots, x_j^k\}$ and new edges $[a \rightarrow b_j]$.

Figure 2 presents the situation before normalisation as it can appear printed on paper when collecting software requirements from requesters who want such a database, for example. Figure 3 shows the same model transformed by our rules into the first graph normal form.

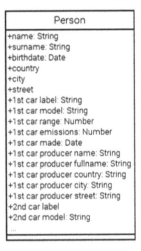

Fig. 2. Unstructured database.

In our example, the repeating group of data was data on owned cars, including data on the manufacturers of those cars. In addition, it was heterogeneous data because we are not interested in *emissions* (environmental pollution) with electric cars, unlike internal combustion cars. However, we are very interested in the *range* of electrical batteries (in km or miles). Of course, from the user's point of view, we need to display all data in one place. Nevertheless, if we implement this database according to Fig. 2, we will have many problems maintaining and storing data, maintaining data consistency, and making querying very complicated.

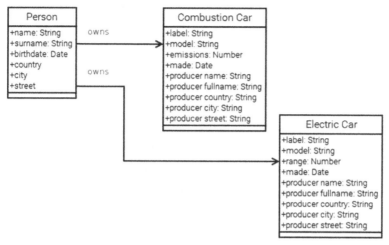

Fig. 3. Database in 1st GNF.

Second Graph Normal Form – no Sharing of Data

Rule 2. *Nodes are in the second graph normal form (2nd GNF) when they are in the 1st GNF and when they do not share identical data. Shared data must be extracted into new nodes and linked to the original nodes by the edges. A database schema is in the 2nd GNF when all nodes are in the 2nd GNF.*

Definition 2. Let us have two nodes a_1, a_2 for $k \geq 1$ (length of a group of shared data) as $data(a_1) = \{\ldots, x_1, \ldots, x_k, \ldots\}$ and $data(a_2) = \{\ldots, y_1, \ldots, y_k, \ldots\}$ having $\forall i \in (1, \ldots, k){:}x_i \equiv y_i$. Then it is required to extract these shared data from nodes a_1, a_2 to create new node b as $data(b) = \{x_1, \ldots, x_k\}$ and create new edges $[a_1 \rightarrow b], [a_2 \rightarrow b]$.

In our example in Fig. 4, we have many vehicles (electric and internal combustion) made by the same produced. Therefore, not primarily for memory-saving reasons but rather for greater data safety with the updating, we must ensure that the same data is stored in the database only once in one node and have them linked to other nodes.

Third Graph Normal Form – no Independent Data

Rule 3. *A node is in the third graph normal form (3rd GNF) when it is in the 2nd GNF and when it does not contain a value or a group of values, which have an independent interpretation of the node identity. The independent values must be extracted into a new node and linked to the original node by an edge. A database schema is in the 3rd GNF when all nodes are in the 3rd GNF.*

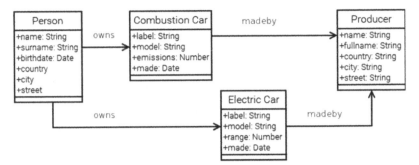

Fig. 4. Database in 2ⁿᵈ GNF.

Definition 3. Let us have a node a for $k \geq 1$ (length of a group of independent data) having $data(a) = \{\ldots, x_1, \ldots, x_k, \ldots\}$, where $\{x_1, \ldots, x_k\}$ is a group of independent data. Then, it is required to extract this group of independent data from the node a, and create a new node b as $data(b) = \{x_1, \ldots, x_k\}$ and new edge $[a \rightarrow b]$.

In our example in Fig. 5, such an independent group is a structured address which we need to use independently, with only the name of the city or country. We can also assume that city names or country names are sometimes changed, although this is rare. However, in any case, the address data values are not controlled and dependent on either the owner or the car manufacturer; they can only place themselves at those addresses.

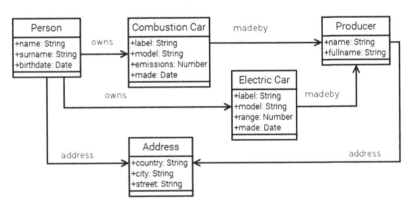

Fig. 5. Database in 3ʳᵈ GNF.

Fourth Graph Normal Form – no Sharing Data Types
Here it is enough to reuse the definition from the 2ⁿᵈ GNF and moved from the data level to the type level (i.e. metadata level). Let's look at the result:

Rule 4. *Nodes are in the fourth graph normal form (4ᵗʰ GNF) when they are in the 3ʳᵈ GNF and when their node types do not share identical data types. Shared data types must* *be extracted into a new node type and linked to the original node type by inheritance. A database schema is in the 4th GNF when all nodes are in the 4th GNF. (The term node type is analogous to the term object class in object-oriented programming.)*

Definition 4. Let us have two node types a_1, a_2 for $k \geq 1$ (length of a group of shared types) as $datatypes(a_1) = \{\ldots, type(x_1), \ldots, type(x_k), \ldots\}$ and $datatypes(a_2) = \{\ldots, type(y_1), \ldots, type(y_k), \ldots\}$ having $\forall i \in (1, \ldots, k):type(x_i) \equiv type(y_i)$. Then it is required to extract these shared data types from node types a_1, a_2 to create a new node type b as $datatypes(b) = \{type(x_1), \ldots, type(x_k)\}$ and create new inheritance links between node types a_1, a_2, b as $[a_1 \succ b]$ and $[a_2 \succ b]$.

Figure 6 shows an example of using inheritance in our database where we have vehicles with an electric or internal combustion engine. However, the question is how to implement this inheritance. It is easy on the client side of the database application because there we have object-oriented programming languages. Nevertheless, it differs on the server side of the database, and we must find a solution. The concept of *node labels*, part of the forthcoming ISO standard [11], has worked for us, as shown in the data creation code fragment in the CYPHER graph query language [17] in Fig. 7. Then, we can work with all nodes of the supertype *Car* or only with the subtype *Electric Car*, as shown in Figs. 8 and 9.

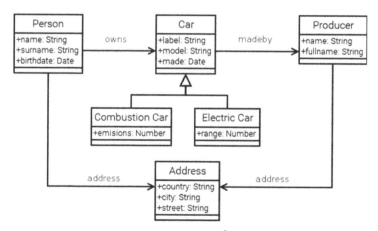

Fig. 6. Database in 4th GNF.

```
CREATE (car1:Car:Combustion {label: "9F7 9987" , model: "Kuga ST-Line"})
CREATE (car2:Car:Electric   {label: "CA 673-998", model: "Tesla S"})
```

Fig. 7. Example of data creation.

According to Fig. 6, the structure of nodes and edges allows more profitable use of specific graph databases' properties. In addition to the queries known from relational databases, such functions can also be smoothly programmed, which in the case of a relational database would require much greater programming effort, going as far as

```
MATCH (car:Car)-[:madeby]->(prod:Producer)-[:address]->(addr:Address)
RETURN car.label , car.model , prod.name , addr.country
```

Fig. 8. Example of a selection of all kinds of cars with their producers.

```
MATCH (addr:Address)<-[:address]-(owner:Person)-[:owns]->(car:Electric)
RETURN owner.name , owner.surname , addr.city , addr.country , car.model
```

Fig. 9. Example of a selection of only electric cars belonging to any owner.

software add-ons of the business intelligence type. The following two examples on Figs. 10 and 11 demonstrate small practical examples supporting our claims.

```
MATCH (addr1:Address)<-[:address]-(owner:Person)-[:owns]->
                              (car:Car)-[prod:Producer]->(addr2:Address)
WHERE addr1.country = addr2.country
RETURN owner.name , owner.surname , addr1.country , car.model , prod.name
```

Fig. 10. Searching for patriots (i.e. owners of any kind of car manufactured in the same country where they live)

```
MATCH path = ((p:Person)-[*]-(addr:Address))
WITH p , nodes(path) AS nodes
WHERE addr.country = "Japan"
    AND size([node IN nodes WHERE ("Car" IN labels(node))]) <= 1
RETURN (p.name + ' ' + p.surname) as person , nodes as connection_to_Japan
```

person	connection_to_Japan
"Haruto Tanaka"	[(:Person {surname: "Tanaka", name: "Haruto"}) , (:Address {country: "Japan", city: "Tokyo"})]
"John Smith"	[(:Person {surname: "Smith", name: "John"}) , (:Car {model: "RAV4 GR", label: "3A2 5619"}) , (:Producer {name: "Toyota"}) , (:Address {country: "Japan", city: "Toyota City"})]

Fig. 11. Searching for people who have something in common with Japan

The example in Fig. 11 searches for everyone somehow related to Japan. Here, the advantages of the graph database are fully shown because the bottom of this query is to find a connection between the nodes defined as "any Person" and "any address in Japan". The result leads through different edges and other internal nodes. We did not have to know the path of edges through internal nodes; instead, we just asked for that unknown path and obtained various kinds of path results:

a) Persons living in Japan have been found (see example in the first row of the table in Fig. 11).
b) Another path was also found, as other people living anywhere but owning a car made in Japan (see example in the second row of the table in Fig. 11).

To avoid bizarre paths, such as someone owning a car made by the same factory which is also producing yet someone else's car who lives in Japan, we restricted the properties of internal path nodes to at most one car of any car type.

7   Conclusion

This article presented our approach to data normalisation techniques in graph databases. This approach enables the generalisation and explanation of some connections with similar techniques from database design and object-oriented programming. Based on our experience, our design allows development team members to improve the quality of their software engineering work, reduce uncertainty, and improve conceptual consistency to better support graph database properties.

The main theoretical contribution of this article is synthetic to current construction techniques, which provides a solid foundation for future theoretical research and for its practical implementation in some CASE tools that support automated or semi-automated data structure modelling. In detail:

1. We added *inheritance* to the graph normalisation rules, which is currently not supported in graph databases but is present in most programming languages on the client side that access graph databases.
2. We have shown new *conceptual connections* (analogy, metamodelling symmetry) between *data composition* and *data inheritance*.
3. We may have found room for a *new inheritance-like concept* of conceptual modelling (3rd normal form in the metamodel).

It remains to decide what can be hidden under the box 5th GNF in Fig. 1. Incomplete classes called *mixins* are offered as possible candidates. Mixins are an object-oriented programming concept that allows a programmer to inject independent code into a class. Mixin programming is a style of software development in which units of functionality are created in a class and then mixed in with other classes. On the conceptual modelling level, this corresponds to the *decorator* (or *wrapper*) design pattern style, where we add more properties to existing object classes. However, since today's graph databases do not even directly support simple inheritance of object classes, we leave this issue open for the future.

Our future research will focus on the further empirical approvement of our claims and programming algorithms for transforming the conceptual model according to our rules in some CASE modelling tools.

References

1. Ambler, S.W.: Agile Database Techniques: Effective Strategies for the Agile Software Developer, Wiley Publishing, Inc., Hoboken (2003). ISBN 978-0-471-20283-7

2. Angles, R., Gutierrez, C.: Survey of graph database models. ACM Comput. Surv. **40**(1) (2008). https://doi.org/10.1145/1322432.1322433
3. Bechberger, D., Perryman, J.J.: Graph databases in action (2020). ISBN: 9789332526280
4. Catell, R., Atwood, T.: The object database standard: ODMG-93, Morgan Kaufmann Series in Data Management Systems (1996). ISBN 978-1558603967
5. Chen, Y., Xing, X.: Constructing dynamic knowledge graph based on ontology modeling and neo4j graph database. In: proceedings of 5th International Conference on Artificial Intelligence and Big Data (ICAIBD) 2022, Chengdu, China, pp. 522–525 (2022). https://doi.org/10.1109/ICAIBD55127.2022.9820199
6. Coad, P., Yourdon, E.: Object-oriented design. Yourdon Press and Prentice Hall Inc. (1991). ISBN 0-13-630070-7
7. Codd, E., Rustin, R.: Further Normalisation of the Database Relational Model in Database Systems, Prentice Hall, Hoboken (1972)
8. Falleri, J.R., Huchard, M., Nebut, C.: A generic approach for class model normalisation. In: Proceedings of the 2008 23rd IEEE/ACM International Conference on Automated Software Engineering (ASE 2008). IEEE Computer Society, Washington, DC, USA, pp. 431–434 (2008). https://doi.org/10.1109/ASE.2008.66
9. Frisendal, T.: Say Hello to Graph Normal Form (GNF), Dataversity publication (2022). https://www.dataversity.net/say-hello-to-graph-normal-form-gnf/
10. Huang, F., et al.: KOSA: KO enhanced salary analytics based on knowledge graph and LLM capabilities. In: proceeding of IEEE International Conference on Data Mining Workshops (ICDMW), vol. 2023, pp. 499–505 (2023). https://doi.org/10.1109/ICDMW60847.2023.00071
11. ISO/IEC FDIS 39075 - Information technology - Database languages (2024). GQL standard under development. https://www.iso.org/standard/76120.html
12. ISO/IEC 24707 - Information technology, common logic - a framework for a family of logic-based languages (2023). https://www.iso.org/standard/66249.html
13. Lissandrini, M., Mottin, D., Palpanas, T., Velegrakis, Y.: Graph-query suggestions for knowledge graph exploration. In: Proceedings of The Web Conference 2020 - WWW 2020 (2020). https://doi.org/10.1145/3366423.3380005
14. Lo, S.H., Shiue, Y.C., Liu, K.F.: Seven steps for object-oriented normalisation in class diagrams: Example of jigsaw puzzle concept for image retrieval. J. Appl. Sci. Eng. **21**, 463–474 (2018). https://doi.org/10.6180/jase.201809_21(3).0018
15. Meier A., Kaufman, M.: SQL & NoSQL Databases, Springer, Cham (2019). ISBN 978-3-658-24548-1
16. Molhanec, M.: Conceptual normalisation in software engineering. In: Proceedings of the Enterprise and Organizational Modeling and Simulation. EOMAS 2019. LNBIP, vol. 366, pp. 18–28. Springer, Cham (2019). https://doi.org/10.1007/978-3-030-35646-0_2
17. Robinson, I., Webber, J., Eifrem, E.E.: Graph Databases - New Opportunities for Connected Data, O'Reilly Media, Inc., Sebastopol (2015). ISBN 978-1-491-93200-1
18. Zhou, B., Li, X., Liu, T., Xu, K., Liu, W., Bao, J.: CausalKGPT: industrial structure causal knowledge-enhanced large language model for cause analysis of quality problems in aerospace product manufacturing. In: Advanced Engineering Informatics vol. 59 (2024). https://doi.org/10.1016/j.aei.2023.102333

Deriving Object Oriented Normalisation from Conceptual Normalisation

Martin Molhanec[(✉)] [iD]

Czech Technical University in Prague, Prague, Czech Republic
molhanec@fel.cvut.cz

Abstract. This article argues that object-oriented normalisation can be derived from conceptual normalisation. First, object-oriented normalisation, which is not generally accepted by default, is introduced. Furthermore, the conceptual normalisation presented by the Author in his previous articles is briefly presented. Finally, the author shows how object-oriented normalisation can be derived from conceptual normalisation. In the end, the author outlines the possible development of his work in this area.

Keywords: Data Normalisation · Conceptual Normal Forms · Object-Oriented Normal Forms

1 Introduction

This article deals with deriving object-oriented normalisation from conceptual normalisation. The author has been addressing this issue for many years and has published articles on this topic [1, 2]. The author is also the originator of conceptual normalisation, which he has published in many of his articles, such as [3–6]. Last year, the author published an article [6] on deriving relational normalisation from conceptual normalisation. The author is convinced that relational and object-oriented normalisation can be derived from conceptual normalisation, which is only a higher and more general abstraction of those above. This concept is illustrated below in Fig. 1.

This article is organised as follows. In the second part, we will address our motivation, attempting to answer why object-oriented normalisation is important and needs to be derived from conceptual normalisation. In this section, we will also provide references to similar works by authors who have already dealt with the issue of object-oriented normalisation. The third part will focus on our method; firstly, we will review conceptual normalisation and primarily recall its four conceptual normal forms. In the fourth part, we will gradually derive four object-oriented normal forms from the abovementioned conceptual normal forms. In the final chapter, we will briefly evaluate the results of our work and potential directions for further future research.

J. P. A. Almeida et al. (Eds.): CAiSE 2024 Workshops, LNBIP 521, pp. 253–263, 2024.
https://doi.org/10.1007/978-3-031-61003-5_22

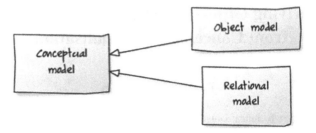

Fig. 1. Conceptual, Relational and Object models.

2 Motivation and Problem Statement

In the classical realm of relational database systems, relational data normalisation is a fundamental and common technique taught in all university database courses. The importance of relational data normalisation cannot be questioned; it is a technique utilised in the design of data systems for many years. We can recall several classic works in this area, for example, the works of the founder of the theory of database systems, Edgar F. Codd [7–9]. Issues of proper design of database systems were also discussed as early as the 70s, starting with the work of Chen [10]. The Author's approach is based on ontology theory, conceptual modelling paradigm and the authors' approaches listed here.

However, in object-oriented systems, something similar has not yet been widely established, even though the reasons for introducing such object-oriented normalisation are identical to the reasons for using relational normalisation in relational systems. Object-oriented normalisation has no standard, and individual approaches to this topic differ significantly.

Efforts to create a theory of object normal forms can be traced back to the 80s [11, 12]. Several different concepts of approaching object normalisation have been developed. Hank Nootenboom [13] says the three relational normal forms also apply to object systems. Nootenboom then adds another object normal form that replaces the relational 4 and 5 forms in the form:

A collection of objects is in OONF if it is in 3NF and contains meaningful data elements only [13].

Another approach can be found in Khodorkovsky [14]. He proposes that the object domain's normal forms correspond to relational normal forms. Finally, he adds the 6th normal form to refine the 5th normal form.

Another approach is in [15]; the authors propose only one normal form for different object functional relations. An object-oriented structure is in ONF when functional dependencies cover user application requirements. This method addresses the behavioural requirements of object databases but is not specifically aimed at conceptual data modelling.

Ambler and Beck are pioneers of the agile approach in programming. They introduced three object-oriented normal forms for object-oriented applications [16]. These normal forms are analogous to the first, second and third relational normal forms.

Our approach is different from all previous approaches. Our approach consists of deriving normal norms for objects from conceptual normal forms, which are higher generalisations of both object and relational normal forms. The method of deriving relational and conceptual normal forms was shown in [6].

3 Presumptions and Our Approach

In our article, we will build upon the existence of conceptual normalisation as defined in articles [3–5]. Here, we will first reiterate briefly the definition of all four conceptual normal forms. In the subsequent sections of the article, we will attempt to propose four object-oriented normal forms based on the conceptual norms provided here. This is the simplest way to derive object-oriented normal forms. Given the nature of object-oriented databases, such a method of defining object-oriented normal forms should be more appropriate and perhaps easier than deriving relational normal forms from conceptual normal forms for relational database systems.

Even entirely false arguments exist for not using any normalisation in object-oriented systems. One is based on the mistaken argument that object-oriented systems do not use any primary keys as is known from relational systems, and therefore, no normalisation is necessary. This argument is completely false; data normalisation itself is based on the fact that data in a database must not be redundant, and this rule generally applies whether it is a relational, object-oriented, or any other type of database, such as a network database. Of course, redundancy may be violated, but only in specific cases, such as achieving greater system performance, for example, in data search or the case of data warehouses. However, in such cases, it is a conscious violation of this rule, and everything related to it must be under our control.

3.1 Conceptual Normal Forms (CNFs)

We now turn to the basic definitions of the four conceptual normal forms; more details are in Molhanec [3–5]. The basic premise of our approach is that our conceptual normalisation approach assumes no redundancy in the real world. Therefore, all further considerations of the author are based on this basic assumption, which is formulated as follows:

AXIOM 1. *About non-redundancy.*

$$\text{There is no redundancy in Real World.} \tag{1}$$

∎

Redundancy can be informally defined as the absence of identical objects (concepts) in a system. Formal definitions of redundancy and non-redundancy follow.

DEFINITION 2. *Redundant system.* – Let S be a system, x and y be concepts of it, and cm be a predicate denoting the conceptual meaning of its argument. We define a predicate RS denoting redundant system formally as:

$$RS(S) \overset{\text{def}}{=} \Box \exists x, y \in S, cm(x) = cm(y) \tag{2}$$

DEFINITION 3. *Non-redundant system.* – Let *S* be a system, *x* and *y* be concepts of it, and *cm* be a predicate denoting the conceptual meaning of its argument. We define a predicate *NRS* denoting a non-redundant system formally as:

$$NRS(S) \stackrel{\text{def}}{=} \Box \forall x, y \in S, cm(x) \neq cm(y) \tag{3}$$

We can now move forward and present the definitions of the conceptual normal forms, which are understood as non-redundancy rules as defined above. I will first give four informal definitions based on the statements presented earlier.

DEFINITIONS 4. *Conceptual Normal Forms*:

- **0CNF**: There is no redundancy in the Real World.
- **1CNF**: A set of object properties is unique in relation to it.
- **2CNF**: An object property is not dividable; in other words, the object property is atomic. If we need to work with its part, this part becomes an object of its own, often abstract, with its own properties.
- **3CNF**: If we need to work with a group of object properties as if it were one concept, the group becomes an object of its own, often abstract, with its own properties.

Detailed formal definitions of these informal definitions were introduced in Molhanec [3]. The following section will briefly repeat these definitions to help you understand the text and our considerations better.

Definition (0CNF): Let *WR* be *Real World* and, *x*, *y* be concepts of it, and, predicate *cm* denotes s conceptual meaning of its argument. We define *0CNF* formally as:

$$0CNF(WR) \stackrel{\text{def}}{=} \Box \forall x, y \in S, \; cm(x) \mathrel{!=} cm(y) \tag{4}$$

∎

Definition (1CNF): Let *WR* be *Real World*, and O be an object from it, and the predicate *in* denotes a set of all properties of that object, and the predicate *cm* denotes a conceptual meaning of these properties. We define *1CNF* formally as:

$$1CNF(WR) \stackrel{\text{def}}{=} \Box \; \forall O \in WR, \forall p, q \in in(O), \; cm(p) \mathrel{!=} cm(q) \tag{5}$$

∎

Definition (2CNF): Let *WR* be the *Real World*, O be an object from it, P_O be a set of all properties of an object *O*, and *p* be a property of that set, and *c* be a concept, finally, predicate *cm* denotes a conceptual meaning of its argument. We define *2CNF* formally as:

$$2CNF(WR) \stackrel{\text{def}}{=} \Box \forall O \in WR, \forall p \in P_O, \; \neg \exists c \sqsubseteq cm(p) \tag{6}$$

∎

Definition (3CNF): Let *WR* be the *Real World*, *O* be an object from it, P_O be a set of all properties of an object *O*, and *s* be a subset of it, and *c* be a concept, and, finally, predicate *cm* denotes a conceptual meaning of its argument. We define a *3CNF* formally as:

$$3\text{CNF(WR)} \overset{\text{def}}{=} \Box \forall O \in \text{WR}, \; \forall s \subset P_O, \; \neg \exists c = cm(s) \tag{7}$$

∎

The grounds for these conceptual normal forms have been introduced previously. The author believes relational and object normal forms can be derived from these generic conceptual forms. The derivation of object normal forms from the conceptual normal forms established above will be shown in the next section.

4   Object Normal Forms (ONFs)

The term normalisation, commonly used in the theory of relational databases, was coined to eliminate data redundancy and errors resulting from it. Data normalisation, therefore, does not occur because someone defined its forms but rather to eliminate redundancy and errors that may arise when working with such a database. Data redundancy as a source of errors is harmful regardless of whether we work with a relational or object-oriented database.

The advantage of deriving object-oriented normalisation from conceptual normalisation is that the conceptual model is essentially object-oriented. This means that, at first glance, such derivation should be seamless, metaphorically described as smooth.

However, there is one problem: in reality, there is no single concept of what constitutes an object-oriented database, and it is precisely for such databases that we are creating our object-oriented normal forms. This is a significant difference from relational normalisation, performed for relational databases.

What constitutes a relational database is relatively well-known. Although there are many variations and degrees of differences, it is still possible to agree on their basic characteristics. However, this does not hold for object-oriented databases; individual databases have far greater differences.

Because, unlike the relational domain, in the object domain, we are not limited to conforming to already well-defined traditional normal forms; we can quite freely define our new normal forms based on already presented conceptual normal forms.

4.1 Zero Object Normal Form (0ONF)

This object normal form states that each object must be uniquely identified. In the conceptual domain, the point is that there must be a certain set of attributes and relationships, the combined value of which is unique for each concept.

Object databases have both attributes and connections that represent the realisation of relationships. This means that each object must have a certain set of attributes and connections whose aggregated value is unique.

Again, these are not internal OIDs but attributes and connections in the real world. You will not identify any person by their OID in a specific database but by their identity card, passport number or social security number, which are values that exist in the real world.

Another important fact is that attributes and connections contribute to unique identification; this is not as clear for object systems as for relational systems. In relational systems, connections are implemented using special attributes, which we call foreign keys. However, object systems are directly related to relationships; how they are realised is not interesting. But in principle, it is the same thing.

PROPOSITION OF 0ONF.

>*Each object in the object database must contain a given set of attributes and connections, the combined value of which is unique for each object.* (8)

4.2 First Object Normal Form (1ONF)

This object normal form asserts that every attribute and relationship of every object should have its unique meaning. This is de facto an analogy of 0CNF, but now related not to a set of objects but to a set of attributes and connections of the given objects.

We can imagine every attribute and relationship inside an object is also an object. We also apply 0ONF to such a group of objects inside the given object. In the opposite direction, we come to the application of 0CNF in creating a metamodel, but we will not deal with these considerations here.

Simply put, each attribute and relationship of a given object must have its unique meaning. For example, I cannot have two attributes with the meaning of *eye* in a *person* object. However, I can have the *left eye* attribute and the *right eye* attribute.

Similarly, using attributes with names such as *address_1* and *address_2* is a mistake, but all have the same meaning as a particular address. It is necessary to remember that the attribute's meaning is not its name! The name of an attribute is something like a sticker on that attribute, which expresses what the meaning of this attribute may be, but the real meaning is something that is only contained in our minds. The real meaning of an attribute is something formally unattainable; it is its thought essence and a philosophical category.

In this particular case, aforementioned, it is necessary to create a collection attribute that can contain multiple addresses or a new class called address, which will contain individual addresses as its objects, and there will be a 1:M relationship between our object and the objects (addresses) of this new address class.

However, of course, having two attributes, one with the meaning *permanent address* and the other with the meaning *transitory address*, is allowed because the two attributes have different meanings. We can also imagine the address class has two subclasses: a *permanent address* subclass and a *temporary address* subclass.

PROPOSITION OF 1ONF.

> *Each attribute and association in a given object must have its own unique meaning. If not, you must create a collection containing such attributes or a new class relative to the original class and move such attributes into it* (9)

4.3 Second Object Normal Form (2ONF)

This object normal form derives directly from 2CNF. Each object attribute contains a value that is always worked with as a whole. In the context of our model, there is no concept that we need to associate with any part of our attribute.

Suppose we have an attribute marked with a *full name* in our object. We know that a *full name* consists of a *first name* and a *surname*; however, our model, a thought pattern, always works with the *full name* and never with its parts. Then everything is fine.

However, it would be wrong if we need to work separately with the *first name* or the *last name* to have only the full name attribute and extract its parts from it using some functions programmatically. This would mean that the given attribute is *not atomic*; its parts also have meaning within our model. This must be considered a bad model.

PROPOSITION OF 2ONF.

> *Each object attribute is atomic; that is, there is no partial meaning of the given attribute at the level of our model.* (10)

4.4 Third Object Normal Form (3ONF)

This object normal form derives directly from 3CNF. Each object attribute and relationship has its meaning. However, suppose I need to work with a group of such attributes and relationships that I assign a certain meaning within a given level of my model. In that case, I have to separate such a group into a new class and thus a new object or create a named tuple.

The point is that each meaning is a concept and has its class in the given model from which I can create instances, i.e. objects. Or it is an atomic attribute that cannot be partitioned by the rule of 2ONF. Or it is a named tuple.

Let's use the example we used in the 2ONF analysis. Let's have an object with *first name* and *last name* attributes. However, if I need to work with the term *full name*, it is necessary to create a tuple with the name *full name* and two components with the names *first name* and *last name*, or it is necessary to create a new class with the name *full name* and two attributes *first name* and *last name*. Or it is necessary to create a named tuple with the *full name* and two named parts: *first name* and *last name*.

The solution method depends on which object-oriented database system we can use. You must use a class or named tuple. A named tuple can also be understood as a form of class.

PROPOSITION OF 3ONF.

Suppose a group of attributes and relationships has its meaning within our model level. In that case, separating such groups from the given object as a separate class or using a named tuple is necessary. (11)

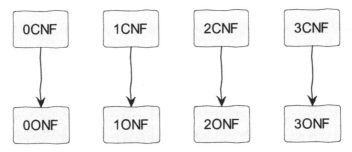

Fig. 2. The connection between conceptual normal forms and object normal forms.

5   Results

Based on the previous propositions, the author claims that the ONFs can be derived from the CNFs proposed in [3–5]; see Fig. 2. They are briefly summarised here. Since the conceptual model is object-oriented, the derivation of normal forms for the object model is inherently seamless. The main difference is that while in the conceptual model, we work purely with concepts and their meanings, in the object model, we have to work with attributes and relationships and their values.

This is very different from deriving relational normal forms from conceptual normal forms. The problem is that relational normal forms were created earlier than conceptual normal forms and, according to the author, chaotically and non-conceptually. And one sinful thought, isn't it time to re-create new relational norms based on conceptual normal forms?

What is the advantage of defining object normal forms based on conceptual normal forms?

– Conceptual normal forms were created based on one strong principle: the fact that there is no redundancy in the real world. Conceptual norms created in this way are strong and elegant, consistently holding the thought pattern together. The same applies to object normal forms derived from conceptual normal forms.

- The derivation of object norms from conceptual ones is simple, given that the conceptual paradigm is also an object paradigm. I will consider the following facts. The real world around us is objectual, and the relational model of such a world is somewhat forcibly grafted onto this essential object model. But are we then trying to redefine the rules for the relational model, i.e. relational normal forms, to object normal forms? So, it's a transformation of *real objects* → *database relations* → *database objects*? That's certainly not smart.

- In the case we advocate, a conceptual model is created, i.e., an essentially object model of the real world and an object model is directly derived from it. The conceptual (object) model rules can easily be transformed into rules for the object model. So, it transforms *real objects* → *conceptual objects* → *database objects*. It is easier than transformation through the relational model.

Perhaps now one heretical remark, fully resulting from the author's experience as a conceptual analyst. The theory of relational database normalisation and its three normal forms shows how to normalise a poorly designed database (database schema). However, in the author's opinion, a correctly performed analysis at the conceptual level automatically leads to a good scheme directly from its principle. A similar situation is, of course, also in the case of an object database.

A properly designed object database using proper analysis, and let's not forget here that the analysis itself is about concepts and not program objects or data tables, leads to a properly designed object database. And I'm not even considering when the programmer first thinks in tables and then designs objects according to them!

It is all the more unfortunate that students greatly underestimate the analysis phase and devote their interest much more to technical matters than thinking about concepts. At this point, I would like to recall a proverb: *measure twice and cut once.*

6   Conclusion and Future Works

The author deals with the connections between conceptual and object normalisation in this paper. A proper understanding of these contexts brings practical benefits to the design of object databases. Object normalisation is not clearly defined yet; in most cases, it is based on relational normalisation. Still, this approach is not considered correct by the author of this article.

The derivation of object normalisation from conceptual normalisation is far more advantageous. This approach allows us to think about the whole problem at a higher level of abstraction. It also allows us to understand the problem better and build the right model. The result can be a correct object model because we start from a higher abstraction of reality.

A better theory for object database normalisation can improve object database design. Database normalisation generally involves organising data to reduce redundancy and improve data integrity. Using normalisation techniques, data is structured to eliminate duplication and ensure all information is stored in one place.

This fundamental topic, i.e. the conceptual foundations of object normalisation, is surprisingly not discussed much by the professional public. Database designers are low-level, seeing the system only as a set of programmer objects and not seeing the object database as a conceptual model of the real world. However, this low level of view brings, in the author's opinion, shortcomings in the database design, which are manifested in various ways, e.g. redundancy, incorrect design of attributes and finally, a faulty database schema.

Another new possibility in the research herein introduced object normalisation is its use in standardising business processes. This topic has not been discussed so much so far. Another option is to evaluate the quality of the final conceptual or object models normalised by the concept proposed here with the standard constructed models. Several articles, for example [17], are dedicated to evaluating the quality of business models, but this is a relatively new concept in the field of general data/object/conceptual modelling.

References

1. Merunka, V., Molhanec, M.: Object normalization as contribution to the area of formal methods of object-oriented database design. In: Sobh, T. (ed.) Advances in Computer and Information Sciences and Engineering, pp. 300–304. Springer, Dordrecht (2008). https://doi.org/10.1007/978-1-4020-8741-7_55
2. Merunka, V., Brožek, J., Šebek, M., Molhanec, M.: Normalization rules of the object-oriented data model. In: Proceedings of the International Workshop on Enterprises & Organizational Modeling and Simulation, pp. 1–14. Association for Computing Machinery, New York (2009). https://doi.org/10.1145/1750405.1750420
3. Molhanec, M.: Towards the conceptual normalisation. In: Proceedings of the 6th International Workshop on Enterprise & Organizational Modeling and Simulation, pp. 133–141. CEUR-WS.org, Aachen, DEU (2010)
4. Molhanec, M.: Some reasoning behind conceptual normalisation. In: Pokorny, J., et al. (eds.) Information Systems Development: Business Systems and Services: Modeling and Development, pp. 517–525. Springer, New York (2011). https://doi.org/10.1007/978-1-4419-9790-6_41
5. Molhanec, M.: Conceptual normalisation in software engineering. In: Pergl, R., Babkin, E., Lock, R., Malyzhenkov, P., Merunka, V. (eds.) EOMAS 2019, pp. 18–28. Springer, Cham (2019). https://doi.org/10.1007/978-3-030-35646-0_2
6. Molhanec, M.: Deriving relational normalisation from conceptual normalisation. In: Babkin, E., Barjis, J., Malyzhenkov, P., Merunka, V., Molhanec, M. (eds.) MOBA 2023, pp. 32–41. Springer, Cham (2023). https://doi.org/10.1007/978-3-031-45010-5_3
7. Codd, E.F.: A relational model of data for large shared data banks. Commun. ACM **13**, 377–387 (1970). https://doi.org/10.1145/362384.362685
8. Codd, E.F.: Recent Investigations into Relational Data Base Systems
9. Codd, E.F.: Further normalization of the data base relational model. Data Base Syst. 33–64 (1972)
10. Chen, P.P.-S.: The entity-relationship model—toward a unified view of data. ACM Trans. Database Syst. TODS. **1**, 9–36 (1976)
11. Yonghui, W., Aoying, Z.: Research on normalization design for complex object schemes. In: Proceedings of the 2001 International Conferences on Info-Tech and Info-Net (Cat. No.01EX479), vol. 5, pp. 101–106 (2001). https://doi.org/10.1109/ICII.2001.983502
12. Mok, W.Y.: A comparative study of various nested normal forms. IEEE Trans. Knowl. Data Eng. **14**, 369–385 (2002). https://doi.org/10.1109/69.991722
13. Nootenboom, H.J.: What is the Object Oriented Normal Form? https://www.sum-it.nl/en200239.html. Accessed 11 Mar 2024

14. Khodorovskiy, V.: On normalization of relations in relational databases. Program. Comput. Softw. **28**, 41–52 (2002)
15. Tari, Z., Stokes, J., Spaccapietra, S.: Object normal forms and dependency constraints for object-oriented schemata. ACM Trans. Database Syst. **22**, 513–569 (1997). https://doi.org/10.1145/278245.278247
16. Ambler, S.W.: Building Object Applications that Work: Your Step-by-Step Handbook for Developing Robust Systems with Object Technology. SIGS, Cambridge (1998)
17. Pavlicek, J., Hronza, R., Pavlickova, P., Jelinkova, K.: The business process model quality metrics. In: Pergl, R., Lock, R., Babkin, E., Molhanec, M. (eds.) Enterprise and Organizational Modeling and Simulation, pp. 134–148. Springer, Cham (2017). https://doi.org/10.1007/978-3-319-68185-6_10

BPMN for Displaying the Progression of Musical Harmony and Chords - Case Study

Josef Pavlicek[1]([⊠]) [iD], Petra Pavlickova[1] [iD], Matej Brnka[2] [iD], and Jan Rydval[2] [iD]

[1] Faculty of Information Technology, CTU, Thákurova 9, 160 00 Prague 6, Czech Republic
{josef.pavlicek,petra.pavlickova}@fit.cvut.cz
[2] Faculty of Economics and Management, Czech University of Life Sciences in Prague,
Kamýcká 129, Praha-Suchdol, 165 00 Prague 6, Czech Republic
{brnka,rydval}@pef.czu.cz

Abstract. This case study discusses the possibility of using process diagrams to formally describe musical dependencies. As a methodological basis, the authors use an example of the tonic C major and its development in the construction of fifth and seventh chords. The authors show how a process diagram provides a good representation of the known dependencies between the notes of a key. They also present a model of the progression of C major chords through the intervals. The paper discusses the problem of how to complete - i.e., harmonize - a melody so that for each quarter note a harmonic and tonal chord is used for a given period. The authors show that musical relations that are now generally formalized by musical notation can be, and in the case of harmony progression, can be usefully modeled in other forms such as a process diagram.

Keywords: Melody · Chord · Harmony progression · Chords progression · Music notation · Music representation · BPMN · Modeling tools

1 Introduction

1.1 Origin of Music

The origin of music is linked to the ancient history of human civilization. Music has its roots in prehistoric times, when humans began to use various sounds and rhythms as a means of communication, expressing emotions, rituals and social events. As time progressed, music became more organized and structured. The first musical systems and notations were created to record and preserve music for future generations. Ancient civilizations such as the Sumerians, Egyptians and Greeks had their own musical traditions and ways of recording music. Throughout history, music has become an integral part of culture and society. In different eras and cultures it has evolved in different directions and styles, reflecting local traditions, religious and social values, political events and technological innovations.

J. P. A. Almeida et al. (Eds.): CAiSE 2024 Workshops, LNBIP 521, pp. 264–274, 2024.
https://doi.org/10.1007/978-3-031-61003-5_23

1.2 Music Research History

The first records of the systematic study of chords probably date from ancient Greece. Pythagoras, the famous mathematician, philosopher and music theorist, was interested in the relationships between notes and musical harmonies. Pythagoras and his school of mathematicians discovered the relationships between the lengths of strings on musical instruments and the fundamentals of musical harmony. Although not directly related to the modern concept of chords, it was one of the first systematic investigations of musical relationships that laid the foundation for the future development of music theory and chord structures. Pythagoras became famous for his discovery that music has mathematical foundations. Ancient sources, which credit Pythagoras with being the philosopher who first discovered musical intervals, also credit him with being the inventor of the monochord. That is, the straight bar on which the relationship of musical intervals could be demonstrated by means of a string and a movable bridge [1].

Another important researcher was Guido of Arezzo [11]. He is known for his contribution to the development of musical notation. He developed a system of marking musical notes using neumes (neumes), which were simple graphic symbols that indicated the pitch and duration of a musical note. This system, known as musical neumes, was the forerunner of modern musical notation. The introduction of musical notation and the use of the key represents a gradual process that took place over several centuries and involved the contributions of many different music theorists and pioneers.

1.3 Current Notation

Contemporary musical notation as we know it today has developed gradually over several centuries. Key steps in its development include [3]:

Medieval Neumes: The first attempts to standardize musical notation date back to the Middle Ages, when neumes were used as simple graphic symbols to indicate melodic lines and rhythmic patterns. Neumes were used from the 9th century to the 11th century and were the forerunner of modern musical notation.

The Development of Mensural Notation: During the 13th and 14th centuries, mensural notation developed, allowing for more accurate notation of note length and rhythm. Mensural notation brought about the introduction of different note values and bar signs (Fig. 1).

The Renaissance: In the 15th and 16th centuries, saw further improvements in musical notation. The introduction of bar lines and the use of fixed note values developed a system that allowed for clearer and more accurate notation of music.

Modern Musical Notation: The modern form of musical notation became established during the 17th and 18th centuries. During this period, notational symbols for different notes, rhythmic values, clefs, bar signs, and other information needed to write music were standardized. These standards are still in use today and form the basis of contemporary musical notation.

All in all, contemporary musical notation was developed gradually over several centuries and was the result of the long-term development and refinement of musical

Fig. 1. Upper voice of the "Christe eleison" part of Barbireau's Kyrie (cf. Lines 4–6 in the manuscript), in mensural notation and modern transcription

notation. Modern notation is often supplemented by numerical notation - usually for stringed instruments (the tablature is marked TAB) where the lines denote the strings and the numbers the fret position.

1.4 Types of Notes According to Their Length

In musical notation, there are several different note lengths that indicate the duration of musical notes. The basic note lengths are:

Whole Note: It lasts for all the periods of a measure. It is marked as a blank ball.

Half Note: Lasts for half the length of the measure. It is marked as an empty ball with a foot.

Quarter Note: A quarter note is worth one quarter of the total length of the note in a given measure. Its basic shape is a black oval with a suspended barred stem.

Eighth Note: An eighth note has a value of one-eighth of the total length of the note in a given measure. Its basic shape is a black oval with a suspended barred stem and a horizontal bar.

Sixteenth Note: A sixteenth note has a value of one sixteenth of the total length of the note in a given measure. Its basic shape is a black oval with a suspended barred stem and two horizontal bars.

More Notes Time: There are also notes with different durations, such as eighth-note dotted notes, thirty-two-note notes, overtones, etc., which are used in musical notation to indicate different rhythmic values. These note durations vary depending on the tempo of the piece and the rhythmic requirements of the composer. They are essential for musical notation, but for the purpose of this study they can be omitted.

1.5 Chords Progression

Composing chords is the process of combining different musical notes into a harmonic whole. There are several ways to compose chords:

Tertian Construction: The tertian construction of a chord consists of composing three notes that are within a third (two musical degrees) of each other. The most common types of tertian chords are major (major third), minor (minor third), and augmented (augmented third). **Quint structure:** the quint structure of a chord involves a combination of notes that are within a fifth (five musical degrees) of each other. Quint chords are usually stable and solid and are the basis of many harmonic progressions. **Septimus construction:** the septimus construction of a chord involves the addition of another note that is within seventh (seven musical degrees) of the chord's fundamental note. Septimus chords are often used to achieve a richer and more complex sound.

Chord Progression: The progression of a chord consists of adding additional notes to the basic chord from some interval 3,5,7 and then 2,4 (sus),6 to create a chord with a richer and more complex sound. Common types of chord modulation also include altering the pitch of the third and seventh (lowering by a half note) and also eight (which is actually the 2nd step up an octave) of the fifth (raising or lowering by a half note). Or chords with the addition of a fifth note (e.g. a note) and others (which is already a limit for some instruments - e.g. guitar). When composing chords, it is important to take into account the harmonic relationships between the notes and the sound characteristics of the chord created.

1.6 Representation of Hamonic Relations Using the Model of Applied Informatics

A number of researchers who have worked on the formalization of musical relations have used the tools of applied computer science. Flowcharts have been utilized by various researchers in the field of music to visually represent complex musical structures, processes, and relationships. One notable example of a researcher who has used flowcharts for music research is Dr. David Temperley [12], a professor at the University of Rochester. In his work on music cognition and music theory, Dr. Temperley [13–15] has employed flowcharts as a means of illustrating harmonic progressions, formal structures, and other aspects of musical analysis.

Another example Brendan Blendell [16] who in the paper Harmony and Syntax in Contemporary Pop Music uses BMP notation. Additionally, various music theorists, educators, and researchers have incorporated flowcharts into their work to explore topics such as composition techniques, improvisation, and music pedagogy. Flowcharts and BPMN provide a visual means of organizing and communicating complex musical ideas, making them valuable tools for music research and analysis.

1.7 Summary of the Introduction

The authors of the probabilistic graphical model for chord procedures see [18] use a Petri net to visualize the display. The authors of the paper Analysis of Chord Progression by HPSG [19] claim that *"the structure of music is to some extent similar to the structure of natural language sentences. When we try to write rules for chord progression in a context-free grammar, we have to add many rules for trivial exceptions."* For a description of the invitational HPSG graph. The authors of the article Predicting the Composer and

Style of Jazz Chord Progressions [20] claim that composers can be reasonably identified by their chord progressions. It is therefore possible to model it.

The overall conception and description of musical harmony and its relationships can be seen as a description of physical laws in mathematical form. As shown by various scientists in the field of music research [12–16] it is possible to use common tools of Applied Computer Science. We will try to look at the progress of harmony as a sequential process that has clear physical laws and use a BPM process diagram to represent it.

2   Material and Methods

2.1   Research Question

The research question focuses on chords progression and are defined as:

> *"Is it possible to use applied computer science methods, more specifically notation for recording BPMN processes, to illuminate and simplify the formulation of chord development?"*

2.2   Chord Types and Their Model

Chords are typically divided into two basic categories based on the character of their sound: major chords and minor chords.

Major Chords: have a bright, joyful, and stable sound. The most common major chord is the major chord, which consists of the root note, major third, and perfect fifth. For example, the C major chord is composed of the notes C, E, and G. Major chords are often used in bright and positive musical contexts, but they can also be used to create tension and contrast in music.

Minor Chords: have a darker, melancholic, and less stable sound than major chords. The most common minor chord is the minor chord, which consists of the root note, minor third, and perfect fifth. For example, the C minor chord is composed of the notes C, Eb, and G. Minor chords are often used in emotionally charged and melancholic musical contexts, but they can also be used to create different moods and atmospheres in music.

In addition to major and minor chords, there are many other types of chords, such as seventh chords, suspended chords, extended chords, etc. Each type of chord has its own characteristics and uses in musical practice.

The question remains how to explain the development of chords in a simplified way. Here, if we study the literature there is a whole wide range of authors who explain them, but we have not come across graphical representations of the development process. This is probably due to the fact that the layman and novice musician uses painted markings, while the experienced professional can construct the chords himself. Therefore, we attempted to formalize this process using BPM notation [4–6] and our applied computer science knowledge [7–9].

2.3 BPMN for Music Progression Expression

For the sake of clarity, we will limit the process of chord progression (in this article we will focus on the development of chords and basic chords - we will not add intervals an octave higher, e.g. add 9 or half chords... sus2, sus4 etc.) to fifth chords (composed of the first, third and fifth degrees) and seventh chords (we will add the seventh degree to the fifth chord). The progression process will use conventional BPM [4–6] notation where we start with an initial symbol (circle), the note (or note step) is then represented by a process symbol, the parallel development of notes is symbolized by a parallel gateway, and the change in interval amount (on the third, fifth and seventh steps) is symbolized by an exclusive gateway. The process model is not terminated because the end is hypothetically un-findable. The chord can theoretically be progressed indefinitely. Practically considered, the end is meaningless.

Start of Chord Progression: we start with the initial note (in this case the note C) and from there we build the next notes on the third and fifth steps. A very clear representation of the fifths of the chord emerges.

C Major Triad Model
The parallel gate symbol models well the process of branching the notes to the desired melody.

C Maj Triad to Progress C Maj 7 to C Dominant 7 and C minor 7
Now we can see, how the process model perfectly represents the development of chords built over the basic (triad) chord C Major (Fig. 2).

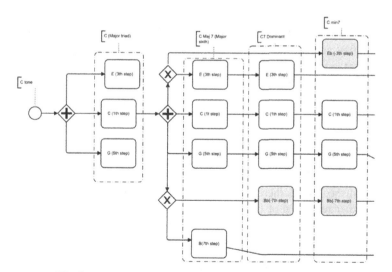

Fig. 2. Chords progression from C Major Triad to Minor 7

In the first step we add the so-called large septum using the paralytic gate. This creates the pure chord C Maj 7. The significance of this chord is not insignificant because it represents the basic melodic and harmonic structure (it is the first note and the prime) from which the melody either begins or usually ends. While the basic C Maj triad is composed of only three notes, this chord has a fourth (the seventh) and this is only a half note lower than the basic C note if we were to add it. This is in fact just in the eighth position (octave). This semitone is significant and creates a harmonic consonance. In truth, we should be a bit more precise (B7 is marked to the prime - i.e. the first note of Sharp Dissonance) but in the overall chord it sounds consonant. That is why it is uncolored. Using BPM notation, we display it as an uncoloured process block located at the bottom of the chord. The fact that the chord is composed of uncolored process blocks allows us to understand it as consonant.

However, if the seventh degree is lowered, then there is a soft dissonance between the seventh and eighth notes and the chord creates tension. This tension is so significant that the chord is called dominant and stands on the fifth degree of the next key, in this case F major. This chord we call C7 Dominant.

If we lower the third degree of the chord (in this case the note E to Eb) then there is an incomplete - imperfect consonance between the first and third degrees. And a minor chord is formed. This is known for its sad characteristic. It's still lilting but at the same time it's emotionally sad. We call it C minor 7. Again, we find an interesting parallel between the processional scheme and the chord colour. There are two coloured elements. The chord will be different from the base chord. But the process pattern tells us even more about the character of the chord. Because the two notes are offset, it won't exude the tension of the previous chord, C7 Dominant. It will be calm and sad.

Progression to C Dim to C Half-Dim and C + Augmented 7

Now there is a further progression of the chord, with a shift of the 5th and a reduction of the already reduced 7th degree. The process model shows a strong dissonance between the first and fifth degrees by changing the colour to purple. Generally, the base of each chord is the first and fifth degrees. We refer to the fifth degree as the dominant (yes, if the fifth degree is with a minor seventh, then it is a dominant seventh chord) and it is generally consonant if it is pure. So, it is not lowered or raised by a semitone. Both the reduction and the increase bring about a fundamental change in the perception of the chord. In the first case, the chord is so called diminished (it is interesting that all the thirds are so called small = i.e. small first third i.e. C, D and Eb and the next -the distance between the third and fifth note is again three... Eb, F and Gb). And it has a special property. It creates tension and power. We await the arrival of a chord that will calm a troubled mind. Very popular with composer Richard Wagner (Fig. 3).

In a diminished chord, there is a double reduction of the seventh (i.e. the B note on Bb and a further reduction of Bbb = A note). It's a musical curiosity and convention says to observe the Bbb though, it's actually the A tone. What's interesting about this chord is that it's fingering stable, i.e., we can move it around in small thirds without changing the fingering and it will still sound the same.

Another chord is the so-called half diminished chord, called an average, and a chord with an augmented fifth. Both chords sound dissonant and are used as a pre-chord (i.e. a tension or through chord) before the chord that follows in the harmony.

Probably the least dissonant chord is the C half-dim. If we look at the BPM display, we can see why. There are two equal blocks, equally diminished, and this (see the

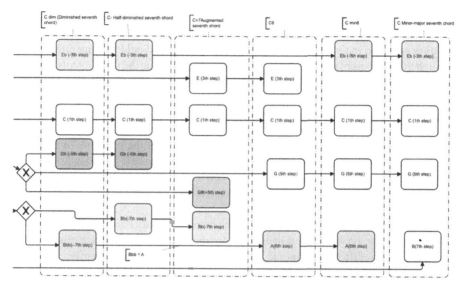

Fig. 3. C dim, C half-dim, C + 7, C6 to C min6 and to C Min-maj

previous C minor 7) creates the consonance. So only the diminished fifth is dissonant. This was known in the Middle Ages as the interval el. Diablo and was even forbidden. Today it is very much in use in modern, especially punk, metal and alternative music.

Progress from C6 to C min6 to C Min-Maj

An interesting chord in terms of its BPM representation is undoubtedly C6. It is a consonant chord. That is to say, between the note C and the note A (that is the sixth degree - hence C6) there is what is called a non-perfect consonance. The perfect consonance is always with the prime and octave (these are identical tones, so they must be physically consonant), then with the pure fifth (from C it is the F tone and is a subdominant - therefore a very common part of songs) and the fifth (G - the dominant. Almost no song can be made without it). However, the procedural model shows it in green (that's just a color) which indicates it is the next step, according to our suggestion. Again, when we play the chord, we find that it is coloured by something. It's not completely dissonant, but it doesn't sound consonant.

The chord that follows has a minor third and is therefore a minor chord. At the same time, it also has a sextuple, and since there is no reduction of two equal intervals, it will sound dissonant. The same can be said of the last chord and it is a C minor major where the first third is major but the seventh is major. It's a chord full of tension. It's used as a final chord to underline the musical and harmonical meaning of the song.

2.4   Results

The result of the investigated problem significantly exceeded the authors' expectations. Not only does the procedural approach to the description of musical harmony apparently make sense. Harmony is, after all, just a respect for physical principles. We perceive a harmonic signal as sound, a discordant one as noise. But the graphical representation and the possibility of expressing the links between intervals in a schematic form gives new dimensions to the study of music and its principles. It should be remembered that although the composers format Amadeus Mozart or let us name the undoubtedly worldly and phenomenal composer Antonín Dvořák knew the principles of music perfectly, they themselves put its notation in musical scores, where its notation is absolutely perfect, but the logical principles and links are neglected. It is logical, the composer composed and the orchestra performed. There is no need to understand the connection between the dominant seventh chord and the tonic. But if we look at the principle of harmony development through a scientific lens, i.e., we don't create music as we feel it, but go back to Mr. Pythagoras, then we see that the procedural model perfectly depicts the steps of harmony development and allows us to understand graphically and even logically why some intervals are consonant and some are dissonant.

The construction of the chords and thus the complementary harmony to the melody depends, of course, on the musical instrument (or musical ensemble) which offers different possibilities to different harmonic patterns. In our case, we are primarily concerned with the guitar. In the case of piano playing, the chord progression could very easily follow the melody line so that the soprano always sounds the melody note, and the remaining chord would transition into the bass. This is possible with piano, but with guitar this principle is more challenging because in some cases the chord cannot be built up with the melody in the sopranos. This fact can be very well illustrated just by a process diagram, where we can see the individual strings as parallel process flows, and thus with the limitation of six (we are thinking of a six-string guitar) strings and then individual process blocks that we compose in succession from left to right (just as we would build a chord on a guitar) we find visually that some types of chords with melody in the soprano are beyond the physical capabilities of the human hand. Of course, this is not true of an entire musical ensemble - meaning a symphony orchestra. The procedural diagram, however, does not suffer from these limits. But we can mathematically define what musical sounds (i.e. chords) are natural to humans, and thus a distance greater than, say, 5 process blocks is inappropriate to build, because no human can play them. This fact can be useful, for example, in teaching artificial intelligences to simulate guitar playing. Thus, our result is not only an optical visualization of harmonic relations, but also a definition of possible harmonic constructions.

We can say that the process model can capture the basic principles of harmony creation. We do not claim that it can be used to record melody (although our research shows this), but we have shown that it can be used to record the process of harmony formation and its harmonic manifestations - that is, the basic 10 chords that can be derived from the basic C triad.

3 Discussion

One of the authors who, like us, are concerned with the scientific knowledge of music is Dr. William Caplin or David Temperly [10]. They used flow charts to symbolically represent musical relationships. It is often the case that a relatively commercially successful composer has not even a minimal awareness of music theory. Technology, however, allows him to assemble music from existing musical fragments in a way that appeals to people. So we try to understand and formalize music scientifically. So, just as linguistic grammars are likely to change their paradigm under the onslaught of contemporary modern technologies such as artificial intelligence will eventually leave the beaten track of traditional musical notation and move towards formal languages. But there will be an effort to formalize it more and more, to digitize it, to translate it as a learning set for the tools of artificial intelligence [21]. One of the favourites of formal notation may be BPMN, or its future, music-extended, form. Martin Molhanec [17] argues in his paper that relational normalization can be derived from conceptual normalization. The relations between tones are given by physical laws. What is conceptually controversial is the relationship between a person's perception of tone and his cultural habit. Whereas the diminished fifth used to sound unacceptable, jazz now uses it routinely. Thus, for mailing these relationships with models that allow them to be captured is probably necessary or at least appropriate.

4 Conclusion

In this paper we discussed the possibility of using process models to formalize musical notation. We have shown that this is possible. It is evident that musical notation, which has evolved into its present form over 1000 years, is certainly the perfect medium for the notation and interpretation of music. We show here that it is necessary to separate musical notation in the form of musical notation for the musical body (here the notation is apparently almost perfect) and musical notation for the understanding of the development of harmony and harmonic-melodic progressions. It should be remembered that harmonic progression, even if it obeys basic physical principles, is always very subjective and dependent on the composer. Artists who practise regularly will, over time, acquire a feel for which melodic harmonies can be perceived as consonant and which cannot. A schematic description of how harmony can be elaborated in musical notation is therefore lacking. For a less experienced composer, such an outline is very valuable. For example, let us look at the schematic representation of the circle of fifths [24]. This harmonically simple but difficult to interpret procedure is also symbolized by a diagram. For example, the authors of the article "Evolutionary composition using music theory and charts" [22] talk about the possibility of formalizing music theory with harmony in the form of graphical representations and suggest to interpret the musical style in their form. This formalization is comprehensive for the use of artificial intelligence training, but also, as we have mentioned, for the teaching of music in music schools.

Our research is therefore directed towards the description of harmony in the form of BPMN and its possible extension for musical purposes so that the harmonic development is as perceptible as possible and the model then perfectly fulfils its educational role.

References

1. Riedweg, C.: Pythagoras: His Life, Teaching, and Influence. Cornell University Press, New York, p. 27 (2008). ISBN 978-0-8014-7452-1
2. Leo van de Pas: Genealogics.org (2003)

3. Hiley, D., Payne, T.B., Bent, M., Chew, G., Rastall, R.: Notation: III and IV. In Sadie, Stanley (ed.). The New Grove Dictionary of Music and Musicians (2nd ed.). Grove, London (2001)
4. BPMN introduction and history. Trisotech, 23 Jan 2022, [online] trisotech.com. https://www.trisotech.com/bpmn-introduction-and-history/. Accessed 15 Dec 2021
5. Kocbek, M., Jošt, G., Heričko, M., Polančič, G.: Business process model and notation: the current state of affairs. Comput. Sci. Inf. Syst. **12**(2) (2015). https://doi.org/10.2298/CSIS14 0610006K
6. Hassen, M.B., Keskes, M., Turki, M., Gargouri, F.: BPMN 4KM: design and implementation of a BPMN extension for modelling the knowledge perspective of ensitive business processes. Procedia Comput. Sci. **121**, 1119–1134 (2017). https://doi.org/10.1016/j.procs.2017.12.121
7. Pavlicek, J., Rod, M., Pavlickova, P.: Usability evaluation of business process modeling standards – BPMN and BORM case study. In: Polyvyanyy, A., Rinderle-Ma, S. (eds.) Advanced Information Systems Engineering Workshops. CAiSE 2021. LNBIP, vol 423, pp. 93–104. Springer, Cham (2021). https://doi.org/10.1007/978-3-030-79022-6_9
8. Pavlicek, J., Hronza, R., Pavlickova, P., Jelinkova, K.: The business process models quality metrics. In: Workshop on Enterprise and Organisational Modelling and Simulation, pp. 134–148. Springer, Cham, June 2017. https://doi.org/10.1007/978-3-319-68185-6_10
9. Pavlicek, J., Pavlickova, P.: Methods for evaluating the quality of process modelling tools. In: Pergl, R., Babkin, E., Lock, R., Malyzhenkov, P., Merunka, V. (eds.) Enterprise and Organizational Modeling and Simulation. EOMAS 2018. LNBIP, vol. 332, pp. 171–177. Springer, Cham (2018). https://doi.org/10.1007/978-3-030-00787-4_12
10. Temperley, D.: The Cognition of Basic Musical Structures. MIT Press, Cambridge (2001)
11. Grier, J.: Guido of Arezzo. Oxford Bibliographies: Music. Oxford University Press, Oxford (2018). https://doi.org/10.1093/OBO/9780199757824-0248
12. Temperley, D.: The melodic-harmonic 'divorce' in rock. Pop. Music **26**(2), 323–342 (2007)
13. Temperley, D.: "The Cadential IV in Rock. Music Theory Online 17 (2011a)
14. Temperley, D.: Scalar Shift in Popular Music. Music Theory Online 17 (2011b)
15. Temperley, D., de Clercq, T.: Statistical analysis of harmony and melody in rock music. J. New Music Res. **42**(3), 187–204 (2013)
16. Blendell, B.: (Year of publication). Harmony and Syntax in Contemporary Pop Music. Digital Library Vassar College. Accessed Jan 2024
17. Molhanec, M.: Deriving relational normalisation from conceptual normalisation. In: Babkin, E., Barjis, J., Malyzhenkov, P., Merunka, V., Molhanec, M. (eds.) Model-Driven Organizational and Business Agility. MOBA 2023. LNBIP, vol. 488, pp. 32–41. Springer, Cham (2023). https://doi.org/10.1007/978-3-031-45010-5_3
18. Paiement, J.-F., Douglas, E., Samy, B.: A probabilistic model for chord progressions. In: Proceedings of the Sixth International Conference on Music Information Retrieval (ISMIR) (2005)
19. Tojo, S., Oka, Y., Nishida, M.: Analysis of Chord Progression by HPSG. Artificial Intelligence and Applications (2006)
20. Hedges, T., Roy, P., Pachet, F.: Predicting the composer and style of jazz chord progressions. J. New Music Res. (2014). https://doi.org/10.1080/09298215.2014.925477
21. Wang, X.: Design of vocal music teaching system platform for music majors based on artificial intelligence. Wirel. Commun. Mob. Comput. (2022). https://doi.org/10.1155/2022/5503834
22. Liu, C.-H., Ting, C.-K.:Evolutionary composition using music theory and charts. In: 2013 IEEE Symposium on Computational Intelligence for Creativity and Affective Computing (CICAC), Singapore, pp. 63–70 (2013). https://doi.org/10.1109/CICAC.2013.6595222
23. Broekhuis, R.: Wheel of Fifths – Harmonic Function. Wheel of Fifths, 11 Oct 2022. Accessed 05 Oct 2023
24. Fig1: https://en.wikipedia.org/wiki/Mensural_notation January 2024

Process-Specific Extensions for Enhanced Recommender Systems in Business Process Management

Sebastian Petter[✉] and Stefan Jablonski

University of Bayreuth, Bayreuth, Germany
{sebastian.petter,stefan.jablonski}@uni-bayreuth.de

Abstract. In Business Process Management (BPM) the integration of advanced recommender systems emerges as a critical strategy to enhance process efficiency and user satisfaction. Despite the dissemination of these systems, there remains a distinct lack of incorporating execution relevant context data, particularly those generated during process execution and prevailing environmental conditions. This paper addresses this gap by proposing process-specific extensions for augmenting an existing recommender system framework. Our approach not only enhances the adaptability and accuracy of recommendations but also sustains the applicability of existing algorithms, ensuring seamless integration into available recommender frameworks. The potential of this refined approach is demonstrated by evaluating a process scenario based on synthetic data.

Keywords: Business process management · Recommender systems · User-centered process improvement

1 Introduction

In today's highly competitive business environment, Business Process Management (BPM) has become a crucial element for the success of organizations [10,22]. BPM involves a systematic approach for improving an organization's workflow to make it more efficient and adaptable in a constantly changing context. The main aims of BPM include boosting performance, minimizing inefficiencies, and fostering innovation within defined sequences of activities that are geared towards achieving specific organizational objectives [13,16]. These activity sequences are formally represented as business process models, which outline the necessary actions in a process and provide information on involved entities like participants and data objects. Such models play an essential role in visualizing and comprehending the flow of activities within processes, serving as a foundation for analyzing, enhancing, and automating business processes. A key component for carrying out these business processes are Process-Aware Information Systems (PAIS), which aid in managing and monitoring the state of process activities to support their execution [20].

© The Author(s), under exclusive license to Springer Nature Switzerland AG 2024
J. P. A. Almeida et al. (Eds.): CAiSE 2024 Workshops, LNBIP 521, pp. 275–290, 2024.
https://doi.org/10.1007/978-3-031-61003-5_24

Despite the advancements in BPM, a significant challenge remains in improving business processes to meet user requirements. Many conventional BPM optimization methods are activity-centered and aim to streamline tasks to reduce inefficiencies [21]. However, they often neglect the importance of human resources [18]. To bridge this gap, there have been attempts to include user preferences in process execution, applying approaches similar to those enacted by recommender systems [5,17,21]. These initiatives mark a paradigm shift from traditional process-centric execution to a more user-centric approach, offering users recommendations on tasks to be performed next based according to their preferences. However, these solutions generally do not take into account data generated during process execution and prevailing environmental conditions. This includes, in particular, *process instance data* on one side and *context (environment) data* on the other side. For instance in a sales order activity , such data embrace activity parameters such as the quantity of a good or context data like weather conditions impacting delivery of goods. The integration of such data allows for a more effective and context-aware generation of recommendations. From now on we refer to these two kinds of data occuring during process instance execution as *execution relevant context data (ERC data)*.

The neglect of context-specific information in process execution can significantly impact the relevance and effectiveness of recommendations. Thus, this paper aims to address this gap by expanding current methods to incorporate process context in generating recommendations. This novel approach promises to improve the flexibility and effectiveness of user recommendations by providing more contextually relevant and personalized recommendations.

The remainder of the paper is organized as follows: Sect. 2 provides an overview of BPM and recommender systems. Section 3 outlines related literature and emphasizes the significance of integrating ERC data. Section 4 showcases a real-world business process from one of our project collaborators. In Sect. 5, we outline the criteria and research inquiries that will shape our study. Section 6 details the expansion of the foundational framework, while in Sect. 7, we showcase the demonstration and evaluation of this framework extension. Lastly, Sect. 8 concludes the paper and looks ahead to future research avenues.

2   Background

2.1   Business Process Management

BPM is a disciplined approach aimed at improving corporate efficiency and effectiveness while striving for innovation, flexibility, and integration with technology. Its primary goal is to increase efficiency and reduce operational costs through the continual optimization of business processes. A business process is a set of sequential activities and tasks that, once completed, will accomplish an organizational goal [10,22].

The BPM lifecycle comprises multiple stages: design, modeling, execution, monitoring, and optimization [10]. In the design and modeling phases, business processes are defined and represented in a process model. This model is then interpreted by a PAIS, enabling the execution of the process. Users engage with the PAIS using a user interface through which they typically receive a worklist containing executable instances of activities (also called tasks) derived from the process model [20]. These tasks are selected and completed by users, with each task's execution recorded as an event within an event log that provides detailed information such as timestamps, involved resources, and executed activities [1]. These events, when collected and organized as part of a specific process instance, form a trace, establishing a chronological record of the process execution.

2.2 Process Perspectives

In BPM, it is crucial to take into account various viewpoints in order to fully grasp and efficiently manage business processes. These perspectives cover different facets of a process, including its organization, timing, participant roles, and related data. By considering these perspectives, organizations can ensure that all aspects of the process are aligned. In the realm of BPM, five distinct perspectives are commonly considered to offer a holistic view of processes and their operational contexts [7,13]; however, this list is not exhaustive and additional perspectives may be added as needed.

- **Functional Perspective:** Focuses on the functional components of a process, such as the specific activities required to complete a business process.
- **Behavioral Perspective:** Also known as control flow; deals with the temporal behavior and ordering of activities, detailing how and in what order tasks should be executed.
- **Organizational Perspective:** Addresses the allocation of process steps to human participants or roles within an organization.
- **Data Perspective:** Concerns the data and information units required, generated, or manipulated at different stages in a process.
- **Operational Perspective:** Focuses on the implementation of each atomic process step, including the applications or tools necessary for execution.

2.3 Recommender Systems

Recommender systems aim to predict user preferences and suggest items accordingly [2]. Most commonly seen in E-Commerce and user-centric web applications, these systems improve user experience and decision-making. Key concepts in recommender systems play a crucial role. An *item* can be anything recommended by the system, such as a product or a movie. A *user* is an individual receiving recommendations based on their distinct preferences and behaviors. *Attributes* are the specific characteristics of either items or users, like genre for movies or age for users. *User Feedback* covers the information provided by users, which can be explicit (like ratings) or implicit (like viewing history) [9]. Recommender systems employ four main methods based on different inputs and use cases:

- **Knowledge-based Filtering:** Recommends items based on a user's specified requirements or preferences, leveraging explicit knowledge about both, the user and the item attributes [2].
- **Content-based Filtering:** Recommends items based on their similarity to other items that the user has liked or interacted with in the past, focusing on the attributes of the items [8].
- **Collaborative Filtering:** Recommends items, based on the preferences of other users with similar tastes and behaviors, not relying on item attributes but rather on user-item interactions [8].
- **Hybrid Filtering:** Combines multiple recommender system methods to improve recommendation quality and overcome the specific limitations of a single method [6].

Each method can be executed using different algorithms and has its unique set of strengths and weaknesses. Personalized recommendations from knowledge-based filtering require extensive user input, which can be overwhelming [2]. Content-based filtering analyzes attributes of items similar to those the user has liked before, providing tailored suggestions but potentially limiting variety in recommendations. Collaborative filtering has the potential to uncover unexpected findings by using the preferences of similar users, though it struggles with new users or items due to the cold start problem [8]. Finally, hybrid filtering combines these approaches to balance their benefits and mitigate downsides, offering a versatile solution, but at the cost of increased system complexity [6].

3   Related Work

In the academic exploration of BPM, the application of recommender systems has been identified as a promising area for enhancing process efficiency and effectiveness [12,21]. Previous studies have focused on providing recommendations for process modeling with the goal of streamlining the development and improvement of business processes [15]. Other research has targeted various optimization goals, including reducing throughput time, showcasing the adaptability and promise of recommender systems in BPM [4,12,21].

The literature review by Petter [18] provides a comprehensive overview of these approaches, highlighting the diversity and scope of existing research. However it becomes apparent that a significant gap remains: the limited attention to user preferences in most of these approaches. In the context of BPM, user preferences refer to the individual likes and dislikes of users, which are articulated explicitly through ratings or inferred implicitly through user behavior. Despite the importance of aligning business processes with these preferences, there has been insufficient integration into the execution phase. Although some efforts have been made, they mostly utilize techniques tailored to a very specific scenario, constraining their applicability [3,5,17].

An exception in the field is our framework [19]. It integrates multiple recommendation methods into one customizable framework. It leverages a variety of recommendation techniques, enhancing the pertinence and usefulness of recommendations for end-users. However, it still lacks in incorporating ERC data, such as activity parameters or environmental parameters. The extension of our approach presented in this paper copes with that issue.

The importance of incorporating ERC data into recommender systems is supported by findings from the broader field, notably by Aggarwal [2]. He indicates that the inclusion of contextual information significantly enhances the effectiveness of the recommendation process. It improves the precision and relevance of recommendations, which in turn contributes to increased user satisfaction and higher process efficiency in BPM scenarios.

4   Running Example

To demonstrate the potential impact of process-specific extensions we provide a running example. Figure 1 outlines a simplified event planning procedure in BPMN[1] notation from one of our project partners in the project PRIME (Process-based integration of human expectations in digitized work environments)[2]. This figure illustrates a business process that is broken down into six key activities, embodying the functional perspective of the process. These activities are essential for the orchestration and realization of an event, engaging three main stakeholders: the event planner, the catering service, and the logistics service, althogether reflecting the organizational perspective.

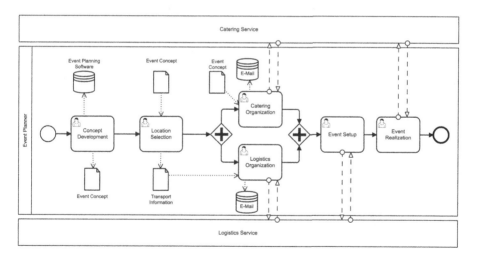

Fig. 1. Event planning process.

Event Concept and *Transport Information* are most important constituents of the process as they represent essential documents from the data-oriented per-

---

[1] https://www.omg.org/spec/BPMN/2.0/.
[2] https://prime-interaktionsarbeit.de.

spective. *Event Concept* outlines the basic parameters like type (such as a networking event or celebration) and target audience of an event, whereas *Transport Information* becomes crucial for logistical planning once the venue has been selected.

The process also employs specific tools facilitating communication and coordination: *E-Mail* and *Event Planning Software (EPS)*. These components are indicative of the operational perspective.

Furthermore, the process encompasses various characteristics and environmental parameters that can have an indirect impact on event planning. Process steps like *Location Selection, Event Setup Catering Organization, Logistics Organization*, and *Event Realization* may heavily be influenced by external factors such as weather or temperature, underpinning the importance of including environmental factors and parameters into the planning process.

5 Requirements Analysis

For enhancing the effectiveness of recommender systems in BPM through ERC data, a thorough requirements analysis is required. Starting with researching literature [18] about what ERC data could enhance recommendations in the context of BPM, a second issue is to analyse how these ERC data could be incorporated into common recommendation algorithms without completely re-implementing them. Finally, an evaluation must reveal how this enhancement could improve recommendations within BPM. The whole analysis results in three research questions:

(i) *What types of ERC data can improve the effectiveness of recommendations in the BPM context?* This question aims at identifying data categories that have the potential to enhance recommendations for process execution. Specifically, we aim at data that are still not considered sufficiently.

(ii) *How can ERC data be incorporated into the generation of recommendations without enforcing a re-implementation of common recommendation algorithms?* This issue embraces data pre-processing, transformation, and integration techniques that can align with current frameworks for recommendation systems, thereby facilitating seamless data incorporation. The goal is to enhance the adaptability of recommendation systems to ERC data while reusing common frameworks and algorithms.

(iii) *What is the impact of ERC data on the accuracy and significance of recommendations?* Here, we explore how incorporating process context affects the production of recommendations. The goal is to measure the advantages of including ERC data and to comprehend its impact on the quality of recommendations.

Addressing these research questions is crucial for enhancing the capabilities of recommendation systems within the BPM domain. By identifying and utilizing ERC data, recommendations become more nuanced and aligned with the specific needs and dynamics of different business processes. Furthermore, comprehending how process context influences the performance of recommendation systems provides valuable insights into their practical usefulness and efficiency.

Research Methodology. This research employs the Design Science Research (DSR) methodology, which consists of five iterative phases [14]. Section 1 initiated this process by explicating the problem, identifying the gaps in current recommendation systems within BPM. This section aims at defining necessary requirements for our proposed solution, aligning with the second phase of DSR. The subsequent phase of the DSR method focuses on designing and developing an improved recommendation framework as an artifact, which will be detailed in the next section. Section 7 will then demonstrate and evaluate this artifact, applying it within a BPM context as outlined in Sect. 4, thus completing the final phases of DSR. This methodology guides our research from problem identification to practical solution evaluation, ensuring a comprehensive and systematic approach.

6   Extension of Framework

In this section, we delve into the *Design and Development of Artifact* phase of the DSR, building upon the foundational work presented in [19]. The paper introduces a framework that facilitates the integration of various recommendation methods into process execution. This integration is facilitated by leveraging enhanced process management systems, which have been augmented to capture explicit user feedback, such as activity ratings, thus providing a more comprehensive dataset for generating recommendations. This framework stands out by focusing primarily on the functional perspective of business processes, analyzing activities and their associated meta-attributes. These attributes, along with explicit user feedback, serve as critical inputs for the recommendation algorithms. One feature of the framework is that it is open to potential input data types for the generation of recommendations in the BPM domain.

Our effort extends both the framework and the input data, placing specific emphasis on process instance data beyond the functional perspective and environmental data as two kinds of ERC data, aspects that have been previously neglected in recommendation generation.

6.1   Extending the Input Data

In order to enhance the effectiveness of recommendation systems within the BPM domain, we focus on incorporating a broader range of ERC data into our framework. Our investigation expands these boundaries, identifying two principal types of ERC data: *process instance (activity) parameters* and *environmental parameters*. This classification not only addresses but also resolves research question (i), emphasizing the necessity for a more nuanced data integration approach. Figure 2 displays the expanded input data categories (dark boxes). The following input data should further be integrated into the framework:

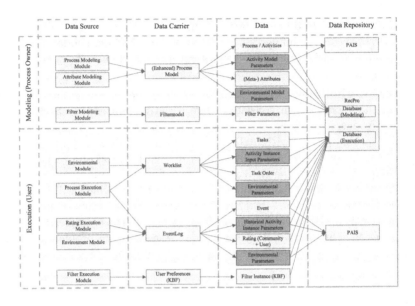

Fig. 2. Enhanced organization of input data (based on [19]).

- **Activity (Model) Parameters:** These are formal parameters of a process model, created in the process modeling phase. In our running example the *Event Type* is such a parameter.
- **Activity (Instance) Input Parameters:** These are actual input parameters of *current* activities, filled through process execution. For instance, *Networking Event* can be an instance value of the formal input parameter *Event Type* of the activity *Location Selection*.
- **Historical Activity (Instance) Parameters:** These are parameters of a previously executed process instance. They provide historical context and data, enabling a deeper understanding of process dynamics and decision-making patterns.

Moreover, we suggest incorporating environmental factors like the time of day, weather conditions, and resource availability into the recommendation system. It is obvious that these parameters has to be selected according to its relevance for the process to perform. For instance, it is more than probable that outdoor jobs (activities) are more attractive when the weather conditions are good. We differentiate between three categories of environmental parameters:

- **Environmental Model Parameters:** These formal parameters are extending a process model. Later during process execution they are automatically captured. In our running example, a good candidate for such a parameter is the ambient temperature.
- **Environmental Instance Parameters (Worklist):** These are specific instances of environmental parameters at the time of process execution, such

as the actual temperature when a task is performed. These parameters are automatically recorded during task execution.

- **(Historical) Environmental Instance Parameters (Eventlog):** These parameters represent the specific instances of environmental conditions recorded during past process executions, offering insights into the environmental context of historical process activities.

6.2 Framework Enhancement

To adapt our recommendation framework for BPM applications [19] to accommodate the new input data identified in Sect. 6.1, its architecture must be expanded. Originally, our framework consists of three core modules:

- *Input Module*: Responsible for providing necessary data for recommendation algorithms.
- *Recommendation Module*: Responsible for generating recommendations.
- *Output Module*: Presents the revised worklist - reflecting the output of the Recommendation Module - to the users.

Addressing research question (ii), we propose a strategic enhancement to our framework. This involves the integration of two new modules as illustrated in Fig. 3: the *Pre-Filtering Module* and the *Post-Filtering Module*. These modules are specifically designed to manage ERC data without comprising the efficiency or integrity of the existing system.

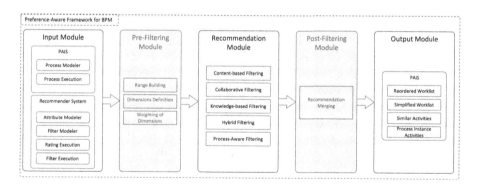

Fig. 3. Enhanced structure of conceptual framework (based on [19]).

Pre-Filtering Module. The pre-filtering module is designed to prepare the enhanced input data for the recommendation engine. It includes three key steps: *Range Building, Dimension Specification,* and *Dimension Weighting*.

The *Range Building* step entails establishing numerical parameter ranges to facilitate meaningful data aggregation and analysis. For instance, temperatures might be grouped in 10-degree intervals. Normally, it is not decisive whether the temperature is 21° or 22°; thus, we abstract from concrete values and work with value ranges instead. These ranges should be determined either by experts or automatically by clustering algorithms, depending on the availability of extensive datasets.

The *Dimension Specification* step enables process owners to determine which ERC data the recommendation module should take into account. The ERC data are allocated in the pre-filtering module. It is possible to consider single ERC data and groupings of them. For instance, it might be interesting to group *temperature* and *humidity* or *catering service* and *event type*. Hereby, not just the parameter types, but also the instance values like *networking* or *celebration* for event types can be regarded. We call single or grouped ERC data considered for recommendations as *dimension*.

Leveraging the expertise of process professionals, the step *Dimension Weighting* enables the prioritization of various dimensions based on their relevance and significance. This guarantees that each dimension's output is accurately represented in the final recommendation, facilitating a customized approach guided by expert insights and priorities.

The pre-filtering module retrieves and processes pertinent data from process-specific sources for recommendation generation, focusing on each specified dimension. Subsequently, the recommendation algorithm is executed for each dimension individually, producing several recommendation outputs that are later consolidated in the post-filtering module.

Post-filtering Module. The *Post-Filtering Module* integrates the multiple recommendations generated by the pre-filtering module into a single, coherent recommendation. This ensures compatibility with the already existing output module of the original framework. This integration respects the weights assigned during the pre-filtering stage, ensuring that the final recommendation reflects the prioritized dimensions.

By incorporating these modules, the enhanced framework enables a more sophisitcated and contextually sensitive method for generating recommendations. The pre-filtering module ensures that data entering the recommendation engine is appropriately structured and prioritized, while the post-filtering module ensures that the final output remains usable and coherent. This extension not only preserves the integrity of the original framework's workflow but also enhances its capability to deliver more personalized and contextually relevant recommendations.

7   Demonstration and Evaluation

Synthetic Data. For the demonstration and evaluation of the enhanced framework, synthetic data is employed as authentic real-world data is not available due to the novelty of the subject being studied. The synthetic data is created to replicate genuine scenarios and encompasses a range of dimensions and features pertinent to the recommendation process. This allows for precise testing and assessment of the enhanced recommender system, offering valuable insights into its efficacy across various settings. In total, we produce an event log consisting of 100 events; an extract of this log is depicted in Table 1.

Table 1. Synthetic event log.

PID	Activity	User	Timestamp	Data	Tool	Environment	Rating
142	Concept Development	U_1	2024-01-10 09:00	Type: Networking	EPS		3
142	Location Selection	U_2	2024-01-12 10:00	Type: Networking		Temperature: 22 Weather: sunny	8
145	Catering Organization	U_1	2024-01-18 11:22	Type: Celebration		Temperature: 22 Weather: sunny Catering: CS_1	9
...	...	...	...	...	...	...	...

In a first step, a basic event log is created according to the process model introduced in Sect. 4. Each event includes details such as execution timestamp, executed activity, resources involved, and activity instance parameters. This fundamental dataset captures common sequences and interactions within an event planning scenario, covering a range of standard procedures and resource involvements. Subsequently, resource ratings are added to the dataset to simulate subjective human ratings and preferences for particular activities and conditions. The enrichment process follows predefined rules reflecting hypothetical user preferences:

- User U_1 prefers activities involving catering service CS_1.
- User U_2 rates the activity *Location Selection* positively if the temperature exceeds 20 °C and negatively if below.
- User U_3 generally dislikes the activity *Catering Organization*.
- User U_4 enjoys activities associated with celebrations.
- User U_5 is a new user without preferences set so far.

In addition, the dataset includes outliers to better capture human behavior, that individual actions and evaluations may not always align perfectly with established preferences or rules. These irregularities contribute to a more authentic simulation, acknowledging the unpredictability and diversity in human behavior.

Nevertheless, it is important to note the limitations associated with artificial data. While the dataset offers valuable insights, it cannot cover all potential scenarios and human responses. The limited set of five user profiles serves as illustrative starting point rather than as comprehensive user scenario.

The generated data is employed to demonstrate and evaluate the enhanced framework through three distinct recommendation approaches: knowledge-based filtering, content-based filtering, and collaborative filtering. We examine the suitable scenarios for applying each method, the influence of the extended framework, and the resulting changes in outcomes.

Knowledge-Based Filtering. This method enables users to explicitly specify their actual preferences by filtering items directly, for instance, stating that *Concept Development* is a favourite for an user. Knowledge-based filtering is used in scenarios when user feedback data is still absent, i.e. among other things it solves the cold start problem.

Originally, manual filtering as main operation of knowledge-based filtering exclusively focuses the functional perspective, allowing users to choose specific activities directly (see example above). Our novel approach facilitates to consider the data-oriented, organizational, and operational perspective as well, meaning that activities are selected that share specific parameters, for instance, a specific tool (operational perspective) or a specific input data (data perspective).

In our running example knowledge-based filtering can now consider event types and temperature ranges, for instance. This makes it easier for user U_5, who is new to the process and lacks historical ratings, to select activities based on their preferences, for instance, stating that events of type *Celebration* are not liked.

Content-Based Filtering. Content-based filtering comes into play when new items are introduced, such as new activities, which lack historical user ratings. This method determines the similarity between items (e.g. activities) and derives recommendation on that.

Previously, this method primarily considered the functional perspective and a limited aspect of the data perspective. For example, it is said that *Catering Organization* and *Event Realization* are similar. We expand content-based filtering across all perspectives of a process. For instance, similarities of activities can be determined when activities are using same tools or producing same results, i.e. output data.

Table 2. Content-based filtering.

(a) Input without ERC data.

	Event Planning Software	Event Concept	Transport Information	E-Mail	Catering Service	Logistics Service	...	Rating	Pearson
Concept Development	1	1	0	0	0	0	...	5	-0.32
Location Selection	0	1	1	0	0	0	...	3	-0.32
Catering Organization	0	1	0	1	1	0	...	5	0.45
Logistics Organization	0	0	1	1	0	1	...	2	-0.45
Event Setup	0	0	0	0	0	1	...	3	-0.2
Event Realization_1	0	0	0	0	1	0	...	*5*	
Event Realization_2	0	0	0	0	1	0	...	*5*	

(b) Input with ERC data.

	Catering Service				Rating	Pearson (CS_1)	Pearson (CS_2)
	CS_1	CS_2	CS_3	:			
...	...	...	...	...	...	...	...
Catering Organization_1	... 1	0	0	...	9	0.61	0.10
Catering Organization_2	... 0	1	0	...	3	0.10	0.61
Catering Organization_3	... 0	0	1	...	3	0.10	0.10
...	...	...	...	...	...	...	...
Event Realization_1 (CS_1)	... 1	0	0	...	*7.5*		
Event Realization_2 (CS_2)	... 0	1	0	...	*3.75*		

To evaluate the efficacy of our enhanced framework, we refer to our running scenario. In Table 2, we present two evaluations demonstrating the behavior of user U_1: the left one excludes, the right one includes ERC data. The rows of the tables indicate activity types (upper section) and instances (lower section), respectively. We first describe the left table. The upper five activities have already been executed, possibly multiple times, the lower two not so far, they are residing in worklists. The assessment of already executed activities is recorded per activity type (upper part of table). In the lower part of the table two instances to be executed are shown; they are depicted in worklists of eligible users. The first block of columns depicts features of an activity. The column *Rating* shows the average rating by U_1 based on the generated event log. The last column shows the calculated Pearson correlation coefficient between the activity (type) in the current row and the still not executed activity instances in the last two rows. The objective is to predict the ratings for these new tasks using the Pearson correlation. It is obvious that both worklist activities are rated equally since preferences are just assigned per activity type. Since *Event Realization* is most similar to *Catering Organization* it inherits rating 5 from the latter one.

The right table considers ERC data and therefore we will incorporate instance data. Thus, we figuratively zoom into the data of the left table. In the right table we exemplary zoom into the process *Catering Organization* depicting three already executed instances of this activity. It is shown that these three instances work on different values of the formal parameter *Catering Service*, namely, CS_1, CS_2, and CS_3. These instances also show different ratings (9, 3, 3), depending on the catering service involved. Consequently, we derive different ratings for the upcoming process instances in the lower part of the table, depending on the actual parameters they are working on. The two ratings depicted in Fig. 2 are computed on basis of the ratings of the process instances above and their Pearson coefficients (Fig. 4) [11]. We are convinced that this reflects user preferences more adequate than just working on an abstract process level without regarding actual process parameters.

$$r_{eventReal.1} = \frac{9*0.61+3*0.10+3*0.10}{0.61+0.10+0.10} = 7.5 \qquad r_{eventReal.2} = \frac{9*0.10+3*0.61+3*0.10}{0.10+0.61+0.10} = 3.75$$

Fig. 4. Rating calculation for task *Event Realization*.

Collaborative Filtering. Collaborative filtering is most effective when exhaustive user feedback is available. It aims to identify similar users and make recommendations based on how these users have rated the activity concerned.

Traditionally, this method considers only the functional perspective, which could lead to inaccuracies due to the too generic treatment of activities. With the framework extension proposed in this paper, collaborative filtering can be enhanced to take into account weighted dimensions. These dimensions can be data oriented (like activity parameters), tool oriented, or behavior oriented. The latter captures the sequence of recent activities performed by the user and their relationship to the current activity.

Figure 5 compares a conventional user-activity matrix without ERC data (on the left) to a multidimensional cube that regards ERC data (on the right). In

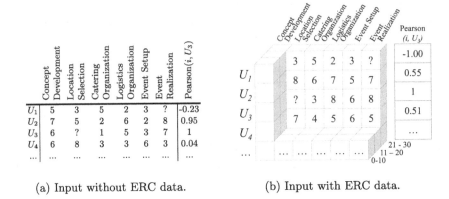

(a) Input without ERC data.   (b) Input with ERC data.

Fig. 5. Collaborative filtering.

the user-activity matrix, each cell denotes the average rating given by a user to an activity, based on historical interactions. A "?" in a cell indicates that the activity has not been rated by the user yet. The rightmost column shows the calculated Pearson correlation coefficients between all users and the target user U_3, demonstrating similarities in preferences based on historical activity ratings. Figure 5b extends this matrix by introducing *temperature* as an additional dimension, categorizing data into three distinct ranges: 0–10, 11–20, and 21-30 °C.

Comparing these two figures highlights notable differences in the Pearson correlation coefficients when ERC data is taken into account. For instance, when ERC data are neglected, user U_4 has almost no impact on User U_3 (0.04). However, when ERC data are considered, in this case *Temperature*, and the outside temperature might been above 20° then $U_4's$ impact on U_3 is essentially higher (0.51).

Now, we want to calculate the recommendation factor for the task *Location Selection* in $U_3's$ worklist. Without considering temperature data, the *Location Selection* task receives an estimated rating of 5.11, based on the Pearson correlation coefficients. However, by incorporating temperature as execution relevant parameter, this potential rating notably increases to 7.52, reflecting the enhanced context-awareness of the recommendation.

Incorporating ERC data, as demonstrated in the examples above, allows for a more accurate reflection of user preferences. Therefore, by aligning the recommendations more closely with actual process and environmental data, we substantiate the resolution of research question (iii), evidencing the critical role of ERC data in enhancing the accuracy of recommendations in BPM systems.

8   Conclusion and Future Work

In conclusion, this study advances the field of recommender systems for BPM by incorporating ERC data. This enhancement increases the adaptability and responsiveness of these systems without altering the underlying recommendation algorithms. By integrating both activity-specific and environmental parameters, the research expands an existing recommendation framework, demonstrating potential for more personalized and situationally aware guidance in BPM. Furthermore, the exploration of pre-filtering and post-filtering mechanisms is a significant focus of our research. The pre-filtering module is created to ensure that data entering the recommendation engine is appropriately structured and prioritized, laying the foundation for more accurate and relevant recommendations. In contrast, the post-filtering module consolidates multiple outputs from the pre-filtering process into a single coherent recommendation, ensuring that the final output is both usable and aligned with user needs and preferences.

Future research should focus on three main areas to enhance BPM recommender systems. The first area involves improving transparency by providing explanations for recommendations, which helps users understand the background of suggested actions. The second area is the empirical assessment of the impact of recommendations on user satisfaction, aiming to evaluate their real-world effectiveness. The final issue is the exploration of diverse algorithmic approaches to refine personalization and accuracy of recommendations, ensuring they are more effectively tailored to user's needs.

References

1. van der Aalst, W.M.P.: Process mining - data science in action, 2nd Edn. Springer, Cham (2016)
2. Aggarwal, C.C.: Recommender Systems - The Textbook. Springer, New York (2016). https://doi.org/10.1007/978-3-319-29659-3
3. Arias, M., Munoz-Gama, J., Sepúlveda, M.: A multi-criteria approach for team recommendation (2016)
4. Barba, I., Weber, B., Del Valle, C.: Supporting the optimized execution of business processes through recommendations. In: Daniel, F., Barkaoui, K., Dustdar, S. (eds.) Business Process Management Workshops. BPM 2011, LNBIP, vol. 99, pp. 135–140. Springer, Berlin (2012). https://doi.org/10.1007/978-3-642-28108-2_12
5. Bidar, R., ter Hofstede, A., Sindhgatta, R., Ouyang, C.: Preference-based resource and task allocation in business process automation. In: Panetto, H., Debruyne, C., Hepp, M., Lewis, D., Ardagna, C., Meersman, R. (eds.) On the Move to Meaningful Internet Systems: OTM 2019 Conferences, OTM 2019, LNCS, vol. 11877, pp. 404–421. Springer, Cham (2019). https://doi.org/10.1007/978-3-030-33246-4_26
6. Burke, R.: Hybrid recommender systems: survey and experiments (2002)
7. Curtis, B., Kellner, M., Over, J.: Process modeling. Commun. ACM **35**, 75–90 (1992)
8. Desrosiers, C., Karypis, G.: A comprehensive survey of neighborhood-based recommendation methods. In: Ricci, F., Rokach, L., Shapira, B., Kantor, P. (eds.) Recommender Systems Handbook, pp. 107–144. Springer, Boston (2011). https://doi.org/10.1007/978-0-387-85820-3_4

9. Douglas, W.O., Jinmook, K.: Implicit feedback for recommender systems. Technical Report (1998)
10. Dumas, M., Rosa, M.L., Mendling, J., Reijers, H.A.: Fundamentals of Business Process Management. Springer, Berlin (2013). https://doi.org/10.1007/978-3-662-56509-4
11. Freedman, D., Pisani, R., Purves, R.: Statistics: fourth international student edition (2007)
12. Haisjackl, C., Weber, B.: User assistance during process execution - an experimental evaluation of recommendation strategies. In: zur Muehlen, M., Su, J. (eds.) Business Process Management Workshops. BPM 2010, LNBIP, vol. 66, pp. 134–145. Springer, Berlin (2011). https://doi.org/10.1007/978-3-642-20511-8_12
13. Jablonski, S., Bussler, C.: Workflow management - modeling concepts, architecture and implementation. International Thomson (1996)
14. Johannesson, P., Perjons, E.: An Introduction to Design Science. Springer, Cham (2021). https://doi.org/10.1007/978-3-319-10632-8
15. Koschmider, A., Hornung, T., Oberweis, A.: Recommendation-based editor for business process modeling. In: Data & Knowledge Engineering, vol. 70 (2011). https://doi.org/10.1016/j.datak.2011.02.002
16. Lawrence, P. (ed.): Workflow Handbook 1997. Workflow Management Coalition. Wiley, New York (1997)
17. Petter, S., Fichtner, M., Schönig, S., Jablonski, S.: Content-based filtering for worklist reordering to improve user satisfaction: a position paper. In: Proceedings of the 24th International Conference on Enterprise Information Systems. ICEIS, vol. 2, pp. 589–596. SciTePress (2022). https://doi.org/10.5220/0011092900003179. ISBN 978-989-758-569-2, ISSN 2184-4992
18. Petter, S., Jablonski, S.: Recommender systems in business process management: a systematic literature review. In: Proceedings of the 25th International Conference on Enterprise Information Systems. ICEIS, vol. 2, pp. 431–442. SciTePress (2023). https://doi.org/10.5220/0012039500003467. ISBN 978-989-758-648-4; ISSN 2184-4992
19. Petter., S., Jablonski., S.: A generic approach towards adapting user preferences in business process execution (2024)
20. Reichert, M., Weber, B.: Enabling Flexibility in Process-Aware Information Systems - Challenges, Methods. Springer, Berlin (2012). https://doi.org/10.1007/978-3-642-30409-5
21. Schonenberg, H., Weber, B., van Dongen, B., van der Aalst, W.: Supporting flexible processes through recommendations based on history. In: Dumas, M., Reichert, M., Shan, MC. (eds.) Business Process Management. BPM 2008. LNCS, vol. 5240, pp. 51–66. Springer, Berlin (2008). https://doi.org/10.1007/978-3-540-85758-7_7
22. Weske, M.: Business Process Management: Concepts, Languages. Springer, Architectures (2007). https://doi.org/10.1007/978-3-642-28616-2

Comparing Process Models Beyond Structural Equivalence

Nicolai Schützenmeier[1]([✉]), Stefan Jablonski[1], and Stefan Schönig[2]

[1] University of Bayreuth, Bayreuth, Germany
{nicolai.schuetzenmeier,stefan.jablonski}@uni-bayreuth.de
[2] University of Regensburg, Regensburg, Germany
stefan.schoenig@ur.de

Abstract. Numerous approaches exist for the structural comparison of processes, focusing on functional and control-flow perspectives. However, such analyses fall short when it comes to facilitating the transfer of processes between different organizations. Successful adoption requires a broader consideration of organizational context, tools, and other pertinent factors. Notably absent from current discussions is an exploration of whether processes that are structurally similar also exhibit similarity across additional perspectives, and to what extent they resemble each other. In this paper, we propose measures of equivalence and similarity for processes beyond their structural aspects. Additionally, we present approaches for aligning processes that exhibit structural similarity but may differ in other important respects. By doing so, we contribute to filling the void in existing research and offer practical insights for process transfer and integration across organizational boundaries. Our findings have implications for both academia and industry, fostering a more comprehensive understanding of process comparison and facilitating smoother transitions in process adoption and adaptation.

Keywords: Model Comparison · Process Modeling · Process Alignment

1 Introduction

In today's dynamic business landscape, mergers and acquisitions have become commonplace strategies for companies striving to expand their market presence, optimize resources, and achieve competitive advantage. However, the integration of disparate organizational structures, systems, and processes often presents significant challenges. One critical aspect of this integration process is the comparison of process models, particularly when merging entities bring their own established workflows to the table [27].

Frequently, when organizations merge, they find themselves confronted with the task of aligning or integrating their respective process models. While these models may appear similar at a superficial level, closer examination reveals nuances that can have profound implications for the success of the integration effort. One of the primary challenges lies in determining the extent to which these seemingly similar process models truly align in terms of their underlying workflows, resource utilization, and data handling procedures [27].

Traditionally, process model comparison has focused on assessing the structural similarities and differences between models, often overlooking critical operational details [5]. For instance, while two process models may depict similar sequences of activities, it remains unclear whether identical tools are employed at each step or if the same personnel are responsible for executing corresponding tasks. Moreover, questions arise regarding the consistency and compatibility of data utilized within these models. Do both models rely on the same data objects? Are they sourced from equivalent datasets, or are disparities present in the availability and quality of information?

Recognizing the limitations of conventional approaches to process model comparison, this paper proposes a novel multi-perspective approach designed to provide a comprehensive evaluation of process model alignment. By adopting a holistic view that considers not only structural congruence but also operational, organizational, and data perspectives, this approach aims to offer insights into the true compatibility and integration potential of disparate process models. By examining the alignment of tools, personnel assignments, and data utilization across multiple dimensions, organizations embarking on integration initiatives can make more informed decisions and devise more effective strategies for harmonizing their processes. In the subsequent sections of this paper, we will delve into the theoretical underpinnings of our multi-perspective approach, outline its methodology, and demonstrate its applicability through a series of practical examples. Through this exploration, we aim to contribute to the evolving field of process management by providing a practical framework for addressing the complexities inherent in process model comparison within the context of organizational mergers and acquisitions.

The remainder of the paper is organized as follows. In Sect. 2, we establish the terminology necessary for the discussions. Section 3 provides an in-depth review of related work in the field. Following this, in Sect. 4, we present our main approach for model comparison. In Sect. 5, we conduct an experimental evaluation to validate our approach. Finally, Sect. 6 concludes the paper with a summary of findings and outlines potential avenues for future research.

2   Basic Terminology

In Sect. 2.1, we delve into Business Process Management (BPM) and process models. Section 2.2 elucidates the various process perspectives, offering insights into different ways of viewing and analyzing processes. Section 2.3 provides the necessary explanations, including our approach of operating language-independently within our conceptual framework, clarifying the rationale behind this methodology. Section 2.4 introduces the concept of equivalence in processes, initiating a discussion on the comparative aspects of different representations.

2.1 Business Process Management and Process Models

BPM is a methodology used by organizations to improve efficiency, effectiveness, and adaptability in their operations. It involves the systematic management of processes throughout their lifecycle, from design and modeling to execution, monitoring, and optimization. One key aspect of BPM is the use of process models, which are visual representations of the sequence of activities, decisions, and interactions that make up a business process [9]. Various languages and notations are used to create process models, including BPMN (Business Process Model and Notation)[1], Declare [17], and DPIL (Data Process Integration Language) [22]. BPMN is a widely adopted standard for modeling business processes. Declare focuses on specifying constraints and rules governing the execution of processes. DPIL is geared towards integrating data processing aspects into models, facilitating seamless data flow within processes.

2.2 Process Perspectives

To depict a process as realistically and accurately as possible, various aspects must be considered. These include not only the arrangement of activities but also individuals or organizations involved in the process and their interactions. Each of these aspects constitutes an *orthogonal block* and is referred to as a *process perspective* [12]. In this context, orthogonal means that these blocks are independent of each other: each block can be changed independently without affecting others, and blocks can be omitted without losing information from other blocks. This allows for describing a process on multiple levels. This work considers the following process perspectives [12]:

- **Functional Perspective:** describes occurring activities and their structures (e.g., subprocesses).
- **Control Flow Perspective:** describes the control flow, such as the causal and temporal arrangement of activities (sequences, parallel processing, etc.).
- **Data and Data Flow Perspective:** describes data objects and documents that may be created, manipulated, or utilized in activities.
- **Organizational Perspective:** describes involved organizations, including individuals, roles, or systems. This perspective captures relationships between organizations and assigns activities to organizations.
- **Operational Perspective:** describes technologies or services used, such as tools, programs, or devices. It records relationships between technologies and assigns activities to technologies.

2.3 Language-Independent Approach: Clarifying Foundations

In this paper, we introduce a novel approach to process model comparison that is independent of specific process modeling languages. While various process modeling languages like BPMN or Declare [17] have been widely used, they often lack

---

[1] http://www.omg.org/spec/BPMN/2.0.

comprehensive support for all process perspectives. For instance, BPMN primarily focuses on operational aspects, neglecting organizational perspectives beyond a superficial level, which can limit its utility in certain contexts [28]. For instance, in BPMN, organizational perspectives are marginally addressed through constructs like pools and swimlanes, but these may not adequately represent complex organizational structures or relationships [28]. Our language-agnostic approach allows organizations to incorporate organizational perspectives seamlessly into their process models, regardless of the modeling language used. Recognizing the inherent limitations of language-specific modeling approaches, we propose a framework that abstracts away from language constraints. Our approach aims to provide a flexible and adaptable methodology for modeling processes, irrespective of the underlying modeling language. By decoupling modeling techniques from language dependencies, organizations can effectively capture diverse process perspectives without being restricted by the limitations of any single language. Furthermore, it is noteworthy that language-agnostic process modeling approaches are not only relevant in practical applications but also in research contexts. In academic literature, it is common to advocate for approaches that are independent of specific languages, recognizing the need for flexibility and interoperability in process modeling methodologies [4,5].

2.4   Equality of Process Models

For our approach, it is assumed that the process models being compared share the same workflow, meaning they are identical in terms of activities and process flow, i.e. the functional and the control flow perspective. To establish this equivalence, we utilize the concept of equality derived from literature, where two workflows are considered equal if they accept the same traces [16]. We assume this equivalence since without it is not feasible to compare processes with regard of the remaining three perspectives (cf. Section 2.2). We denominate these processes as *structurally equivalent*:

Definition 1. *Two processes are called strucurally equivalent if they are equivalent in terms of both functional perspective and control flow perspective.*

Additionally, it is presumed that all external models, such as organizational models, have been matched, thereby identifying identical elements across the models. This assumption facilitates a consistent basis for comparison, allowing our approach to focus on capturing and analyzing variations in process behavior beyond the control flow perspective, while ensuring alignment with organizational, operational, and data related structures and relationships.

3   Related Work

The identification of similarities and common characteristics in process models is of great importance both in industry and research [27]. It is essential to identify duplicates [15] and various model variants [26] that may arise when process models are changed or developed. Another focus is on the correctness of models, aiming to ensure the verification of transformations of process models between different modeling languages [1] as well as supporting the theoretical correctness of process models [2]. In general, the literature distinguishes four different dimensions of equality and similarity for process models [21]:

- The *(natural) language dimension* describes the identification of the same objects, activities, etc.
- The *graph dimension* compares process models based on similar structures in the corresponding graph (e.g. subgraphs).
- The *behavioral dimension* examines process models based on language comparisons.
- The *(human) estimation dimension* is based on the subjective assessment of process experts.

The language dimension describes the comparison of the functional perspective. This is often done through the assessment of domain experts or approaches from the field of Natural Language Processing [14,20]. However, since the comparison of the functional perspective mainly serves to make process models comparable in principle, it is not further elaborated in this work or in the literature.

The graph dimension examines process models for similarities in the associated graph structure. However, this approach faces the challenge that not all process modeling languages have a graphical representation. For example, the declarative modeling language DPIL [22] does not have a graphical form of representation. Additionally, the graphical structure can be misleading: two process models that appear similar at first glance can be very different [27]. Nevertheless, comparing graph structures can provide indicators to quantify similarities for process models [27]. However, this work does not further consider the graph structure, as qualitative concepts and methods for comparing process models should be developed independently of the modeling language used.

In the realm of the behavioral dimension, the languages associated with process models are examined theoretically. This area is the most pursued approach in the literature for comparing process models [27]. For example, there are approaches to compare the complexities of languages [19]. However, for comparing process models, their complexity is not the most essential aspect but rather the concrete behavior in terms of eventually executed traces [27].

The last dimension, the estimation dimension, deals with the subjective assessment of process experts and/or domain experts. While a trained eye can provide insights into different process models and assess whether and to what extent the underlying processes are similar, an automated method is preferable due to its less error-prone nature and generally higher efficiency. It can be concluded that the behavioral dimension is the most important and informative dimension for process model comparison. This paper focuses on this dimension.

Current approaches can be divided into two categories: approaches for imperative process modeling languages and approaches for declarative process modeling languages. While there are numerous approaches for imperative process modeling languages [8], the number of methods for declarative process models is comparatively limited. The study in [10] demonstrates that declarative process models with few constraints can be well analyzed, while handling models consisting of a large number of constraints poses significant challenges. The increasing complexity of models with the number of constraints is undoubtedly one of the causes for this limitation. Nonetheless, there are isolated approaches for declarative languages. For instance, in [7], an automaton-based approach is introduced to detect redundant constraints and conflicts between different constraints. Often, all traces up to a certain length are simulated to gain a better understanding of the process models and to identify potential deadlocks [13]. This is also the standard procedure for checking mutual subset relationships between declarative process models [6]. The approaches in [24,25] present two different comparison methods for Declare [17] models.

Due to the lack of approaches for declarative process modeling languages, there are hardly any methods for comparing imperative and declarative process models. In [18], the imperative and declarative modeling paradigms are generally compared on a very abstract level. However, such an approach seems unhelpful when it comes to examining the expressive power of concrete process models. In [11], the authors define equality between two process models (regardless of their imperative or declarative nature) based on all possible execution traces, which is tackled by the approach in [23]. However, it remains unclear how to handle the problem of a potentially infinite set of traces, which is an obvious characteristic of declarative process models and therefore must be considered. In conclusion, there are hardly any methods for aligning multi-perspective process models. All previously mentioned comparison methods focus solely on the functional perspective and the control flow perspective. While there are some approaches in the literature for aligning additional perspectives, e.g., [4,5], they only allow for the direct comparison of elements without considering the complete process model. For example, the components of the process models are compared pairwise, ignoring all potential dependencies between them.

This paper develops innovative approaches to close existing research gaps in the comparison of the organizational, operational and the data and dataflow perspectives of process models. By considering all perspectives, this work provides a comprehensive basis for comparing process models. The developed approaches address the mostly neglected multi-perspective view. Thus, an important contribution is made to the development of generally applicable methods for comparing process models to meet the requirements in industry and research.

4   Model Comparison

Our approach encompasses the examination of various perspectives to comprehensively assess the equivalence of process models. Therefore, it is assumed for all perspectives that the two process models being compared are structurally equivalent. Furthermore, it is assumed that external administrative structures (e.g., organizational models) have already been checked for equivalence and adjusted if necessary. For instance, roles that are used equally but are denoted differently in process models to be compared are denoted equivalently. In general, the methods presented for comparing additional perspectives are completely independent of each other. This means that depending on a specific use case, the most interesting perspective(s) can be selected. Particularly, the order of comparing additional perspectives is irrelevant and can be chosen arbitrarily.

4.1 Comparison of the Organizational Perspective

In this subsection, we examine structurally equivalent process models with a focus on the organizational perspective. It is customary in the literature to conduct such investigations independently of specific modeling languages [4,5]. Therefore, we consider conditions formulated in any logic (e.g., propositional logic). Such conditions impose restrictions on the organizational perspective regarding the actors eligible to execute certain activities of a process. For instance: "Activity A must always be performed by Bob" or "The person performing a certain activity must be at least 18 years old." Such conditions can typically be implemented in any common process management system.

We assume that the organizational perspective for declaring the performers of a certain activity A in a process is expressed by a formula $C(A)$ in any logic. Then $C(A)$ can be equivalently decomposed into conjunctive normal form (CNF), such that

$$C(A) = C_1(A) \wedge \cdots \wedge C_n(A),$$

where the terms $C_i(A)$ are pairwise distinct and each term $C_i(A)$ contains only one elementary condition [3]. An "elementary condition" refers to a condition that is only tied to one variable, e.g., "Age > 18" or "Gender $= $'m'". The CNF is calculated because in this standardized form, the elementary conditions are linked by a logical AND ($\wedge$), making the complete formula easy to oversee [3]. Assuming that all assignments are in CNF, the comparison of the organizational perspective is generally carried out according to the following procedure:

1. Determine relevant domains $D_i(A)$ for all subformulas $C_i(A)$ and their cardinalities $d_i(A) := \#D_i(A)$ for all activities A.
2. Calculate the number of different configurations for A: $D(A) := \prod_{i=1}^{n} d_i(A)$
3. Determine the set of domains relevant for $C(A)$ for the processes to be compared.
4. Calculate similarities for each activity.
5. Calculate similarity for processes as the average of activity similarities.

The above-described procedure is explained step by step below. For this purpose, conjunctive normal forms are examined in more detail. Let $C(A) = C_1(A) \wedge \cdots \wedge C_n(A)$ be a formula in conjunctive normal form as described above. Then, let $D_i(A)$ denote the set of different relevant domains for $C_i(A)$ and $d_i(A) := \#D_i(A)$ the associated cardinality (Step 1). This refers to the number of different configurations for $C_i(A)$, each leading to a different result. For example, the formula "Age > 18" has two different relevant configurations: Either the age is

≤ 18 (resulting in evaluating the formula to *false*), or the age is > 18 (resulting in evaluating the formula to *true*). Thus, for the case where the data type of age is defined as a natural number, the two domains are $[0, 1, ..., 18]$ and $[19, 20, ...]$. Applying this process to all elementary formulas $C_i(A)$ yields a total number $D(A)$ of different and relevant configurations (Step 2):

$$D(A) := \prod_{i=1}^{n} d_i(A)$$

Now, for a process model P and an activity A, the number of relevant domains for A can be defined (Step 3):

Definition 2. *Let P be a process model, A an activity of P, and $C(A) := C_1(A) \wedge \cdots \wedge C_n(A)$ a formula regarding A in conjunctive normal form. Then,*

$$D_i(A, P) := \{d \in D_i(A) \mid d \text{ satisfies } C_i(A)\} \subseteq D_i(A)$$

*is called the **set of domains relevant to** $C_i(A)$ **of** P. Furthermore,*

$$D(A, P) := \prod_{i=1}^{n} D_i(A, P)$$

*is called the **set of domains relevant to** $C(A)$ **of** P.*

The above definition is now illustrated by a small example. For this purpose, the following formula $C(A)$ in conjunctive normal form, assigning the organizational perspective to an activity A of a process P, is considered:

$$C(A) = \underbrace{(\text{Age} > 18)}_{C_1(A)} \wedge \underbrace{(\text{Gender} = 'm')}_{C_2(A)}$$

As described above, there are two different domains for both age and gender (i.e., $\#D_i(A) = 2$ for $i = 1, 2$). The two domains for age are $[0, 1, ..., 18]$ and $[19, 20, ...]$, and for gender, $\{m\}$ and $\{f, d\}$. This results in a total number of relevant configurations $D(A) = 2 \cdot 2 = 4$, namely:

- Age $\leq 18 \wedge$ Gender $\in \{m\}$
- Age $> 18 \wedge$ Gender $\in \{m\}$
- Age $\leq 18 \wedge$ Gender $\in \{f, d\}$
- Age $> 18 \wedge$ Gender $\in \{f, d\}$

For both age and gender, exactly one domain is allowed by the above formula, i.e., $d_i(A, P) = 1$ for $i = 1, 2$. Thus, the number of relevant domains for $C(A)$ is $1 \cdot 1 = 1$. The second configuration of the above list represents this single permissible one. Now, the introduced terminologies and definitions are used to compare the organizational perspective of two different process models. Let P_1 and P_2 be process models, A a common activity, and $C(A) = C_1(A) \wedge \cdots \wedge C_n(A)$ and $C'(A) = C'_1(A) \wedge \cdots \wedge C'm(A)$ the formulas describing activity A with regard to the organizational perspective in conjunctive normal form in the respective models. Let $d_i(A)$ be the number of relevant domains for $C(A)$ and $C'(A)$. Then, the similarity $SimOrg_{P_1,P_2}(A)$ regarding the organizational perspective of P_1 and P_2 concerning activity A is defined as follows (Step 4):

$$SimOrg_{P_1,P_2}(A) := \frac{\#\left(D(A,P_1) \cap D(A,P_2)\right)}{\#D(A,P_1) + \#D(A,P_2)}$$

So far, similarity values have only been computed for activities being compared pairwise. Finally, the approach is extended to entire process models (Step 5). Let P_1 and P_2 be two process models with a common (finite) set of activities $\mathcal{A}$. Then, the similarity between P_1 and P_2 regarding the organizational perspective is defined as follows:

$$SimOrg(P_1, P_2) := \frac{\sum_{A \in \mathcal{A}} SimOrg_{P_1,P_2}(A)}{\#\mathcal{A}}$$

To illustrate the calculation, consider an example consisting of two processes P_1 and P_2 with a common activity A. The organizational perspective is given by the following formulas $C(A)$ and $C'(A)$:

$$C(A) = \underbrace{(\text{Age} > 60 \;)}_{C_1(A)} \wedge \underbrace{(\text{Gender} = \;'m')}_{C_2(A)} \;\Big|\; C'(A) = \underbrace{\text{Age} > 59}_{C'_1(A)}$$

(i) Age > 60 ∧ Gender = 'm'   (ii) Age > 60 ∧ Gender ≠ 'm'
(iii) 59 < Age ≤ 60 ∧ Gender = 'm'   (iv) 59 < Age ≤ 60 ∧ Gender ≠ 'm'
(v) Age ≤ 59 ∧ Gender = 'm'   (vi) Age ≤ 59 ∧ Gender ≠ 'm'

Fig. 1. Six distinct domains for organizational perspective

Setting up the domains relevant to both process models yields the six distinct domains $(d_i(A) = 6)$ as illustrated in Fig. 1. Formula $C(A)$ is only satisfied by domain (i). Thus, $\#D(A,P_1) = 1$. Formula $C'(A)$ is satisfied by domains (i), (ii), (iii), and (iv), i.e., $\#D(A,P_2) = 4$. Since domain (i) satisfies both $C(A)$ and $C'(A)$, it follows that $\#\left(D(A,P_1) \cap D(A,P_2)\right) = 1$. Therefore, the similarity with respect to the organizational perspective is:

$$SimOrg_{P_1,P_2}(A) = \frac{1}{5} = 20\%$$

With a similarity of 20%, it can be inferred that the two processes P_1 and P_2 are quite dissimilar in terms of their organizational perspective. Thus, merging or directly aligning the two processes would initially require a considerable effort. However, a domain expert might recognize that the significant difference between the two processes lies in the assignment of gender to activity A. Therefore, it would be worth reconsidering and potentially adjusting the assignment of gender as necessary. For detailed interpretations of the procedures and calculations presented in this section, reference is made to Sect. 5.

4.2 Comparison of the Operational Perspective

In this subsection, we turn our attention to the operational perspective. Similar to the organizational perspective discussed in Sect. 4.1, activities in a process model are also assigned the operational perspective. Therefore, all definitions and methods introduced for the organizational perspective in Sect. 4.1 can equally be applied to the operational perspective. The only difference between the two perspectives lies in the underlying model (organizational vs. operational model) [12]: Instead of organizations (e.g., people, roles, companies), elements of the operational perspective (e.g., tools, programs) are managed. Hence, the structuring of the approach from Sect. 4.1 can be applied in the same way, as the background models are structurally equivalent. Consequently, the entire approach from Sect. 4.1 can be adopted for the operational perspective. The similarity of two process models P_1 and P_2 regarding an activity A with respect to the operational perspective is defined as follows:

$$SimOp_{P_1,P_2}(A) := \frac{\#(D(A, P_1) \cap D(A, P_2))}{\#D(A, P_1) + \#D(A, P_2)}$$

Here, the domains $D(A, P_i)$ for $i = 1, 2$ are defined as in Sect. 4.1. Now, the above definition can be further extended to entire process models P_1 and P_2 over a set of activities $\mathcal{A}$:

$$SimOp(P_1, P_2) := \frac{\sum_{A \in \mathcal{A}} SimOp_{P_1,P_2}(A)}{\#\mathcal{A}}$$

4.3 Comparison of Data and Dataflow Perspective

As a final perspective beyond the perspective constituting the principle structure of a process, i.e. functional and behavioral perspective, the data and data flow perspective is examined. In this section, a comparison method is developed to enable the comparison of process models with respect to this perspective.

The data and data flow perspective describe data objects and documents occurring in the process. These are assigned as inputs and outputs to activities defining the data flow between them. Thus, data objects can be processed or created by executing activities. For the conceived comparison method, initially, only individual activities and their assigned data objects are considered. Let P_1 and P_2 be process models, A a common activity of P_1 and P_2, and D the set of data objects used in P_1 and P_2. Furthermore, let $I_{P_i}(A) \subseteq D$ be the set of inputs of A in P_i for $i = 1, 2$. Then, the similarity $SimInput_{P_1,P_2}(A)$ of P_1 and P_2 regarding A with respect to the inputs is defined as follows:

$$SimInput_{P_1,P_2}(A) := \frac{\#(I_{P_1}(A) \cap I_{P_2}(A))}{\#I_{P_1}(A) + \#I_{P_2}(A) - \#(I_{P_1}(A) \cap I_{P_2}(A))} \in [0, 1]$$

This means that the similarity is defined based on the ratio of common inputs to all inputs. Similarly, the similarity of the outputs is defined as:

$$SimOutput_{P_1,P_2}(A) := \frac{\#(O_{P_1}(A) \cap O_{P_2}(A))}{\#O_{P_1}(A) + \#O_{P_2}(A) - \#(O_{P_1}(A) \cap O_{P_2}(A))} \in [0, 1]$$

Now, the similarity of P_1 and P_2 regarding A with respect to the data and data flow perspective can be defined by averaging the similarities for inputs and outputs:

$$SimData_{P_1,P_2}(A) := \frac{SimInput_{P_1,P_2}(A) + SimOutput_{P_1,P_2}(A)}{2} \in [0,1]$$

Finally, the similarity regarding the data and data flow perspective is extended to complete process models P_1 and P_2 over a set of activities $\mathcal{A}$:

$$SimData(P_1, P_2) := \frac{\sum_{A \in \mathcal{A}} SimData_{P_1,P_2}(A)}{\#\mathcal{A}}$$

To illustrate the calculation of similarity, let's consider an example of two process models P_1 and P_2 with a common activity. Suppose A has input $I_{P_1}(A) = \{D_1, D_2, D_3\}$ and output $O_{P_1}(A) = \{D_1, D_3\}$ in P_1. Additionally, A has input $I_{P_2}(A) = \{D_1, D_3\}$ and output $O_{P_2}(A) = \{D_1, D_2\}$ in P_2. Therefore, the similarity regarding the data and data flow perspective is:

$$SimData_{P_1,P_2}(A) := \frac{SimInput_{P_1,P_2}(A) + SimOutput_{P_1,P_2}(A)}{2}$$

$$= \frac{\overbrace{\frac{2}{3+2-2}}^{SimInput_{P_1,P_2}(A)} + \overbrace{\frac{1}{2+2-1}}^{SimOutput_{P_1,P_2}(A)}}{2} = \frac{\frac{2}{3} + \frac{1}{3}}{2} = \frac{1}{2} = 50\%$$

A similarity of 50% suggests that the two processes, P_1 and P_2, are quite dissimilar in terms of their data and data flow perspective. This can already be deduced from their respective outputs: significant adjustments would be necessary to align the two processes as they differ completely in an output object. This results in an overall similarity of only 33.3% for outputs. For a interpretation of the procedures and calculations presented, we refer to Sect. 5.

5   Methodology and Practical Application

5.1   Methodology

The approaches developed for comparing the organizational, operational, and data and data flow perspectives (Sects. 4.1–4.3) share a commonality: all approaches yield a quantitative value between 0 and 1. These values merely serve as indicators for assessing the similarity of the process models involved. A high value (e.g., 0.95) suggests a substantial similarity, whereas a low value (e.g., 0.1) indicates that the process models may differ significantly. We have established a methodological approach predicated on the analysis of the organizational structures underlying the processes as follows:

1. **Initial Metric Computation**: Begin by calculating various metrics to evaluate and compare the two processes. This step serves to quantify the similarities and differences between the organizational structures of the two models.
   If the similarity metrics indicate that the differences are minor, the process
   may be concluded at this point. However, if there are still small differences
   but they are deemed acceptable, proceed to manually make adjustments to
   better align the models. This manual adjustment is mandatory and aims to
   refine the comparison by addressing and minimizing these discrepancies.
2. **Analysis of Different Organizational Assignments**:
   (a) **Adjustment of Organizational Structures**: In cases when the orga-
       nizational assignments within the process models to be compared differ,
       undertake a targeted adjustment of the corresponding segments of the two
       organizational structures. This step is executed in a cooperative manner,
       ensuring that any changes are made with consensus and aim to align the
       organizational frameworks more closely.
   (b) **Restart the Process**: Following the cooperative adjustments, the
       method mandates a restart of the entire comparison process. This is not
       merely a repetition of the initial steps but an informed re-evaluation,
       taking into account the adjustments made to ensure a more accurate and
       comprehensive comparison.

This iterative process of adjustment and re-evaluation allows for a nuanced and
detailed comparison of the business process models, focusing on their organizational aspects. It ensures that the comparison accounts for both broad metrics
and specific organizational assignments, leading to a thorough understanding of
how the models relate and differ from an organizational perspective. Although,
in this sub-section we are merely presenting an example related to the organizational perspective, the above introduced method can similarly be applied to the
operational and data perspective.

5.2 Practical Example

Let's consider a simple business process model P_1 for processing customer orders
within *company 1*. This model outlines the flow from receiving an order to delivering the product to the customer, with each step assigned to a specific organizational unit.

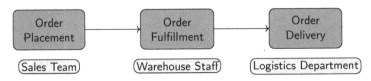

For another *company 2* with a more granular approach to its organizational
structure, the process model P_2 of processing customer orders involves the same
activities - this is a prerequisite for the comparison of the organizational perspective - but with responsibilities assigned to more specific sub-units within the

originally mentioned departments. The important information here is that the *Online Sales Team* is a sub-unit of the *Sales Department*, the *Order Processing Unit* is a specialized team within the *Warehouse Staff*, and the *Domestic Shipping Team* is a specific division within the *Logistics Department*.

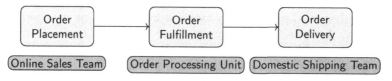

Based on the concepts of Sect. 4.1 we can calculate the model similarity as follows: Firstly, we construct the two CNFs for the activity *Order Placement*:

$$C_1(\textit{Order Placement}) = (\text{organisation} = \text{Sales Team}),$$

$$C_2(\textit{Order Placement}) = (\text{organisation} = \text{Online Sales Team}).$$

The CNFs yield the following four relevant domains (S denotes the set of all organizational elements): (i) Sales Team, (ii) Online Sales Team, (iii) Sales Team \ Online Sales Team, (iv) S\ Sales Team. $C_1(\textit{Order Placement})$ is fulfilled by domains (i), (ii) and (iii), whereas $C_2(\textit{Order Placement})$ is only fulfilled by domain (ii). Hence, we get a similarity for activity *Order Placement* of

$$SimOrg_{P_1,P_2}(\textit{Order Placement}) = \frac{1}{3+1} = \frac{1}{4} = 25\%.$$

A similar procedure leads to the same results for the other two activities, i.e. $SimOrg_{P_1,P_2}(\textit{Order Fulfillment}) = SimOrg_{P_1,P_2}(\textit{Order Delivery}) = 25\%$. Overall, we thus obtain an organizational similarity of

$$SimOrg(P_1, P_2) = \frac{25\% + 25\% + 25\%}{3} = 25\%.$$

The calculation of the organizational similarity between the two companies results in a match of 25%. This suggests that despite similar activities in both process models, significant differences exist for organizational assignments. This is due to the refinements of organizational structures in the second process, e.g. from *Sales Team* to *Online Sales Team*. "Harmonizing" the organizational structure of the second organization, such that also the *Sales Team* is now eligible to execute the first process step results in an organizational similarity of 50%. In such a way dissimilarities must be investigated and cleared if required.

6   Conclusion and Future Work

In this paper, we introduced comparison methods for the organizational, operational, and data and data flow perspectives. These methodologies serve as valuable tools for assessing processes within various contexts. However, it's imperative to emphasize that the values derived from these methods must always be interpreted within their respective contexts. Domain experts play a crucial role in providing nuanced insights that enrich the interpretation of these metrics. Looking ahead, there are promising avenues for future research. One potential direction is the application of our approach to specific process modeling languages such as BPMN or Declare. By tailoring our methods to these languages, we can refine our analyses and provide more targeted insights into process performance and efficiency. Additionally, conducting a user study could provide invaluable feedback on the usability and effectiveness of our comparison methods. Understanding how practitioners interact with and perceive these tools in real-world scenarios can guide further enhancements and refinements. Ultimately, integrating user perspectives into our research agenda will ensure that our methodologies remain relevant and impactful in practical settings.

References

1. Ackermann, L., Schönig, S., Jablonski, S.: Towards simulation- and mining-based translation of process models. In: Pergl, R., Molhanec, M., Babkin, E., Fosso Wamba, S. (eds.) EOMAS 2016. LNBIP, vol. 272, pp. 3–21. Springer, Cham (2016). https://doi.org/10.1007/978-3-319-49454-8_1
2. Aiolli, F., Burattin, A., Sperduti, A.: A business process metric based on the alpha algorithm relations. In: Daniel, F., Barkaoui, K., Dustdar, S. (eds.) BPM 2011. LNBIP, vol. 99, pp. 141–146. Springer, Heidelberg (2012). https://doi.org/10.1007/978-3-642-28108-2_13
3. Andrews, P.B.: An Introduction to Mathematical Logic and Type Theory: To Truth Through Proof, Springer eBook Collection Mathematics and Statistics, vol. 27, Second edition edn. Springer, Dordrecht (2002). https://doi.org/10.1007/978-94-015-9934-4
4. Baumann, M.H., Baumann, M., Schönig, S., Jablonski, S.: Towards multiperspective process model similarity matching. In: Barjis, J., Pergl, R. (eds.) EOMAS 2014. LNBIP, vol. 191, pp. 21–37. Springer, Heidelberg (2014). https://doi.org/10.1007/978-3-662-44860-1_2
5. Baumann, M., Baumann, M.H., Schönig, S., Jablonski, S.: Resource-aware process model similarity matching. In: Toumani, F., et al. (eds.) ICSOC 2014. LNCS, vol. 8954, pp. 96–107. Springer, Cham (2015). https://doi.org/10.1007/978-3-319-22885-3_9
6. Corea, C., Nagel, S., Mendling, J., Delfmann, P.: Interactive and minimal repair of declarative process models. In: Polyvyanyy, A., Wynn, M.T., Van Looy, A., Reichert, M. (eds.) BPM 2021. LNBIP, vol. 427, pp. 3–19. Springer, Cham (2021). https://doi.org/10.1007/978-3-030-85440-9_1
7. Di Ciccio, C., Maggi, F.M., Montali, M., Mendling, J.: Resolving inconsistencies and redundancies in declarative process models. Inf. Syst. 64 (2017)
8. Dijkman, R., Dumas, M., van Dongen, B., Käärik, R., Mendling, J.: Similarity of business process models: metrics and evaluation. Inf. Syst. 36(2) (2011)
9. Dumas, M., La Rosa, M., Mendling, J., Reijers, H.: Fundamentals of Business Process Management. Springer, Berlin, Heidelberg (2013). https://doi.org/10.1007/978-3-662-56509-4
10. Haisjackl, C., et al.: Understanding declare models: strategies, pitfalls, empirical results. Softw. Syst. Model. 15(2) (2016)

11. Hidders, J., Dumas, M., Aalst, W., Ter, A., Verelst, J.: When are two workflows the same? CATS, CRPIT **41** (2005)
12. Jablonski, S., Bussler, C.: Workflow Management: Modeling Concepts, Architecture and Implementation. ITP Internat. Thomson Computer Press, London (1996)
13. Käppel, M., Schützenmeier, N., Schönig, S., Ackermann, L., Jablonski, S.: Logic based look-ahead for the execution of multi-perspective declarative processes. In: Reinhartz-Berger, I., Zdravkovic, J., Gulden, J., Schmidt, R. (eds.) BPMDS/EMMSAD -2019. LNBIP, vol. 352, pp. 53–68. Springer, Cham (2019). https://doi.org/10.1007/978-3-030-20618-5_4
14. Klinkmüller, C., Weber, I., Mendling, J., Leopold, H., Ludwig, A.: Increasing recall of process model matching by improved activity label matching. In: Daniel, F., Wang, J., Weber, B. (eds.) BPM 2013. LNCS, vol. 8094, pp. 211–218. Springer, Heidelberg (2013). https://doi.org/10.1007/978-3-642-40176-3_17
15. La Rosa, M., Dumas, M., Ekanayake, C.C., García-Bañuelos, L., Recker, J., ter Hofstede, A.H.: Detecting approximate clones in business process model repositories. Inf. Syst. **49** (2015)
16. Li, C., Reichert, M., Wombacher, A.: On measuring process model similarity based on high-level change operations. In: Li, Q., Spaccapietra, S., Yu, E., Olivé, A. (eds.) ER 2008. LNCS, vol. 5231, pp. 248–264. Springer, Heidelberg (2008). https://doi.org/10.1007/978-3-540-87877-3_19
17. Pesic, M., Schonenberg, H., van der Aalst, W.M.: Declare: full support for loosely-structured processes. In: Enterprise Distributed Object Computing Conference (EDOC) (2007)
18. Pichler, P., Weber, B., Zugal, S., Pinggera, J., Mendling, J., Reijers, H.A.: Imperative versus declarative process modeling languages: an empirical investigation. In: Daniel, F., Barkaoui, K., Dustdar, S. (eds.) BPM 2011. LNBIP, vol. 99, pp. 383–394. Springer, Heidelberg (2012). https://doi.org/10.1007/978-3-642-28108-2_37
19. Polyvyanyy, A., Solti, A., Weidlich, M., Di Ciccio, C., Mendling, J.: Monotone precision and recall measures for comparing executions and specifications of dynamic systems. ACM Trans. Softw. Eng. Methodol. **29**(3) (2020)
20. Sànchez-Ferreres, J., van der Aa, H., Carmona, J., Padró, L.: Aligning textual and model-based process descriptions. Data Knowl. Eng. **118** (2018)
21. Schoknecht, A., Thaler, T., Fettke, P., Oberweis, A., Laue, R.: Similarity of business process models—a state-of-the-art analysis. ACM Comput. Surv. **50**(4) (2018)
22. Schönig, S., Ackermann, L., Jablonski, S.: Towards an implementation of data and resource patterns in constraint-based process models. In: MODELSWARD 2018. SCITEPRESS - Science and Technology Publications Lda (2018)
23. Schützenmeier, N., Jablonski, S., Käppel, M., Ackermann, L.: Comparing the expressiveness of imperative and declarative process models. In: Babkin, E., Barjis, J., Malyzhenkov, P., Merunka, V., Molhanec, M. (eds.) Model-Driven Organizational and Business Agility. MOBA 2023. LNBIP, vol. 488, PP. 16–31. Springer, Cham (2023). https://doi.org/10.1007/978-3-031-45010-5_2
24. Schützenmeier, N., Käppel, M., Ackermann, L., Jablonski, S., Petter, S.: Automaton-based comparison of declare process models. Softw. Syst. Model. (2022)
25. Schützenmeier, N., Käppel, M., Petter, S., Jablonski, S.: Upper-bounded model checking for declarative process models. In: Serral, E., Stirna, J., Ralyté, J., Grabis, J. (eds.) PoEM 2021. LNBIP, vol. 432, pp. 195–211. Springer, Cham (2021). https://doi.org/10.1007/978-3-030-91279-6_14
26. Tealeb, A., Awad, A., Galal-Edeen, G.: Context-based variant generation of business process models. In: Bider, I., et al. (eds.) BPMDS/EMMSAD -2014. LNBIP,

vol. 175, pp. 363–377. Springer, Heidelberg (2014). https://doi.org/10.1007/978-3-662-43745-2_25

27. van der Aalst, W.M.P., de Medeiros, A.K.A., Weijters, A.J.M.M.: Process equivalence: comparing two process models based on observed behavior. In: Dustdar, S., Fiadeiro, J.L., Sheth, A.P. (eds.) BPM 2006. LNCS, vol. 4102, pp. 129–144. Springer, Heidelberg (2006). https://doi.org/10.1007/11841760_10

28. Wohed, P., van der Aalst, W.M.P., Dumas, M., ter Hofstede, A.H.M., Russell, N.: On the suitability of BPMN for business process modelling. In: Dustdar, S., Fiadeiro, J.L., Sheth, A.P. (eds.) BPM 2006. LNCS, vol. 4102, pp. 161–176. Springer, Heidelberg (2006). https://doi.org/10.1007/11841760_12

A Meta-Design Method for Modeling Customer Value

William Sniekers[1] and Ben Roelens[1,2(✉)] (iD)

[1] Open Universiteit, Valkenburgerweg 177, 6419 Heerlen, AT, The Netherlands
william.sniekers@live.nl, ben.roelens@ou.nl
[2] Ghent University, Tweekerkenstraat 2, 9000 Ghent, Belgium

Abstract. Customer value, which is the utility of goods and services assessed from the perspective of a customer, is at the core of every healthy organization. As Enterprise Modeling focuses on the systematic modeling and analysis of structures and activities within an organization, it supports the interaction between customer and supplier as a communication and analysis tool of value co-creation. However, existing methods for creating these models require support from scarce model experts to realize concrete model instantiations. This research examines how the modeling of customer value through enterprise models can be made practically applicable in a business context. In this respect, a meta-design modeling method is proposed, which is developed according to a first cycle of the build-and-evaluate loop of the Design Science Research Methodology. The results show that the meta-design modeling method is suitable to model customer value in a business context. However, further improvements can make this method better practically applicable for both domain experts and end-users. In this respect, interesting opportunities for future research are the use of a questionnaire to fill in the front-end models and the integration of the customer value model with, e.g., improvement projects or service management practices.

Keywords: Customer Value · Enterprise Modeling · Meta-Design Method

1 Introduction

Customer value is a central concern to the healthy functioning of any organization [16]. In an era where the agility of organizations is challenged, supporting the creation of customer value is essential to domain experts in areas such as marketing, sales, and service management. Customer value is defined as the utility of goods and services assessed from the perspective of a customer [13]. Over the past decade, the focus on customer value in service organizations has shifted towards the paradigm of value-in-use, which is based on the outcome and process of the service provider's domain, the customer's domain and the interaction between both [4]. More specifically, there are activities in the customer domain, which occur outside the realm of supplier interaction and yet contribute to customer value resulting from the delivered services [15].

J. P. A. Almeida et al. (Eds.): CAiSE 2024 Workshops, LNBIP 521, pp. 307–318, 2024.
https://doi.org/10.1007/978-3-031-61003-5_26

An enterprise model of customer value can support the interaction between customer and supplier as a communication and analysis tool. By modeling customer value, a necessary dialogue emerges between them, which allows to better co-create value [4]. Enterprise Modeling (EM) focuses on *the systematic analysis and modeling of processes, organization and product structures, Information Technology (IT) systems and any other perspective relevant for the modeling purpose* [14, p.70]. However, existing EM methods for customer value require scarce knowledge of modeling experts and require a collaboration between modeling and domain experts to develop model instantiations [14]. Sandkuhl et al. [14] propose that a solution to this usability problem could be found in lightweight EM methods, where the focus is on usability and impact. Their resulting research agenda includes the following design requirements that such a lightweight method should meet: modeling should be (i) part of daily work, requiring (ii) little to no additional training, and (iii) allowing, if necessary, relaxation of the usual requirements of completeness and coherence [14]. Given the importance of modeling customer value and the limited knowledge in the literature on how to make enterprise models widely applicable in practice, this research aims to answer the following research question: *How can the modeling of customer value through enterprise models be made practically applicable in a business context?*

This paper proposes a meta-design modeling method to tackle this problem. Fischer et al. [2, p.65] characterize meta-design in the field of Human-Computer Interaction as *design for design after design*. In other words, one expert (i.e., the modeling expert in customer value) designs a model that leaves freedom for another expert (i.e., the domain expert who is responsible for managing customer value in an organization) to finalize the design of the model by customizing it to the specific needs of the end-users (i.e., stakeholders with an interest in customer value). This results in a tool through which end-users can provide input in an independent manner, combined with a method that can generate model instantiations based on this input. The modeling method is designed according to the Design Science Research Methodology (DSRM) [7], of which a first cycle of building the method and evaluating it by a real-life case study is presented.

The paper is structured as follows. Section 2 explains how we applied DSRM for the design of the modeling method, which is substantiated in Sect. 3. Afterwards, the results of the case study demonstration (Sect. 4) and the evaluation of the method and the models (Sect. 5) are presented. Finally, Sect. 6 reviews related work and Sect. 7 concludes this work and discusses future research options.

2   Methodology

DSRM is used as the research methodology in this study as it addresses the need to build an IT artifact (i.e., the meta-design modeling method) and evaluate it within its application context by solving the identified organizational problem(s) [7]. In this respect, existing literature is used as the knowledge base to build the initial meta-design modeling method. Furthermore, the demonstration (i.e., application) and subsequent evaluation of the modeling method are performed by a single exploratory case study, which includes an in-depth inquiry of the application of the modeling method within a real-life context [17]. As meta-design is a new modeling approach to the EM field, the exploratory character of the case study is suited to investigate whether the following propositions persist in a real-life application context:

S1 The meta-design modeling method is suitable for domain experts to independently create customer value models.
S2 The customer value models are suitable for end-users to analyze customer value and engage in a mutual dialogue.

The formative nature of the evaluation primarily requires an understanding of the outcome of the demonstration and how the artifacts can be improved. The evaluation of the method's suitability (S1) is carried out based on quantitative questionnaire data collected using the Method Evaluation Model [10], which differentiates between three dimensions: (i) perceived ease of use, (ii) perceived usefulness, and (iii) intention to use. These data are supplemented with a qualitative semi-structured interview, which delves deeper into these three dimensions. The evaluation of the suitability of the customer value models (S2) is based on quantitative data collected using a quality model for conceptual models [8]. This measurement instrument assesses the quality of model instantiations based on user perceptions. These instantiations are the type of models relevant to end-users, and their perception is essential to assess whether the quality of the models is sufficient. The instrument uses four constructs: (i) perceived ease of understanding, (ii) perceived semantic quality, (iii) perceived usefulness, and (iv) user satisfaction. This evaluation is supplemented with a focus group interview, during which these four dimensions are further explored.

3   Meta-Design Modeling Method

Section 3.1 discusses the theoretical knowledge base of the meta-design modeling method, while we explain its design in Sect. 3.2.

3.1   Theoretical Knowledge Base

The ArchiMate Value Pattern Language [13] is a suitable EM language to analyze customer value. To address the semantic ambiguity that exists about the concept of 'value', Sales et al. [13] introduce seven modeling patterns that translate specific elements and relationships from the Common Ontology of Value and Risk to ArchiMate. Given its conformance to the principles of the Unified Foundation Ontology and the ArchiMate meta-model, this language is primarily oriented to modeling experts. Besides, Heinonen and Strandvik [6] propose Customer-Dominant Logic that depicts how a client and a service provider interact from the perspective of the customer. This marketing perspective argues that customer value is based on the outcome and process of the service provider's domain, the customer's domain and the interaction between both [6]. As the model of Heinonen and Strandvik represents a supplier's logic that prioritizes customer value, it aligns with the domains experts' perspective of the service provider. More information about these models can be found in the referenced papers.

3.2 Design

Domain experts can capture their domain and customer knowledge using the model of Heinonen and Strandvik [6]. However, translating this knowledge into a complete and coherent ArchiMate model would be too complex for them. To solve this issue, we propose a meta-design approach[1] that consists of three levels: (i) meta-design, (ii) design and (iii) use.

1. At the meta-design level, a generic front-end model of customer value is provided by the modeling experts to the domain experts. Furthermore, a procedure is developed to translate such a front-end model into a complete and coherent ArchiMate back-end model by a modeling expert. The front-end model facilitates communication between domain experts and end-users, while the back-end model ensures integration with existing enterprise models. To realize this, an ArchiMate model based on the Value Pattern Language [13] was combined with the content of the model presented in Heinonen and Strandvik [6] to populate the generic Value Pattern Language with concepts relevant to modeling customer value. Confirming to the meta-design approach, the modeling experts then worked towards a model that matches the requirements and competencies of domain experts. These domain experts should be able to independently add their domain knowledge to the model. Therefore, the ArchiMate back-end model was translated to a canvas-based front-end model in Excel. The main advantage of this canvas-based model is that it allows to hide the complexity of the underlying ArchiMate models for domain experts and end-users. Furthermore, a PowerPoint presentation was developed for domain experts serving as a guide to the relevant concepts, the steps of the method, and the various visual components of the front-end model. In this generic front-end model, the design freedom for domain experts is limited to determining the essential concepts of customer value [13]: (i) functional and quality goals, including their weight factors, (ii) events that influence these goals and thus create value to a greater or lesser extent, (iii) experiences that consist of multiple events forming a logical grouping, along with their weight factors, and (iv) three roles, namely: the subject that experiences the value, the object from which the value is experienced, and the assessor that determines the value.
2. At the design level, it is the task of the domain expert to develop a domain-specific version (i.e., for a particular product or service) of the front-end model

---

[1] Via https://doi.org/10.13140/RG.2.2.29818.67528/1 all supporting material can be consulted.

supported by the guiding PowerPoint presentation. For each experience, a canvas (see Fig. 1) is built by adding functional and quality goals (see Fig. 2) and events (see Fig. 3) to it.

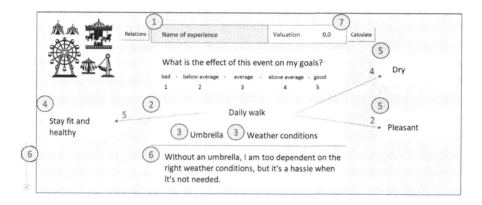

Fig. 1. Front-end canvas per experience

The various elements of the canvas are schematically depicted in Fig. 1: (1) name of the experience, (2) an event element, (3) in this case with two value enablers, (4) a functional goal, (5) two quality goals, and (6) the possibility to add a more elaborate explanation. Upon pressing the "Calculate" button in (7), the total weighted valuation of the experience is displayed. The "Relations" button provides a visual representation of the relationships between events and goals. In this example, the analysis could reveal that a good weather forecast, as a value enabler, may increase the experienced value.

Figure 1 displays two available types of goals: functional goals that are placed in box (4), and quality goals that are placed in box (5) on the canvas. Figure 2 shows that goal elements further consist of the following components: the respective goal is selected in (8), after which a short name for this goal appears in (9), and the relative weight of the goal is displayed in (10). These properties (name, short name, and relative weight) of goals are populated in a separate canvas. The cells in (11) then calculate the average value of all events that have an impact on the respective goal.

Events, placed in box (2) on the canvas of Fig. 1, are further specified in the canvas of Fig. 3. The name of the event is entered in (12). In (13), the effect of this event on the functional goals is evaluated, and in (14), the effect on the quality goals is assessed. These goals are linked to the goal elements in Fig. 2 through their short names. For box (15), fixed patterns are available that are able to model the most common situations.

Finally, it is also the task of the domain expert to prepare the modeling session to complete the front-end model in collaboration with the end-users.

3. At the use level, the end-users give input to the domain expert to create a customer-specific front-end model and use it to understand and

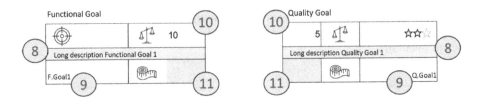

Fig. 2. Front-end canvas per quality or functional goal

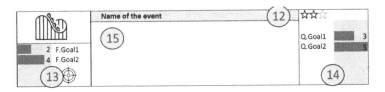

Fig. 3. Front-end canvas per event

communicate about the creation of customer value. Suitable end-users are product managers, solution consultants, account managers, service managers, and especially the customers themselves. The work sessions with end-users to complete the front-end models are supported by a PowerPoint presentation that describes the working method and essential concepts.[2] These sessions should be hands-on and collaborative to efficiently complete the customer-specific front-end model. Finally, the modeling expert ensures the translation between the customer-specific front-end model to ArchiMate back-end models using the procedure developed at the meta-design level. Figure 4 provides an example of one of these mapping steps, visually illustrating how to build an ArchiMate value pattern starting from a front-end model in Excel.

4   Case Study Demonstration

In Sect. 4.1, the case organization is presented, after which we discuss the demonstration of the meta-design modeling method in Sect. 4.2.

4.1   Organizational Context

The case study included analyzing the creation of customer value within the context of outsourcing IT services. The IT service provider is a Dutch organization of about 350 employees. The customer that was involved was AgroCooperation (i.e., a fictitious name), which is a Dutch agricultural cooperative. This customer receives a service that is named the Modern Workplace, which includes

---

[2] The presentation in the supporting material is based on a specific customer case, where theoretical concepts are kept to a minimum. Nevertheless, a significant portion of this presentation is applicable to other contexts.

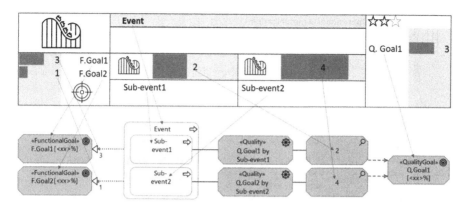

Fig. 4. Example mapping between front-end model and an ArchiMate value pattern

office automation services. AgroCooperation started using this service in 2021 with an approximate daily user count of 100. The modeling method is demonstrated and evaluated by a team consisting of two modeling experts (i.e., the authors), one domain expert (i.e., product manager of the Modern Workplace), and four end-users active in both organizations. The two end-users of AgroCooperation were a business controller and an IT coordinator, while an account manager and a service manager were involved from the side of the IT service provider.

4.2 Meta-Design Modeling Method

In three sessions, the domain expert applied the meta-design modeling method by creating a customer-specific front-end model of the Modern Workplace with support of the modeling experts. During the first session, the method was explained and the Modern Workplace was selected as the relevant value object (i.e., the service from which value is experienced). During the two remaining sessions, the domain expert showed a growing understanding of the method resulting in a domain-specific front-end model. The growing ability to apply the available patterns was demonstrated by an increased expressiveness in the customer value model of the Modern Workplace. Figure 5 shows an example of this evolution of a value event from a very basic pattern to a pattern with several value enablers. The domain expert finally used this domain-specific front-end model to prepare a group session with the end-users to develop a customer-specific front-end model.

5 Evaluation

Section 5.1 substantiates the evaluation of the method by the domain expert, while the end-user evaluation of the customer value models is presented in Sect. 5.2.

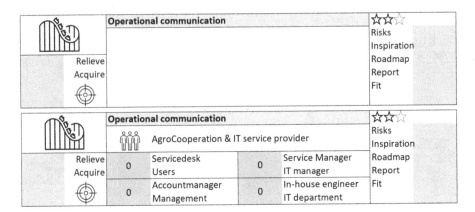

Fig. 5. Refinement of a value event by the domain expert (top: basic model, bottom: resulting model)

5.1 Meta-Design Modeling Method

Quantitative Data. The constructs of the Method Evaluation Model were scored by the domain expert on a 7-point Likert scale ranging from 'strongly disagree' to 'strongly agree'. The scores show that this expert agrees with the perceived ease of use (i.e., a score of 6.0) and usefulness (i.e., a score of 6.0) of the modeling method, while there is a more than slight agreement with the intention to use this method in practice (i.e., a score of 5.5).

Qualitative Data. The insights from the semi-structured interview with the domain expert can be summarized as follows.

Perceived Ease of Use. The modeling method can be easily adopted when accompanied by proper guidance to its functioning through training by the modeling experts. Additionally, it requires significant preparation time, such as selecting appropriate end-users and formulating concrete goals or events as a starting point for the analysis. Understanding the structure of the method can be challenging. Therefore, the domain expert proposes to structure the development process of the customer-specific front-end model by creating a questionnaire.

Perceived Usefulness. The strength of modeling customer value lies in the ability to recognize factors that are beyond the scope of the IT service provider. The domain expert does not expect to be capable of independently establishing a customer value model without the meta-design method, as the direct use of ArchiMate for the analysis would be too complex. Before implementing the method, the Excel implementation must be made more robust to prevent user mistakes. The outcome in ArchiMate is visually stronger than the front-end model, but it is advantageous that a moderately complex model can be displayed on a single page in Excel as opposed to multiple views in ArchiMate.

Intention to Use. The domain expert sees opportunities to use the method as part of service management or business consultancy, especially after further optimizations. However, the method only becomes useful if there is proper follow-up. This means that after gaining insights, actions should be taken to act on the results. Currently, the method does not yet provide these follow-up actions.

5.2 Customer Value Models

Quantitative Data. Table 1 shows the scores for the constructs of the quality model for conceptual models [8] on a 7-point Likert scale ranging from 'strongly disagree' to 'strongly agree'. The figures show that the customer-specific front-end models score better than the back-end ArchiMate models. For the back-end models, the general sentiment is more neutral to their quality, while end-users tend to slightly agree with the quality of the front-end models.

Table 1. Evaluation of the quality of the model instantiations

Quality construct	Back-end model	Front-end model
Perceived ease of understanding	3.4	4.4
Perceived semantic quality	4.4	5.0
Perceived usefulness	4.8	5.2
User satisfaction	3.8	4.6

Qualitative Data. The focus group interview with the four end-users yielded the following insights to understand the given scores.

Perceived Ease of Understanding. There is a considerable variation in the perceived ease of understanding among the respondents. The service manager, who only participated during the validation of the front-end model, struggles to comprehend the subject matter. On the other hand, the business controller finds the model understandable. The two end-users of AgroCooperation (i.e., the business controller and IT coordinator) express that the provided assistance to understand and complete the front-end model was essential and that their mutual interaction during the modeling process proved beneficial.

Perceived Semantic Quality. Customer value is a relevant subject for the end-users. In their current practice, it takes time for the IT service provider to realize that the customer faces a particular challenge. In this respect, the modeling method reveals blind spots that are overlooked by the currently used approach in the case organization, which only focuses on customer satisfaction. The business controller feels that the model aligns well with the Modern Workplace, but finds it challenging to envision how it would apply to other services.

Perceived Usefulness. Discussing customer value is particularly beneficial as it is facilitated by the creation of the front-end model. Nevertheless, the service manager thinks the structure of the model needs to become more lightweight as it is quite different from the usual dialogue with the IT coordinator.

User Satisfaction. The business controller finds the front-end model more user-friendly than the back-end model, given that the latter was only briefly seen during the demonstration. The service manager suggests including a concise explanation of the thought process to support the numerical data in the models.

6   Related Work

Model-driven development [12] aims at separating the concerns of modeling experts (i.e., building generic modeling artifacts) and domain experts (i.e., describing key aspects of particular domains). Although this idea partly overlaps with the proposed meta-design modeling method, model-driven development makes use of models that can automate the creation of concrete solution artifacts. As this focus is fundamentally different from the use of enterprise models as a communication and analysis tool, we developed a novel modeling method.

Several EM techniques are suited to model customer value. At the meta-design level of the modeling method, these techniques could be relevant as alternative back-end model to ensure integration with other enterprise models. The Value Delivery Modeling Language is a modeling language that has *a particular focus on the creation and exchange of value inside an organization* [11, p.1]. This language is developed as a standard that integrates other value modeling techniques, such as Value Network Analysis [1], the Resource-Event-Agent ontology [9], e^3-value [3], capability maps [5], etc. As can be seen in Table 2, these approaches capture a particular value aspect inside organizations. In contrast, the ArchiMate Value Pattern Language was chosen for the proposed modeling method as it implements the Common Ontology of Value and Risk, which is a well-founded reference ontology that is relevant for customer value as it follows the paradigm of value-in-use [13]. Besides, it conforms to ArchiMate as a modeling standard, which supports the integration with EM efforts in practice [13].

Table 2. EM approaches oriented towards customer value

EM approach	Value aspects
Value Network Analysis	Value conversion of tangible and intangible assets in networks [1]
Resource-Event-Agent ontology	Generalized framework for accounting systems in a shared data environment [9]
e^3-value	Development of innovative e-commerce business models [3]
capability maps	Determining the key capabilities inside organizations [5]

7   Discussion and Conclusion

With regard to the validity of evaluation data, it should be noted that several respondents are evaluating their own work when assessing the modeling method or models. As this could lead to inflated scores, the absolute figures from the evaluation instruments should be interpreted cautiously. This effect could be alleviated by involving respondents in the evaluation, who were not part of the application of the modeling method. Furthermore, since the modeling method is applied in a single exploratory case study, it could be argued that the results are limited in generalizability outside the particular application context. However, this issue can be solved by replicating the current case study design [17].

The empirical part of this research is designed as an exploratory case study, in which two propositions were put forward (see Sect. 2). The case study showed that both the domain experts and the end-users require support and time to familiarize themselves with respectively the modeling method and the resulting customer value models. The domain expert seems capable to independently design domain-specific front-end models using the meta-design modeling method and also sees potential for applying the method in practice. However, the end-users are more skeptical in this regard. While they acknowledge the value of analyzing and communicating about customer value, they question whether an enterprise model adds significant value to this purpose. All respondents agree that the modeling method and resulting models should be further simplified. It has been shown that meta-design can be applied to existing EM approaches for customer value. The expectation was that using the ArchiMate Value Pattern Language in the back-end would enable an easy integration with existing enterprise models. However, some quality issues were observed in the created back-end models, which currently results in a limited possibility to integrate them.

In summary, the evaluation has shown how the meta-design modeling method supports the application of customer value modeling in a business context. However, further improvement steps still need to be taken before this is considered practically applicable by both domain experts and end-users. In this respect, interesting opportunities for future research arise. First, several respondents in this study reported that when creating the front-end models, they would like to be guided by a structured way of questioning. They envision a questionnaire derived from the main elements of a domain-specific front-end model. This approach could enable the distribution of the questionnaire to a larger group of end-users, thereby broadening support for the model. An important aspect of this future research effort would be to empirically test the practical applicability of such a structured questionnaire. Furthermore, end-users want to experience a more direct benefit from their modeling efforts. To enable this, it should be investigated how the development of a customer value model can be incorporated into, e.g., improvement projects or service management practices. An appropriate research design could involve using the meta-design modeling method as part of a case study within one of these application contexts. This further case study research could also help to investigate the generalizability of the current findings.

References

1. Allee, V.: Value network analysis and value conversion of tangible and intangible assets. J. Intellect. Cap. **9**(1), 5–24 (2008). https://doi.org/10.1108/14691930810845777
2. Fischer, G., Fogli, D., Piccinno, A.: Revisiting and broadening the meta-design framework for end-user development. In: Paternò, F., Wulf, V. (eds.) New Perspectives in End-User Development, pp. 61–97. Springer, Cham (2017). https://doi.org/10.1007/978-3-319-60291-2_4
3. Gordijn, J., Akkermans, J.: Value-based requirements engineering: exploring innovative e-commerce ideas. Requir. Eng. **8**(2), 114–134 (2003). https://doi.org/10.1007/s00766-003-0169-x
4. Grönroos, C., Voima, P.: Critical service logic: making sense of value creation and co-creation. J. Acad. Mark. Sci. **41**, 133–150 (2013). https://doi.org/10.1007/s11747-012-0308-3
5. Hafeez, K., Zhang, Y., Malak, N.: Determining key capabilities of a firm using analytic hierarchy process. Int. J. Prod. Econ. **76**(1), 39–51 (2002). https://doi.org/10.1016/S0925-5273(01)00141-4
6. Heinonen, K., Strandvik, T.: Customer-dominant logic: foundations and implications. J. Serv. Mark. **29**(6/7), 472–484 (2015). https://doi.org/10.1108/JSM-02-2015-0096
7. Hevner, A.R., March, S.T., Park, J., Ram, S.: Design science in information systems research. MIS Q. **28**(1), 75–105 (2004). https://doi.org/10.2307/25148625
8. Maes, A., Poels, G.: Evaluating quality of conceptual modelling scripts based on user perceptions. Data Knowl. Eng. **63**(3), 701–724 (2007). https://doi.org/10.1016/j.datak.2007.04.008
9. McCarthy, W.: The rea accounting model: a generalized framework for accounting systems in a shared data environment. Account. Rev. **57**, 554–578 (1982). https://www.jstor.org/stable/246878
10. Moody, D.L.: The method evaluation model: a theoretical model for validating information systems design methods. In: ECIS 2003 Proceedings, vol. 79 (2003). https://aisel.aisnet.org/ecis2003/79
11. OMG: Value Delivery Modeling Language (VDML) 1.1 (2018)
12. Pastor, O., España, S., Panach, J.I., Aquino, N.: Model-driven development. Informatik-Spektrum **31**, 394–407 (2008). https://doi.org/10.1007/s00287-008-0275-8
13. Sales, T.P., Roelens, B., Poels, G., Guizzardi, G., Guarino, N., Mylopoulos, J.: A pattern language for value modeling in archimate. In: Giorgini, P., Weber, B. (eds.) CAiSE 2019. LNCS, vol. 11483, pp. 230–245. Springer, Cham (2019). https://doi.org/10.1007/978-3-030-21290-2_15
14. Sandkuhl, K., et al.: From expert discipline to common practice: a vision and research agenda for extending the reach of enterprise modeling. Bus. Inf. Syst. Eng. **60**, 69–80 (2018). https://doi.org/10.1007/s12599-017-0516-y
15. Strandvik, T., Heinonen, K., Vollmer, S.: Revealing business customers' hidden value formation in service. J. Bus. Ind. Mark. **34**(6), 1145–1159 (2019). https://doi.org/10.1108/JBIM-11-2017-0259
16. Stępień, B.: In search of apprehending customers' value perception. Int. J. Econ. Manag. **53**(1), 99–117 (2017). https://doi.org/10.1515/ijme-2017-0007
17. Yin, R.: Case Study Research and Applications: Design and Methods, 6th edn. SAGE Publications Inc, Thousand Oaks (2017)

DigPro

1st Workshop on Digital Transformation with Business Process Mining (DigPro)

The workshop DigPro2024 (Digital Transformation with Business Process Mining) aimed to provide a platform for the introduction of Process Mining as a keystone in Digital Transformation, offering fertile ground for influential research. Advancements in Information System research are witnessing the impact of Process Mining as data-driven techniques to extract insights while discovering and analyzing processes and workflows within a business. The convergence of Digital Transformation approaches like process automation with emerging techniques of Process Mining promises to deliver high value in creating a modern and efficient Information System.

With business process automation already a crucial part of Digital Transformation, it is not only a matter of automating previously manual processes but also about bringing overall efficiency to the organization while leveraging advancements in Process Mining. Process Mining has already shown the capability to provide a wholistic picture of all events, processes, and workflows in an organization. This emerging technology is currently streamlining organizational workflows while suggesting substitutions of mundane tasks with efficient workflow and optimized process automation.

By leveraging the data-driven approach with Event logs, various Process Mining approaches are endeavoring to optimize organizational workflows with process discovery, process conformance, and process enhancement techniques. The DigPro workshop, focusing on the impact of Process Mining research on Digital Transformation, proposed to incorporate both case study and research paper presentations to provide new insights and a data-driven approach that is useful to Software Engineers, System Managers, IT Professionals, along with Students, Research Scholars, and Faculty members in the broad field of Information Systems Engineering.

The workshop attracted 15 submissions, out of which 4 papers were selected for final inclusion in the proceeding as full papers. With a keynote by Sander Leemans of RWTH Aachen University, Germany, the workshop took place on June 4th, 2024, to facilitate cross-disciplinary brainstorming.

June 2024

Om Prakash Vyas
Sander Leemans
Ranjana Vyas
Jerome Geyer-Klingeberg
Praveen Ranjan Srivastava

Organization

Program Chairs

Om Prakash Vyas	IIIT Allahabad Prayagraj, India
Sander Leemans	RWTH Aachen, Germany
Ranjana Vyas	Indian Institute of Management, Rohtak, India
Jerome Geyer-Klingeberg	Celonis, India
Praveen Ranjan Srivastava	IIIT Allahabad Prayagraj, India

Program Committee

Praveen Ranjan	IIM Rohtak, India
J.C. Bose R. P.	Skan.ai, India
Monika Gupta	Celonis, India
Prof.Vivek Ranga	ICFAI Business School, Ahmedabad, India
Emilio Sulis	University of Turin, Italy
Johannes De Smedt	KU Leuven, Belgium
Sebastiaan van Zelst	Celonis Labs GmbH, Germany
Han van der Aa	University of Vienna, Austria
Wolfgang Kratsch	FIM, Germany
Felix Mannhardt	Eindhoven University of Technology, The Netherlands
Neeraj Pandey	IIM Bombay, India

Empirical Insights into Context-Aware Process Predictions: Model Selection and Context Integration

Marc C. Hennig(⊠) [ID]

University of Applied Sciences Munich, Lothstraße 64, 80335 Munich, Germany
mhennig@hm.edu

Abstract. The prediction of service process performance is fraught with challenges from the selection of suitable recurrent neural network architectures. In this study, we evaluate the effectiveness of various recurrent neural network (RNN) architectures, including Long Short-Term Memory (LSTM) and Gated Recurrent Unit (GRU) networks, for predictive process monitoring in service processes. We analyze the impact of incorporating contextual process information from event logs by benchmarking the model performance across multiple IT service management datasets, RNN architectures, and integration strategies. Our empirical results highlight that context-aware models improve prediction performance, but the extent varies with the dataset and the specific RNN architecture. Time-aware LSTMs demonstrated superior performance for remaining time and next timestamp predictions, while GRUs were particularly effective in predicting the next activity. This research underscores the need to carefully consider model architecture and context integration to enhance predictive process monitoring. It also provides insights that can guide the selection of models and integration techniques, leading to future research directions in refining these methods for service process applications.

Keywords: predictive process monitoring · IT service management · recurrent neural networks · context-aware prediction · TLSTM · GRU · LSTM

1 Introduction

Predictive process monitoring faces the challenge of predicting future process performance indicators and outcomes. This is particularly demanding in service processes that significantly differ from "standard" production processes [1]. Such service processes are heterogeneous and time-critical, as process instances rely heavily on user input, and the outputs of process steps cannot be produced and stored beforehand [1]. Additionally, adhering to contractual service-level agreements (SLA) while correcting service quality issues demands efficient operational decision-making that offers the potential for process maturation [2] and cost reduction in service-oriented areas such as IT service management (ITSM). Therefore, assisting operational decision-making in service processes is crucial and requires accurate assessments to identify process instances at risk of

© The Author(s), under exclusive license to Springer Nature Switzerland AG 2024
J. P. A. Almeida et al. (Eds.): CAiSE 2024 Workshops, LNBIP 521, pp. 323–334, 2024.
https://doi.org/10.1007/978-3-031-61003-5_27

violating SLAs and initiate counteractions [3]. Service processes are fraught with high complexity in organizational interdependencies and process artifacts [1, 4], which hampers the efficacy of predictive process monitoring methods. The event logs also reflect this complexity, often containing additional attributes with context information [5] about ongoing process instances, such as responsible resources, affected infrastructures, and prioritizations.

While many predictive process monitoring models have been developed over the years, a comprehensive comparison and an assessment of different integration methods for additional event log attributes are missing. This work, therefore, benchmarks multiple state-of-the-art models with a focus on recurrent neural networks (RNN) and their gated derivatives like long short-term neural networks (LSTM), gated recurrent units (GRU), and their bidirectional variants. RNNs are especially relevant as they are among the most popular machine learning models used in predictive process monitoring [6, 7]. Thus, this research attempts to answer the question: *How does the choice of RNNs and context integration techniques affect prediction model performance?*

As part of an ongoing research project to develop a general approach for improving ITSM processes using predictive process mining, the approach of this paper is twofold. First, the related literature is analyzed, focusing on sequential neural network architectures. Second, multiple sequential neural network architectures are developed and benchmarked with a focus on integrating process context information [5]. The developed models are compared using available datasets from ITSM's incident management to assess how different architectural properties affect predictive process monitoring performance, thereby contributing to a better understanding of neural network architectures and context integration techniques. Due to their relevance for the highly operational incident management [3], the focus lies on the directly execution-related [8] next activity, remaining time, and next timestamp predictions.

2   Research Background

2.1   Recent Trends in Neural Network Designs for Process Prediction

In predictive process monitoring, a range of machine learning techniques [6, 7] are leveraged to predict various target variables from an ongoing process's event log. Despite considerable research efforts to enhance the efficacy of predictive process monitoring solutions, the field lacks robust, evidence-based guidelines for selecting neural network architectures. Historically, the focus has primarily been on adapting existing models to suit different event logs, leading to an iterative enhancement of models. Over time, a trend toward more diverse neural network architectures has emerged. Within the current literature [6, 7], one can observe three significant trends:

First, recurrent neural networks have been refined through innovations in their architecture and training processes. For instance, a time-aware LSTM (TLSTM) [9], which incorporates the temporal intervals between events, has been introduced. The performance has also seen advancements by executing class weighting strategies [9] to address imbalances in the event data and ensemble learning [10].

Secondly, there is increasing employment of attention mechanisms independently [11] or in combination with RNNs, resulting in multi-layered hierarchical structures that offer more precise predictions by focusing on salient parts of the input data. Such models [12, 13] commonly employ layer-wise abstractions to improve their prediction quality at the cost of a significantly increased model complexity.

Thirdly, the advent of combined architectures merges the strengths of different machine learning approaches with established neural networks, like LSTM or attention-based models. One example is the use of clustering methods [14, 15] before further processing, showing a blend of neural networks with other algorithms. Using other machine learning models, such as random forests [16], also falls under this observation.

Despite these methodological advancements, there remains an absence of clear indicators showing the general superiority of one model over another due to the inherent challenges in ensuring comparability [17] across different datasets, preprocessing methods, performance metrics, and prediction goals. A noteworthy observation is the prevalence of LSTMs as a predominant choice [6, 7], which is intriguing given that research suggests GRUs might deliver similar performance with more efficient training [6]. Bidirectional RNNs, especially BiGRUs, also remain underexplored, indicating a research gap. The trends also pinpoint a necessity for more comparative analysis to determine effective predictive process monitoring architectures in a task- and domain-specific manner. Such work would contribute to developing model selection guidelines, ultimately advancing process management's predictive capabilities.

2.2 Usage of Static and Dynamic Process Context Information

Considering additional event log attributes, or process context, is a common practice in predictive process monitoring. However, the definition of process context is inherently ambiguous and often varies across literature. For our study, we define every attribute of the data that provides information beyond the baseline event log attributes – activity, timestamp, and case identifier – as contextual, aligning with [5]. Attributes that remain consistent for all events within a process instance are termed static [5], whereas dynamic attributes [5] fluctuate in value throughout a process instance. The treatment of these attribute types is markedly different in sequential neural networks [18], making them a noteworthy area for examination in predictive process monitoring due to variations in their integration across different predictive models.

Although some approaches only use timestamp and activity data, it is common to derive features from timestamps [6, 9, 19], enriching the data for predictive process monitoring. Typically, static or dynamic attributes are employed exclusively. Standard practice involves transforming these attributes to maintain consistency – for static contexts, by updating to the latest dynamic attribute state, a technique known as last-state encoding [20], and for dynamic contexts, by repeating static attributes across events to form "fake sequences" [18], which allows their analysis as if dynamic, potentially improving prediction accuracy.

Despite evidence that handling static and dynamic attributes separately can bolster prediction outcomes in sequence-related tasks [18, 21], such methods are rarely [22] employed in predictive process monitoring. Additionally, there's a shortfall in comparing models applying different process context integrations.

3   Research Method

Given the state of the art, the ongoing research in predictive process monitoring, and the gaps detected therein, we provide a comprehensive benchmark of different recurrent neural network architectures. This benchmark is conducted on publicly available incident management event logs. The design science research method described by [23] provides the overarching framework for the steps, which are outlined in Fig. 1.

After analyzing the literature, we were able to narrow down the research problem and identify the research gap of lacking grounds for informed prediction architecture choice and contextual attribute integration. We prioritize investigating dynamic (event-specific) and static (case-specific) contextual attributes [5], as this is a division commonly made in predictive process monitoring [20]. Also, these types can be easily distinguished with limited domain knowledge about the datasets.

After that, multiple event logs are analyzed and preprocessed using a streamlined and reproducible approach. Strict temporal splitting [17] and a unified preprocessing are applied therein to ensure comparable results. Then, the models are developed and trained on the prepared event logs, and their performance is measured. To compare their performances, metrics appropriate for the prediction tasks, i.e., regression metrics for the next timestamp and remaining cycle time prediction and classification metrics for the next activity prediction, are selected. Finally, the results are evaluated and compared with other solutions in the field.

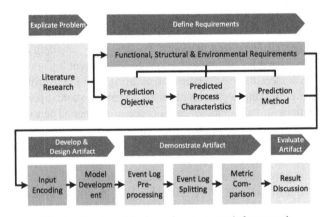

Fig. 1. Employed design science research framework

4   Design and Development

To assess the impact of adding additional attributes on the prediction quality of predictive process monitoring solutions and the effectiveness of different RNN types, multiple models and variations of them are developed and evaluated. For this, several general RNN mechanisms are used for processing the sequential data:

- LSTM and BiLSTM, as de-facto standard [6, 7, 19] in predictive process monitoring.
- GRU and BiGRU, as an underused and potentially superior [6, 15] alternative.
- TLSTM, as a novel solution [9] in the field.

Each of these fundamental RNN mechanisms is used as the central component of multiple models to investigate the influence of the model choice and the relevance of context for the prediction performance. Three general kinds of context inclusion are used:

- No context attributes are used, i.e., only activity and timestamp. These models are denoted as *RNN*, where *RNN* is to be replaced by the used architecture.
- All attributes are treated as dynamic. Static attributes are sequentialized [18] to mimic dynamic attributes. These models are denoted by $RNN_{Dyn.C}$ and are comparable to those without context but using all available attributes.
- Static and dynamic attributes are treated separately. Dynamic attributes are handled by the RNN, while the static data is integrated using a multi-layer perceptron's (MLP) latent states similar to [21]. RNN_C denotes these models.

All models are developed as multi-task learning models, which use the added individual losses [9] to learn the next activity, next timestamp, and remaining time tasks concurrently in the same model. The same hyperparameters are applied to all models and event logs. Thus, no optimization is performed, focusing on the relative comparison.

4.1   Recurrent Neural Networks

Recurrent neural networks that can work with sequential data are common in predictive process monitoring as they are designed to handle temporal dependencies in sequential prediction problems. Given an input sequence $x_1, x_2, \ldots, x_m$, a sequence of outputs $h_1, h_2, \ldots, h_m$ is calculated. Gated RNNs, such as LSTMs and GRUs, have shown better performance across the board [6, 7], so they are primarily used nowadays and inspected in this work. The common LSTM uses the following approach for the jth cell at the timestep t, with W, U, and V being trained weights and a bias b [24]:

$$
\begin{aligned}
i_t^j &= \mathrm{sigmoid}(W_i x_t + U_i h_{t-1} + V_i c_{t-1} + b_i)^j & \text{(input gate)} \\
f_t^j &= \mathrm{sigmoid}(W_f x_t + U_f h_{t-1} + V_f c_{t-1} + b_f)^j & \text{(forget gate)} \\
o_t^j &= \mathrm{sigmoid}(W_o x_t + U_o h_{t-1} + V_o c_t + b_o)^j & \text{(output gate)} \\
c_t^j &= f_t^j c_{t-1}^j + i_t^j \tanh(W_c x_t + U_c h_{t-1} + b_c)^j & \text{(current memory)} \\
h_t^j &= o_t^j \tanh\left(c_t^j\right) & \text{(activation)}
\end{aligned}
$$

The novel TLSTM [9] adds the following amendments to the LSTM, thus changing the calculation of the long- and short-term memory based on the time difference to the previous sequence element. Thus, the previous memory is altered to c_{t-1}^*:

$$
\begin{aligned}
c_{t-1}^S &= \tanh(W_d c_{t-1} + b_d) & \text{(short-term memory)} \\
\hat{c}_{t-1}^S &= c_{t-1}^S * \mathrm{decay}(\Delta_t) & \text{(discounted short-term memory)} \\
c_{t-1}^T &= c_{t-1} - c_{t-1}^S & \text{(long-term memory)} \\
c_{t-1}^* &= c_{t-1}^T + \hat{c}_{t-1}^S & \text{(adjusted previous memory)}
\end{aligned}
$$

The GRU simplifies the LSTM by omitting a separate output gate. GRUs thus provide a computationally more efficient variant than the LSTM and TLSTM [24]:

$$z_t^j = \text{sigmoid}\left(W_z x_t + U_z h_{t-1}^j + b_i\right) \text{ (update gate)}$$
$$r_t^j = \text{sigmoid}\left(W_r x_t + U_r h_{t-1}^j\right) \quad \text{(reset gate)}$$
$$\tilde{h}_t^j = \tanh\left(W x_t + U\left(r_t \circ h_{t-1}^j\right)\right)^j \quad \text{(candidate activation)}$$
$$h_t^j = \left(1 - z_t^j\right)h_{t-1}^j + z_t^j \tilde{h}_t^j \quad \text{(activation)}$$

Regular RNNs take sequences from one side. As a result, the RNN is trained using historical data and current input. Since it can be advantageous to include information about future elements, a bidirectional RNN considers two sequences, one in regular order and one in reverse order [13]. The forward and backward outputs are concatenated at each time step, where *RNN* is to be substituted by the employed architecture.

$$\vec{h}_t^j = \overrightarrow{RNN}\left(x_t^j, h_{t-1}^j\right) \text{ (left-to-right)}$$
$$\overleftarrow{h}_t^j = \overleftarrow{RNN}\left(x_t^j, h_{t+1}^j\right) \text{ (right-to-left)}$$
$$h_t^j = \left[\vec{h}_t^j, \overleftarrow{h}_t^j\right] \quad \text{(activation)}$$

4.2 Input Encoding

The input to the neural networks varies for the different types of attributes included in the datasets and follows a general approach depending on the data type.

Numerical Attributes. Min-max scaling is applied to all numerical attributes, fitted on the training part of the dataset. Thus, attributes are scaled linearly to a range between 0 and 1 using the following approach:

$$x_{scaled} = \frac{x - x_{min}}{x_{max} - x_{min}}$$

Timestamp Attributes. The timestamp attribute in the dataset is handled similarly to previous work [9, 19], which includes the extraction of custom time attributes.

Categorical Attributes. Categorical attributes can be either ordinal or nominal. Ordinal ones are numbered and min-max scaled, while nominal ones are encoded using learnable embeddings to reduce high dimensionality, which is what the standard one-hot encoding [6, 7] would result in. This approach balances expressiveness and dimensionality, potentially improving the model performance via learned embeddings.

4.3 Models Without Context and Sequentialized Dynamic Context

A similar approach is applied for the models without context and the model using the dynamic context. First, the encoded attributes are concatenated to form an input $x =$

$\langle x_1, x_2, \ldots, x_m \rangle$ consisting of the events of the trace as timesteps x and the encoded attributes as values x_t. The input sequence is subjected to a shared RNN layer, returning a sequence consisting of the outputs of the recurrent cells j for the element x_t. The shared outputs are then separately used as inputs for output-specific RNN layers, where the inputs for each layer are the previously generated outputs. Therefore, the model without context attributes uses a setup similar to [9, 19] with additional output.

4.4 Models with Static and Dynamic Context

The model handling static and dynamic content separately presents itself similarly to the setup for handling dynamic and no context. However, it is extended by an MLP handling the static context, similar to the proposal of [21]. Given a vector of static, non-sequential attributes $x = [x_1, x_2, \ldots, x_m]$, , a single perceptron uses the following formula using a gaussian error linear unit (GELU) [25] as activation function, with w_i and b being the trained weights and bias respectably.

$$h_{stat} = \text{GELU}\left(b + \sum_{i=i}^{m} x_i w_i\right)$$

As shown in Fig. 2, one MLP is set up and trained for each output MLP. The latent states derived from the MLPs are concatenated with the result of the RNN, h_{dyn} of the last cell from the RNN, and then also used as input for the corresponding output layers.

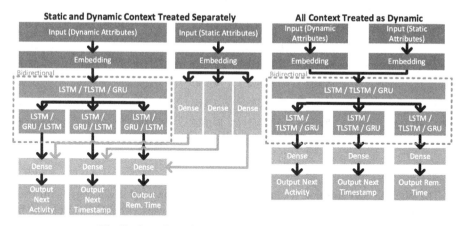

Fig. 2. Overview of the developed context-aware models

5 Experimental Evaluation

Five different datasets are used to compare the developed models. These datasets contain event logs from incident management processes from various industries and show different properties regarding the number of events, cases, and attributes.

- The "enriched event log of an incident management process" [26] is derived from an IT company's ServiceNow platform and is referred to as "Incident V1."
- The "Dataset belonging to the help desk log of an Italian Company" [27] originating in an Italian software company referred to as "Italian Company".
- The well-known "Helpdesk" event log [28] is also from an Italian software company. Please note that this dataset does not contain additional attributes.
- The BPIC 2014 [29] event log was created by Rabobank's IT organization.
- The BPIC 2013 [30] from the IT organization of the car manufacturer Volvo.

5.1 Preprocessing and Splitting

A unified cleaning process is applied to ensure suitable data for further processing. Empty and duplicate events are removed, along with highly correlated attributes (≥ 0.9 or ≤ -0.9). For event logs consisting of multiple files, all parts are joined by provided identifiers. The event logs are divided into 80/20 splits using strict temporal splitting [17] to ensure unbiased and reproducible partitions. Chronological outliers are filtered, and the top 5% of the longest cases are removed, similar to [17]. The resulting train and test sets are shown in Table 1. Chronological outliers at the start and end of the BPIC 2014, BPIC 2013, and Incident V1 datasets are also filtered as advised by [17], leading to the total events in the train and test sets shown in Table 1.

Table 1. Event logs after filtering and strict temporal splitting

	Train		Test		Total	
	Abs.	Rel.	Abs.	Rel.	Abs.	Rel.
Incident V1	96,350	77.69%	27,670	22.31%	124,020	87.52%
Italian Company	15,807	77.08%	4,700	22.92%	20,507	96.06%
Helpdesk	11,029	81.45%	2,512	18.55%	13,541	98.77%
BPIC 2013	8,653	31.15%	19.124	68.85%	27.777	42.39%
BPIC 2014	318,228	80.13%	78,901	19.67%	397,129	85.09%

The filtering and splitting results are satisfactory for most event logs, with over 85% coverage of events compared to unfiltered logs. However, BPIC 2013 cannot be split using the chosen approach without producing many invalid events in the overlaps between the train and test sets, making it unusable [17] for strict temporal train-test-splitting and disqualifying it for further use in this work.

5.2 Performance Metrics

The prediction of the remaining time (RT) and the next timestamp (NT) in days (or any other time unit) is a regression task, which requires the use of metrics for determining the deviation between the label y and the predicted values $\hat{y}$. Although the mean absolute error (MAE) shows some sensitivity to outliers, it is less than other metrics [31].

$$MAE = \frac{1}{n} \cdot \sum_{i=i}^{n} |y_i - \hat{y}|$$

The forecast of the next activity constitutes a multi-class classification problem, which necessitates a different approach. The classification metrics are based on true positives (TP), true negatives (TN), as well as false positives (FP), and false negatives (FN), respectively [32]. The accuracy is calculated class-wise and averaged. While class imbalances bias the accuracy, it is a standard measure in predictive process monitoring and consequently chosen to simplify comparisons.

$$Accuracy = \frac{1}{n} \cdot \sum_{i=1}^{n} \frac{TP_i + TN_i}{TP_i + TN_i + FP_i + FN_i}$$

To assess whether the models have learned adequately, a naïve model, predicting only the median for the remaining time, the next timestamp, and the mode for the next activity of the train set, is added for reference.

5.3 Evaluation Results

Table 2 shows the evaluation results and indicates that most models have learned to predict the three target variables better than most naïve predictions, except for the BPIC 2014 dataset, where for the next timestamp predictions, the naïve model performs best along with multiple other models. This indicates that the additional model complexity is not effectively leveraged.

The performance metrics for context-included models show that the context may bring considerable benefits, as demonstrated by the Italian company event log. This event log contains a reasonable number of attributes; the more convoluted event logs show worse results, indicating that different preprocessing or context integration methods might be more suitable in these cases. The TLSTMs perform strongly on time-related predictions, being among the best models for these tasks across all datasets. No such distinct observation can be made regarding the next activity prediction, although the GRU models perform quite well. The bidirectional models perform mediocrely, hinting that bidirectionality remains situational rather than generally advisable.

5.4 Insights and Contributions

The exploration and empirical performance assessment of various recurrent neural network architectures, shown in the previous section, yields critical insights that extend to the broader field of predictive process monitoring. While no one-fits-all solution could be identified, we provide empirical evidence that specific models, like TLSTMs, are better suited for temporal predictions. At the same time, GRUs excel in categorical next activity prediction, thereby contributing to the evidence base required for architecture selection in various predictive tasks. The benefits of GRUs [6, 15] were also found previously, but the use cases in predictive process monitoring are sparse, hinting at further applications. A novelty of this study is the focus on the analysis of integrating contextual

Table 2. Results of the benchmark with MAE in days

	Incident V1			Italian Company			Helpdesk			BPIC 2014		
	MAE_{RT}	MAE_{NT}	Acc_{NA}	MAE_{RT}	MAE_{NT}	Acc_{NA}	MAE_{RT}	MAE_{NT}	Acc_{NA}	MAE_{RT}	MAE_{NT}	Acc_{NA}
Naïve	3,26	1,48	0,17	15,97	8,06	0,19	5,05	2,43	0,29	1,94	**0,23**	0,18
T-LSTM$_C$	2,79	0,67	0,68	**12,43**	5,62	0,73	–	–	–	1,94	0,25	0,52
TLSTM$_{Dyn.C}$	2,42	0,74	0,68	22,08	7,93	0,56	–	– .	–	1,92	0,25	0,40
T-LSTM	2,21	**0,64**	0,67	21,40	7,74	0,72	4,88	2,43	**0,85**	**1,78**	**0,23**	0,46
LSTM$_C$	2,55	0,76	0,68	14,77	5,99	0,71	–	–	–	1,96	0,27	0,51
LSTM$_{Dyn.C}$	2,79	0,8	0,67	21,42	7,79	0,74	–	–	–	2,02	0,24	0,35
LSTM	2,29	0,79	0,71	21,61	7,86	**0,75**	4,94	2,40	0,83	1,79	**0,23**	0,45
BiLSTM$_C$	2,55	0,77	0,66	15,76	6,05	0,73	–	–	–	2,00	0,25	0,53
BiLSTM$_{Dyn.C}$	3,00	0,92	0,68	21,87	7,87	0,70	–	–	–	1,96	0,24	0,41
BiLSTM	2,24	0,67	0,71	22,91	7,91	0,73	**4,84**	**2,39**	0,83	1,80	0,25	0,49
GRU$_C$	2,53	0,76	0,70	12,49	5,79	0,73	–	–	–	1,91	0,25	0,53
GRU$_{Dyn.C}$	2,31	0,76	0,66	21,48	7,69	0,73	–	–	–	1,93	**0,23**	0,53
GRU	**2,17**	**0,64**	**0,72**	21,74	7,99	0,69	4,88	2,40	**0,85**	1,81	0,32	0,52
BiGRU$_C$	2,70	0,75	0,69	14,51	**5,59**	0,72	–	–	–	1,95	0,26	0,55
BiGRU$_{Dyn.C}$	2,38	0,83	0,70	22,42	8,42	0,54	–	–	–	1,98	0,24	**0,57**
BiGRU	2,57	0,7	0,68	21,97	7,90	0,69	4,85	2,40	**0,85**	1,90	0,28	0,53

process information different for static and dynamic attributes, combining the formal framework from [5] with a predictive process monitoring specific application of the MLP integration [21], demonstrating empirically that context-aware models enhance prediction performance, albeit to varying degrees dependent on the architecture and dataset utilized. The study revealed that more event log attributes do not always result in better predictive outcomes, suggesting that further refinement in context integration and feature engineering could be beneficial. The results of this work include a comprehensive review of the use of RNN architectures, some of which are only rarely used in the field, giving insights for more complex and hybrid future architectures.

6 Conclusion and Future Research

This work contributes valuable empirical insights that future model selection and development in ITSM incident management can build upon by inspecting further integration techniques and contextual data. Contrary to some other work, no hyperparameter optimization was performed, potentially limiting the understanding of the full potential of each model variant and affecting the comparisons made, as many other works employ some form of optimization. Comparisons to other work are also complicated as implementations are usually unavailable, and the preprocessing differs [6]. For this reason, we focused on a repeatable and understandable preprocessing strategy following published guidelines [17].

While we concentrated on RNNs, future research should explore the efficacy of other architectures in process monitoring tasks, such as increasingly popular transformer models, possibly assessing how different model types can be applied in hybrid solutions and ensemble learning setups. Many relevant data sources in ITSM, such as configuration management databases and organizational technical structures, form multi-layered networks. In this regard, the work with non-tabular network data remains especially interesting for future analyses. It will form a significant part of our future research to extend the insights with a holistic view of the socio-technical IT organization.

References

1. Bardhan, I.R., Demirkan, H., Kannan, P.K., Kauffman, R.J., Sougstad, R.: An interdisciplinary perspective on IT services management and service science. JMIS **26**, 13–64 (2010). https://doi.org/10.2753/mis0742-1222260402
2. Marrone, M., Kolbe, L.: ITIL and the creation of benefits: an empirical study on benefits, challenges and processes. In: 18th European Conference on Information Systems, Pretoria, South Africa, p. 66 (2010)
3. Mao, H., Zhang, T., Tang, Q.: Research framework for determining how artificial intelligence enables information technology service management for business model resilience. Sustainability **13**, 11496 (2021). https://doi.org/10.3390/su132011496
4. Loewenstern, D., Shwartz, L.: IT service management of using heterogeneous, dynamically alterable configuration item lifecycles. In: Cordeiro, J., Filipe, J. (eds.) 10th International Conference on Enterprise Information Systems, Barcelona, pp. 155–160 (2008)
5. Brunk, J.: Structuring business process context information for process monitoring and prediction. In: 22nd Conference on Business Informatics, Antwerp, Belgium, pp. 39–48. IEEE (2020). https://doi.org/10.1109/cbi49978.2020.00012
6. Rama-Maneiro, E., Vidal, J., Lama, M.: Deep learning for predictive business process monitoring: review and benchmark. IEEE Trans. Serv. Comput. **16**, 739–756 (2022). https://doi.org/10.1109/tsc.2021.3139807
7. Neu, D.A., Lahann, J., Fettke, P.: A systematic literature review on state-of-the-art deep learning methods for process prediction. Artif. Intell. Rev. **55**, 801–827 (2022). https://doi.org/10.1007/s10462-021-09960-8
8. Poll, R., Polyvyanyy, A., Rosemann, M., Röglinger, M., Rupprecht, L.: Process forecasting: towards proactive business process management. In: Weske, M., Montali, M., Weber, I., vom Brocke, J. (eds.) BPM 2018. LNCS, vol. 11080, pp. 496–512. Springer, Cham (2018). https://doi.org/10.1007/978-3-319-98648-7_29
9. Nguyen, An., Chatterjee, S., Weinzierl, S., Schwinn, L., Matzner, M., Eskofier, B.: Time matters: time-aware LSTMs for predictive business process monitoring. In: Leemans, S., Leopold, H. (eds.) ICPM 2020. LNBIP, vol. 406, pp. 112–123. Springer, Cham (2021). https://doi.org/10.1007/978-3-030-72693-5_9
10. Metzger, A., Neubauer, A., Bohn, P., Pohl, K.: Proactive process adaptation using deep learning ensembles. In: Giorgini, P., Weber, B. (eds.) CAiSE 2019. LNCS, vol. 11483, pp. 547–562. Springer, Cham (2019). https://doi.org/10.1007/978-3-030-21290-2_34
11. Bukhsh, Z.A., Saeed, A., Dijkman, R.M.: ProcessTransformer: predictive business process monitoring with transformer network (2021). http://arxiv.org/abs/2104.00721
12. Wang, J., Yu, D., Liu, C., Sun, X.: Outcome-oriented predictive process monitoring with attention-based bidirectional LSTM neural networks. In: 13th International Conference on Web Services, Milan, Italy, pp. 360–367. IEEE (2019). https://doi.org/10.1109/icws.2019.00065
13. Jalayer, A., Kahani, M., Pourmasoumi, A., Beheshti, A.: HAM-Net: Predictive Business Process Monitoring with a hierarchical attention mechanism. Knowl. Based Syst. **236**, 107722 (2022). https://doi.org/10.1016/j.knosys.2021.107722

14. Ni, W., Zhao, G., Liu, T., Zeng, Q., Xu, X.: Predictive business process monitoring approach based on hierarchical transformer. Electronics **12**, 1273 (2023). https://doi.org/10.3390/electronics12061273
15. Hinkka, M., Lehto, T., Heljanko, K.: Exploiting event log event attributes in RNN based prediction. In: Ceravolo, P., van Keulen, M., Gómez-López, M.T. (eds.) SIMPDA SIMPDA 2018 2019. LNBIP, vol. 379, pp. 67–85. Springer, Cham (2020). https://doi.org/10.1007/978-3-030-46633-6_4
16. Gunnarsson, B.R., van den Broucke, S.K.L.M., De Weerdt, J.: Predictive process monitoring in operational logistics: a case study in aviation. In: Di Francescomarino, C., Dijkman, R., Zdun, U. (eds.) BPM 2019. LNBIP, vol. 362, pp. 250–262. Springer, Cham (2019). https://doi.org/10.1007/978-3-030-37453-2_21
17. Weytjens, H., De Weerdt, J.: Creating unbiased public benchmark datasets with data leakage prevention for predictive process monitoring. In: Marrella, A., Weber, B. (eds.) BPM 2021. LNBIP, vol. 436, pp. 18–29. Springer, Cham (2022). https://doi.org/10.1007/978-3-030-94343-1_2
18. Leontjeva, A., Kuzovkin, I.: Combining static and dynamic features for multivariate sequence classification. In: 2016 IEEE International Conference on Data Science and Advanced Analytics, Montreal, pp. 21–30. IEEE (2016). https://doi.org/10.1109/dsaa.2016.10
19. Tax, N., Verenich, I., La Rosa, M., Dumas, M.: Predictive business process monitoring with LSTM neural networks. In: Dubois, E., Pohl, K. (eds.) CAiSE 2017. LNCS, vol. 10253, pp. 477–492. Springer, Cham (2017). https://doi.org/10.1007/978-3-319-59536-8_30
20. Di Francescomarino, C., Ghidini, C.: Predictive process monitoring. In: van der Aalst, W.M.P., Carmona, J. (eds.) Process Mining Handbook. LNBIP, vol. 448, pp. 320–346. Springer, Cham (2022). https://doi.org/10.1007/978-3-031-08848-3_10
21. Miebs, G., Mochol-Grzelak, M., Karaszewski, A., Bachorz, R.A.: Efficient strategies of static features incorporation into the recurrent neural network. Neural. Process. Lett. **51**, 2301–2316 (2020). https://doi.org/10.1007/s11063-020-10195-x
22. Stevens, A., De Smedt, J.: Explainability in process outcome prediction: guidelines to obtain interpretable and faithful models. Eur. J. Oper. Res. (2023). https://doi.org/10.1016/j.ejor.2023.09.010
23. Johannesson, P., Perjons, E.: An Introduction to Design Science. Springer, Cham (2021). https://doi.org/10.1007/978-3-030-78132-3
24. Chung, J., Gulcehre, C., Cho, K., Bengio, Y.: Empirical evaluation of gated recurrent neural networks on sequence modeling (2014). http://arxiv.org/abs/1412.3555
25. Hendrycks, D., Gimpel, K.: Gaussian error linear units (GELUs) (2023). https://doi.org/10.48550/arXiv.1606.08415
26. Amaral, C., Fantinato, M., Peres, S.: Incident management process enriched event log (2018). https://doi.org/10.24432/c57s4h. https://archive.ics.uci.edu/dataset/498
27. Polato, M.: Dataset belonging to the help desk log of an Italian Company (2017). https://doi.org/10.4121/uuid:0c60edf1-6f83-4e75-9367-4c63b3e9d5bb
28. Verenich, I.: Helpdesk (2016). https://doi.org/10.17632/39bp3vv62t.1
29. van Dongen, B.F.: BPI challenge 2014 (2014). https://doi.org/10.4121/uuid:c3e5d162-0cfd-4bb0-bd82-af5268819c35
30. Steeman, W.: BPI challenge 2013 (2013). https://doi.org/10.4121/uuid:a7ce5c55-03a7-4583-b855-98b86e1a2b07
31. Plevris, V., Solorzano, G., Bakas, N., Ben Seghier, M.: Investigation of performance metrics in regression analysis and machine learning-based prediction models. In: 8th European Congress on Computational Methods in Applied Sciences and Engineering, Oslo, Norway (2022). https://doi.org/10.23967/eccomas.2022.155
32. Sokolova, M., Lapalme, G.: A systematic analysis of performance measures for classification tasks. Inf. Process. Manag. **45**, 427–437 (2009). https://doi.org/10.1016/j.ipm.2009.03.002

Online Next Activity Prediction Under Concept Drifts

Thaddeus Kosciuszek and Marwan Hassani[(✉)] [ID]

Eindhoven University of Technology, Eindhoven, The Netherlands
t.l.kosciuszek@student.tue.nl, m.hassani@tue.nl

Abstract. Existing research in predictive process maintenance has recently focus on designing models for an online prediction where both training and testing should be performed efficiently, sequentially and in a scalable manner. However, less attention has been given to the realistic requirement of detecting concept drifts on the fly during training. Additionally, the retraining frequency as well as the training dataset size are used to be statically pre-decided. In this work, we address the previous shortcomings when designing our dynamic concept drift detection and online next activity prediction framework DynaTrainCDD. Our framework first uses a PrefixTree-driven method to detect drifts online then utilizes the Weibull distribution to estimate the retraining parameters. An extensive experimental evaluation using 10 real world datasets shows that our model additionally performs on par with or better than state-of-the-art methods in terms of accuracy while requiring a comparable running time.

Keywords: Predictive Process Monitoring · Concept Drift Detection

1 Introduction

Due to its wide application in real life, predicting trace next activity has attracted a lot of research in predictive process monitoring [4]. Recently (e.g. [11] and [12]), more attention has been given to performing this prediction task *online* (i.e. both training and inference are performed efficiently and sequentially in a test-then-train setting). [11] has elaborated further into the updating of these models when changes are detected in the underlying business process by using a method called incremental updating. While much of the existing research covers extensive applications in the field of process mining, no studies were found which combine the online detection of concept drifts with dynamic setting of training parameters. There is a significant amount of research that has detailed methods used to represent business processes efficiently alongside other analyses identifying changes in such processes [3,5,7,9]. [5] includes online methods for analyzing event streams which we will discuss in Sect. 2. However, there are no studies on dynamically setting parameters or on utilising the identification of concept drifts to update underlying next activity prediction models. Two largest gaps left in

J. P. A. Almeida et al. (Eds.): CAiSE 2024 Workshops, LNBIP 521, pp. 335–346, 2024.
https://doi.org/10.1007/978-3-031-61003-5_28

these works are (i) the assumption of accessing all concept drift moments in the stream in advance (despite assuming an online solution), and (ii) dealing with all concept drifts equally, regardless of severity, instead of dynamically updating the prediction model.

Recently, a research has developed a framework to online detect drifts in event streams by building an efficient representation of processes using tree structures [5]. Our paper seeks to apply the dynamic concept drift detection adopted from our previous work [5] in an on-the-fly manner as events are observed in the stream. Additionally, we dynamically adapt the training frequency and the training data size. This way, drifts can be detected and accounted for when updating a process model. Using tree structures to detect drifts combined with incremental updates to the model, the combination works to maintain optimal performance of the model. Once changes are detected, new updates are made. As variation in incoming data stabilizes after a concept drift, updates and training are considered to be less important for maintaining accuracy until new changes are identified and the model is again updated to reflect such changes. In doing so, the main goal of this paper is to identify factors that influence overall performance when retraining next activity prediction models in an online environment. The result is a framework, called *DynaTrainCDD*, that performs well in correcting for concept drift in datasets with *previously unknown* drifts. In addition to filling above-mentioned gaps, an extensive experimental evaluation using 10 real-world datasets against state-of-the-art solutions, highlights the superiority of our retraining model on prediction accuracy while delivering satisfying running-time efficiency results. The remainder of this paper is organized as follows: Sect. 2 introduces required background and surveys the related work. Section 3 introduces in details our DynaTrainCDD framework. Section 4 extensively evaluates DynaTrainCDD using 10 real datasets. We conclude the paper in Sect. 5.

2   Preliminaries and Literature Review

An **event** e is the individual row-level record that holds m attributes $(a_1, a_2, ..., a_m)$ which are captured at the time of the event occurrence. The event is described here as a tuple $e = (c, r, a, t)$ which contains multiple attributes. For the purpose of this analysis, events have been abridged to only include the case c, the resource completing the event r, activity or event type a, and the time at which the event occurred t. We also note the total space of all events as E. The overall set of events is stored in a multiset which is referred to as an **event log**.

A **trace** is a temporally ordered sequence of events ordered by t, all sharing the same case identifier c. Formalizing the definition of a trace, we present the character $<$ meaning "directly follows". When two events $e_1 = (c_1, r, a, t_1)$ and $e_2 = (c_2, r, b, t_2)$ are correctly ordered according to their timestamps $t(e)$: $t_1 < t_2$ where $c_1 = c_2$ (corresponding to the same case/being of the same trace) and no e_3 exists where $t_1 < t_3 < t_2$. An event log file not only consists of many events but also many traces. The log is ordered by time and can be considered a mapping $S : \mathbb{N} \to \mathbb{E}$ defining an **event stream**. When examining any two events e_1 and

e_2 where $S(m) = e_1$ and $S(n) = e_2$, the mapping holds if $t(e_1) < t(e_2)$ for $m < n$ [3]. This can be simplified through the following representation of an event stream: $S = <e_1, e_2, ...>$. Streaming process logs provide the ability to be analysed only in real time as the data is acquired as opposed to previously recorded data whereby all the available data is known at the time of analysis. **Predicting next activity** [2,11,14]. [1] has attracted a lot of research, both under traditional settings and online, due to the wide real-life applications [4]. In this work, we are using next activity prediction as a challenging use case. However, the concept of our model works essentially for all predictive process monitoring tasks. In our experimental evaluation, we compare our model to several variants of the state-of-the-art model [11].

Concept drift in our context is the phenomenon of a change in the underlying process behind a model. Processes can change with respect to three main process perspectives: control-flow, data, and resource [5]. [9] presents two points needed to successfully deal with concept drifts: capturing the characteristics of those traces as well as identifying when those characteristics change. Drifts create difficulties in predicting future information as the accuracy in predictions output by the model lose their relevance and performance as time progresses. This occurs as the current observed time $t(e_i)$ grows farther from the time the model was last updated $t(e_{update})$ There are four different classifications of drifts according to [7]: sudden drift, gradual drift, recurring drift, and incremental drift.

In the case of big data, it can become unreasonable to store all historical data to build a representation of a process due to storage sizes, running times, and efficiency of comparison to other processes. Recent literature details the representation of such prefixes (or former events) in processes with many different forms. Some have tried abstract domains to represent prefixes as multidimensional polygons in the case of the apron library [10]. Others have used a tree structure, called **Prefix Tree** as seen in [5] for use in identifying concept drifts. A prefix tree can be used to represent the possible outcomes that some modeled process $\hat{p}$ can follow. In applying this back to the idea of concept drift, two trees are maintained with respect to some time t in the event stream, with the number of leaves (in this case referred to as nodes with no children) signifying the number of possible outcomes which a trace can follow. [5] describes a formal representation of the prefix tree as composed of nodes n holding the following attributes: $n = (i, a, p, pL, ch, f)$ Whereby n is the prefix tree, i is a random unique identifier for the node, a is the activity label, p is the parent node or predecessor, pL is the list of parents up until the root node, ch is a dictionary of all children nodes of this node, and f is the frequency of this node (being the amount of times this event has been seen) [5].

Adaptive window, otherwise known as ADWIN, is an additional tool which allows for comparisons within two subsets of events. The method compares the two windows, denoted as: W_{i-1}, W_i within the same stream over time. By joining an adaptive window with the methods of a prefix tree, a "distance metric" is created through which a concept drift can be identified. The value of this distance metric determines how significant a change from the previously modeled process has occurred, with larger distances signifying a greater change in the process. The function of an adaptive window operates in a way such that two windows are compared to each other with a prefix tree representing the process observed from the events contained in each window. If no differences are identified between the two windows when using statistical tests for comparison, the test window grows until it hits the maximum size of the test window parameter. This parameter is set by the user in the *PrefixTreeCDD* algorithm [5]. When no changes are identified and the window size of the test window has already reached the maximal set parameter, the test window begins sliding forward in time. The sliding action drops events from the beginning of the test window which expire as they leave its context. Once a change is identified at any point in this process, a new reference window is created at the point of the change and the testing window moves beyond the identified change and is set back to the minimum window size. The reasoning is that the longer it takes for a change to be detected, the more gradual the change is expected to be (although not necessarily). On the contrary, once a change is detected, another may occur very quickly and be missed if the test window is too large. A visualization of this is displayed in Fig. 1.

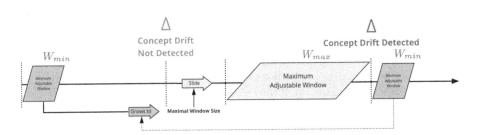

Fig. 1. Adjustable Window Procedure (Figure adapted from [3])

Incremental updating is the process of fitting new data to a previously trained model without having to retrain the model again. This process involves using data which is coming from a test set in the case of a static model or from the actual incoming data for which there is now a known outcome for. When retraining a model, all of the previous computation is lost when it is overwritten by a new model. On the contrary, when performing incremental updates, there is the opportunity to incorporate new data into the seen context of the model by updating the weights which have been learned by the previously trained model. Not only does this take significantly less time than full retraining, but it also means that the most recently fitted data has become the most relevant (leading to more accurate predictions). [11] tests the performance of both incremental updates and retraining with respect to accuracy and running time. The findings suggest that incremental updates provide a boost in performance in both metrics. One key point missing in [11] however, is the optimization and dynamic setting of these parameters. Their work predetermined the drift points on a static dataset and presented the improvements of updating the model exactly at those drift points. We propose a solution to address these shortcomings below in Sect. 3 through adopting *PrefixTreeCDD*.

The Single Dense Layer (henceforth referred to as **SDL**) is a neural network developed specifically for process models [11]. The authors specifically developed these SDL methods for the purpose of providing a light and thus fast framework to facilitate an accurate process model. The SDL is made up of a number of input layers which are fed into a concatenation layer, then a dense layer (hence the name), and finally a softmax layer. The softmax layer predicts the probability of each of the categorical outputs in the layer. In this case the categorical outputs are the number of unique activities $\#a(e)$ which an event can assume in the data. The event with the highest output probability is then selected as the predicted event in the process.

The **Kaplan Meier survival curve** is a widely used estimator to examine differences between two or more populations when analyzing individual factors relating to survival of different groups. One very commonly used function in survival and reliability analysis is the Weibull distribution due to its versatility. Within its distribution, it is able to take on the form of the exponential function while also offering the flexibility to accommodate a number of other curve shapes. The two most common forms are shown in Eqs. 1 and 2 [8].

$$F(t) = 1 - \exp(-(\frac{t-\tau}{\alpha})^{\beta}), t \geq \tau \tag{1}$$

$$F(t) = 1 - \exp(\lambda(t-\tau)), t \geq \tau \tag{2}$$

where α is the scale parameter, β is the shape parameter, τ is the location parameter, and λ is a combination scale and shape parameter ($\lambda = \alpha^{-\beta}$). In Dyna-TrainCDD, we utilize this estimator to infer a drift recovery formula through which values can be chosen for both the update frequency and training size.

3   Methods

In this section we layout the procedures used to develop our framework, which we name *DynaTrainCDD*. Figure 2 shows an overview of our framework with pointers to the sections explaining the different components or evaluating the framework. In the following, we will focus on explaining the DynaTrainCDD algorithm and on setting its parameters.

3.1   Developing the Dynamic Framework

In making a determination as to how severe a drift is, we propose the development of two heuristics; one heuristic each to set the dynamic value for the update frequency as well as the training size. The metadata regarding drifts can be utilised in a way that determines the "reliability of the information" based on the number of events since the last drift. When a drift has not been observed for

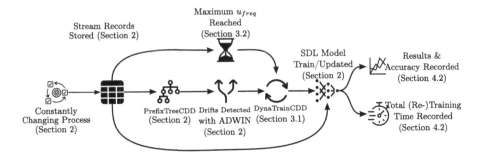

Fig. 2. DynaTrainCDD Framework Structure and Workflow

some time, intuition is that less frequent updates and smaller update sizes are needed to maintain the performance of the prediction model. With less frequent drifts, we can place more trust in the trained model and hold the expectation that we can increase the timing between updates (update frequency) and decrease the amount of data used in each of those updates (train size).

Taking our learnings from the exploration of update frequency and training size from Sect. 4.1, we introduce a Weibull function used to set each of the stated parameters dynamically. This Weibull function can be considered to track the reliability of the model as it experiences drift over time. The intuition in developing this model is as follows: the more time since the last drift, the more lenient the values of update frequency and train size can be. Parallels can be made to the adjustable window approach whereby the window expands until its maximum size and then continues sliding until another drift is found which we covered in Sect. 2 [3,5,11]. In this case, however, the Weibull function is utilised to help dynamically loosen the "reigns" on our algorithm parameters as increasing amounts of data are trained and the model is considered to be more trustworthy due to a lack of drifts. Within this framework, safeguards are built to make incremental updates to the model with the parameters u_{min}, t_{min}, u_{max}, and t_{max}. Through the implementation of these ranges, the minimum and maximum number of events between (u)pdates as well as the minimum and maximum number of events that must be included in the (t)raining of each update to the prediction model are explicitly set.

3.2 Drift Recovery Formula and Setting of Algorithm Parameters

Using the model incremental update parameters introduced in Sect. 3.1, two arrays of integers are created seen in Eqs. 3 & 4. Each array contains all integers between and including minimal and maximal values respectively for both update frequency and train size. Important to note is that the training size is in reversed order from maximal to minimal. This reversal is significant in that the parameters in the leading part of both arrays represent values for when drift is present and models are considered less trustworthy while the trailing half contains values used when the process model is considered more trustworthy; at this point the model no longer requires such frequent and large updates.

$$updateArray = <u_{min}, u_{min} + 1, u_{min} + 2, ..., u_{max} - 1, u_{max}> \qquad (3)$$

$$trainArray = <t_{max}, t_{max} + 1, t_{max} + 2, ..., t_{min} - 1, t_{min}> \qquad (4)$$

We now define the *dynamic drift recovery* formula using the second Weibull function found in Formula 2. In creating this formula, we want an equation which begins at a value of 1 indicating the need for maximal correction after a drift, then trailing off to our minimal value of 0 indicating the ability to relax our parameters. The output is a float in the range of $[0, 1]$ which is then used to determine the parameter to use by multiplying this value by the length of the *updateArray* and *trainArray* from Eqs. 3 & 4. By multiplying these two, we identify the index of the parameter chosen as input in updating the model at time t, with t being the number of events after the most recent drift is identified. As we want all of our values to start from time $t = 0$ after a drift occurs, there is no need to use the location parameter τ. We can set τ to zero and remove it from Formula 2. We are now left with the equation seen in Formula 5 whereby the only remaining parameter we need is λ as t is set automatically by the number of events which have passed since the last drift divided by u_{max} such that the value for t is never greater than 1. Thus:

$$Recov_{drift} = 1 - \exp(\lambda t) \qquad (5)$$

In choosing a value for λ we consider first what we know regarding [5]'s work whereby there is an expected delay in reporting of an identified concept drift. [5]'s research indicates that we should expect around a 3500 event delay with the default parameters for the *PrefixTreeCDD* algorithm. With this in mind, we know that once a drift has been identified, it likely holds some level of history which can be used to update the model.

To create the final formula we will use as the drift recovery curve in our framework we must find the value of λ. To do so, we take the chosen value for d (which must be lower than our u_{max}) parameter and formulate the equation by filling in t with our $\frac{d}{u_{max}}$. This essentially sets d as a number of events to maintain the integrity of retraining of the model above the parameter k. In this case we have chosen k as 0.8 as we believe that after holding the drift recovery curve output at 80% until d events have passed, this should yield favorable results with respect to accuracy. To set the value of our λ we layout the equation filled in as follows:

$$1 - \exp \lambda(\frac{d}{u_{max}} - 1) = k \qquad (6)$$

We calculate λ by having an equation that has outputs which start at 1 and end at 0 going through the point $\frac{d}{u_{max}}$ at the value k. $\ln(1 - k) = \lambda(\frac{d}{u_{max}} - 1)$

$$\lambda = \frac{\ln(1 - k)}{(\frac{d}{u_{max}} - 1)} \qquad (7)$$

Now we have our final equation which we have determined by making measured decisions which will serve as the foundation for dynamically changing u_{freq} and t_{size}. When integrating this together with the values we have for u_{freq} and t_{size} as well as our arrays $updateArray$ and $trainArray$ we use the input index parameters $\in [0,1]$ to retrieve values form these arrays. To calculate the input to send to the *drift recovery function*, we utilize the tree distance metric from *PrefixTreeCDD* [5]. In the case that we have identified fewer than 5 drifts in a given dataset, the input to the *drift recovery function* is set to 1 and considered to be the most severe. After 5 drifts have been detected, the sixth and all subsequent drifts are compared against the existing stored library of drifts and their tree distance metrics and a percentile is calculated of where it falls within the distribution of those drifts to serve as the input to the *drift recovery function*. In the case that a drift is not detected yet the value for u_{max} events since the last training event has been reached, we run an update anyway with the input to the drift detection formula set at a value of 0.5 which can be viewed as half severity. The algorithm for this can be seen in Algorithm 1.

Algorithm 1. Drift Recovery Calculation

1: $drifts \leftarrow$ list of drift objects containing drift location, severity
2: **for** every *event* in dataset **do**
3:      $lastDrift \leftarrow 0$
4:      **if** CDDAlgo detects *drift* at *event* **then**
5:          $drifts \leftarrow drifts + drift$
6:          $lastDrift \leftarrow 0$
7:          **if** length of drifts < 5 **then**
8:              $DriftRecCurveInput \leftarrow 0$
9:          **else**
10:             $DriftRecCurveInput \leftarrow quantile(drift, driftSeverities)$
11:     **if** $lastDrift > u_{max}$ **then**
12:         $DriftRecCurveInput \leftarrow 0.75$

The output of the Drift recovery function is a value $\in [0,1]$ which is then multiply by the number of elements in the arrays $updateArray$ and $trainArray$ before rounding to a whole integer to determine the index in the respective array of the u_{freq} and t_{size} values for the current batch. These batches are then updated as would normally be done during *Incremental Update* methods [11].

4   Experimental Evaluation

We use here the commonly used datasets: *Helpdesk*, *BPIC11*, *BPIC12* and the five files of *BPIC15*. For the previous datasets we perform a separate parameter tuning using the training data before evaluating the models. Then, we additionally apply the *merged BPIC15* dataset and the *BPIC17* dataset for evaluating the model without a separate parameter tuning or a model training. *merged BPIC15* dataset is created by appending the five datasets of *BPIC15*. This way we can see how the method performs when experiencing sudden drifts with new, never before seen data. To create more room for testing under concept drifts, each dataset (except *BPIC17*) was split temporally into 50% training data and 50% test data. An open source implementation of *DynaTrainCDD* is available under: https://github.com/m-h/DynaTrainCDD/.

4.1 Parameter Settings, System Specifications and Baselines

After an extensive parameter setting tuning over all real datasets except for *BPIC2017*, we found that for the drift detection parameters, selecting window size of 1000, number of prefix trees as 10, and $\lambda = 0.25$ yields the best results in detecting the expected number of drifts while minimizing the running time. These values are also the recommendation as reported in [5]. For setting the *initial* update frequency and the training dataset size, we performed also extensive parameter tuning using accuracy and running time evaluations. The results show the expected trade off between the running time on the one hand and both the training data size and the updating frequency (in number of events) on the other hand. A general best performance was observed for an update frequency of 200 and training size of 500. For the competitors, we followed the suggested values in [11], whenever available. All results were obtained on a Mac OS 12.4 machine with a 2.4 GHz Quad-Core Intel Core $i5$ processor and 8 GB memory.

The methods to be compared are: *DynaTrainCDD* (Ours), *IncrementalUpdate* ($w = 1$) [11], *IncrementalUpdate* ($w = LastDrift$) [11] and No Retrain (no update after the initial training of the model). The running time evaluation excludes, for all models, the initial training time.

4.2 Results and Discussion

Online Next Activity Prediction Accuracy. Looking at Table 1, we present the results of *DynaTrainCDD* alongside the methods used by [11]. We see that for every dataset except for *BPIC11*, *BPIC12*, and *Helpdesk*, *DynaTrainCDD* was able to outperform the others. Particularly with the *BPIC15* data, we see significant improvements of around 1–2% improvement on average. For *BPIC11*, *BPIC12*, and *Helpdesk DynaTrainCDD* was the second with a minor difference behind the winner. Overall all methods on *BPIC11* suffered with respect to accuracy. This can be attributed due to the significantly higher number of unique activities. In an online setting we are unsure when or if drifts are occurring as the event stream is constantly incoming. Running a model with the assumption that drifts will not occur, assuming that a business process will never change, is unrealistic. While never retraining would be ideal in terms of running time, assuming we need to spend no time in training updates leaves a model highly vulnerable to unexpected drifts. Any drift encountered by a model which is not updated (dynamically or not) could cause the accuracy to unexpectedly plummet. Thus utilising the method whereby no retraining occurs could be risky in the case a future drift is encountered, leading to a lower expected accuracy.

Table 1. Average Accuracy Results (**Best** in bold, <u>Second Best</u> underlined, *Worst* italicised)

Method	Helpdesk	BPIC11	BPIC12	BPIC15_1	BPIC15_2	BPIC15_3	BPIC15_4	BPIC15_5
DynaTrainCDD	<u>0.8377</u>	<u>0.2473</u>	*0.7479*	**0.7615**	**0.7538**	**0.7816**	**0.7888**	**0.7671**
IncrementalUpdate (w = 1) [11]	**0.8426**	0.2282	<u>0.7502</u>	<u>0.7447</u>	<u>0.7445</u>	<u>0.7613</u>	<u>0.7773</u>	<u>0.7406</u>
IncrementalUpdate (w = LastDrift) [11]	0.8323	*0.2280*	0.7474	0.6743	0.6572	0.7127	0.7161	0.6977
No Retrain	*0.7642*	**0.2646**	**0.7930**	*0.2425*	*0.2843*	*0.2981*	*0.2592*	*0.2428*

Table 2. Total Training Time in Seconds (**Best** in bold, *Worst* is italicised)

Method	Helpdesk	BPIC11	BPIC12	BPIC15_1	BPIC15_2	BPIC15_3	BPIC15_4	BPIC15_5
DynaTrainCDD	44.439	**2830.526**	*444.673*	407.256	348.296	426.515	299.566	438.440
IncrementalUpdate (w = 1) [11]	**29.784**	*3680.473*	167.456	**360.305**	**293.987**	**353.182**	**262.477**	**397.981**
Last Drift [11]	*120.137*	3535.270	**120.895**	*2430.327*	*2122.920*	*1567.416*	*1376.079*	*1474.330*
No Retrain	-	-	-	-	-	-	-	-

Next, we examine the running times. In Table 2. We see that while the *Incremental Update* methods run faster on the *Helpdesk*, *BPIC12* as well as all *BPIC15* datasets, *DynaTrainCDD* outperforms other methods on *BPIC11*. Specifically, we note only about 1.5 times running times of the fastest training times on the *BPIC15* dataset. Not only did accuracy increase on the *BPIC15* dataset, however we also observe minimal increases in running times.

Validation Data Results. Next we present the results observed on an external validation set. When looking at Table 3, we notice that *No Retrain* performs the best. The second best performance is *DynaTrainCDD* followed by *IncrementalDrift* methods respectively [11]. This is also reflected in Table 3 where all the results for accuracy and running time are displayed for our two validation sets. However, this doesn not tell the full story. Any unexpected drift would cause the baseline model to become unreliable and lose accuracy. Around the $450k$ event, we notice exactly that whereby the accuracy starts falling from 0.85 to 0.7 on the *No Retrain* methods and *IncrementalUpdate* ($w = 1$) while it stays stable for our method. In looking towards the *BPIC15* (Merged) Dataset we see that *DynaTrainCDD* performs the best with respect to accuracy around 4% higher than its nearest competitor (being *IncrementalUpdate* ($w = 1$) with 0.191). Overall the accuracies experienced across the *BPIC15* (merged) dataset are significantly lower than any other accuracies we have seen in our results. We attribute this to the extremely high number of activities to predict, similar to the results seen on the *BPIC11* dataset in Table 1. The number of unique activities is the sum of all unique activities present in the *BPIC15* datasets combined. Table 3 shows that *DynaTrainCDD* performs better than *IncrementalUpdate* ($w = LastDrift$) *BPIC15* (merged) but not on *BPIC17*. The higher running time of *DynaTrainCDD* is justified in accuracy for *BPIC17* however, as it performs better overall for everything except for the *No Retrain* method.

Lastly, in Fig. 3 and Table 4 we examine the results of the *BPIC15* (merged) dataset and note that *DynaTrainCDD* is the best performer when observing the overall results in the period of $20,000$ events following each sudden drift.

Table 3. Validation Results (**Best**, <u>Runner up</u>, *Worst*)

Method	BPIC15 Merged		BPIC17	
	Accuracy	Total Update Train Time	Accuracy	Total Update Train Time
DynaTrainCDD	**0.234**	<u>3460.941</u>	<u>0.843</u>	*3335.099*
IncrementalUpdate (w = 1) [11]	<u>0.191</u>	**2701.935**	0.842	2656.926
IncrementalUpdate (w = LastDrift) [11]	0.165	*10240.607*	*0.836*	**1539.348**
No Retrain	*0.133*	–	**0.845**	–

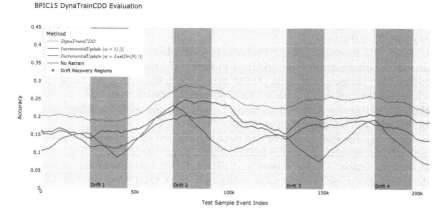

Fig. 3. Online Next Activity Prediction over *BPIC15* Dataset.

Table 4. BPIC15 Merged Post-Drift Performance (**Best** in bold, *Worst* italicised)

Method	Drift 1	Drift 2	Drift 3	Drift 4
DynaTrainCDD	**0.192**	**0.260**	**0.220**	**0.248**
IncrementalUpdate (w = 1) [11]	0.130	0.203	0.152	0.197
Last Drift [11]	*0.124*	*0.197*	*0.144*	*0.175*
No Retrain	0.184	0.255	0.182	0.217

Surprisingly, not retraining at all is the second best performing method. The results in Table 4 further show the strength of *DynaTrainCDD* following sudden drifts as those created when merging all subsets of *BPIC15* dataset.

5   Conclusions and Future Directions

In this work, we developed and evaluated a framework for an incremental online retraining of online next activity prediction. Our framework has the unique ability of detecting the drifts online and then adapting the training data size and the retraining frequency accordingly. The experimental results over several real-world datasets highlight the added prediction accuracy value that *Dyna-TrainCDD* has when compared to state-of-the-art online next activity prediction models. In most of the results, our framework was able to achieve similar running times to the best models despite spending time to detect drifts. In the future, we would like to experiment the performance of our model using synthetic and real datasets with other drift types. We would like also to examine the ability of our model to avoid catastrophic forgetting by including continual learning concepts [6,13].

References

1. Benzin, J.V., Rinderle-Ma, S.: A survey on event prediction methods from a systems perspective: bringing together disparate research areas (2023). https://arxiv.org/abs/2302.04018
2. Böhmer, K., Rinderle-Ma, S.: Probability based heuristic for predictive business process monitoring. In: Panetto, H., Debruyne, C., Proper, H.A., Ardagna, C.A., Roman, D., Meersman, R. (eds.) OTM 2018. LNCS, vol. 11229, pp. 78–96. Springer, Cham (2018). https://doi.org/10.1007/978-3-030-02610-3_5
3. Hassani, M.: Concept drift detection of event streams using an adaptive window. In: ECMS, vol. 33, pp. 230–239 (2019)
4. Hassani, M., Habets, S.: Predicting next touch point in a customer journey: a use case in telecommunication. In: ECMS 2021, pp. 48–54 (2021)
5. Huete, J., Qahtan, A.A., Hassani, M.: PrefixCDD: effective online concept drift detection over event streams using prefix trees. In: COMPSAC, pp. 328–333 (2023)
6. Hurtado, J., Salvati, D., Semola, R., Bosio, M., Lomonaco, V.: Continual learning for predictive maintenance: overview and challenges. Intell. Syst. Appl. **19**, 200251 (2023)
7. Jagadeesh Chandra Bose, R., van der Aalst, W., Zliobaite, I., Pechenizkiy, M.: Dealing with concept drifts in process mining. IEEE TNNLS **25**(1), 154–171 (2014)
8. Lai, C.D., Murthy, D., Xie, M.: Weibull distributions and their applications. In: Pham, H. (ed.) Springer Handbook of Engineering Statistics. SHB, pp. 63–78. Springer, London (2006). https://doi.org/10.1007/978-1-84628-288-1_3
9. Martjushev, J., Bose, R.P.J.C., van der Aalst, W.M.P.: Change point detection and dealing with gradual and multi-order dynamics in process mining. In: Matulevičius, R., Dumas, M. (eds.) BIR 2015. LNBIP, vol. 229, pp. 161–178. Springer, Cham (2015). https://doi.org/10.1007/978-3-319-21915-8_11
10. Miné, A.: The apron numerical abstract domain library (2021). https://github.com/antoinemine/apron
11. Pauwels, S., Calders, T.: Incremental predictive process monitoring: the next activity case. In: Polyvyanyy, A., Wynn, M.T., Van Looy, A., Reichert, M. (eds.) BPM 2021. LNCS, vol. 12875, pp. 123–140. Springer, Cham (2021). https://doi.org/10.1007/978-3-030-85469-0_10
12. Rizzi, W., Di Francescomarino, C., Ghidini, C., Maggi, F.M.: How do i update my model? On the resilience of predictive process monitoring models to change. Knowl. Inf. Syst. **64**(5), 1385–1416 (2022)
13. Serra, J., Suris, D., Miron, M., Karatzoglou, A.: Overcoming catastrophic forgetting with hard attention to the task. In: Proceedings of the 35th International Conference on Machine Learning, vol. 80, pp. 4548–4557 (2018)
14. Taymouri, F., Rosa, M.L., Erfani, S., Bozorgi, Z.D., Verenich, I.: Predictive business process monitoring via generative adversarial nets: the case of next event prediction. In: Fahland, D., Ghidini, C., Becker, J., Dumas, M. (eds.) BPM 2020. LNCS, vol. 12168, pp. 237–256. Springer, Cham (2020). https://doi.org/10.1007/978-3-030-58666-9_14

Overstock Problems in a Purchase-to-Pay Process: An Object-Centric Process Mining Case Study

Dina Kretzschmann[1]([envelope]) [iD], Gyunam Park[1] [iD], Alessandro Berti[1] [iD],
and Wil M. P. van der Aalst[1,2] [iD]

[1] Process and Data Science (PADS), RWTH Aachen University, Aachen, Germany
{dina.kretzschmann,gnpark,a.berti,wvdaalst}@pads.rwth-aachen.de
[2] Celonis, Munich, Germany

Abstract. This paper addresses overstock issues in a real-life Purchase-to-Pay process in cooperation with the industry leader in pet retail in Europe. It highlights the development of solutions for more efficient inventory management, thereby reducing overstock. Our approach involves identifying patterns leading to overstock and proposing specific improvement measures within the existing logistics systems. This includes technical modifications in the order suggestion and purchase order processes using Logomate and SAP systems. The research utilizes object-centric process mining techniques as a crucial tool to uncover these patterns, with a focus on the practical solutions derived for overstock reduction. The case study conducted with the PM^2 methodology demonstrates potential benefits in optimizing inventory structure and suggests a path for future research in generalizing these findings across various sectors and automating overstock pattern detection.

Keywords: Object-Centric Process Mining · Case Study · Purchase-to-Pay Process

1 Introduction

The Purchase-to-Pay process is one of the core business processes across different industries. The overarching objective of this process is to ensure the availability of goods for the customers. This includes ensuring that the right *products* are available at the right *time, quantity, quality, place*, and at the right *costs*. Reaching this objective and controlling the related supply chain is one of the most important success factors for companies [11].

In this study, we examine a pet retail company with a notable market presence, characterized by a sales volume of 4 billion euros in 2023 and over 18,000 workers. The company's ability to provide a diverse array of pet products is underpinned by an extensive supply chain comprising hundreds of suppliers, ten warehouses across five countries, more than 1900 physical stores in Europe, and

We thank the Alexander von Humboldt (AvH) Stiftung for supporting our research.

J. P. A. Almeida et al. (Eds.): CAiSE 2024 Workshops, LNBIP 521, pp. 347–359, 2024.
https://doi.org/10.1007/978-3-031-61003-5_29

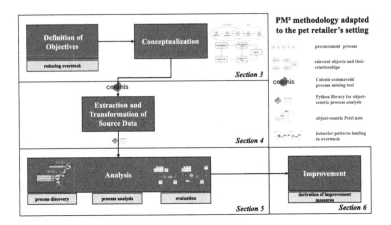

Fig. 1. PM² methodology adapted to the pet retailer's setting

an online shopping platform. The supply chain mechanism involves procuring pet products from various suppliers, primarily storing them in a central warehouse before distribution to regional warehouses, physical stores, or directly to customers. Managing such a widespread supply chain is highly complex. Talking to the logistics management of the pet retailer, it becomes clear that high stock levels compensate for current challenges along the supply chain. As a result, the company is facing inefficiencies in the inventory structure regarding overstock. There is currently overstock worth several million euros. All Purchase-to-Pay process activities leading to overstock should be reduced accordingly [21].

In this context, the pet retail company opted for the commercial process mining tool Celonis[1], aiming to analyze and enhance its supply chain operations. However, the traditional approach has its limitations when it comes to realistically representing the complexity of the supply chain. Recognized for its robust traditional process mining capabilities, Celonis also offers support for object-centric data models. This study is one of the first documented real-life cases for object-centric process mining and demonstrates that the object-centric feature is particularly beneficial for understanding complex supply chain dynamics, where multiple interrelated objects, such as purchase orders, items, and materials, interact within the same process. For example, a single purchase order in this process might encompass numerous items, these items distributed across various shipments [1]. This approach not only overcomes the constraints of traditional methods but also unveils patterns that otherwise remain hidden. Despite their significant potential, object-centric techniques are still not extensively utilized in practice, highlighting the importance of their application in real-world scenarios such as this study. By expanding traditional process mining to object-centric process mining, the pet retailer aims to gain new comprehensive insights, address bottlenecks, optimize inventory management, and enhance order processing efficiency more effectively.

---

[1] https://www.celonis.com.

This case study focuses on addressing the overstock issues within the Purchase-to-Pay process. In particular, we aim to identify and categorize general patterns that lead to overstock using the application of object-centric process mining techniques. The overstock patterns, potentially common across various Purchase-to-Pay processes in different sectors, are analyzed with the goal of developing targeted improvement measures. These measures are designed to optimize inventory structure, addressing the core challenges in the supply chain and contributing to more efficient operations.

The case study applied the PM^2 methodology to the pet retailer's setting (see Fig. 1) [9]. The paper is structured as follows: Sect. 2 reviews related work. Section 3 sets the objective of reducing future overstock and outlines the target data format. Section 4 details the extraction of source data with Celonis and its transformation into an object-centric event log. In Sect. 5, process models are discovered and analyzed using a tool for object-centric process analysis [3], identifying overstock patterns. This section also covers the evaluation of case study results with the pet retailer's logistics management. Section 6 proposes measures to decrease overstock-causing activities. The conclusion and future research directions are presented in Sect. 7, emphasizing the need to generalize and automate these findings.

2 Related Work

The paper tackles overstock problems by detecting patterns leading to overstock in a real-life Purchase-to-Pay process using the application of object-centric process mining techniques. Therefore, we consider the scientific results of previous work related to overstock problems in a real-life Purchase-to-Pay process and traditional/object-centric process mining.

Overstock Problems in a Real-Life Purchase-to-Pay Process: In Purchase-to-Pay processes, companies across different industries face challenges like supply bottlenecks and often maintain high stock levels to ensure product availability, leading to frequent overstock situations and inefficiencies in inventory structure. Overstock, or excess stock without demand, hinders flexibility in responding to customer demand changes, adversely affecting sales and costs [19,21]. The studies [8,12,14,15,19] have analyzed the root causes of overstock in efforts to mitigate its impact. In [8,14,15], a mathematical model from operations research is used to optimize the inventory structure, the *economic order quantity* calculation. The mathematical model, which relies on assumptions such as constant demand and ordering costs, is often not applicable in real-world scenarios. In [12], the business process management method *process mapping* is used to visualize the control-flow of the supply chain processes. In [19], the *fishbone diagram* is used, which also belongs to the business process management, to determine the root causes of overstock. The applied operations research mathematical model and the business management methods lack the capability for event-data-driven process analysis and optimization, highlighting a research gap in identifying and addressing overstock patterns through process mining techniques.

Traditional Process Mining in ERP: Recent research highlights process mining's role in improving logistics and supply chain management. A systematic review demonstrated process mining's utility in identifying inefficiencies and aiding data-driven decision-making within manufacturing organizations [4]. Another study introduced a maturity model for integrating process mining in supply chain management, offering a framework for organizations to assess readiness and pinpoint areas for improvement [11]. Further, research on optimizing order processing with process mining has shown its effectiveness in enhancing order processing efficiency, offering valuable insights for business practices [20]. These studies underscore process mining's significant benefits in streamlining supply chain and logistics operations, notably in the Purchase-to-Pay process.

Object-Centric Process Mining in ERP: Object-centric process mining enhances traditional process mining by linking events to multiple objects, offering a more nuanced view of complex processes [1]. Applied particularly in SAP ERP systems, methodologies have evolved from artifact-centric approaches [17,18] to object-centric behavioral constraint models (OCBC) [16], and multi-graph techniques for capturing interactions among different object types [2,5]. These developments utilize object-centric event logs, following the OCEL specification [10], with research also exploring semi-automated extraction from SAP ERP systems [7] and practical applications in processes like Purchase-to-Pay [6]. Despite challenges in data extraction and analysis complexity, such studies indicate potential for process improvement.

Industry adoption, exemplified by Celonis, reflects this shift. Celonis integrates object-centric concepts through features like multi-event logs and the process sphere, offering advanced process visualizations and analysis capabilities to pinpoint inefficiencies. Yet, the broader application of object-centric process mining in the industry remains limited, highlighting a gap for further exploration and documented real-life implementation studies to harness its full business potential.

3   Preparation

In this section, we prepare the object-centric process mining case study. We present the defined objectives and the target data format of the object-centric event data in terms of Object-to-Object (O2O) and Event-To-Object (E2O) relationships.

3.1   Definition of Objectives

From the logistics management of the pet retailer, we know that the current overstock is worth several million euros. The goal is to optimize the inventory structure to build up less overstock in the future. The following research questions aim to create transparency about the Purchase-to-Pay process activities leading to overstock by using object-centric process mining:

1. How do the relevant objects in the Purchase-to-Pay process behave and interact with each other?
2. Which behavior and interaction of the objects in the Purchase-to-Pay process
   lead to overstock?

3.2   Conceptualization

To achieve the mentioned objectives and to answer the research questions, we
focus on the purchase part of the Purchase-to-Pay process. The considered part
refers to all process activities from predicting demand, ordering goods to goods
receipt [13]. Accordingly, we assume that the predicted demand is equal to the
actual demand. In reality, these may differ from each other. The Purchase-to-Pay
process can be simplified as depicted in Fig. 2.

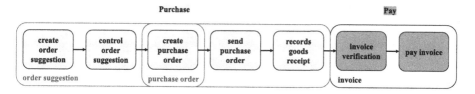

Fig. 2. Standardized representation of a Purchase-to-Pay process

The figure shows that there are two sub-processes in the purchase part of the
Purchase-to-Pay process: (1) order suggestion process and (2) purchase order
process. In the order suggestion process, a merchandise planning tool suggests
an order regarding multiple factors like predicted demand, stock levels, and
additional factors. These suggestions are manually controlled and transformed
into a purchase order. In the purchase order process, a purchase order is created
and sent to the supplier. Afterward, the purchase order gets delivered.

The relevant object types of a general Purchase-to-Pay process are the following: *order suggestion, order suggestion item, purchase order, purchase order
item*, and *material*. To show the cardinalities of the Object-to-Object (O2O)
relationships of the object types we use a "UML-like notation" (see Fig. 3) [1].

The figure illustrates classes and associations where an *order suggestion*
includes one or more *order suggestion item(s)*, and a *purchase order* contains
one or more *purchase order item(s)*, indicated by *1* and *1..**. An *order suggestion* may or may not refer to a *purchase order*, shown by *0..1*, highlighting that
not every suggestion leads to a purchase order. Similarly, the relation holds for
order suggestion item and *purchase order item*. Quantities, though not shown in
the figure, are important; for instance, an *order suggestion item* for 100 pieces
might become a *purchase order item* for 50 pieces. Each item links to one *material*, which can be suggested or purchased any number of times, indicated by
0..*, reflecting the varying frequency of suggestions or purchases for different
materials.

The relevant events of a general Purchase-to-Pay process are events of the event types: *create order suggestion, control order suggestion, create purchase order, send purchase order,* and *records goods receipt.* The cardinalities from Event-to-Object (E2O) relationships and from Object-to-Object (O2O) relationships are depicted in Fig. 4 [1].

In the figure, the left area indicates how often the events of the event types are executed for objects of the object types on the right side. The right area indicates how many objects of the object types are involved in events of the event types on the left side [1]. For example, the event type *create order suggestion* occurs once for each *order suggestion* and once for one or more *order suggestion item(s).* The event type *control order suggestion* occurs once or more for each *order suggestion* and for each *order suggestion item.*

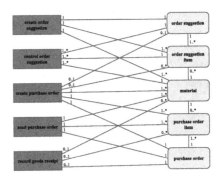

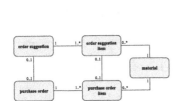

Fig. 3. Object-to-Object (O2O) relationships

Fig. 4. Event-to-Object (E2O) relationships where the left area shows event types and the right area shows object types including Object-to-Object (O2O) relationships

Next to the O2O and E2O relationships, we assume that one *order suggestion* can be completely, partially, or not transformed into one *purchase order.* One *purchase order* can also include one or more *purchase order items* that were not suggested (see Fig. 5).

4   Extraction and Transformation of Source Data

In this section, we present the extraction of the event data from Celonis and the data processing steps to create an object-centric event log using OCEL Standard format[2].

We explain how we extract the event data for the conceptually defined objects and events. For this case study, we extract all required event data for the

---

[2] https://ocel-standard.org.

Purchase-to-Pay process from Celonis. All event data in Celonis are previously extracted from two source systems: (1) Logomate[3] and (2) SAP[4].

The Logomate information system is a tool designed to optimize inventory management and replenishment processes in retail and distribution. Its primary purpose is to automate order suggestions. This system analyzes sales data, inventory levels, and other relevant parameters to forecast demand and recommend the most efficient purchase orders. This helps in maintaining optimal stock levels, reducing overstock or stockouts, and improving overall inventory management efficiency. The system employs algorithms to predict future demand patterns and suggests purchase orders accordingly, ensuring that inventory is aligned with anticipated sales. The order suggestion process and the purchase order process can be described as follows concerning the source systems: Logomate suggests automatically at the item level which *materials* should be ordered, in which quantity, and at what time. The automatic generation of the *order suggestion* is rule-based. The *order suggestion* is checked manually by an employee, who decides whether the *order suggestion* should be transformed into a *purchase order*. If the *order suggestion* is approved, then the *purchase order* is created in SAP and sent to the supplier. When the supplier delivers the *purchase order*, the receipt of the goods is posted in SAP.

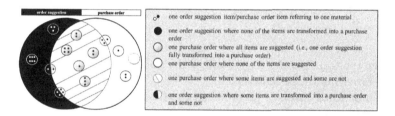

Fig. 5. Connection between order suggestions and purchase orders

For the Purchase-to-Pay process in this study, we extracted the necessary event data from the source systems, namely Logomate and SAP, using Celonis. In consultation with the logistics management of the pet retailer, we applied a set of criteria to pre-filter the event data for clarity and focus. These criteria included selecting data within the date range from January 1, 2023, to April 30, 2023. We specifically concentrated on events associated with one central warehouse located in Krefeld, Germany. Further, we filtered for materials that have a purchase order lead time of less than 10 days, are part of the standard assortment, and have a status of 'listed and active'. Then, we extract the event data from Celonis to a CSV file. The extraction, in general, produces three tables: (1) an order suggestion activity table (2) a purchase order activity table, and (3) a relationship table. These are related to the predefined conceptually relevant

---

[3] https://www.remira.com/en/products/purchasing/logomate.
[4] https://www.sap.com.

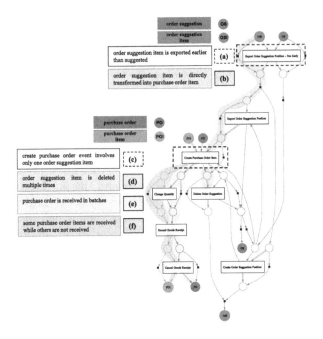

Fig. 6. An object-centric Petri net describing a holistic view of the Purchase-to-Pay process

five object types, i.e., order suggestion, order suggestion item, purchase order, purchase order item, and material.

Data processing involves preprocessing extracted data and constructing an object-centric event log. Preprocessing focuses on removing duplicate events from the order suggestion and purchase order activity tables and filtering activities deemed relevant by logistics management. The data is then transformed into an object-centric event log in OCEL standard format, resulting in a log with 13,151 events, encompassing 1,918 order suggestions, 39,853 order suggestion items, 3,144 purchase orders, 49,176 purchase order items, and 5,144 materials.

5   Analysis

In this section, we present the discovered process models, we analyze the behavior and interaction of the relevant object types, and evaluate the results to answer the research questions using an iterative approach in cooperation with the logistics management.

Using a tool for object-centric process analysis [3], we generate object-centric Petri nets from the event log to model the Purchase-to-Pay process. These nets combine multiple control-flows for different object types, addressing concurrent actions and interactions within the process. They support conformance checking, comparing events to models to identify deviations. This approach provides

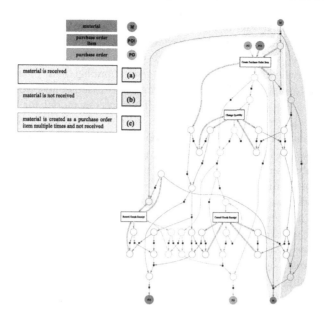

Fig. 7. An object-centric Petri net describing a detailed view with a focus on the material processes

Table 1. Assessment of the patterns in the order suggestion processes

Patterns	Assessment
order suggestion item is exported earlier than suggested	potential overstock
order suggestion item is directly transformed into purchase order item	high level of automation, but risk of errors
create purchase order event involves only one order suggestion item	inefficient
order suggestion item is deleted multiple times	rework

Table 2. Assessment of the patterns in the purchase order processes

Patterns	Assessment
purchase order is received in batches	shortfall
some purchase order items are received while others are not received	shortfall
some materials are received while others are not received	shortfall
material is created as a purchase order item multiple times and not received	shortfall and potential overstock

a detailed view of the process phases. The choice of this open-source library over Celonis is based on its superior preprocessing, performance analysis, and conformance checking capabilities, offering a deeper and more accurate process analysis.

We developed two process models: a holistic view in Fig. 6 and a detailed view on material processes in Fig. 7. Figure 6 outlines a model with *order suggestion, order suggestion item, purchase order,* and *purchase order item* object types, incorporating eight event types like *create order suggestion position* and *record goods receipt.* Color coding differentiates between order suggestion and purchase order processes. The model illustrates the flow from creating order suggestions to the delivery outcomes of purchase orders, emphasizing the central role of *create purchase order item* in connecting sub-processes. We presented the process model describing the holistic view to the logistics management of the pet retailer and conduct interviews with the management to discuss noteworthy patterns and relevant aspects of the holistic view. The process model for order suggestion and order suggestion item processes outlines several patterns as depicted in Fig. 6. These include the premature exportation of the order suggestion item, its direct conversion into a purchase order item, the creation of purchase orders that involve only a single order suggestion item, and the repeated deletion of an order suggestion item.

Figure 7 presents a detailed process model focusing on material processes with *material, purchase order item*, and *purchase order* as object types and includes *create purchase order item, change quantity, record goods receipt*, and *cancel goods receipt* as event types. Pink denotes material processes, while dark purple and orange signify purchase order item and purchase order processes. The model highlights the initiation of material processes with the creation of a *purchase order item*, shown by pink double lines in Fig. 7, where one *material* becomes a *purchase order item* multiple times. After presenting this process model to the pet retailer's logistics management and conducting interviews, the model's significant patterns for material processes include the receipt and non-receipt of *material* and the repeated creation of *material* as a purchase order item without receipt.

In the order suggestion and order suggestion item processes, we discovered previously the following noteworthy patterns and these patterns are assessed as follows (see Table 1). Exporting *order suggestion items* to *purchase order items* prematurely results in overstock before actual demand. Assuming daily recalculations of predicted demand, early exports rely on less accurate forecasts, inhibiting response to demand fluctuations and increasing overstock risk. This manually decided pattern was observed 1, 123 times in the review period. In the purchase order and purchase order item processes, we discovered previously the following noteworthy patterns which are assessed as follows (see Table 2). The pattern that *material* is created as a *purchase order item* multiple times and not received leads to overstock. This pattern and how it leads to overstock is illustrated by the following data-based example: predicted demands for *Material 1 (M1)* at 100 units and *Material 2 (M2)* at 200 units lead to a purchase order *(PO1)* containing both items. *M1* is not received, prompting a new order for *M1* through *PO2*, which also includes *Material 3 (M3)* due to minimum order requirements or capacity utilization of the truck. *M1* remains unreceived, while *M3* is received without initial demand, resulting in overstock. This pattern, affecting 171 materials, highlights the complexities in linking orders and understanding material flows, challenges not addressable with traditional process mining.

It is important to note, that we would not be able to detect these patterns using traditional process mining approaches. For example, in the previously explained pattern, we would not be able to establish the link between PO1 and PO2 based on M1 and analyze the interaction of these objects. Instead, we could only analyze the life cycle of a single object (i.e. one purchase order).

The two identified patterns leading to overstock are not specific to the pet retailer's environment, indicating that these patterns may be generalizable and can occur in Purchase-to-Pay processes in different sectors. The initial research questions can be answered as follows:

1. **How do the relevant objects in the Purchase-to-Pay process behave and interact with each other?** We developed two object-centric Petri net models: a holistic model covering *order suggestion, order suggestion item, purchase order*, and *purchase order item*, starting with order suggestions merging into a single suggestion and focusing on the *create purchase order item* activity, including *purchase order* statuses. The second model, centered on materials, features *material, purchase order*, and *purchase order item*, emphasizing the repeated listing of *material* as a *purchase order item* and tracking its reception.

2. **Which behavior and interaction of the objects in the Purchase-to-Pay process lead to overstock?** In analyzing the Purchase-to-Pay process, two main patterns contributing to overstock were identified. The first involves prematurely converting *order suggestion items* to *purchase order items*, leading to overstock before actual customer demand arises, noted $1,123$ times in the analysis period. The second pattern features *materials* repeatedly listed in *purchase orders* but not received, often including new items without demand, further contributing to overstock, observed in 171 materials during the review period.

After discussing these patterns with the logistics management of the pet retailer, they acknowledged the importance of these findings in understanding and reducing overstock within the Purchase-to-Pay process.

6 Improvement

In this section, we derive important improvement measures for the two detected patterns leading to overstock in cooperation with the logistics management of the pet retailer, which need to be operationalized:

1. **Adjustment in Order Suggestion Process:** Within the Logomate system, a modification is required to manage the premature export of order suggestion items. The current system allows manual overrides that can lead to early exports. This capability should be restricted, with overrides permitted only in exceptional circumstances, such as an impending promotional event. This change aims to align order suggestions more closely with actual demand, reducing the likelihood of overstock due to premature ordering.

2. **Technical Modification in Purchase Order Process:** A dual-system adjustment involving Logomate and SAP is necessary. When a material, listed

as a purchase order item, experiences a delivery failure, an automated notification should be sent to the designated employee. This notification's role is to prompt an inquiry into the cause of these delivery issues, such as potential shortages at the supplier's end. Furthermore, Logomate should temporarily cease generating order suggestions for the affected material until the supplier confirms its availability. This approach ensures that orders are not placed for materials facing supply chain disruptions, thereby preventing overstock.

The logistics management of the pet retailer acknowledged, that there will be less overstock if these measures are operationalized. Future research will focus on a more comprehensive analysis of the overstock problems. The aim is to assess whether the identified patterns of overstock are applicable across various industry sectors. This will involve establishing a systematic framework for the automatic detection of these patterns, enhancing the efficiency of the Purchase-to-Pay process. Additionally, we plan to refine and implement specific strategies to effectively address the overstock challenge, based on the insights gained from this study.

7   Conclusion

In this paper, we addressed overstock problems in a real-life Purchase-to-Pay process of a pet retail company. Through the adapted PM^2 methodology, we identified key patterns contributing to overstock and developed corresponding improvement measures [9]. The use of object-centric process mining was crucial in uncovering these patterns, demonstrating its utility in such analyses. The study indicates that these overstock patterns may be common across Purchase-to-Pay processes in different sectors. This observation suggests a wider relevance for the proposed solutions. Future efforts will aim to deepen the understanding of these patterns, improve automatic detection methods, and apply effective overstock reduction strategies across various industries.

References

1. van der Aalst, W.M.P.: Object-centric process mining: unraveling the fabric of real processes. Mathematics 11(12), 1–11 (2023)
2. van der Aalst, W.M.P., Berti, A.: Discovering object-centric petri nets. Fundam. Inform. 175(1–4), 1–40 (2020)
3. Adams, J.N., Park, G., van der Aalst, W.M.P.: ocpa: a python library for object-centric process analysis. Softw. Impacts 14, 100438 (2022)
4. Alnahas, J.: Application of process mining in logistic processes of manufacturing organizations: a systematic review. Sustainability 15(15), 11783 (2023)
5. Berti, A., van der Aalst, W.M.P.: OC-PM: analyzing object-centric event logs and process models. Int. J. Softw. Tools Technol. Transf. 25(1), 1–17 (2023)
6. Berti, A., Jessen, U., Park, G., Rafiei, M., van der Aalst, W.M.P.: Analyzing interconnected processes: using object-centric process mining to analyze procurement processes. Int. J. Data Sci. Anal. (2023)

7. Berti, A., Park, G., Rafiei, M., van der Aalst, W.M.P.: A generic approach to extract object-centric event data from databases supporting SAP ERP. J. Intell. Inf. Syst. **61**, 835–857 (2023)
8. Biswas, S.K., Karmaker, C., Islam, A.: Analysis of different inventory control techniques: a case study in a retail shop. J. Supply Chain Manage. Syst. **6**(3), 35–45 (2017)
9. van Eck, M.L., Lu, X., Leemans, S.J.J., van der Aalst, W.M.P.: PM^2: a process mining project methodology. In: Zdravkovic, J., Kirikova, M., Johannesson, P. (eds.) CAiSE 2015. LNCS, vol. 9097, pp. 297–313. Springer, Cham (2015). https://doi.org/10.1007/978-3-319-19069-3_19
10. Ghahfarokhi, A.F., Park, G., Berti, A., van der Aalst, W.M.P.: OCEL: a standard for object-centric event logs. In: Bellatreche, L., et al. (eds.) ADBIS 2021. CCIS, vol. 1450, pp. 169–175. Springer, Cham (2021). https://doi.org/10.1007/978-3-030-85082-1_16
11. Jacobi, C., Meier, M., Herborn, L., Furmans, K.: Maturity model for applying process mining in supply chains: literature overview and practical implications. Logist. J.: Proc. **2020**(12) (2020)
12. Jie, F.: Supply chain design for global competitiveness. In: Proceeding International Conference on Science and Engineering, vol. 1 (2017)
13. Khabbazi, M., Hasan, M.K., Sulaiman, R., Shapi'i, A.: Business process modeling for domain inbound logistics system: analytical perspective with BPMN 2.0. J. Basic Appl. Sci. Res. **3**(9), 569–578 (2013)
14. Kusuma, Y.A.: Supply arrangement of raw material and sugar stock to organize overstock risk in warehouse. J. Phys: Conf. Ser. **1375**(1), 012048 (2019)
15. Lestari, N.F., Handayati, Y.: Analysis of inventory management in order to reduce overstock (case study of TVF footwear). Int. J. Curr. Sci. Res. Rev. **5**(09) (2022)
16. Li, G., de Carvalho, R.M., van der Aalst, W.M.P.: Automatic discovery of object-centric behavioral constraint models. In: Abramowicz, W. (ed.) BIS 2017. LNBIP, vol. 288, pp. 43–58. Springer, Cham (2017). https://doi.org/10.1007/978-3-319-59336-4_4
17. Lu, X., Nagelkerke, M., van de Wiel, D., Fahland, D.: Discovering interacting artifacts from ERP systems. IEEE Trans. Serv. Comput. **8**(6), 861–873 (2015)
18. Nooijen, E.H.J., van Dongen, B.F., Fahland, D.: Automatic discovery of data-centric and artifact-centric processes. In: La Rosa, M., Soffer, P. (eds.) BPM 2012. LNBIP, vol. 132, pp. 316–327. Springer, Heidelberg (2013). https://doi.org/10.1007/978-3-642-36285-9_36
19. Rahansyah, V.Z., Kusrini, E.: How to reduce overstock inventory: a case study. Int. J. Innov. Sci. Res. Technol. (2023)
20. Schuh, G., Gutzlaff, A., Cremer, S., Schoppen, M.: Understanding process mining for data-driven optimization of order processing. Procedia Manuf. **45**, 417–422 (2020)
21. Zakka, U.R., Khairunisa, A.: Integration of deterministic and probabilistic inventory methods to optimize the balance between overstock and stockout. In: IOP Conference Series: Materials Science and Engineering, vol. 722, no. 1 (2020)

Exploring Object Centric Process Mining with MIMIC IV: Unlocking Insights in Healthcare

Anukriti Tripathi[1]([⊠])(iD), Aneesh[1](iD), Yuvraj Shivam[1](iD), Swetank Pandey[1](iD), Aamod Vyas[2](iD), and O. P. Vyas[1](iD)

[1] Indian Institute of Information Technology Allahabad, Prayagraj, India
{rsi2023003,iib2021010,iib2021006,iit2021266,opvyas}@iiita.ac.in
[2] Hof University of Applied Sciences, Hof, Germany

Abstract. The vast Medical Information Mart for Intensive Care (MIMIC IV) dataset offers a goldmine for process mining in healthcare, yet traditional approaches often struggle with complex object interactions like patients, medications, and diagnoses. Object Centric Process Mining (OCPM) unlocks deeper insights into patient care, leading to improved coordination, resource allocation, and ultimately, better patient outcomes. This work explores how OCPM overcomes these limitations. By analyzing data flow within the MIMIC IV dataset through an OCPM lens, we illuminate intricate relationships between objects across clinical processes like heart patient or medication administration. By leveraging OCPM on MIMIC IV data, this study offers a novel perspective on emergency department processes of healthcare. We propose a method that leverages the inherent structure of MIMIC IV to directly extract relevant objects, visualizing the convergence and divergence picture and their relationships, bypassing the traditional conversion from XES to OCEL. Our approach focuses on key clinical entities like patients, hospitals admission, and transfer of patients across various departments in hospitals to construct an Object Centric Event Log (OCEL) that captures patient journeys within the hospital system. This direct object-centric approach aims to streamline the process discovery phase and potentially unlock new insights into patient flow patterns and clinical care pathways.

Keywords: MIMIC-IV · Object Centric Process Mining · Process Mining in Healthcare · Convergence and Divergence in OCPM

1 Introduction

The healthcare domain comprises a large number of complex processes as it involves intricate interactions of patients across various departments, allocation of specific departments for patient treatment, etc. The traditional methods of analyzing these processes often fall short. This is where process mining emerges as a game-changer. It may be imagined as a digital detective, meticulously examining a trail of digital breadcrumbs - appointment bookings, lab test results,

J. P. A. Almeida et al. (Eds.): CAiSE 2024 Workshops, LNBIP 521, pp. 360–372, 2024.
https://doi.org/10.1007/978-3-031-61003-5_30

medication administration records - left behind by patients as they navigate the healthcare system [10]. However, the initial approach of case-centric process mining, focusing on individual patient journeys, can be restrictive. It's like analyzing a single patient's experience in isolation, neglecting the broader context of how their care interacts with various departments and healthcare professionals. This can lead to blind spots, hindering efforts to optimize patient flow, identify bottlenecks, and ensure adherence to best practices [12].

OCPM offers a novel perspective by shifting its focus from individual cases to the objects which represent entities crucial to patient care. These objects could be patients themselves, medications, lab results, or even referrals. By analyzing events related to these objects and their interactions across different departments and specialties, OCPM paints a more comprehensive and interconnected picture [2].

Medical Information Mart for Intensive Care (MIMIC), a credential accessible database, offers de-identified medical data from critically ill patients. This treasure trove includes details like patient information, vital signs, lab results, medications, and clinical notes. Researchers leverage MIMIC for various purposes, including training machine learning algorithms for tasks like predicting patient risks, studying treatment effectiveness, and developing tools to improve healthcare delivery [5]. The latest version, MIMIC IV, released in 2023, boasts significant improvements: a significantly larger dataset, enhanced data quality through rigorous cleaning and validation, modular organization for easier access, and strengthened privacy measures [8]. OCPM in MIMIC IV can be enhanced to extract more complex relationships beyond co-occurrence, by incorporating additional data sources like patient demographics and lab results. Improved scalability and explainability of OCPM models would increase their trustworthiness and usefulness for healthcare professionals. Furthermore, evaluating generalizability of OCPM findings across different healthcare institutions is crucial.

The objective of this work is to transform event logs from the MIMIC IV healthcare database into Object-Centric Event Logs using a novel approach of selecting relevant objects and their relationships. By extracting and analyzing these object interactions, we aim to gain deeper insights into patient journeys within the MIMIC IV data. This conversion process, focusing on carefully chosen objects and their connections to other objects and events, enables a more comprehensive understanding of healthcare workflows and patient care pathways.

2   Related Work

The proposed work focuses on object centric process mining with MIMIC IV dataset to gain the deeper insights of healthcare processes. In this regard authors in [4] proposed a framework specifically designed to extract usable event logs from the comprehensive MIMIC-IV database. This framework, including a method, event hierarchy, and log extraction tool, facilitates the use of MIMIC-IV in healthcare process mining research, improving data accessibility and research reproducibility. The authors in [1] proposed a new approach to bridge the gap between real-world event data and the data required by traditional process mining techniques. They argue that current methods require *flattening* the data, which leads to disconnected views and a loss of context. It proposes a specific logging format that allows events to be linked to different types of objects, along with notations and a baseline discovery approach to improve process mining analysis. Authors in [11] tackles the challenge of analyzing complex processes with many interacting objects. They proposed a method to automatically convert existing, limited *flat* event data into a more informative *object-centric* format. This conversion unlocks more accurate analysis by revealing hidden relationships between objects and events. This is significant as most data currently resides in the less informative flat format. In [3], the authors proposed OCEL which represent events involving collections of different object types. These OCELs are then used to discover Object-Centric Petri Nets, where places represent object types and transitions handle collections of these objects. The approach implemented in PM4PY tool, allows for the creation of more comprehensive process models that capture the complex relationships between the objects within a process. These models can be further explored from specific object-centric viewpoints.

After conducting the intense literature review it is observed that the limited amount of work has been done on OCPM with MIMIC IV dataset. Additionally, the OCPM comprises the power to gain the deeper information from the processes. Hence, to strengthen the healthcare domain and reducing the obstacles for the patients as well as for the hospitals, it is much required to have a deeper analysis of healthcare domain with OCPM by using some large datasets like MIMIC-IV.

3   Event Log Extraction from MIMIC IV

This section provides a brief description of the MIMIC IV dataset, the process of generating an event log from its relational data, and the analysis of this event log using process mining techniques. The MIMIC IV dataset is analysed by the process mining technique in which the process discovery and conformance checking is applied. The dataset and the employed techniques are discussed below.

3.1   The Dataset

MIMIC-IV is a large healthcare database (over 60,000 patients) from a Boston hospital (until 2018). It includes detailed information on patients' stays, like procedures, tests, and activities. Timestamps are shuffled to protect privacy, but the order of events is preserved to maintain the integrity of the data for analysis [8]. MIMIC-IV dataset is organized into modules as follows. These module offers a rich resource for healthcare research. The event log for the analysis in the proposed work is obtained by combining these modules.

- **Core:** Basic patient information like demographics.
- **Hosp:** Hospital-wide data on a patient's journey, focusing on continuity of care.

- **ED:** Information from the Emergency Department, including initial diagnoses and triage.

3.2   Event Log Generation

Building our foundation to the existing work [4], we developed a Python script to extract and analyze healthcare data from the MIMIC-IV database. The script allows users to define a patient cohort based on criteria like admission and subject IDs, as well as age ranges. Further refinement of the cohort can be achieved using ICD (International Classification of Diseases) and DRG (Diagnosis-Related Group) codes for targeted analysis. The script extracts case attributes such as gender, age, admission type, and diagnostic/procedural codes. Users can choose between subject-level or admission-level data. For flexibility, both cohort and case attribute data can be optionally saved as CSV files.

The script is well-organized and utilizes utility functions for tasks like SQL query creation, ID list preparation, and timestamped filename management. By applying the script to the entire dataset and focusing on specific output needs, we can obtain event logs like the one shown 10 rows of the log in Table 1. The generated event logs contain 431,232 cases (hospital stays) and encompass 40 unique activity types. The timestamps span a 10-year period. Additionally, the logs include attributes for subject ID (subjectID), hospital admission ID (hadmID), and transfer ID (transferID) for better patient context.

Table 1. Generated Event Log Data-frame **Abbreviations**: ED: Emergency Department, DL: Discharge Lounge, M/S/G: Med/Surg/GYN, CID:Case ID, etype: event-type, hID: hospitalId, subID: subjectId and tranID: transferId.

CID	Activity	Timestamp	etype	outtime	hId	subId	tranId
19.0	ED	2159-03-20 18:56:00	ED	2159-03-20 22:48:00	19.0	1047237	3907130
19.0	Medicine	2159-03-20 22:48:00	admit	2159-03-23 16:54:19	19.0	1047237	3796519
19.0	Discharge	2159-03-23 16:54:19	discharge		19.0	1047237	3836374
24.0	ED	2151-05-25 15:03:00	ED	2151-05-26 00:03:00	24.0	1695328	3548147
24.0	Medicine	2151-05-26 00:03:00	admit	2151-05-26 18:36:48	24.0	1695328	3340796
24.0	Discharge	2151-05-26 18:36:48	discharge		24.0	1695328	3270447
34.0	Medicine	2174-05-22 19:14:02	admit	2174-05-24 17:27:40	34.0	1940048	3110114
34.0	Discharge	2174-05-24 17:27:40	discharge		34.0	1940048	3837048
41.0	DL	2143-09-03 04:53:44	admit	2143-09-03 18:25:56	41.0	1890522	3073395
41.0	M/S/G	2143-09-03 18:25:56	transfer	2143-09-06 13:58:45	41.0	1890522	3139342

3.3   Process Discovery and Conformance Checking

In process mining, process discovery reveals the fundamental structure of a business process by analyzing event logs. It tells 'who, what, when, and where' of activities within the process where conformance checking then takes the discovered process model and event log to compares it to how the process actually executes in reality. This highlights any deviations between the intended process flow and its real-world implementation [13].

After generating the event log, the next objective is to comprehend the process flow depicted in this log through process discovery. We utilized the 'Interactive Data-Aware Heuristic Miner' algorithm [9] within the ProM tool [14], with customized threshold values (Frequency: 0.054, Dependency: 0.097, Binding: 0.643, Condition: 0.11). This analysis results in a process model (as depicted in Fig. 1). To further assess the alignment between the log and the discovered model, we employ an optimal alignment conformance technique. This technique highlights three types of deviations: log, model, and no deviation. In Fig. 1, the yellow colour represents log deviation, magenta indicates model deviation, and green areas depict where the log and model aligns.

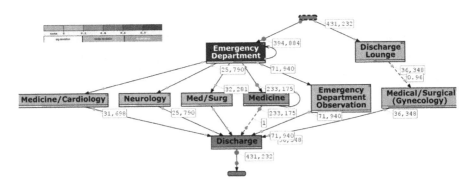

Fig. 1. Process Discovery(Interactive data aware heuristic Miner) and Process Conformance checking(Optimal Alignment) using PM4PY Tool

4   Unlocking Patient Journeys with Object-Centric Process Mining in MIMIC IV

Traditional process mining analyzes each patient journey as a single, linear path. However, healthcare journeys are often complex and have variations (e.g., some patients need additional tests). The OCPM solves this by allowing events to relate to multiple objects, like patients, medications, and procedures. This enables deeper analysis of MIMIC IV data, revealing intricate dependencies, pinpointing bottlenecks, and uncovering variations in treatment. In this section, we explore OCPM within MIMIC IV event logs by identifying relevant objects and their relationships. We then visualize the relationships between objects and events. Next, we transform the data into an Object Centric Event Log and applied the discovery process using Petri nets and finally end with our analysis of OCPM in MIMIC IV.

4.1 Selection of Object from Traditional Event Log of MIMIC IV Datasets

Although OCPM takes a unique approach to analyzing processes, shifting the focus from individual cases to the interconnected journeys of real-world entities called 'objects'. These objects, like patients, medications, or procedures in healthcare, can interact and evolve throughout a process, revealing complex relationships and pinpointing bottlenecks. Our investigation of patient flows within a hospital setting is paramount to understanding and optimizing healthcare delivery. This study delved into the complexities of patient trajectories using an event log, focusing on three critical attributes: **subjectId, hadmId** and **transferId**.

- Subject ID (SubjectId): Uniquely identifies a patient across admissions.
- Hospital Admission ID (hadmId): Uniquely identifies a specific hospital stay for a patient.
- Transfer ID (transferId): Tracks patient transfers between different units or facilities (optional, depending on the discovered model).

The process commenced with the extraction of these attributes from an extensive XES event log, which records a sequence of events or activities related to processes within a hospital.

4.2 Finding the Relation Between the Objects

OCPM goes beyond single cases, allowing diverse relationships between objects to be captured. This includes single object participating in multiple events (e.g., one patient having multiple appointments), multiple objects contributing to a single event (e.g., surgery involving surgeon, nurse, and equipment), and intricate networks of interactions between multiple objects (e.g., a patient's treatment journey involving various medications, procedures, and professionals). To obtain the relationship between the objects in an event log the values for the corresponding attributes in the event log is checked for its relation with the other attributes in the event log. To check such relationship between the attributes the algorithm 1 given as follow is employed. The relation is obtained by taking two attributes at a time. The result of the relation represents that the hadmId may have one subjectId but it may also have more than one transferId.

4.3 Visualization of Divergence and Convergence

Process mining analyzes event logs to understand how processes actually function. Two crucial concepts in this analysis are divergence and convergence. Divergence occurs when a single case (patient journey) exhibits multiple occurrences of the same activity. Imagine a patient in the emergency room undergoing repeated tests due to changing medical needs. This creates a loop-like structure in the process model, indicating divergence. Conversely, convergence happens when a single event appears in multiple cases. For example, a medication dispensing event might appear for various patients within the same timeframe, suggesting

Algorithm 1. Attribute Relationship Extraction (Let attr1 and attr2 belongs to an event log.)

for each trace in log **do**
    for each event in trace **do**
        if attr1 and attr2 exist in event **then**
            attr1_value → attr2_value //Store Relationship
            attr2_value → attr1_value //Store Relationship
        end if
    end for
end for
for each unique attr1_value and its associated attr2_values **do**
    Store in aggregated_attr1_to_attr2
end for
for each unique attr2_value and its associated attr1_values **do**
    Store in aggregated_attr2_to_attr1
end for

a shared resource (a nurse) being utilized across different patient visits [1]. From the MIMIC IV event log, we selected three objects: hadmID, subjectID, and transferID. We then investigated the visual relationships between these three objects and 40 activities using Algorithm 2 and the result are shown in Figs. 2 and 3.

Algorithm 2. Relationship Visualization in Objects and Activities

for all trace in the event log **do**
    Get attr1 and attr2
    Increment count for the connection between attr1 and attr2
    for all event in the trace **do**
        Get attr3 and activity_name
        Update counts for activities and connections
    end for
end for
Add nodes for attr1, attr2, attr3 with labels
Add nodes for each activity with labels including counts
Add edges between nodes without specifying labels

The Fig. 2 depicts that each subjectId (S1-S5) was positioned as the source node at the top, emphasizing the starting point of the interaction within the hospital system. Directly below, the hadmid (H1–H5) nodes served as the gateway through which the patient's journey within the hospital unfolded. Branching out from each hadmId node, multiple transferId nodes (T1.1, T1.2, etc.) illustrated the patient's trajectory across different hospital departments. This structured and layered approach illuminated the patterns of divergence and convergence. For instance, subjectId S2 is linked to hadmId H2, which further fans out to five distinct transfers, highlighting a case of high conversion where the patient interacted with numerous departments. Conversely, other subjects displayed fewer departmental interactions, suggesting a more streamlined course of treatment. in Fig. 3, It is noted that 'hadmID' and 'transferId' are closely associated with nearly all activities out of 40, whereas 'subjectID' is linked to only a limited number of activities. 'subjectID' represents the patient ID, directly connected to other objects such as 'hadmID', but not directly to activities.

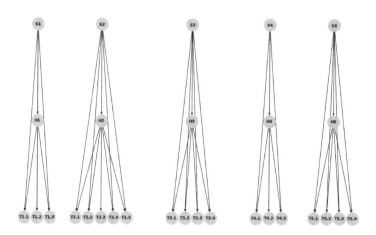

Fig. 2. Convergence and Divergence between the Objects

The findings from this reduced and focused analysis are pivotal. It highlights the areas where the patient journey can be streamlined, potential bottlenecks in departmental transfers can be identified, and resources can be better allocated. By simplifying the discovery model and concentrating on the core elements of patient admissions and transfers, the study provides valuable insights into the operational dynamics of hospital processes, paving the way for enhanced healthcare delivery and administration.

4.4   Conversion from XES to OCEL

Our initial dataset was stored in the extensible event stream (XES) format, a standard for case-centric event logs. However, OCPM applications require the Object centric event log [7] format for further analysis. Therefore, we converted our base dataset to OCEL format (specifically, .xmlocel files) using the PM4PY tool [6]. Within this converted format, we defined the objects of interest as subjectID, hadmID, and transferID. The statics of OCEL shown in Table 2.

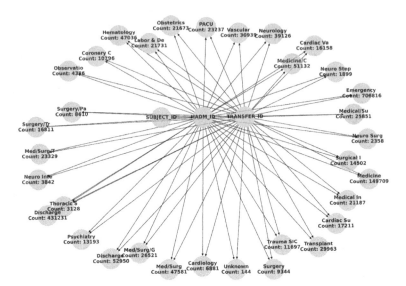

Fig. 3. Convergence and Divergence Between the Objects and Activities

Table 2. Statistics of OCEL dataset of MIMIC-IV

Statistic	Value
Number of Objects	5,342,892
Total Types of Objects	3
Total Number of Events and Traces	1,890,972

4.5   Discovery with Petri Net

Understanding activity objects and associated attributes is crucial for effective conversion of OCEL to process models using PM4PY. OCEL tightly links events to objects, expressing activities within their context. It begins by loading the OCEL file via PM4PY, then extracts this critical information to prepare for the Petri Net transformation. Due to its long scale size, Fig. 4 shows only part of the model. In this model the eclipse shape is terms as starting point of any object, rectangle as activities and circle as states. So there are three colours of eclipse shows three different objects and there are 40 activities. The complete process model is available on Github repository (view here).Although the process model is extensive in scale, it is more clearly visualized compared to the traditional approach of process discovery. When all activities are covered, our model may resemble spaghetti-like complexity, but with the application of OCPM, our model encompasses all paths and activities while remaining clear and comprehensible.

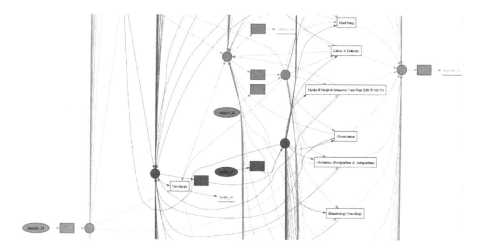

Fig. 4. Discovery in Petri Net Model of OCEL using PM4PY Tool

4.6   Analysis

The OCPM plays a vital role in enhancing the process model and deepening our understanding of the workflow. Within the MIMIC IV dataset, it was challenging to make it readable for both traditional process mining and OCPM. Thus, we explored OCPM within the MIMIC IV dataset. Our findings are as follows:

1. We transformed the dataset, originally structured as a relational database, into an executable object-centric event log. Our focus was on specific objects to trace their relationships throughout the patient journey.
2. We investigated the transformed log using OCPM and identified relationships between objects, including one-to-many and one-to-one connections, as depicted in Fig. 5. This figure demonstrates that upon each patient visit to the organization (e.g., hospital), they are assigned a diagnosis-based hospital and subsequently visit multiple departments. Additionally, patients may also visit another hospital as needed.
3. Our analysis revealed a more comprehensive understanding of the patient journey by employing OCPM techniques and tools, which facilitated the exploration of object involvement.

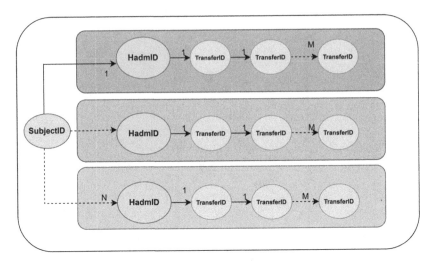

Fig. 5. Objects Visits through the other objects

5   Conclusion and Future Work

This study successfully demonstrated the application of Object-Centric Process Mining to the MIMIC IV dataset. We began by extracting an event log from the relational data, a crucial step in transforming the information into a format suitable for OCPM analysis. Subsequently, relevant objects within the emergency department setting were identified, enabling us to explore the relationships between these objects and the associated events. The analysis revealed one-to-many and many-to-many relationships between the objects and also between 40 unique activities, providing valuable insights into the interactions between various entities within the Emergency department environment. Following the object identification and relationship analysis, the event log was converted into the OCEL format, a prerequisite for OCPM exploration using PM4PY tools. The final stage involved the application of discovery algorithms for the generation of an OCPM Petri net. This Petri net serves as a visual representation of the process dynamics within the emergency department, incorporating the identified objects and their interactions. By leveraging OCPM on MIMIC IV data, this study offers a novel perspective on emergency processes. The extracted knowledge regarding object relationships and the generated Petri net provide valuable insights for healthcare professionals and researchers. This approach allows for a deeper understanding of complex workflows and interactions within the emergency department, potentially leading to improved patient care and resource allocation strategies. This research opens doors for further exploration. Future studies could investigate the application of specific OCPM algorithms to specific clinical questions within the healthcare dataset. Additionally, the generated petri net could be validated with domain experts to ensure its accuracy and relevance to real-world practices. Ultimately, the integration of OCPM with healthcare data holds immense potential for improving our understanding and management of critical care processes.

Acknowledgement. The work acknowledges the Risk Averse Resilience Framework for Critical Infrastructure Security (RARCIS) project, funded by the Department of Science and Technology (DST), and C3i-Hub (Indian Institute of Technology Kanpur), India, for their partial funding.

References

1. Aalst, W.M.P.: Object-centric process mining: dealing with divergence and convergence in event data. In: Ölveczky, P.C., Salaün, G. (eds.) SEFM 2019. LNCS, vol. 11724, pp. 3–25. Springer, Cham (2019). https://doi.org/10.1007/978-3-030-30446-1_1
2. van der Aalst, W.M.: Object-centric process mining: unraveling the fabric of real processes. Mathematics **11**(12), 2691 (2023)
3. van der Aalst, W.M., Berti, A.: Discovering object-centric petri nets. Fundam. Inform. **175**(1–4), 1–40 (2020)
4. Cremerius, J., Pufahl, L., Klessascheck, F., Weske, M.: Event log generation in mimic-iv research paper. In: Montali, M., Senderovich, A., Weidlich, M. (eds.) ICPM 2022. LNBIP, vol. 468, pp. 302–314. Springer, Cham (2022). https://doi.org/10.1007/978-3-031-27815-0_22
5. Edin, J., et al.: Automated medical coding on MIMIC-III and MIMIC-IV: a critical review and replicability study. In: Proceedings of the 46th International ACM SIGIR Conference on Research and Development in Information Retrieval, pp. 2572–2582 (2023)
6. Ghahfarokhi, A.F., van der Aalst, W.: A python tool for object-centric process mining comparison. arXiv preprint arXiv:2202.05709 (2022)
7. Ghahfarokhi, A.F., Park, G., Berti, A., van der Aalst, W.M.P.: OCEL: a standard for object-centric event logs. In: Bellatreche, L., et al. (eds.) ADBIS 2021. CCIS, vol. 1450, pp. 169–175. Springer, Cham (2021). https://doi.org/10.1007/978-3-030-85082-1_16
8. Johnson, A., Bulgarelli, L., Pollard, T., Horng, S., Celi, L.A., Mark, R.: MIMIC-IV. PhysioNet. https://physionet.org/content/mimiciv/1.0/. Accessed 23 Aug 2021
9. Mannhardt, F., De Leoni, M., Reijers, H.A.: Heuristic mining revamped: an interactive, data-aware, and conformance-aware miner. In: 15th International Conference on Business Process Management (BPM 2017). pp. 1–5. CEUR-WS. org (2017)
10. Munoz-Gama, J., et al.: Process mining for healthcare: characteristics and challenges. J. Biomed. Inform. **127**, 103994 (2022)
11. Rebmann, A., Rehse, J.R., van der Aa, H.: Uncovering object-centric data in classical event logs for the automated transformation from XES to OCEL. In: Di Ciccio, C., Dijkman, R., del Río Ortega, A., Rinderle-Ma, S. (eds.) BPM 2022. LNCS, vol. 13420, pp. 379–396. Springer, Cham (2022). https://doi.org/10.1007/978-3-031-16103-2_25
12. Tayebati, S.K., et al.: Process mining case study approach: extraction of unconventional event logs to improve performance in hospital information systems (HIS). Int. J. Comput. Sci. Inf. Secur. **17**(4), 117–128 (2019)

13. Van Der Aalst, W.: Process mining: overview and opportunities. ACM Trans. Manage. Inf. Syst. (TMIS) **3**(2), 1–17 (2012)
14. van Dongen, B.F., de Medeiros, A.K.A., Verbeek, H.M.W., Weijters, A.J.M.M., van der Aalst, W.M.P.: The ProM framework: a new era in process mining tool support. In: Ciardo, G., Darondeau, P. (eds.) ICATPN 2005. LNCS, vol. 3536, pp. 444–454. Springer, Heidelberg (2005). https://doi.org/10.1007/11494744_25

Author Index

A
Abgrall, Théo 135
Afonina, Valeriia 85
Aghakhani, Ghazaleh 217
Allan, James 53, 200
Aneesh, 360

B
Bazazzadeh, Hassan 53
Bellizio, Federica 53
Beránek, Pavel 229, 241
Berti, Alessandro 347
Bianchini, Filippo 147
Bigiotti, Alessandro 5
Bottoni, Maria Paola Francesca 5
Brnka, Matej 264

C
Cai, Hanmin 53
Calamo, Marco 147
Campos, Nathalie 200
Cui, Heming 25

D
De Luzi, Francesca 147
Ding, Yuntian 18

E
Efthymiou, Vassilis 180
Ehrenthal, Joachim C. F. 59

F
Franconi, Enrico 135
Fricker, Reto 53
Füßl, Anne 72

G
Gachnang, Phillip 59
Ghiran, Ana-Maria 156

González, Sergio Acero 53
Guan, Rongxin 25

H
Hassani, Marwan 335
Heer, Philipp 53
Hennig, Marc C. 323
Herbaut, Nicolas 18
Heringklee, Stefan Horst 72
Hinkelmann, Knut 85

I
Iga, Vasile Ionut Remus 156, 168

J
Jablonski, Stefan 275, 291

K
Kirikova, Marite 186
Kolp, Manuel 217
Kondylakis, Haridimos 180
Kosciuszek, Thaddeus 335
Kretzschmann, Dina 347
Kumarasinghe, Aritha 186

L
Laurenzi, Emanuele 200
Lohachab, Ankur 37
Loran, Louisa 59

M
Macrì, Mattia 147
Mäder, David 97
Mavromatidis, Georgios 53
Mecella, Massimo 147
Merunka, Vojtěch 229, 241
Molhanec, Martin 253
Montazeri, Mina 53

J. P. A. Almeida et al. (Eds.): CAiSE 2024 Workshops, LNBIP 521, pp. 373–374, 2024.
https://doi.org/10.1007/978-3-031-61003-5

Printed in the United States
by Baker & Taylor Publisher Services